Praise for *The Baby Bond*

"Babies would tell you to buy this book! *The Baby Bond* is the latest word on responsive baby care, warmly written and backed up by a wealth of research references and academic articles. This is the book I wish I'd had when my son was born. I would have had an abundance of helpful information, I would have been reassured that it was OK—in fact, essential—to trust what my heart told me, and I would have had the perfect book to show skeptical friends and relatives."—**Jan Hunt, MSc, author of** *The Natural Child: Parenting from the Heart*

"An instant classic. A must-read for all parents. Dr. Palmer's book is the best book on the hard science behind attachment parenting that I've ever read. I plan to make it a baby gift for every pregnant friend. I wish I had read this book before I became a mother. I cannot recommend this book highly enough. It's the most exciting new book on parenting that I've read in a number of years." —**Katie Allison Granju, author of** *Attachment Parenting*

"*The Baby Bond* was invaluable to me in dealing with my baby's pediatrician. I brought in references from the book and was actually able to enlighten her position and foster a solution that worked better for my baby."—**Sandra Seastedt, MFCC**

"A viewpoint different from what I was taught in school…seems much healthier. I believe that reading this book prior to having children would have helped me to be a better father."—**V. Paul Kater, MD, family practice**

"Filled with scientific research regarding key issues of infant care. Provides parents information on healthy parenting choices in easy-to-digest language. It is a must-read for new and expecting families and also an important text for educators."—**International Childbirth Education Association**

"[An] excellent book. I had to have my highlighter at the ready the entire time I was reading it. The references are fantastic. Thank you so much for your great work. We quote *The Baby Bond* at our conferences and feel it would be helpful for the students, mostly labor and delivery nurses, to have it available."—**Carole Peterson, MS, IBCLC of Lactation Education Consultants**

"Parents need to know this information in order to make informed decisions about their children's health. Her book is extremely well-referenced and, as a lactation consultant, I use her book in my work at the hospital and with the mothers in my breastfeeding support group."—**Sharon Johnson, RN, BSN, PHN, IBCLC**

"A long-needed in-depth investigation and discussion...covers topics ranging from the chemistry of bonding to the health advantages of breastfeeding and in each case, her comments are well-substantiated by very impressive and extensive scientific citations."—**Rosalind C. Haselbeck, PhD, biochemist**

"This is truly a valuable resource for attachment parents...shows what you (and your great-grandma) knew in your heart was right all along." —***Vegetarian Baby and Child* magazine**

"*The Baby Bond* is a well-referenced compendium of information from highly authoritative sources written by a dedicated healthcare professional—for caring parents seeking a source book to understand their baby's physiology." —**George J. Pratt, PhD, clinical psychologist, author of *Instant Emotional Healing***

"Provides a straightforward examination of many key issues new parents might be unfamiliar with...in "reader friendly" down-to-earth terms... *The Baby Bond* is an excellent and highly recommended reader for the new mother!"—**Midwest Book Review, "The Motherhood Shelf"**

"The extensively documented *The Baby Bond*...could serve as an attachment parenting primer, covering breastfeeding, bonding, and co-sleeping. Palmer also pays a lot of attention to food allergies and immunity protection."—**Mothering magazine**

"From the health aspects to the emotional bonding that takes place between a mother and a baby, Dr. Palmer does a great job of summarizing the research associated with the first year of baby's life and writing in a style that makes you feel like you're talking to a girlfriend over tea and cookies." —**Vegfamily.com**

"In *The Baby Bond*, Linda Palmer combines current psychological, bio-chemical, and nutrition research with good common sense. A sophisticated professional, yet she understands the needs of ordinary families with a new baby."—**A. Christine Watson, PhD, clinical psychologist**

"This is the book for which many lactation professionals have been waiting, because it is the perfect book to recommend to clients. Well researched and hard hitting, the text provides a comprehensive and truthful discussion of current issues related to birth and the infant period."—**Denise Pickett-Bernard, PhD, RD, *The Journal of Human Lactation***

"Find out what is truly important for the well-being of your baby in this intriguing book...Problems with cow's milk and the benefits of breastfeeding are thoroughly explored. There is a wealth of information on infant nutrition and issues related to food allergies...thought-provoking addition to the expectant mother's bookshelf."—**Living Without magazine**

"*The Baby Bond* explains in reader-friendly scientific detail why parents should often follow their own hearts and avoid many widely accepted parenting practices."—**InnerSelf magazine**

THE

BABY BOND

The New Science Behind What's Really
Important When Caring for Your Baby

THE BABY BOND

The New Science Behind What's Really Important When Caring for Your Baby

Dr. Linda Folden Palmer

SOURCEBOOKS, INC.®
NAPERVILLE, ILLINOIS

Published by Sourcebooks, Inc.
P.O. Box 4410, Naperville, Illinois 60567-4410
(630) 961-3900
Fax: (630) 961-2168
www.sourcebooks.com

Originally published in 2001 by Lucky Press

Library of Congress Cataloging-in-Publication Data

Palmer, Linda Folden.
  The baby bond : the new science behind what's really important when caring for your baby / by Linda Folden Palmer.
      p. cm.
  "Originally published in 2001 by Lucky Press."
  Includes bibliographical references and index.
  1. Infants—Care. 2. Child care. 3. Pediatrics—Popular works. I. Title.
RJ61.P16 2009
618.92—dc22
                                  2009016450

Printed and bound in the United States of America.
  DR 10 9 8 7 6 5 4 3 2 1

Contents

Unfortunately, a new problem developed for families—that of crying, sleepless infants vying for attention.

Enter Dr. Luther Emmett Holt, considered the father of pediatrics. Around the turn of the century, he started to teach that babies should never be played with. He came up with the idea that infants would be "spoiled" if parents gave in to their requests for "indulgences." A baby's desires to be frequently fed, carried, rocked, comforted, and to have something to suck on were "bad habits" that should not be obliged. Infant crying increased from this advice, but mothers were relieved by the (very erroneous) advice that infants needed to be allowed to cry for extended periods in order to develop their lungs.

> Suddenly, male doctors, educated only by formula companies, became experts on how mothers should feed their babies.

Also during the early 1900s, as sanitation awareness increased, orphans and other infants were starting to survive on artificial feeding formula far more often than they had in the past. Nestlé and other formula manufacturers mounted enormous campaigns to promote their infant feeding substitutes. They even sent saleswomen dressed as nurses to hospitals or to new mothers' homes as "milk nurses." Companies also gave gifts and grants to doctors and hospitals to encourage them to distribute free formula samples. They used aggressive TV, billboard, radio, and neon sign campaigns to convince mothers that they may not have enough breastmilk, and that formula was elite, convenient, sterile, and "scientific." These companies provided huge grants to promote the development of the American Academy of Pediatrics. Suddenly, male doctors, educated only by formula companies, became "experts" on how mothers should feed their babies. The companies' milk stations, which promoted their formulas, were soon converted to "well-child" clinics. Eventually these became the first pediatricians' offices, providing "nutritional advice" and regular weighing for infants. "Scientific" weight charts developed by the formula companies were used to convince the majority of mothers they were not supplying enough nourishment for their infants. In truth, these charts only reflected the obesity resulting from overeating by formula-fed infants attempting to obtain adequate nutrients. Nevertheless, an "epidemic" of imagined breastmilk insufficiency occurred, which led to a real insufficiency as mothers breastfed less and started producing less, and soon, artificially feeding infants with cow's milk formulas became the norm.

Robbed of the proper nutrition and immune protection of mother's milk, these infants suffered untold cases of diarrhea, illness, and death. Additionally, some doctors began to recognize that not all symptoms related to formula and cow's milk were caused by infection or malnutrition. Cow's milk allergies became widely recognized. Later, however, this observation went out of vogue in favor of describing the problem as colic, colitis, and nervous mothers.

As women began to work outside the home, and scheduled bottle feedings became the norm, pediatric and hospital visits for illnesses became more and more frequent, behavior problems increased, and nighttime crying issues and night terrors became common problems. A new kind of child expert, the sleeping specialist, became popular.

In the middle of the twentieth century, after noticing that certain kinds of behavior problems were increasing in children, Dr. John Bowlby and others began to study parent-child bonding. They noticed that children who had been evacuated from war zones (and separated from their parents) were far more disturbed by their wartime experiences than those who had stayed with their mothers during the bombing of London. It became clear to these researchers that the availability of parents was a key factor in the behavior patterns developed by children. In recent decades, the diagnosis of "hyperactivity" has become very common. Researchers have linked such symptoms not only to a need for greater parental attention, but often to cow's milk sensitivities and other food reactions, all products of "modern" parenting. Still, these observations are seldom taken into account when recognizing such hyperactive behaviors. The usual treatment for this behavior is addictive stimulant drugs. Now we see up to 35% of children in some classrooms being diagnosed and medicated for attention-deficit disorder even as we teach the mantra "just say NO to drugs."

While new sanitation practices and miracle medicines have been curing diseases and saving the lives of young and old alike, many children's health problems have actually increased by orders of magnitude.

Thanks to medicine and sanitation, the infant death rate has dropped drastically over the last hundred years (after rising greatly with the onset of industrialization). But there is an enigma in the United States—while often leading the way in medicine, the United States actually has one of the lowest infant survival rates among industrialized nations. Childhood diseases and behavior problems are considerably higher than in most other nations as well.

We have also been watching puberty occur at increasingly earlier ages. Now that many of these twentieth-century babies are beyond their third or fourth decades of life, we are faced with geometric increases in bowel diseases, obesity, and several kinds of cancers and autoimmune diseases. We have also noticed that the "unspoiled," "early independence" children are having more problems than ever with adult independence, intimacy issues, and lasting marital relationships.

Now that many of these twentieth-century babies are beyond their third or fourth decades of life, we are faced with geometric increases in bowel diseases, obesity, and several kinds of cancers and autoimmune diseases.

Science is just now finding some keys to what is going on in our children's bodies. First, we are learning, at a chemical level, about the consequences of our lost art of touch. Additionally, we are discovering some of the adverse effects of children's exposures to pesticides, antibiotics, vaccinations, and consumption of milk from cows.

This volume represents my wish to give parents the tools to evaluate their young children's environment and understand how it can affect their development. The intent is to arm parents with information, so they can make better parenting and healthcare choices.

1

Finding Out What Matters

TODAY, PARENTS FACE MANY PROBLEMS CREATED BY PARENTING AND FEEDING techniques introduced over the last century. Colic, for instance, is far more common in the United States than in many other places around the world. I will show how two chief causes for its rise are the stress suffered by babies being regularly separated from their mothers and the common difficulties babies have tolerating the large cow's milk proteins in infant formulas and breastfeeding mothers' diets. Cow's milk is a foreign substance that has pervaded every corner of our diets—starting with artificial infant feeds, but finding its way into mother's breastmilk through the foods she eats as well. As it turns out, health problems such as diabetes, obesity, bowel disease, and cancer, on the rise in both children and adults, are strongly linked to infant feeding choices. This book discusses the most important problems that have flourished over the last century, and those that parents have the most power to change.

We begin with a story about a mother, who we'll call Jenny, whose newborn behaved wildly at the breast—wanting to nurse, but not wanting to nurse, flailing his head back and forth. After his first several days of life, he would do little more than scream and cry. Even though Jenny was a new mother, she was sure this was a cry of pain and frustration. Her baby's bowels did not move, except for a weekly watery explosion that no diaper on the planet could hold. He would awaken during naps and during the night with screams. He lost more than the usual amount of weight for a newborn, and then did not show much gain.

The doctors diagnosed Jenny's infant with colic and sent her back home, assuring her that he would "grow out of it" someday. They provided an "increased" feeding schedule, which was actually much less frequent than his attempts already. But making him wait to eat only found him in such a crying frenzy that he couldn't even try to nurse. Well-meaning visitors tried to force him to nurse, which made him protest more, force bottles of formula on him, which made him vomit, or force pacifiers and water bottles, which made him lose interest in feeding at all. The doctor also eventually recommended formula supplements, but these still did not stay down. Jenny looked frantically through all her baby books to find out just what colic was, and what could be done. She found an answer: crying 2 hours per day is "normal"; crying 3 hours or more per day is "colic"—a condition of crying a lot.

This, she thought, was no diagnosis; it was simply an excuse. But why? Apparently hers was not the first child to ever behave this way. The first clue came from another mother. She suggested that the baby might be allergic to something in Jenny's milk. Jenny had never heard of this, but she thought back over her diet before the miserable night that had just passed. It contained three of the foods her friend mentioned as the most common offenders. She went home and found a couple vague references to these food reactions in her baby books, so she tried eliminating a few foods from her diet and saw immediate improvement, although her son was far from recovery.

Jenny thought she was well educated in diagnosis, health, and nutrition. Her training included basic pediatric concerns as well. Not only that, but she owned quite a stack of the standard baby care books, and her pediatrician was so popular that he was frequently seen on local TV. She felt rather embarrassed and concerned that her education did not include such basic dietary information. She wondered why it was not readily available.

Okay, so this mom's name wasn't Jenny. It's Linda, Linda Palmer—me, the author.

By this time, it was very clear that my son was in pain. He would arch his back and clench his fists. I began searching through medical textbooks and found little help. Finally I began to find information in some well-recognized research journals. Strangely, however, I noticed that most of the helpful research and information came from Europe, Australia, Israel, and many parts of the world, but rarely from the United States.

The more answers I found, the more questions I had. It would take a book to tell you about even a small portion of the vast amount of, shall I say, "secret" research and information out there about colic and many other challenges that parents might face. Then I found some incredible reasons for why this sound, scientific, and important information is not available in most medical offices in the United States: Basically, a few stray misconceptions and a century of exploitation for industry profit are behind the story. It would take a book to tell you even a little of what I learned… and you are reading that book.

Herein, I only discuss situations where choices can be made and where there are important potential differences in the mental and physical outcomes for children based on those choices. Of course, it is precisely these matters, those where there are choices, that are influenced by industry and advertising (propaganda). Some child-rearing ideas are woven so deeply into the fabric of our culture that even most of our well-meaning infant care scholars are victims of the scheme.

To understand the problems of modern child rearing, we must recognize the impact of industrialization, which brought rapid and frequent transport of families from their friends and extended families. Busy people in rapid transit, who were also busy with their new radios and televisions at home, lost a great deal of community interaction, and therefore support. Industrialization has also shaped a society where both parents often work, reducing contact not only with the neighborhood, but even within the nuclear family. The "village" is now a thing of the past. The village not only more easily provided the significant attention and stimulation a child needs, but it also gathered and passed on a collection of parenting knowledge and discoveries.

Why did it take me so long to realize that my baby, although still suffering food sensitivity problems, actually did feed quite well first thing in the morning and during the night? Rather than relying on a stream of lactation nurses and relatives hovering around, trying to force my baby to feed, I finally found some mothers who explained that my sensitive and already uncomfortable young baby was hyperstimulated by all the noise and strangers. Having recently arrived from a peaceful womb, where he mainly heard only two voices, my son finally found a little peace in his new existence, one break from his crying and frustration. Babies are not all alike, but finally, alone with me in a quiet, dimly lit room, my tiny son could nurse soundly and happily, in between his bouts of painful crying and snatches of sleep. In fact, he seemed to find relief from pain in the act of nursing itself. This, I found later, could be soundly explained by some of the secret science.

I should have known all about child rearing since playing house as a child; I should have learned this from being a part of a village. The truth is, however, that I had never even seen a baby nurse before. I am most frightened to realize that I may never have "gotten" it, that my son may never have begun to gain weight, that...who knows?

Since our villages are all but gone in the industrialized world, members of La Leche League, International, have taken it upon themselves to again gather up the wisdom from experienced mothers and share these experiences, the trials, and the successes. This breastfeeding organization, founded in 1956, now acts as a valuable information source for new mothers. Hopefully, with efforts such as these and others, our new generation of babies will not have to be the guinea pigs of modern society. Hopefully, mothers can collect evidence and experience and pass this information on, for more consistently healthy, happy, and brighter results.

I came into parenting with little agenda beyond every parent's hope for a healthy child. Challenges came quickly however, and answers were limited, didn't seem to help, and generally were not well supported with sound research. I embarked on a large amount of research and established contact with hundreds of families whose lives I probed, aiming initially to solve my own parenting dilemmas. Over time, it became apparent that infant care choices could make huge differences, and that the research evidence pointed to certain choices rather definitely. It is stunning that this information is widely unknown in parenting circles, parenting books, and in pediatric offices. The information in this volume will empower parents by revealing a large amount of the latest scientific, medical, sociological, and psychological research about how babies are affected by parenting choices.

Somewhat insidiously over time, child care has drifted into a regimen that aims to make strong, independent "adults" out of our innocent children, starting from day one. Parents have been encouraged to ignore baby's cries and their own very strong instinctual urges to respond, to disconnect themselves from their infant very quickly, to create a detached, "independent" infant. I've certainly obtained this programming from social cues all my life: If you pick up the baby, coddle him, "give in" to baby's requests, you will "spoil" him—"Don't spoil the baby!" Yet, I have found that there is no sound research to support any long-term benefit from this advice. In fact, mountains of psychology studies suggest the opposite, and a look at cultures with differing practices bears this truth out.

This reminds me of an incredible embarrassment. I am haunted by a sick feeling every time I recall the number of times I regurgitated my own cultural programming to my patients—that babies need to cry frequently and at length to develop their lungs.

Quite contrary to the popular idea that babies are out to control their parents, I intend to demonstrate that babies are helpless immature beings with feelings and instinctual drives for survival and social imprinting. They thrive when they are tenderly cared for, nursed, and closely nurtured. Psychology and sociology researchers have found that, in reality, the significant result of today's coveted early independence is poorly bonded children who often become poorly functioning adults. The outcome of our ubiquitous detached parenting is most clearly seen during adolescence when poorly attached children often exhibit highly destructive behavior toward themselves or others—often gently referred to as "antisocial" behavior. This behavior is the independent behavior that was sought—now, unfortunately, independent of the wishes of parents or society. It is the consequence of successfully preventing close bonding from birth.

Self-destructive and violent behavior has been a growing problem throughout the twentieth century. Nearly all who study it find it is strongly linked to the earliest treatment of children. In fact, it has been found that the level and quality of maternal care, especially during the earliest months, provides an incredibly consistent indicator of a child's future behavior and socialization. Well-bonded, securely attached children are more responsive to parental requests, a kind of "dependence" that is preferable. Of course, the results of this behavior carry on into adult life. Furthermore, many adult diseases, both mental and physical, including the now common inability to form long-bonded marital or partner relationships, stem from this lack of strong early attachment.

> This anti-social behavior is the independent behavior that was sought—now, unfortunately, independent of the wishes of parents or society. It is the consequence of successfully preventing close bonding from birth.

Leaving babies crying alone in cribs and otherwise maintaining physical distance through plastic bottles, playpens, and plastic baby carriers contributes to poor attachment. Although the results are obvious, those who study the functioning of our nerves and hormones have now demonstrated that a hormonally conducted bonding occurs when two people consistently touch, protect, and care for each other, and that brain patterns are permanently altered by bonding patterns between parent and child.

Most would agree that children probably do not consciously remember the way they were treated during early infancy. Many recount this observation as support or comfort for their ideas about ignoring babies' cries for attention and providing minimal stimulation. Yet, it can be shown that while the specifics may be lost, unconscious memories are developed on the neurological and biochemical level from birth—a baby's brain develops according to its environment, from day one. Childhood, adolescence, and adulthood are all affected by this early programming. And, as far as the coveted independence goes, it has been shown that those who receive the most affection early on display the highest levels of independence as adults.

At the same time that emotion and behavior are being influenced by detached parenting, health and survival are also taking a beating. Formula feeding is a facet of detached parenting. Not only does withholding breastmilk lead to more illness and death when this important part of an infant's immune protection is lost, but an untold number of babies, children, and adults suffer from physical and behavioral ailments linked to food intolerance reactions. These reactions are an immune system response, stemming especially from the early introduction of cow's milk and milk formulas.

We know that the intestinal irritation and bleeding commonly associated with infants consuming cow's milk proteins eventually allow heavy proteins to pass through the intestinal walls before they have been digested, causing further destructive immune reactions. Our increasing exposure to chemical contaminants in our environment and the enormous amount of drugs and chemicals fed to milk-producing cows may be partially respon-

sible for the ever-increasing number of cases of food allergies, asthma, and auto-immune illnesses. At the same time, medical recognition of these immune mechanisms has actually waned considerably, especially in the United States. Therefore, treatable cases of colic and many other problems remain unrecognized, and children continue to suffer and parents continue to be frustrated. At the same time that milk formulas became popular infant feeds, huge numbers of children suddenly started suffering from a wide array

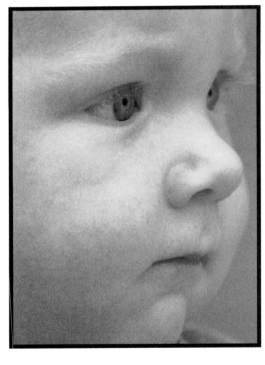

of symptoms that were recognized as food sensitivities. Unfortunately, it appears that the response to this "coincidence" was to change the definition of food allergy. Today, most reactions to milk products are still considered to be somehow different from other validly recognized allergies, causing them to become entities unto themselves, such as "colic" or "reflux," or they are attributed to psychological behavior problems of the child or the parents.

Other connections between cow's milk and disease are also not widely advertised. Today, there is little doubt that early and frequent feeding of dairy products leads to a greatly increased incidence of childhood diabetes. It has been confirmed that high cow's milk consumption is a major cause of osteoporosis. Alas, this information has been stifled, apparently because the National Dairy Council governs the National Osteoporosis Foundation. With huge contributions to pediatric education, the dairy industry and formula manufacturers have managed to keep their products in the high regard of baby doctors. Their other advertising efforts have caused these products to become widely accepted in the eyes of the public as well. Pediatricians and the public have been successfully convinced that formula is a quite reasonable substitute for mother's milk. In fact, however, formula-fed infants suffer twice as many illnesses as breastfed ones, and approximately twice as many bottle-fed infants die compared to breastfed babies (from all causes, as an average). Supplementing breastfed babies with formula not only slows early weight gain, but interferes greatly with the valuable immunity provided by breastmilk. Somehow, this information never quite makes it into mainstream media, whose chief advertisers are…you guessed it. Even after infancy, a significantly higher risk of childhood cancer exists for those who never received breastmilk compared to those who nursed exclusively and for extended periods.

Other parenting practices changed as a result of formula feeding. Today's babies are kept in a separate room so that breastfeeding is not encouraged. Since these babies don't nurse throughout the night while mom and dad sleep, they frequently wake up crying, wanting to eat. Babies often also suffer from chronic intestinal inflammation or indigestion due to irritating and difficult-to-digest foreign bovine proteins, which also makes them wake up crying many times during the night. Parents of these formula babies have to find ways to get a good night's sleep. Measures designed to alleviate this sleep dilemma, such as imposing deep sleep by having babies sleep unnaturally on their stomachs, or exhausting children by allowing long periods of crying, have greatly backfired. We are now discovering that this once-coveted deep sleep has led to countless sudden infant deaths. Formula-fed crib babies also miss the comforting nursing and warm breastmilk throughout the night, as well as the sleep-inducing hormones acquired from nursing closely between two warm parents. Nature designed everything for the most peaceful, restful night for the entire family.

Other potentially harmful practices may be motivated by other industries. Fever-reducing medications are strongly advertised and prescribed, yet for most infections, illness and death increase when fevers are reduced. These are the statistics, the research findings, yet, what message do we receive? Antibiotics continue to be prescribed for ear infections even though there is little doubt that there is a higher rate of recurring ear infections in those who receive antibiotic therapy than in those who do not. In fact, the return of chronic middle ear fluid is 2 to 6 times higher in those treated with antibiotics. Serious sinus infections (mastoiditis) are currently on the rise as a direct result of strongly resistant bacteria developed through the common use of antibiotic therapy for ear infections. Ear infection is a topic well covered in this text because it is so pervasive, but its frequent occurrence doesn't make sense and is not universal. It is largely preventable.

Although some of these modern problems have been largely ignored, the number of people who react to cow's milk is so significant that the problem can't be entirely swept under the rug. Instead, the discussion has become misguided. Parents and doctors have been led to believe that the chief cause of intestinal pain from dairy consumption is lactose intolerance, a condition that can be easily overcome even without excluding dairy products from the diet. Lactose intolerance *is* a real problem that increases with age (evidently, adults are not intended to drink milk, a baby food). It occurs sooner and more often in genetic populations that have consumed dairy for a much shorter history: actually most of the world except for those of Northern European descent. But lactose is a chief component of mother's milk, and, until quite recently, a baby who could not digest lactose would never have lived to pass on his genes. Intestinal intolerance to *cow's milk protein, not lactose,* is the major cause of undiagnosed colic in infants, and of other GI symptoms in the young and old alike.

I have come across many other startling matters. For example, did you know that vitamin K injections at birth are associated with childhood leukemia? Did you know that how you feed and treat your infant can strongly affect your child's IQ? There are also some important concerns surrounding common practices such as vaccination and circumcision that I feel parents have the right to know about.

I have found overwhelming evidence for these assertions and others. I will explain how the health, behavior, intelligence, and success of our children, and the adults they become, can be positively influenced by parental behavior. For various reasons this information does not permeate our common medical or social knowledge; therefore, I wish to arm parents with the best information available. I hope that parents and parents-to-be will find this data provocative, so they will be aware that they have choices and will understand what some of the consequences of their choices may be. I wish parents to know that what you feed your baby matters. How you treat your baby matters. Our future will be significantly affected by the choices that parents make today.

I have high hopes for the children of the twenty-first century.

2

The Attachment Advantage

"The spoiled baby is not one who is pampered, it is one who is being disciplined...its trust in mother and father is being eroded—in the true sense, it is being spoiled."
—Desmond Morris, *Human Beings*, a television documentary

GRADUALLY, MORE AND MORE PARENTS ARE FINDING THAT BY FOLLOWING THEIR deep inborn instincts for baby care, they feel attuned to their child rather than confused about child rearing. They are rewarded for their efforts as their children reach school age, adolescence, and adulthood. However, without appropriate support from doctors and the community, isolated from their extended families who are often in conflict and lacking information about child rearing themselves, and with much of the maternal wisdom of the ages lost, new families often have to blaze their own trails.

The Big Experiment

For a brief period in man's multimillion-year history (the twentieth century), in a small part of the world (Western civilization), one of nature's miraculous innate powers was terribly abused. Down through ages of natural selection, mothers and their infants learned how to recognize each other, how to communicate, and how to imprint and bond. Mothers also knew how to provide all the necessary nurturing, nutritional, and developmental care for their infants, and how to warmly, lovingly, and gently develop a sense of security that allowed their offspring to grow and eventually achieve a healthy independence. While extraordinary medical advances have increasingly provided for the physical survival of the mother and infant, emotional well-being has taken a beating. Failure to thrive, behavior disorders, illness, and occasionally even death are some of the unfortunate consequences.

At the end of the nineteenth century, Dr. Luther Emmett Holt Sr., considered the father of pediatrics, published *Care and Feeding of Children*, which became a child care bible. This book and others instructed parents to never give in to babies' cries for "indulgences." Indulgences included being picked up, held, rocked, comforted, or provided with something to suck on, whether for attention, warmth, simply because baby was hungry, or for any other "bad habit." Dr. Holt demanded that infants should never be played with and should never be allowed in their parents' bed. Next came the psychologists such as John Watson. Watson preached in his widely revered 1928 book, *Psychological Care of Infant and Child*, that children should never be hugged or kissed or allowed on your lap—except for maybe a good-night kiss on the forehead, a morning handshake, or an occasional pat on the head for a job well done.[1]

Throughout the twentieth century infant care "professionals" pushed tremendously for artificial feeding, insisted that children should "cry it out," and advised that responding to infants would seriously "spoil" them. This advice forced bewildered mothers to repress the very essence of their maternal instincts, creating an unnaturally cold, harsh environment for infants. Over time, as weak bonds occurred, this method became easier for mother to uphold. And as more and more people who had failed to form deep attachments during infancy and childhood became parents, these insidious rules became easier and easier for each successive generation to follow. Many problems developed, but there were "expert" answers around every corner.

Some mothers weakened and secretly gave in to their infants' needs behind closed doors, but would then provide mixed messages to their babies when others were near. In the end, many lived with incredible guilt over the whole ordeal. Certainly, no power on earth can prevent mothers from deeply loving their babies or from finding ways to reveal their love. For attempting to provide the best possible environment for us, our fore-mothers' finest intentions must be highly honored, but at the same time, we must be aware that there were consequences to the negligence that was culturally imposed upon both mother and child.

Over the last decades, we have been encouraged to avoid comforting our infants for fear they may ask for more. On one hand we have been told that babies are totally blank slates to be molded as we please. On the other hand we are supposed to believe that they are devious, scheming creatures who spend their days conniving to control the household and come between the parents. If we allow them to have their way, they will become spoiled and will continue to cry for more and more indulgence.

This hands-off approach has not been the only experiment in infant care, but it has been notably unsuccessful, as were many others, and it is the one we need to correct now. The consequences of this great experiment in human health and nature have been far from healthy, and often very destructive. Mid-century researchers such as John Bowlby and Mary Ainsworth studied in depth the psychology behind the explosion of aggressive children, socially irresponsible adolescents, insecure and behaviorally disordered adults, and

> *The explosion of aggressive children, socially irresponsible adolescents, insecure and behaviorally disordered adults, and growing divorce rates stems from frequent rejection by caretakers who ignored the infants' earliest and most primal needs: security, a deep bonding with a primary caregiver, and tender, responsive maternal care.*

growing divorce rates. They found the strongest links to the individuals' early environments. Their studies provided powerful insight into what they labeled "insecurely attached" children. These psychologists found that many developmental and adult shortcomings stemmed from frequent rejection by caretakers who ignored the infants' earliest and most primal needs: security, a deep bonding with a primary caregiver, and tender, responsive maternal care.

As time passed, these psychologists' words were partially heeded, and a gradual softening of position started to appear in the writings of child care experts. Consider the career of one of the most popular advisors, Dr. Benjamin Spock. Much evolution can be seen from his first 1945 baby care book to his last 1998 edition. But as far as matching advice to psychological and scientific findings, there is a long way to go. At the same time that we've seen some softening, we've developed a new hardening of sorts. We have become masters of the baby container. Children are carried in plastic carriers from crib to car seat, transported in strollers, strapped into bouncy seats, and otherwise confined in high chairs, walkers, jumpers, and playpens—often for 95% of their day.

Mixed Feelings

Generations of parents following the advice of the experts who cautioned them not to allow their babies to develop strong attachments to them, or to expect comfort from them, have come to wonder why their teenagers won't trust and confide in them. By withholding parental responsiveness and affection, we have grown generations of adults who are unable to trust, and who act out to acquire attention. Many lack the foundation, security, and trust required to maintain a lasting relationship with a mate. By not respecting the feelings of our infants, we raise children who do not respect the feelings of their peers, adolescents who do not respect the feelings of their parents, and adults who often can't respect even their own feelings.

One major facet of the advice given to parents was the counsel that "autonomy" or "independence" must be developed in their infants. Infants, however, are not meant to be independent, and humans are not solitary animals. Out of a totally protective, secure, nutritive, life-sustaining, and nurturing womb, we are born, helpless, to adults who are tuned by evolution to provide nutrition, protection, and social development during our continued growth. As a reward, this relationship forms the foundation for continued nurturing and guidance, and eventually creates a loving, self-sustaining adult. Not responding to infants' needs has been shown to often reduce their efforts to have their needs met, sometimes resulting in a less-demanding "good baby." In others, prolonged periods of crying ensue, unheeded, when baby is hungry or alone in a crib. Either way, the mother and baby have successfully avoided becoming "too attached" to each other, as the standard advice recommends, so that separations will be easy. Withdrawn or crying alone, whichever path the infant takes, she may appear to be more independent, but ultimately the sad fact is that she is merely very much on her own.

> *Withdrawn or crying alone, whichever path the infant takes, she may appear to be more independent, but ultimately the sad fact is that she is merely very much on her own.*

Countless investigations have revealed the behavioral consequences of these methods: a high risk for behavioral disorders in growing children as well as in the adults they will become. School-age children may be more outwardly aggressive and less in control of themselves, or sometimes they are quite withdrawn. Parents often have little control over their detached and now very independent teenagers, and these teens often demonstrate a wide variety of antisocial behaviors. Anxiety disorders, depression, intimacy issues, and an inability to form stable, lasting bonds are also prominent in adults from insecurely attached beginnings.

To put this issue more simply, when infants' feelings are consistently ignored, they cannot be expected to confide in their caretakers when they become teenagers. When their needs and desires (which are one and the same at this age) are consistently unmet early on, the resulting teenagers cannot be expected to trust that their parents are the ones to turn to. Furthermore, fear may appear to work well as a behavior control for young children, but this tactic runs out of steam for young adults. Only strong bonding and deeply embedded respect and trust will positively influence behavior at this stage of life and beyond.

Popular Psychological Models of Attachment

Children from very understaffed orphanages, such as those in Romania, who were supplied almost no affection or stimulation, provide a sad view of the opposite extreme to strong infant bonding with a responsive, affectionate caregiver. Even in institutions where food and medical treatment are adequate, few of the infants live. Those who do may cry for long hours, but more often a trance-like state manifests. They have minimal intellectual development and poor motor development. Those who are rescued into homes become very difficult to control. They show little response to caregiver overtures, but may be overly friendly to strangers. They often grow into adolescents and adults whose pathological behavior seems unresponsive to nearly any kind of therapy. Many of these males end up institutionalized for crimes, while females frequently become victims. The more "successful" ones use their interpersonal detachment in pathological ways to advance their careers and to frequently enter into and out of relationships. The fate of these emotionally abandoned youngsters is explained by their lack of early bonding to a consistent caregiving figure. As they grow up, they lack a secure emotional foundation, they are unable to develop trust in others, and they seldom initiate fulfilling affectionate relationships. In short, the skills necessary for productive interpersonal interactions have never been learned. These children are not neurologically well developed and are unable to form bonds with other human beings. They suffer from severe attachment disorder.

Boosted by her work with Bowlby, and after years of painstaking observation and research during the 1950s and 1960s, Mary Ainsworth divided children, chiefly from less severe situations than just described, into three categories. According to her nomenclature, which continues to be used in psychology today, children can be "avoidantly attached," "ambivalently attached," (two forms of insecure attachment), or "securely attached." As defined in this work, secure attachment is observed in just over half of all infants. A "disorganized attachment" category was later added by psychologist Mary Main and is sometimes, but not always, used in studies. Seeking to find a standard for measurement of infant attachment, Ainsworth recorded detailed observations of infant behavior toward their mothers and strangers in a consistently performed laboratory sequence of events dubbed the "strange situation." Her work became very popular in the 1970s because she was able to recognize distinct behaviors in infants that consistently reflected distinct maternal practices. Many others went on to confirm and expand her work, and some investigators even followed infants into adolescence and adulthood.

According to the widely accepted Ainsworth model, infants develop secure attachment when their mothers provide tender, responsive care from the very beginning. Their mothers quickly respond to their cries, validate their feelings, and are affectionate, well attuned to them, and consistently concerned. Securely attached infants are confident, display upset when mother leaves, greet her warmly when she returns, respond to her soothing, and enjoy her comfort. They explore away from their mother, glancing back or returning frequently to their mother, using her as a secure base, and seeking her comfort when alarmed or upset. The secure child develops good peer relationships and expresses empathy. While occasionally testing limits, they are elementally trustworthy.

Avoidantly attached infants come from mothers whose availability, both emotionally and physically, has been limited. This child's mother pushes for his independence and doesn't like his "neediness." She often rejects him and is emotionally unresponsive. While Ainsworth never directly implied any connection, this perfectly describes the expert pediatric advice of the times—force independence and do not respond to cries. Avoidantly attached infants do not look for physical contact with their mothers, and they don't respond to an embrace, although they may express upset at being put down. They actively ignore mother's return after separation and avoid mother when in distress. This is the "good" or "independent" baby many have been told to strive for. The avoidant child often appears complacent and less distressed over separation, although he eventually can become very demanding. The avoidant child may be alternatively clingy, demanding, withdrawn, aggressive, and angry. He may randomly attack or express anger at his mother, and isolate himself when in pain. As he grows, he is unenthusiastic and has poor peer relations.

The ambivalently attached baby is anxious, cries a lot, does not explore, and resists being soothed. Her body does not mold to that of her caregiver when being held, rather she may arch away or become limp. She may act overly cute and ply for favor. She actively seeks her parents' affections yet responds with hostility. As she grows, she shows immaturity and often becomes the victim of the avoidant child's aggressiveness. This infant's behavior is the result of receiving inconsistent attention from her parents. (These parents tried to follow the no-spoiling rules, but often gave in.) She becomes angry and unsure of her parents' ability to be there when needed.

More seriously abused or neglected infants generally fall into the disorganized attachment classification. To the less familiar observer, they may appear very attached, but they may greet a parent with actions such as falling to the floor or leaning their heads against a wall. As children, they attempt to control their parents as well as take care of them. They seldom make eye contact, seldom smile, and often exhibit speech problems. They act overly attractive and cute toward strangers. They are least able to regulate their emotions and may exhibit self-destructive behaviors.

Securely Attached

I emphasize the mid-century models of attachment because a great number of studies are available, based on these models, that give us insight into the results of various parenting attitudes. The idea of secure attachment has now grown. Many parents seek a greater depth of attachment through even more natural means, such as breastfeeding on cue, than these early researchers were ready to consider.

Having been provided with consistently responsive and affectionate care, children classified as securely attached, and the adults they become, usually develop more successful marriages, maintain better relationships with their parents, suffer fewer behavioral disorders, and show higher levels of integrity, including the ability to trust. In contrast to the results of trying to instill "independence" through early detached parenting, which creates emotionally insecure adults, securely attached infants become secure adults of high self-esteem who are strongly independent, but who can also be interdependent in relationships.

Researchers investigating various attachment levels in mother-infant pairs report that mothers of securely attached infants seem to enjoy their babies more, are better able to recognize and understand their cues, and are better able to use those cues to guide their infants' behavior.[2] It is logical to view the maternal ability to act on cues as a cause of attachment as much as a result of it. Greater joy for all participating family members is the typical outcome.

Securely attached children are able to delay gratification much longer than their poorly attached peers (a measure of independence).[3] Higher IQ, regardless of mother's working status, and greater success in school, regardless of intelligence, are shown to be other benefits reaped by securely attached children.[4,5] It has even been shown that securely attached infants use acute care services about half as often,[6] perhaps because the attuned mother has better skill at determining the actual level of illness in her child, or feels more secure about her observations and her ability to care for him. Also, it is more likely that these children have been breastfed, and a reduction in illness results from breast-feeding alone. Although it is sometimes difficult to ascertain how much influence each of the factors in child rearing has, a healthier child is the common denomina-tor of a more secure attachment.

Many studies have shown success-ful outcomes from training mothers of high-risk mother-infant pairs to respond sensitively to their babies' cues. One study specifically reported more pleasingly social-ized babies who cried less and performed more intellectually challenging types of exploration.[7] A preschool-age follow-up showed that the effects of sensitive moth-ering were lasting, finding that the babies had become secure children who displayed positive peer interactions.[8]

> *In contrast to the results of trying to instill "independence" through early detached parenting, which creates emotionally insecure adults, securely attached infants become secure adults of high self-esteem who are strongly independent, but who can also be interdependent in relationships.*

One valuable achievement in young children that helps promote positive social behavior for years to come is developing a good conscience. Research on children between the ages of 2 and 5 discerned that while gentle mater-nal discipline (one attachment guideline) successfully promoted conscience in fearful toddlers, only a high level of responsiveness from mother and

secure attachment resulted in a well-developed conscience in toddlers classified as fearless.[9]

Although pacifier use does not disqualify a child from being described as attached, securely attached children are seldom found to have strong attachments to pacifiers.[10] Looking beyond the securely attached classification to the "attachment-parented" child (soon to be described), one will see that these children seldom develop long-term attachments to thumbs, pacifiers, or inanimate objects of any kind.[11] The key is that these children are more attached to their caretakers. Later on, this ability to derive more long-term security and satisfaction from a mate than from "things" is reported to be an advantage for developing a more secure marriage.

Seeds of Behavior Disorders

So what happens to the many children who do not gain the benefit of strong bonding experiences with a consistent caretaker? Inborn temperaments cause all children to respond to a given caregiving environment in their own way. However, certain strong patterns do reveal themselves in sociological studies, which provide insight and help us predict the general results of certain parenting patterns for children of all temperaments. A large number of studies have confirmed that weakly or insecurely attached children manifest unproductive behaviors throughout their lives as a result of their relationship with their mothers and the level and quality of caregiving, not generally as a result of genetic or other factors.[12,13]

Insecurely attached youngsters, those from "early independence" and "let them cry" households, often evolve into adults who dread emotional intimacy or are hostile, insecure, or manipulative with romantic partners.[14,15] Not only does poor attachment lead to poor adult romantic relationships, but often to the development of psychological disorders.

Psychologists know well that a child's level of attachment strongly predicts behavior problems at school age.[16] In addition, *researchers have found that anxiety disorders,[17] deviant behavior,[18] and other personality disorders[19] during adolescence are strongly linked to poorly developed early bonding,* with only a minimal influence from other factors such as parental death, maternal anxiety, or initial temperament. Aggressive and self-destructive behavior, eating disorders, and substance abuse are some of the results[20]—all common problems in recent decades. Adolescents hospitalized for psychiatric disorders overwhelmingly display insecure attachment patterns,[21] as do those involved in criminal behavior and hard drug use.[22]

As attachment theory studies gradually worked their way up to studying the effects on adulthood, romantic failings were the first focus. Gradually, the connections between infant attachment and adult mental behavior and stress reactions became recognized. In fact, a recent large survey confirms that most adults with mental disorders suffer from childhood-based attachment disorders.[23] Much current research has shown interest in the strong connection between impaired attachment and the development of depression.[24,25] New hormone studies reveal that adults with poor coping abilities for dealing with stress were infants whose stress hormone regulation did not organize well due to poor maternal responsiveness (*as explained in the next chapter*). And, today's ever-so-prominent workaholics are considered to be adults raised with insecure attachment, now hiding from the intimacies of real life.

Clues from Immigration

The psychological results of different bonding practices are clearly revealed by following the health patterns of people from cultures who transition from one kind of child-rearing society to another. The people of Mexico, who generally practice a more attached style of parenting than people in the United States, suffer mental disorders only half as much as non-Hispanic U.S. whites. This difference persists in recent Mexican immigrants to the United States;

however, the mental health of their U.S.-born children is reduced. By the third generation, U.S.-born Mexican Americans have rates of mental illness just as miserable as those in non-Hispanic U.S. whites. This same effect has been shown for immigrants from other Central and South American regions studied. It has been proposed that the increasing incorporation of standard U.S. child-rearing practices over generations is responsible for the declining rate of mental health seen in successive generations of immigrants.[26–29]

Seeds of Violence

Psychologists, psychiatrists, sociologists, and others agree that reduced motherly responsiveness leads to the poor early attachment patterns that predispose children to aggressive behavior.[30,31] In addition to being associated with mild and moderate behavior disorders such as depression and anxiety, the quality of infant attachment has been found to be strongly linked to aggression, violence, and criminality in adolescence and adulthood.[32]

It has been proposed that the increasing incorporation of standard U.S. child-rearing practices over generations is responsible for the declining rate of mental health seen in successive generations of immigrants.

These patterns are found to be remarkably unyielding to change throughout a child's development and during adulthood.[33] Once seen, childhood aggression and associated poor peer relations are strong predictors of aggressive adolescent behaviors,[34] which in turn can often result in adult violence. Dr. Ken Magid, author of *High Risk: Children without a Conscience*, has studied the issue of adolescent and adult violence in depth and concludes that poor early attachment is the key.

Bonding Effects on Puberty

One striking consequence of the childhood stress of insecure attachment is early puberty. While this has been noticed in both males and females, the early onset of menstruation in girls, the most objective measurement, is the most frequently measured indicator in puberty studies.[35–37] There are several unfortunate results from early puberty. One is that children develop adult feelings before they are old enough to understand and handle them. Another, encouraged by the behavioral results of parental detachment, is an increase in teen pregnancy. Possibly the most devastating result is the increased risk of breast cancer and other cancers associated with early menstruation.[38,39] The incredible rise in consumption of cow's milk during the 1900s, also a factor in decreased attachment (via decreased breastfeeding), provides an additive effect to the early onset of puberty as well as to increased cancer rates (*as discussed in the chapter on cow's milk*).

Psychologist Jay Belsky provides a possible explanation for this accelerated maturity. He has proposed that a pattern of detached parenting has naturally occurred throughout our history, and in animals as well, in response to hard times when food is scarce or survival is otherwise in danger.[40] Ample food and safety generate the time and stability for providing warm, responsive care, thereby resulting in quality evolution of the species; hard times switch the focus to mere survival. Theoretically, reduced attachment would serve to reduce the pain of lost family members. Harsh parenting would lead to the development of early puberty and would encourage behaviors that promote multiple sexual partners, thus increasing chances for survival of the species during bleak times. Detached parenting would also foster aggressive behavior, increasing the ability to compete for food and mating opportunities.

Other Factors

Certainly, an increasing level of psychological aftermath, aggression, or violent behavior correlates with a more insecure level of attachment. Most researchers agree that withholding maternal responsiveness, often characterized as "not spoiling the child," which was encouraged by experts over the last one hundred years, is the major source of undesirable behavior, but other factors compound these problems. These are the more obvious elements of marital conflict, divorce, parental substance abuse, parental crime or psychiatric disorder, and overprotective and controlling parents. Note, however, that these conditions are those that occur chiefly in parents with insecurely attached beginnings. Fortunately, it is comforting to know that, at least statistically, the effects on children experiencing hardships such as divorce can be mostly overridden when at least one long-term caregiver maintains a strong, sensitive bond with them.

Another major cause of infant and child behavior problems is food sensitivity reactions and other allergies. These are much more far-reaching than most are led to believe. The reduction in breastfeeding and the resultant mass use of cow's milk largely causes this growing predicament. (*This topic is covered in depth in the last chapters of this book.*) It's clear that less-responsive parenting and formula use often go hand-in-hand, making it sometimes difficult to entirely discern which of these factors is leading to which behavioral effects. Yet, with the thousands of studies on the adverse effects of dairy consumption, it is quite clear that this ingredient on its own is highly responsible for many behavioral problems now becoming prevalent. Over and over again, we will see similar behavior and health problems from detached parenting practices and from early and heavy cow's milk feeding.

Separation Sensitivity

Extended mother-infant separation is another key issue affecting infant bonding. In the early years, repeated long separations, such as parental vacations, can be harmful to the attachment relationship.[41] Children may learn that they can't depend on mother to always be there, and trust diminishes. Along with long-term separation comes the delicate issue of day-long separations and day care. There were bursts of studies on this issue in the mid 1980s as well as the late 1990s, but the results are conflicting. None of the results appear to be overwhelming. Overall, it appears that less-attached mother-infant pairs may decide to use day care somewhat more frequently, which may perpetuate the reduced attachment, but many of these infants end up finding attachments through day care that instill the ability to trust. Infants who repetitively lose predominant caregivers seem to suffer most. Using data on the *quality* of day care produces more certain statistics, but ideas on quality also vary. When visiting a daycare center, one tends to notice beauty and cleanliness, at least at first, but the nature and level of the attention given to each child is far more important. There seems to be agreement that part-time day care has less effect on the mother-infant bond than does full-time, and other factors being the same, many behavioral differences between in-home and daycare children seem to fade over time after kindergarten. Unfortunately, most families today, having generally lost the valuable access to a close-knit neighborhood or tribe or highly available extended families, are sometimes caught between what parenting levels are desired and what is emotionally (and financially) possible.

Twins: The "Beginnings Don't Matter" Studies

Lawrence Wright, a staff writer for the *New Yorker,* wrote *Twins and What They Tell Us About Who We Are.*[42] He summarizes and speculates from studies performed on twins who were raised in separate households. Studies of separated twins aim to discover how totally different environments affect the outcome of genetically identical humans, in an attempt to throw light on the age-old nature versus nurture debate. Because Wright found similar behaviors in adults who came from supposedly different beginnings, Wright suggests that early environment has little effect on behavior. Judith Harris, in *The Nurture Assumption,* uses the same arguments to suggest that only peers influence how children will behave and what kind of people they will become—that the actions of the parents matter little. Again, she bases her arguments on the assumption that the separated twins in the studies had entirely different beginnings, having been adopted by different families. Although parenting practices were not strongly altered by the large number of attachment studies of the 1970s and 1980s, which added much weight to the parental nurture side of the equation, there has been a sigh-of-relief reaction from factions of society for these new nature- and peer-based arguments, demonstrating that the issue has remained a prominent concern in the minds of many.

I believe, however, that the subjects in these studies had much more similar beginnings than Wright and Harris realize, and this is a very critical point that washes out their arguments from the start. First of all, each pair shared the same womb and intrauterine exposure to maternal emotions, stress levels, nutrition, drugs, and so forth. Since the subjects were nearly all adopted, few, if any, were breastfed. Since most or all of the adoptive families were unaware they were raising separated twins, it can be assumed that none of the adoptive parents were present at the births or were available for early bonding experiences. In fact, the average age of these subjects at adoption was *5 months!* (Only after the severe effects of institutionalizing babies were recognized in the 1960s did newborn adoptions occur to any degree.) Since most twins are low-birth-weight babies, in all likelihood most of these babies spent their first weeks in hospitals. Then these children, depending on the year of their birth, spent the next months of their lives either in inattentive orphanages, or in foster homes where caretakers typically protect themselves by not becoming too attached to the infants. Furthermore, all these subjects not only shared a critical separation with their first bonded caretakers (after non-bonded hospital beginnings), but they also suffered separation from their closely bonded twin, whom they knew for several months in the womb plus for whatever time they spent together after birth. Initially, their adoptive parents would not have been influenced by the hormonally induced reorganization of brain receptors that goes on during pregnancy, promoting early parental behaviors. Additionally, the infants would not have an initial imprinting on these adoptive parents, generally formed in the womb and the first weeks of life. Their bottle-feeding and less intimate relationships would predict more of a crib-crying, textbook-of-the-times (stressful) upbringing. Finally, particularly at the time of these births, there were set parameters for families who were allowed to adopt, creating more similarity.

None of this is meant to suggest that adoption is anything less than an absolutely priceless opportunity. Adopted infants can develop as strong an attachment as any other baby—and can even be breastfed in most cases if the desire is there. I make this comparison only to point out that Wright's and Harris's subjects have far less random beginnings than they suggest.

For instance, Wright describes two girls who similarly displayed prolonged thumb-sucking and "blanket clenching." Neither girl could be easily controlled, both had poor peer relations, and both hid their emotions. Each girl told the researchers that she received a very low level of affection from her mother—the one who reported a somewhat higher level being the one with better behavior and peer relations. To me, the girls' behavior sounds like genetically similar responses to similar low-attachment environments and the shared early loss of primary caregivers and a sibling. Other symptoms they displayed, such as prolonged bedwetting and learning disorders, are often signs of intolerance to cow's milk products (beginning with formula feeding) and possibly other foods. This sensitivity and the resulting behavior require a certain genetic disposition, but depend on environmental circumstances to manifest.

Because researchers found close similarities in behavior in many sets of separated twins, they conclude that early environment has little to do with shaping personality. However, when one examines the truly important factors, the early environments of these twins were very similar indeed. The early conditions these twins shared are the ones that attachment researchers emphasize as the most important for shaping behavior.

Consider another example. Other researchers showed that when one twin was divorced, there was a much higher than average chance the other would be.[43] This *could* demonstrate a genetic predisposition for divorce, as they suggest; more likely (to me), however, divorce was a genetically similar response to the shared experience of poor attachment and separations during infancy.

Most importantly, when these studies reported "similar behaviors," they usually described shared personality quirks. In contrast, more reliable statistics, gathered by comparing identical twins (identical genetics) to fraternal twins (some dissimilar genetics) who were all raised together, indicate that *social* behavior, discipline, criminality, and depression were all influenced more by family environment than by genetics, as was "happiness." Attachment studies suggest the very same thing; furthermore, these behaviors are the most important aspects of personality, not the mere quirks of personality upon which much of the nature and peer arguments were built.

As with our appearance, much of our personality, preferences, and mannerisms are genetically determined. So are the ways we will respond to certain kinds of social exposure. But there is a definite pattern to the responses that correlate most strongly with the earliest environment, which then governs how we will react later on in life. I find no contradiction between the studies on twins and the attachment study findings. No one discounts genetics, but it seems clear that parental responsiveness and bonding play a major role in psychological and social outcomes.

Reattachment

Psychologists do have ways of intervening when poor attachment has occurred in a child. Before the age of 7 months, extra holding, nurturing, and availability generally do the trick. Children adopted or placed into foster homes before this age show little difficulty in forming healthy attachments when strong measures are taken. Professional intervention needs to be more focused the older the child is. Fairly good results are still expected when efforts begin before the age of 7 years.[44] These windows of opportunity also exist for the father who was not involved from the beginning. Beyond this age, positive lasting change is very difficult to produce and treatments become more radical. For this reason, psychologists and sociologists emphasize the overwhelming importance of nurturing parenting from the very beginning.

Breaking the Cycle

The findings of attachment research suggest that insecurely attached children not only end up in poorly attached marriages and relationships, but in turn also raise insecurely attached children. Fortunately, however, it has been shown that some adults who explore their own insecurely attached shortcomings can heal and become more attached as adults and parents. Belsky found that adults who simply have a coherent understanding of the negative consequences of their own insecure attachment, and who can remain effective parents during highly stressful situations, are able to raise securely attached children.[45] He calls these adults "earned secures." Others have similarly found that the cycle can be broken through intellectual means.[46] Ultimately, many heal themselves by successfully developing a strongly attached relationship with a mate or child.[47]

Social behavior, discipline, criminality, and depression were all influenced more by family environment than by genetics, as was "happiness."

Going Beyond Secure Attachment

The distinct categories of secure or insecure attachment serve to provide a valuable basis for research into the outcomes of various parental patterns, but the picture is certainly not as simple as some literature describes it. There are very severe examples of improper attachment resulting from abandonment and abuse, but there are many shades of attachment between this and the securely attached infant, whose parents respond quickly and sensitively to cries, and provide consistent affectionate attention.

Many also believe there are many levels of secure attachment, possibly including a level beyond it of highly attuned, strongly bonded, gentle, and intimate relationships. Today, parents around the United States are rediscovering their natural parenting options and are following a style that has become known as "attachment parenting." The results of the multitude of in-depth studies on attachment have lent permission to many to provide the responsive, affectionate care parents are naturally driven to offer. Some deeper issues are not addressed in the popular psychological models of the twentieth century, such as the immense value of nursing for emotional, physical, and intellectual development, as well as for physical health. Even beyond this, there is a huge gap between common breastfeeding advice and the most beneficial nursing measures. The provision of skin-to-skin contact and frequent holding and carrying may not be part of these models either, but the great value of around-the-clock close contact has been described by many and can be clearly seen around the world.

> Cultures around the world that practice more natural forms of parenting have healthier infants who cry much less, toddlers who do not exhibit "terrible twos," generally respectful teenagers, and independent adults who participate in family matters.

Thus, the attachment-parenting model may look at traditional twentieth-century parenting as the cause of mild to moderate forms of attachment disorders. Moreover, some of the relationships approved as securely attached may be viewed as still lacking some ideal qualities. While only 41% of U.S. infants have been classified as insecurely attached, the percentage of adults who generally suffer from security, trust, control, or intimacy issues, who are not able to sustain long healthy relationships, who are depressed or anxious, or who deal poorly with stress, is larger than this.

Cultures around the world that practice more natural forms of parenting have healthier infants who cry much less, toddlers who do not exhibit "terrible twos," generally respectful teenagers, and independent adults who participate in family matters.

Attachment parenting practices are based on the wisdom of our natural parenting instincts and baby's natural abilities to provide instructions for care. In addition to instinctual guidance, more complex species are known to pass wisdom down from generation to generation. But we have lost a few generations. It's no wonder new mothers in the Western world have so many problems and questions. Most have never witnessed a birth before their own child's, nor seen a baby nurse—the most basic essentials are missing. Actually, a large portion of attachment-parented infants are the third or fourth child in a family that has given up "modern" methods in favor of practices they found over time to be easier and to provide superior results.

Those who wish to gain all the benefits of securely attached parent-child relationships find it easy to follow their natural drives to feed baby when hunger is expressed, to nurse, console, and comfort him in response to his needs, to hold and be with their infants as much as possible, using snuggies, slings, and backpacks to give the infant moment-to-moment body contact, to provide consistent caretaker availability and response, and to offer enriching exposure to the daily world. Nightly cries of abandonment and hunger, which tear at a parent's heart, are enjoyably avoided by naturally sharing sleep and nursing throughout the night.

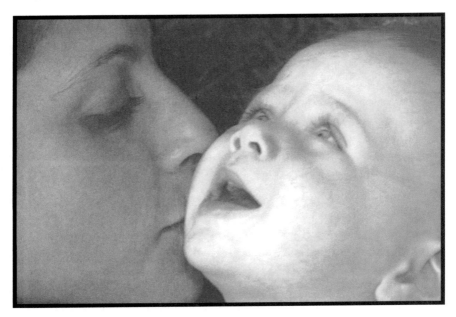

Follow Your Instincts

Human babies are born much more prematurely than most babies are. While most animal babies can walk or swim at birth, humans are unable to even make their way to mother's milk or other food for a year. Two years must pass before they can recognize danger signs. At birth, they only have needs: to be fed when their tummies are hungry, to be kept warm by warm bodies, to be protected and cared for, and to develop social attachments for emotional security.

Nature and evolution have provided sufficient means for babies to have all their needs met. Their tiny size, softness, precious smiles, and heart-rending cries elicit powerful drives in adult females to respond to them and hold them, and in males to protect them. When there is no interference, human instincts, hormones, neurotransmitters, and neurons provide for a strong bonding process between infants and their caretakers so that the providers of the infants' milk and safety will never be far away. At the same time, infants' brains are stimulated and educated by regular social interaction, expressions, touching, and words from caretakers, and they are therefore nurtured into intelligent, inde-

> *An infant who is fed when he is hungry feels satiated, loved, and respected, and trusts that he is safe. A baby whose parents respond to her feelings knows she can confide in them.*

pendent, secure, trusting beings. A gesture or a whimper and mother knows they need to be fed, dried, spoken to, or warmed. When you pick up a crying baby, you provide security and comfort and build the baby's trust in her caretakers. An infant who is fed when he is hungry feels satiated, loved, and respected, and trusts that he is safe. A baby whose parents respond to her feelings knows she can confide in them.

By following nature rather than fighting it, parenting can be far more fulfilling, as can the results. Many parents are comforted to discover permission to be with their children in the way their hearts tell them. The idea of being natural parents includes considering what feels natural for each person in the relationship. Thus, *every family will practice parenting in its own unique way*—and even differently with each child. Most find that parenting is easier when the feeling is right.

3

Bonding: The Inside Story

FALLING IN LOVE CAN BE INTOXICATING. WE MAY FEEL EUPHORIC, GIDDY, OR forgetful as our minds become saturated with endorphins (natural opioids, pleasure hormones) and norepinephrine (adrenaline). These are our rewards for closeness. Furthermore, our bodies maintain relationships by secreting hormones such as oxytocin, prolactin, and vasopressin that make us feel good when we interact with others. Under proper conditions, this experience can emerge during parent-infant bonding. If it does, we as parents will follow the advice of our hormones and will continue to nurture our babies and maintain physical closeness with them. We "fall in love" with our babies over and over as our brains undergo physical changes that reinforce parenting behaviors. The infant experiences similar hormonal responses and is permanently affected by them, becoming strongly attached to his closest caretakers.

Humans could not have become complex, intelligent creatures without a long evolutionary social development that taught them to live with each other, learn from each other, care for each other, and depend upon each other for survival and fulfillment. This social development begins in the womb, where we become accustomed to the scent and sounds of our mother, and to the rhythm of her day. Once we are born, our hormonal control systems and brain synapses begin to permanently organize according to the human interactions we experience. We are designed to seek fulfillment for all our basic health and social needs so we can blossom into healthy, intelligent, and socially well-adapted individuals; however, we may find ourselves in an environment where our solicitations do not always receive a healthy response. When this is the case, we are programmed to become more self-centered and aggressive and less-bonded, in proportion to the severity of conditions. Toward the harsher extreme, where touching is seldom experienced and comfort rarely received, we stop secreting growth hormone and reduce brain development in order to conserve energy for a more independent survival.

> *While an adult may be able to be romantically neglected, deceived, or uninvolved without major long-term consequences, an infant's permanent brain development is shaped by the level of attentiveness she receives from her "first loves."*

In the brains of infants and children, permanent patterns are created. Unneeded brain receptors and neural pathways are disposed of, while those appropriate to the given environment are enhanced. Early social responses, stress responses, and intellectual attention build a foundation that will guide our interaction with our environment for the rest of our lives (moderated by our own genetic slants). The initial availability of responsive care and the pursuant level of bonding with consistent caregivers determine to what degree responsible social beings will develop. While an adult may be able to be romantically neglected, deceived, or uninvolved without major long-term consequences, an infant's permanent brain development is shaped by the level of attentiveness she receives from her "first loves."

While many clues have been found along the way, over the last decade research has described the chemical bases of bonding reactions, confirming many people's suspicions that attentiveness and touching enhance a child's development. Recent advances in measuring stress hormones have spurred a deluge of research into infant responses to stresses such as maternal separation. Amazingly, or perhaps not, these findings tie in very well with earlier psychological findings. By becoming familiar with baby's biochemistry, one can clearly understand how parents' actions can affect their children's psychological health. Moreover, parents can better recognize their parenting instincts, plan their parenting choices, and understand the feelings of their spouse and child.

Oxytocin: A Bonding Hormone

Oxytocin is a chemical messenger released in the brain. It is very important for developing bonding between mothers and their infants, and between mother and involved father. To a lesser extent, oxytocin is elicited by friendships and general social contact, even by relationships with pets. The most common stimulus for its release in both men and women, in adults as well as in children (and mammals in general) is social contact—especially physical contact, being most pronounced with skin-to-skin contact. After it is released, oxytocin promotes the desire for further social interaction. Therefore, frequent close proximity develops a continuous drive to maintain a given relationship, and physical touch heightens this drive. Over time, the sight, sound (especially a cry), or even thought of the individual can cause oxytocin release.

Oxytocin calms and relaxes and reduces stress responses, playing a likely role in the health benefits reportedly seen with long marriages and social relationships,[1] or when the elderly keep pets. By promoting lower blood pressure and reduced heart rate as well as certain kinds of artery repair, long-term social interactions that increase oxytocin levels actually reduce heart disease.[2] In fact, adults who display the symptoms of poor childhood attachment, such as bouts of depression or anxiety, face a tripled risk of dying from heart disease.[3] Oxytocin lowers pain sensitivity, which is why a parent's kiss is effective treatment for a scraped knee. It also helps to regulate bodily functions such as digestion and hormone secretion, promoting absorption of nutrients and growth in the well-attended baby.

Oxytocin and the Mother

When the process is uninterrupted, oxytocin is one of nature's chief tools for creating a mother. Roused by the high levels of estrogen ("female hormone") during pregnancy, the number of oxytocin receptors in the expectant mother's brain increases dramatically near the end of her pregnancy. This makes the new mother highly responsive to the presence of oxytocin. These receptors increase in the part of her brain that promotes maternal behaviors.[4]

Oxytocin's first important surge is during labor, when labor is allowed naturally, that is. Serving to encourage uterine contractions for the passage of the infant from the uterus to the birth canal, this is the beginning of highly elevated oxytocin levels that assist the initial bonding after birth. Beyond this stage, further release of oxytocin is stimulated by the infant's passage through the birth canal.

When all goes well, the oxytocin level is very high in a mother at the moment her infant is born. It continues to rise until 45 minutes after birth, returning to its pre-labor level at the end of 1 hour,[5] if no nursing has occurred. This high level is one of several factors that create the imprinting opportunity during the first hour after birth. Initially high levels of oxytocin and the mother's high receptivity to its presence help mother imprint strongly onto her new infant. High oxytocin levels promote mother's maternal feelings and behaviors, as well as her tendency to bond. Oxytocin also causes mother to become familiar with the odor of her infant and attracted to it, preferring it above all others.[6] By influencing maternal behavior and stimulating milk "let down" (allowing milk to flow) during nursing, oxytocin helps make the first attempts at breastfeeding feel entirely natural. High levels after birth also help reduce mother's pain recognition. The first nursing attempts after birth then cause further oxytocin release, which not only continues the bonding process, but serves to help shrink the uterus, preventing hemorrhage.

Much higher levels of oxytocin are found in a mother after a vaginal delivery than after an elective C-section.[7] A cesarean section after some labor produces oxytocin levels somewhere in between elective C-section and vaginal delivery. It has been found that the oxytocin levels secreted during nursing remain low even 2 days following a C-section, with a notable increase in mother's anxiety level[8,9] and decrease in her breastfeeding success. Furthermore, the infant is receiving less of this comforting and bonding hormone from mother's milk.

After the first hour following labor and birth, mother continues to produce elevated levels of oxytocin as a consequence of nursing and holding her infant. She may be aware of helpful uterine contractions during breastfeeding for days or weeks. Her increased level of oxytocin receptors also remains high for more than several months. This hormonal condition provides calm, pain tolerance, reduced blood pressure, and a sense of well-being for her, and also promotes bonding and maternal behaviors that help her to fall in love with her baby.

Oxytocin causes mother to be more caring, to be more eager to please others, to become more sensitive to others' feelings, and to recognize nonverbal cues more readily. Under the early influence of oxytocin, certain nerve junctions in certain areas of her brain actually undergo reorganization, thereby making her maternal behaviors rather permanent. High oxytocin in the female has also been shown to promote preference for whatever male is present during its surges[10] (one good reason for dad to hang around during and after the birth).

Elevated levels of oxytocin also promote what is referred to as social memory—developing increased memory for people's faces, odors (subconsciously), and impressions, although the highest doses of oxytocin create an amnesia-like effect[11] that helps the mother forget some of the trauma of childbirth and makes her a bit forgetful at other times during the first months spent close to her infant. Oxytocin levels create increased social behavior as well. Having spent much time at home "nesting" during pregnancy, new mothers now seek the company of other family members and other mothers. We see her comparing baby's teething schedules, forming play groups, attending parenting classes and support groups, or just cruising the malls. But this attached mother may not be buying many fancy clothes and accessories for herself because her brain receptors have been reorganized by oxytocin (and prolactin). Her priorities have been altered and her brain no longer signals her to groom and adorn in order to obtain a mate, and thus a pregnancy. Now that the child has been created, mom's grooming instincts are directed toward baby.

Even though estrogen helps oxytocin secretion in the non-mother, estrogen levels in the mother gradually decrease in the days after an infant's birth in order to sustain lactation (breastmilk development). At this point it is safe for the body to do this because a strong and lasting imprinting and neural reorganization should have already taken place, and mother still has more oxytocin receptors than usual, thanks to the high estrogen of pregnancy. Estrogen stays low for about the first year of nursing, then gradually increases to normal levels, even when lactation continues.[12] Even though estrogen levels drop, oxytocin levels are not necessarily depleted in a nursing mother. The reduced estrogen can be more than made up for with a lot of physical contact during nursing, holding, and sharing sleep (parents and children in the same bed). Oxytocin levels are higher in mothers who exclusively breastfeed than in those who use supplementary bottles.[13]

Oxytocin and the Infant

Just like his mother, an infant is born with highly elevated oxytocin levels, but the first attempts at nursing during the initial hour of bonding will cause these levels to surge even more. The initial bonding of an infant to its parents appears to be mostly, but not entirely, inspired by odors (pheromones). When the infant is born, he is already imprinted on the odor of his amniotic fluid.[14,15] This imprinting occurs shortly before birth with the help of oxytocin, and this imprinting is then heightened during the high oxytocin window just after birth. In the days following birth, the infant can be comforted by this odor—babies who remain exposed to these odors cry far less than those who do not.[16] Gradually over the next days, baby starts to prefer the odor of his mother's breast. A newborn can quickly find mother's nipple even on his first couple of tries because mother's breast odor resembles that of the amniotic fluid. While this pre-birth imprinting must have a partial role in helping a newborn find his food, continued imprinting upon his mother is not food related. In fact, formula-fed infants are more attracted (in laboratory tests) to their mother's breast odor than to that of their formula, even 2 weeks after birth.[17] Elevated oxytocin levels created by body contact and nursing help the infant continue to develop odor preferences, especially in the first weeks of life. To me, this suggests that father has a very good chance of having baby imprint on him in the early days after birth if the newborn learns his father's odors, even though father is not feeding the baby. Mates can imprint on each other's odors throughout adulthood, but the early abilities of the infant are much stronger.

Although baby makes her own oxytocin in response to nursing, mother also transfers oxytocin to the infant in her milk.[18] This oxytocin serves to promote continuous relaxation and closeness for both mother and baby, over and above the oxytocin-induced experiences of breastfeeding. Often the calming granted an infant during nursing helps her to drift off to sleep naturally, with mother joining in on occasion. A more variable release of oxytocin is seen in bottle-fed infants, but is definitely higher in an infant who is "bottle-nursed" tightly in the arms (causing oxytocin release in the feeder as well), rather than with a propped bottle.

Oxytocin also provides some relief from hunger, helping the infant to end nutritive nursing (taking in milk), even though she may continue non-nutritive nursing (taking little or no milk) for many more minutes for its calming and bonding effects.

Regular body contact and other nurturing acts by parents produce a constant, elevated level of oxytocin in the infant, which in turn provides a valuable reduction in the infant's stress hormone responses. It has been demonstrated that, *depending on the practices of the parents, the resulting high or low level of oxytocin will control the permanent organization of the stress-handling portion of the baby's brain* — promoting lasting securely attached or insecure characteristics in the adolescent and adult. Psychiatrist Michael Commons suggests that the now-common poor stress regulation is responsible for the proliferation of post-traumatic stress disorder (PTSD) seen today in Americans.[19] Others liken this tendency to overreact to stress to what is known as "type A" behavior.

Oxytocin and the Father

It has been shown in various mammals that a live-in father's oxytocin levels rise toward the end of his mate's pregnancy.[20] In humans, an involved father can discriminate between the odor of his newborn's amniotic fluid and that of others, and can associate it with his infant and his late-pregnancy wife.[21] Apparently, nature means for father to bond with his infant, and at the same time develop heightened bonding with his mate.

When the father spends significant amounts of time in contact with his infant, oxytocin encourages him to become more involved in the ongoing care in a self-perpetuating cycle. Oxytocin in the father also increases his interest in physical contact with the mother, but not for sexual contact.[22] After a birth, some fathers have a long wait before their mates have much sexual interest (or their babies allow the time), but just as sexual drive is a hormonal event, nature now provides a hormonal boost for father to become more interested in being a devoted and satisfied part of the family picture through his involvement with the baby. Just as with the hormonal effects on mother, this design is primarily for baby's benefit, to provide another caretaker and a protector for him and his mother. The parents certainly benefit too; in fact, the health benefits they receive help keep them around for baby.

Oxytocin: Love and the Heart

The existence of oxytocin in humans and its elevated presence in parents and in infants at birth in no way guarantees bonding, nurturing, and growing love. Only by acting on your instinctive desires to enjoy close contact will your oxytocin levels continue to surge, thereby continuously stimulating your desire to be physically close. Once the initial imprinting has occurred in the first days of the infant's life, it will persist, but it can fade over time without continued involvement. If you provide sensitive, responsive care to your infant through breastfeeding and prolonged body contact, high levels of oxytocin in you and your baby will continue to promote strong long-term bonding, assuring each of reciprocal love. In addition, your infant's brain will be organized so that stress responses are minimal and well-handled, thereby improving future behavior and relationships and reducing later risk of heart disease to one-third that of an insecurely attached child. Bonding creates a happier individual who can form strong adult bonds with a mate.

The father who is physically involved with his infant will become more and more attracted to the child, enjoying strong paternal feelings and becoming more in tune with the mother as well. Everyone benefits from his enhanced role as father and husband. He will reap heart and health rewards as well as a better future relationship with his child. High oxytocin levels in mother help prevent her from feeling like a beast of burden. Instead, she will beam with love and continue to nurse and cling to what feels like her bundle of joy. She will feel much desire to nurture and to be socially responsive. She'll feel good and remain calmer, allowing her to handle her busy new job with composure and joy,

> When the father spends significant amounts of time in contact with his infant, oxytocin encourages him to become more involved in the ongoing care in a self-perpetuating cycle.

and pass that joy on to her baby and those around her. She, too, reaps heart benefits from the long-term effects of oxytocin. Incidentally, alcohol reduces oxytocin levels.[23] Regular consumption can reduce one's ties to the family, replacing that rewarding sensation with the rewards of the bottle. (Wonder where this bottle attachment started?)

With all of its powers, oxytocin is but one of a list of many chemicals that nature uses to ensure that baby finds the love and care he needs.

Vasopressin and Protection

Although present and active during bonding in the mother and infant, vasopressin plays a bigger role in the father. Vasopressin is largely dependent on testosterone ("male hormone"), and in a male it modifies testosterone's effects. Animal studies have found that vasopressin causes some reorganization in the male brain, but not in the female's.[24] Although these studies report that this starts after mating, mating generally leads to pregnancy in animals, so mating and pregnancy effects cannot easily be separated in these studies. Other studies indicate that, in humans, brain reorganization is stronger when males are living with a partner, and strongest when cohabiting with a pregnant mate. After this has occurred, the male is more dedicated to his mate and expresses paternal behaviors of protection and maintaining nearness. Virgin male prairie voles (a small mammal) injected with vasopressin were found to begin touching, grooming, and huddling over nearby pups, where normally they would have avoided them.[25] While evidence indirectly

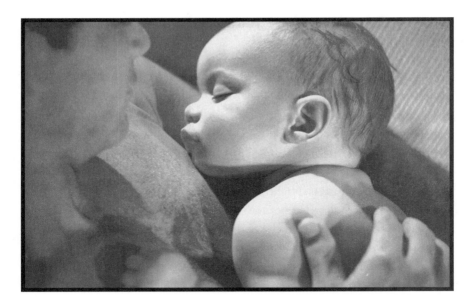

suggests that touch elevates vasopressin (as with oxytocin), it seems to develop from close proximity alone.

Like oxytocin, vasopressin promotes bonding between the father and the mother,[26] helps the father recognize and bond to his baby, and makes him want to be part of the family, rather than alone. It has gained a reputation as the "monogamy hormone." Dr. Theresa Crenshaw, author of *The Alchemy of Love and Lust*, says, "Testosterone wants to prowl, vasopressin wants to stay home."[27] She also describes vasopressin as tempering the man's sexual drive.

Vasopressin reinforces the father's testosterone-promoted protective inclination regarding his mate and child, but tempers his aggression, making him more reasonable and less extreme. By promoting more rational and less capricious thinking, this hormone induces a sensible paternal role, providing stability as well as vigilance.

Vasopressin helps to control stress responses[28] in baby, mother, and father, thus providing calm, but also encouraging positive social interaction and behavior. Vasopressin also improves learning and memory.[29] Although it has a weaker effect than oxytocin, vasopressin plays a role in odor attachment, at least in infants, as well as the onset of maternal behaviors.[30]

> *High oxytocin levels in mother help prevent her from feeling like a beast of burden. Instead, she will beam with love and continue to nurse and cling to what feels like her bundle of joy.*

Prolactin and Behavior

Prolactin is released in all healthy people during sleep, helping to maintain reproductive organs and immune function. In an expecting mother, prolactin levels are elevated throughout pregnancy, preparing the breasts for milk production and speeding the onset of maternal behavior after birth. Then, after a woman gives birth, her prolactin promotes milk production for lactation as well as maternal behavior. But prolactin production is not stimulated by baby's hunger cries, as is oxytocin. Prolactin is produced in response to suckling during nursing. While some milk is produced and stored between nursing sessions, most is made during nursing. Prolactin also relaxes mother, and in the early months, creates a bit of fatigue during a nursing session so she has no strong desire to hop up and do other things.

Prolactin promotes caregiving behaviors and over time directs brain reorganization to favor these behaviors.[31] Father's prolactin levels begin to rise during mother's pregnancy, but most of the hormone's elevation in the male occurs after many days of cohabitation with the infant,[32] increasing his responses to typical infant cues.[33]

As a result of hormonally orchestrated brain reorganization during parenthood, prolactin release patterns are altered. Fathers release prolactin in response to intruder threats, whereas childless males do not,[34] thus indicating that prolactin plays a role in creating protective paternal behavior. On the other hand, nursing mothers do not release prolactin in response to loud noise, whereas childless females do.[35] In children and non-parents, prolactin surges are related to stress levels, so it is generally considered a stress hormone. In parents, it serves as a parenting hormone. Research indicates that the brain uses different pathways during acute stress responses and during parental care, and parental care in the attached parent does not cause the release of other stress hormones.[36]

Prolactin not only promotes maternal and paternal behaviors in parents but also reduces their sex drive. In childless adults, prolonged elevations are associated with the fatigue and infertility that often accompany long periods of stress, and with depression and other emotional difficulties as well.[37] Just as an infant's early attachment levels will permanently affect her stress responses, adults who had less-attached infancies will typically experience more stress-like prolactin elevations, actions, and responses. A common link between elevated prolactin levels and mood disorders provides one explanation for the psychological difficulties that are more prevalent in insecurely attached adults.

In a child, prolactin is a stress hormone, not a parenting hormone. Pediatrician Betsy Lozoff found that children with high prolactin levels were described as hesitant and unhappy during stressful test situations.[38] She noted that different children had different levels of stress response (measured here by prolactin release). Other studies (*discussed in the previous chapter*) have strongly correlated these differences with the levels of early maternal responsiveness. One researcher suggests that prolonged periods of elevated prolactin in poorly bonded infant males (reducing testosterone levels during a sensitive brain organization period) could influence their sexual orientation.[39]

Elevated prolactin levels in both the nursing mother and the involved father cause some reduction in their testosterone levels, which in turn reduces their libidos (but not their sexual functioning).[40,41] Their fertility can be reduced for a time as well.[42] This reduction in sexual activity and fertility is entirely by design for the benefit of the infant. First, it focuses parental time and affection on the baby, which will ultimately lead to the highest degree of behavioral development and bonding. More important, preventing another child from entering the picture for at least a couple years helps assure the infant ample breastfeeding and holding time, parental attention and energy, and access to his parents' resources. The infant is also more likely to have a consistently low-key, level-headed mother who is not subjected to the mood swings and energy drops of premenstrual syndrome (PMS) or pregnancy. When the father is intimately involved with the infant along with the mother, there should be some accord between the desires of the two, and oxytocin and other chemicals provide for heightened bonding and non-sexual interest in each other, which serves to retain a second devoted caretaker for the infant.

Opioids and Rewards

Opioids (endorphins and enkephalins) are natural morphine-like chemicals created in our bodies. They reduce pain awareness and create feelings of elation. Social contacts, especially those between parent and child, and most especially touch, induce opioid release, creating good feelings that will enhance bonding. Play, including rough and tumble play, also causes opioid release,[43] as does smiling. Some of the most special smiles are those intently shared between parent and child. Odor, taste, activity, and even place preferences can develop as the result of opioid release during pleasant social contacts, and certainly the sight of a loved one's face stimulates surges of this hormone. Opioid released in a child's brain as a conditioned response to a parent's warm hugs and kisses can be effective for helping reduce the pain from a tumble or a disappointment.

Parents "learn" to enjoy beneficial activities such as breastfeeding and holding, and infants "learn" to enjoy contact such as being held, carried, and rocked, all as a response to opioid release. Babies need milk, and opioids are nature's reward to them for obtaining it, especially during the initial attempts. The first few episodes of sucking organize nerve pathways in the newborn's brain, conditioning her to continue this activity.[44] This can create a problem for an infant who is given bottles in the newborn nursery. Any incidental sensations experienced during rocking, touching, and eating that aren't noxious can become part of a child's attachment and will provide comfort. It could be the warmth of mother's body, father's furry chest, grandma's gentle lullaby, the background aroma of grandpa's cooking, a blanket, the wood-slatted side of a crib—or a bottle. Psychologist Jaak Panksepp has extensively researched the relationship between opioids and infant bonding. He believes that those stimuli that are encountered prior to weaning, in particular, can cause opioid releases in both the child and adult.[45]

Opioids initially suppress the young infant's curiosity for his environment during nursing so that he can focus on obtaining milk and becoming familiar with his mother's face and voice. Later, opioids can enhance learning during nursing, as the reward of obtaining milk connects the infant to other experiences at the nipple such as the specific patterns of mother's speech or her comments on surrounding objects and sounds.[46] Opioids also reduce appetite and help the nursing infant know when he has obtained enough breastmilk.

Prolonged elevation of prolactin in the attached parent stimulates the opioid system,[47] heightening the rewards for intimate, loving family relationships, possibly above all else. Just as with codeine and morphine, tolerance to natural opioids can occur, which will reduce the reward level for various opioid-releasing activities over time. But this is not a problem for infants and parents, because the desired learning will have already taken place. Furthermore, higher levels of oxytocin, especially when created through frequent or prolonged body contact, actually inhibit opioid tolerance,[48] protecting the rewards for maintaining close family relationships. On the other hand, consuming artificial opioid drugs replaces the brain's need for maintaining family contacts.

Once a strong opioid bonding has occurred, separation can become emotionally upsetting, and in the infant possibly even physically uncomfortable when opioid levels decrease in the brain, much like the withdrawal symptoms from cocaine or heroin. When opioid levels become low, one might feel like going home to hold the baby, or like crying for a parent's warm embrace, depending on one's point of view. Sometimes alternate behaviors are helpful. For instance, thumb-sucking can provide some relief from partial or total withdrawal from a human or rubber nipple and can even provide opioid-produced reminiscences for a while.

Norepinephrine and Learning

Breastfeeding also causes dopamine and its product, norepinephrine (adrenaline), to be produced, which help maintain some of the effects of the early bonding. Dopamine and norepinephrine enhance energy and alertness along with some of the pleasure of attachment.[49] Norepinephrine helps organize the infant's stress control system, as well as other important hormonal controls in accordance with the nature of the early rearing experiences.[50] It is elevated in mother and infant just after birth and is a factor that helps create the initial window for imprinting, including odor imprinting.[51] Beyond birth, norepinephrine promotes learning—especially learning by memorization that is carried out by oxytocin, opioids, and other chemical influences.

Pheromones and Basic Instincts

How does a man's body know to initiate hormonal changes when he is living with a pregnant female? Of course, he may consciously know that his mate is pregnant (although sometimes not at first), but it is not the conscious mind that causes prolactin and vasopressin production. Also, how can an infant accurately interpret mother's "odors" that adults often can barely detect? The answer is pheromones. Very recently, proof of their role in human perception has become quite conclusive.[52] Between 1 and 2% of our DNA (genetic information) is devoted to sensors inside the nasal cavity—a rather large amount in light of our limited sense of smell, but we now know there is another set of receptors in our nose besides those for smelling. Vomero-nasal organs are chemosensory receptors situated along our nasal septum[53] that are sensitive to the pheromones released by other humans. Among other things, pheromones are hormones, such as estrogen and testosterone, that are made in our skin.[54] Our bodies are instinctually programmed to react accordingly when we detect these pheromones around us.[55]

Newborns are much more sensitive to pheromones than adults. Unable to respond to verbal or many other cues, they apparently depend on this primitive sense that controls much of the behavior of lower animals. Most likely the initial imprinting

Prolonged elevation of prolactin in the attached parent stimulates the opioid system, heightening the rewards for intimate, loving family relationships, possibly above all else.

of baby to odors and pheromones is not just a matter of preferring the parents' odors, but is also a way nature controls brain organization and hormonal releases to best adapt baby to its environment. Baby's earliest, most primitive experiences are then linked to higher abilities such as facial and emotional recognition. Through these, baby most likely learns how to perceive the level of stress in the caretakers around her, such as when mother is experiencing fear or joy. Part of an infant's distress over separation may be caused by the lost parental cues about the safety of her environment. Of course, the other basic sensation an infant responds to well is touch, and coincidentally, body odors and pheromones can only be sensed when people are physically very near each other.

The powerful effects olfactory and chemical sensations have on infants' hormone levels and brain development, as well as those of the parents, lead one to wonder what future research will uncover regarding the effects of close contacts with infants.

Other Chemical Bonding

Growth hormone is increased by touch and by good sleep, and is decreased by separation from the mother.[56] Melatonin is increased by good sleep, only in the dark, and in turn enhances prolactin and growth hormone. Cholecystokinin, diazepam, GABA, serotonin, somatostatin, progesterone, androgens, and other biochemical systems, including the immune system, all affect the parent-infant attachment process, and most are likely influenced in some way by our caregiving choices as parents.

Cortisol and Stress

The HPA (hypothalamic–pituitary–adrenocortical) axis, a relationship between specific brain organs and the adrenal glands, is the chief regulator of stress reactions. While several hormones direct stress reactions, often in concert with each other and with some playing more than one role, cortisol is probably the most typical of the stress hormones. It is the subject of many recent reports. During stress, stress hormones are released under control of the HPA axis to help the body cope. Cortisol can elevate the blood pressure and the heart rate, increase blood sugar, and interrupt digestive and kidney functions.

Norepinephrine responses and cortisol responses are connected. Both are released in reaction to excitement, exercise, and stress. Both cause increased heart rate, blood sugar, and brain activity. I have discussed how surges of norepinephrine during affection and play can promote learning in infants (you may remember how you occasionally learned better under the stress and excitement of last-minute studying), as well as bonding (since bonding occurs in children and adults when they share exciting activity). However, chronic exposure to negative stress causes *chronic* elevations of cortisol, instead of *surges* that have a positive effect. Chronically elevated cortisol in infants and the hormonal and functional adjustments that go along with it are shown to be associated with permanent brain changes that lead to elevated responses to stress throughout life, such as higher blood pressure and heart rate.[57] This elevated response begins quite early. Even infants regularly exposed to stress already demonstrate higher cortisol releases and more sustained elevations of cortisol in response to stressful situations,[58,59] as do toddlers.[60]

Occasional surges of cortisol throughout the day can be beneficial, but continuously elevated stress hormone levels in infancy from a stressful environment are associated with permanent negative effects on brain development. Some evolutionary theories even go so far as to suggest that the heightened stress responses that apparently lead to aggressive behavior and early puberty serve a purpose, aiding survival of the species during drought, war, or other hardships.

Studies have shown that infants who receive frequent physical affection have lower overall cortisol levels,[61] while psychological attachment studies reveal higher levels in insecurely attached children.[62–64] Women who breastfeed also produce significantly less stress hormone than those who bottle-feed.[65–67]

Stress in Infancy

What causes stress during infancy? Laboratory and psychology research on animal and human infants gives us many clues. Certainly, pain from unfortunate medical conditions can create stress. So would pain from sensitivity reactions to formula or to foods passed along in breastmilk. Physical abuse and extreme neglect provide a very high degree of stress, but the effects of these severe cases are not the point of this text. Even short-term separation from mother leads to elevated cortisol in infants, indicating stress.[68,69] In fact, after 1 full day of separation, infant rats already show altered brain organization of chemical receptors.[70] A similar rat study revealed that *1 day without mother actually doubled the number of normal brain cell deaths.*[71]

Animal findings demonstrate that isolation from mother, decreased skin stimulation, and withholding of breastmilk have biochemical and permanent brain consequences. Correlating these findings with human behavioral research suggests which events lead to chronic stress and its permanent consequences:

- allowing a child to "cry it out" without parental attention and affection[72]
- not feeding the child when hungry
- not offering comfort when the child is disturbed or distressed
- limiting body contact during feeding, through-out the day, and during stressful parts of the night
- low levels of human attention, stimulation, "conversation," and play

When these occur regularly, they can lead to early chronic releases of high levels of stress hormones, as well as low expression of favorable hormones, as previously discussed. All these practices have been promoted during the last century in the form of scheduled feedings, "don't spoil the child" tactics, bottle feedings that lead to propped bottles, and physical separation during the day and night.

While it is evident that genetic makeup and life experiences influence behavior, it has been demonstrated that experiences during infancy have the strongest and most persistent effect on adult hormone regulation, stress responses, and behavior.[73] Research has demonstrated that high levels of early physical contact and maternal responsiveness can even mitigate genetic predisposition for more extreme stress reactions.[74]

Biological psychology researcher Megan Gunnar and her colleagues did infant studies that confirmed animal research findings. In their work, infants 3 months of age who received consistent responsive care produced less cortisol. Also, 18-month-olds classified as insecurely attached (who had received lower levels of responsiveness) revealed elevated levels of stress hormone.[75] These same children at age 2 continued to show elevated levels of cortisol and appeared more fearful and inhibited. Again, these children were those who had been classified as having lower levels of maternal responsiveness.[76] Other investigations have confirmed these findings.[77] Dr. Gunnar reports that the level of stress experienced in infancy permanently shapes the stress responses in the brain, which then affect memory, attention, and emotion.[78]

Results of Infant Stress

Without regular closeness to a caregiver, an infant not only suffers from elevated stress hormones, but also receives less benefit from oxytocin surges and other positive biochemical influences. The biochemical environment imposed on an infant's brain during critical development stages affects the anatomy and functioning of the brain permanently.[79,80] A poor biochemical environment results in less desirable emotional, behavioral, and intellectual abilities for the rest of a child's life.

Chronically elevated cortisol in infants and the hormonal and functional adjustments that go along with it are shown to be associated with permanent brain changes that lead to elevated responses to stress throughout life, such as higher blood pressure and heart rate.

As previously described, a brain developed in a stressful environment overreacts to stressful events and controls stress hormones poorly throughout life. The constant irregular cortisol levels eventually lead to inflammatory changes that are typically related to inadequate cortisol. This brings on a high risk of heart disease, stroke, and adult-onset diabetes.[81] Interestingly, one psychiatrist found that the poor health consequences for adults who received restricted mothering during childhood—high blood pressure and high cortisol responses—closely resemble those in adults who lost a parent as a child.[82] The effects, however, go way beyond one's blood pressure and ability to deal with stress.

The hippocampus, a structure important in learning and memory, is one brain site where development is affected by stress and bonding hormone

> *Studies have shown*
>
> *that infants who receive*
>
> *frequent physical affection*
>
> *have lower overall*
>
> *cortisol levels.*

levels. The level of the stress hormones circulating in an infant affects the number and types of receptors here.[83] It has also been demonstrated that nerve cells in the hippocampus are destroyed as a result of chronic stress and elevated stress hormone levels, producing intellectual deficits as a consequence.[84] Memory and spatial learning deficits have been demonstrated in rats that suffered prolonged stress in infancy.[85] Similarly, children with the lowest scores on mental and motor ability tests have been shown to be the ones with the highest cortisol levels in their blood.[86]

Premature development of puberty has also been associated with significantly higher levels of cortisol and other stress indicators.[87] This study additionally reports that these children have more depression, more behavior problems, and lower intelligence scores. *Here again, the laboratory studies fully confirm psychological attachment studies.* Furthermore, premature puberty increases one's risk of developing cancer.

In individuals who suffer from various psychological disorders, irregular production of cortisol is a very consistent finding.[88,89] Oversecretion of stress hormones has also recently been implicated in obesity, Alzheimer's disease,[90] accelerated aging symptoms,[91] and suicidal behavior.[92] Animal studies have demonstrated decreased immune system functioning in infants subjected to the stresses of prolonged separation from mother,[93,94] which coincides with the increased incidence of illness shown in less-attached children.

Beginnings

Much has been written about the first moments after a child is born. The infant, if not entirely intoxicated by drugs used in labor, has been primed by hormones during the birth process to be born wide awake and alert for a short while. During this time the initial imprinting takes place. Already familiar with the voices of his parents, the baby, who can distinguish faces from other objects and body parts, gazes intently into the eyes of his parents, as if to record their images for life. He recognizes the odor of the amniotic fluid, which is chiefly his own, but is also that of his mother. His important early programming guides his mouth to seek and find a new physical method of maternal nourishment, and he is immediately attracted to the specific odor of the nursing vessels that will now replace his umbilical cord. The newborn, barely able to maintain his body temperature, finds comfort and ideal temperature regulation in contact with mom's warm body. Having known only the firm secure confinement of his womb, he feels comfortable against a warm body or in secure arms, and he will cry loudly, uncomfortable and anxious, if left to flail on a cold, hard surface. With his first taste of concentrated nutrition and immunity-providing colostrum, and hearing the familiar beating and gurgling sounds of mother's body, he soon falls into a peaceful sleep—even his heartbeat and breathing are regulated by mother's rhythms. As he sleeps, his first breaths and tastes of his mother establish normal, healthy flora in his digestive tract, providing defense against the less friendly microbes all around him.

Although all is not lost if an infant's life did not begin this way, this is the first chance for attachment and the first choice made regarding baby's health. There is a long life ahead for parents and child, and there are many directions a family can take. While a child is born seeded with specific potential (nature), parenting style (nurture) will greatly influence whether these latent abilities will come to fruition, to the benefit or detriment of the child, family, and society.

The greatest lesson from these studies is that while nature has a very good plan, failure to follow it may lead to less desirable results.

Bonding Matters

Research on the biochemical factors influenced by child care methods demonstrates that with responsive parenting the body produces substances to help generate effective, loving, and lasting parents for an infant, as well as infants who are strongly bonded to their parents. Over time, these bonds mature into love and respect. Without a doubt these chemicals permanently organize an infant's brain toward positive behaviors and later development of strong, lasting attachments. However, the greatest lesson from these studies is that while nature has a very good plan, failure to follow it may lead to less desirable results. In other words, when parents heed instinctive desires to enjoy a great deal of closeness with their infants, by feeding them naturally and responding quickly to their needs and desires (which in the infant are truly one and the same), nature is designed to develop sensitive, responsible adults. Withholding attention from an infant allows the vital chemical messengers to quickly diminish, and as a result, weak bonds are formed, and parenting becomes more arduous and less successful. At the same time, the infant manifests the effects of stress. Moreover, stress reactions and other behaviors in a child and the adult he will become are permanently altered in unfortunate ways. Aspects of the intellect and health may suffer as well.

The incredible, extensive, innate human system of hormonal rewards for consistent, close, and loving physical and social contact between parent and infant, and the just as incredible consequences, combined with the psychological research findings about attachment, provide overwhelming evidence for nature's intended plan for infant care, at least for me.

I once witnessed an older pediatrician strongly disapprove of the way a toddler clung to his mother and demanded that she hold him while his blood was drawn. He said to the mother, "It all starts the first day you pick him up when he cries."

My only answer to this is, "Yes, it does."

4

Crying and Caring

"Contrary to earlier belief, the genetic constitution of each cell of the body (nature) is subject to modulation by environmental factors (nurture)...The effects begin during early development."
     —Bruce S. McEwen, MD, Rockefeller University, 1988[1]

"Major brain pathways are specified in the genome; detailed connections are fashioned by, and consequently reflect, socially mediated experience in the world."
     —Leon Eisenberg, MD, Harvard Medical School, 1995[2]

WE HAVE SEEN THAT RESEARCHERS HAVE LEARNED A GREAT DEAL ABOUT how early parental care affects the development of an infant. We have also seen that many elements of infant care can profoundly impact a child's behavior into adolescence and shape his mental and physical health and his bonding abilities through adulthood. Now let's consider some specific caring and nurturing patterns.

Whether to allow children to cry it out is one key issue, emblematic of many others. Many old-school child care advisors promoted the idea that children should be left alone to cry without being consoled. As a rationale, they suggested that long bouts of crying were needed to develop the lungs. This lung theory has since been disproved, but many of today's popular authorities continue to come up with (unproven) reasons why an infant should be left to cry it out, particularly when they are learning to sleep alone. In fact, crying is a result of much of the advice given by those who are considered experts in child rearing.

As many cultures are proudly imitating the affluent Western picture of artificial infant feeding, separate bedrooms, and fancy baby containers, Western-style ill health is increasing.

The Western world's familiar crying baby is far different from what is seen in cultures where parental responsiveness and affection are the unquestioned norm. It is disturbing that health problems in Western adult populations tend to coincide with the history of detached child-rearing practices—the West being plagued by eating disorders, high blood pressure, heart disease, diabetes, ulcers, colitis, depression and anxiety disorders, as well as a fear of intimacy. The prevalence of these problems in the non-nurturing world is in stark contrast to their limited occurrence in traditionally more nurturing cultures—at least until lately. As many cultures are proudly imitating the affluent Western picture of artificial infant feeding, separate bedrooms, and fancy baby containers, Western-style ill health is increasing. As you will see, a discussion of these practices and their consequences must also lead to a discussion of sudden infant death syndrome or SIDS, which frightens all parents.

Crying Babies

A newborn child cannot speak. She is helpless, unable to mobilize or feed herself. She can't even lift her head. She is trapped inside a mysterious existence where unusual and often painful sensations come frequently, where sights and sounds buzz around her, some frightening and some comforting. Having spent her prenatal life connected to her mother, she is driven by instincts to remain connected to her until her brain and motor development grow, gradually giving her independence and the ability to be a contributing member of the family and village. She begins with only one chief communication tool—crying. Crying is intended to be a highly successful means for youngsters to communicate. Any parent flooded with parenting hormones or past experience is biologically predisposed to be deeply affected by the sight and sound of an infant crying. Unless parents have rehearsed away their natural reactions (their innate intelligence), they strongly desire to respond to crying—and quickly!

If baby's communication works and his discomfort is relieved, he will develop an intimate relationship with the caretakers who provide comfort and companionship. Baby will then gradually learn that when a caretaker is nearby, other gestures can often be just as effective. A smile can lead to eye-to-eye contact and friendly facial "conversation." A grunt, whimper, or

mouth gesture can successfully express hunger. Eventually, an infant won't always need to cry when other cues are well responded to. More advanced communication develops. Still, there is not always going to be someone looking directly at him for such communication to work, and in an infant, pain and fear lend themselves to crying. Stress strongly lends itself to crying unless an infant or child is encouraged to hold the stress inside, releasing it in other, less healthy ways. In fact, infants with responsive mothers quickly develop the ability to create different cries, to indicate different levels of distress. Their communicative intelligence grows naturally through maternal interaction. This ability cannot manifest and flourish in infants whose cries are regularly ignored.[3]

For Crying Out Loud

While crying is intended to be purposeful, it can also be stressful. Extended crying is physically exhausting for an infant, consuming large amounts of precious energy. The digestive system is impaired and tensed during crying. Cortisol, the damaging stress hormone, is released into the bloodstream and persists at least 20 minutes after a crying bout has stopped.[4-6] During crying, an infant's blood pressure rises dramatically and blood oxygenation falls. The return of oxygen to the brain is hindered; thus, oxygenation of the brain is diminished.[7] Crying also suppresses the body's immune system, decreasing its ability to fight infections and weakening its infant defenses. Moreover, prolonged crying continues to perpetuate the sensation of sadness that initiated it.[8,9]

It is normal for infants to cry in response to fear, stress, sleepiness, or pain, or when they wish to request food, entertainment, or comfort. Yet, such cries, when frequently unanswered, are responsible for much of the stress that interferes with the attachment process and causes brain cell death, stress control disorganization, adolescent behavior problems, and physical and psychological difficulties in adults. Since crying is exhausting to the infant and mother, both mentally and physically, it is understandable that mothers feel the urge to answer crying quickly. A mother attempting to ignore crying also becomes quickly exhausted because she is being helplessly exposed to prolonged and annoying wails. She also becomes flooded with cortisol. Responsive parenting is best for an infant in terms of immediate safety, health, and comfort, as well as for long-term development. It is healthier and generally more comfortable for mother, too.

"Normal" Crying

We have long been conditioned to think of the normal newborn as red-faced and loudly crying. However, when a newborn is treated with affection and comfort, this is not the case. In fact, one study found that responsive treatment led to 2 minutes of crying during the first 3 hours of life, compared to over 18 times that amount in infants treated by the culturally accepted hospital routine.[10] Thus, it is reasonable to conclude that the "normal" newborn American infant is crying from sudden abandonment. Another study found infants who received peaceful, warm physical contact during their first hours actually cried much less during their 1-year physical examinations,[11] suggesting a profound and lasting effect probably on the parenting behaviors as well as those of the infant.

U.S. child care experts provide descriptions of what they refer to as "normal" amounts of crying in infants, generally suggesting that 2 to 3 hours per 24-hour period is normal. Yet, these "normal" crying measurements are made in hospital nurseries where newborns are severed from their mothers, and in traditional homes where the practice of ignoring crying is commonplace. Crying beyond this amount is then defined as "colic." In the absence of an obvious medical disorder, the diagnosis of colic is intended as an explanation that will provide some sort of relief to parents. At a certain point, crying goes beyond what is classified as normal; then long crying is termed "colic"; the problem is now "explained," thus no further investigation or action may be suggested. Often, parents are offered assurances that "this time will pass." Many researchers have made detailed observations of child care practices in cultures around the world. Quite consistently they have found that when frequent natural feeding, close

Quite consistently they have found that when frequent natural feeding, close contact, and quick responsiveness are the norm, the average amount of infant crying is far below that seen in the United States, and furthermore, colic is generally unknown.

contact, and quick responsiveness are the norm, the average amount of infant crying is far below that seen in the United States, and furthermore, colic is generally unknown.[12-14] Since these cultures represent by far a greater portion of the world population, *their* infant crying behaviors should more accurately be considered the norm.

Studies show that in U.S. families with long-crying infants, when parents are taught how to quickly respond to their infant's cries and learn how to understand their cues, the amount of crying drops dramatically.[15] Also, when American mothers in La Leche League (an organization that promotes breastfeeding, whose members generally feed their infants on cue and are otherwise responsive to their infants) were compared to American mothers using typical care techniques, far less crying was measured.[16] Both frequent feeding and regular responsiveness, measures that reduce infant stress, were found to be independently responsible for decreased crying.

If children are left alone in bed and start to cry, responding to that crying greatly reduces it. Also, breastfed infants cry less in the night,[17] in part because bottle-fed infants have to wait for their formulas to be mixed and warmed, in part because breastfed infants experience fewer digestive problems and illnesses, and in part because of the calming, soothing effects of nursing. Yet night waking and night crying are two very different things. A healthy, cosleeping (sleeping with mom), breastfed infant seldom finds need to cry during the night, but may feed frequently as a result of some degree of arousal several times through the night. This natural stirring can be very helpful in preventing SIDS.

To Respond or Not: "Spoiling" Myths

The stress of isolation and infrequent feeding can cause infants to cry a great deal, which in turn causes more physical and emotional stress. Infants who have succumbed to the idea that crying for desired feeding and attention is futile suffer possibly even more stress, having no outlet for their ongoing frustrations. As seen in the last two chapters, the consequences of regular stress for an infant are far-reaching. Some parents believe that little they do before the age of 3 to 5 matters, since there are no memories before this time. Quite the contrary, early brain organization is a very powerful memory. *While the specifics may be lost, unconscious memories are developed neurologically and biochemically from birth.* Just as the tiny body needs to grow, the brain needs to discover what kind of environment it exists in, so it can develop accordingly.

Yet, many advisors suggest that delaying or avoiding response to infants and allowing them to cry over easily resolvable stresses is in their best interest. Some suggest that "giving in" to their "controlling demands" will cause them to become more demanding. But the extensive amount of research performed on this subject has shown that about half the children whose needs were neglected actually became more demanding, fussier infants. The other half became withdrawn, learning to suppress their emotions and not trusting their parents to be there for them, often making no attempts to engage their mothers at all. Some of the latter are what many call "good babies." Desmond Morris refers to these kinds of infants as those who have been truly "spoiled," in the sense of spoiled fruit. Their potential is being wasted.

Infants' reactions to unresponsive caregivers is like that of patients in a busy hospital ward: When patients' call button requests are not answered for very long periods of time, nurses know well that some patients will begin to signal over and over, eventually crying out frequently for assistance. Others simply stop trying, resolving to bear their pain, thirst, or other discomfort until help arrives on its own. For a telling comparison, let's translate today's prevalent baby care advice into marital advice: From the very start, withhold affection from your mate or he may come to expect it, or even worse, ask for it. Ignore his wishes for comfort so he does not become spoiled. Do not validate his feelings, and refuse to console him when he is sad or lonely so he will not bother you with those feelings. Forbid him to eat unless your watch says it's time for him to eat…Needless to say, strong marital bonds could not be developed this way. Nor would you care for your helpless bedridden mother in this fashion.

Twentieth-century Western culture has stressed independence. Many experts assert that if an infant doesn't learn to be independent quickly, it never will learn. Yet, attachment studies have shown that infants who receive strong responses from caregivers request holding less often and appear to enjoy holding more. *Attached children also become more responsive to parental requests, a kind of "dependence" that is preferable.* Lozoff studied a sample of contemporary hunter-gatherer cultures around the world to observe the relationship between the kind of infant care provided and the outcome in the children. She found that the mothers were the chief nurturers of infants, providing lots of body contact throughout the day and night, prolonged breastfeeding, and quick, affectionate response to crying. The children in these cultures achieved independence by 2 to 4 years of age, spending more than half their days away from their mothers.[18] Apparently, infants are able to develop confidence in themselves and their environment when they are able to obtain what they need through their communication attempts. By contrast, delayed response creates a sense of helplessness.

One common bit of advice has been to respond to a baby only when she is being "good." That is, when she is not expressing fear or sadness, or any desire for food or help. Psychologists have found that this kind of behavioral conditioning is very effective for creating individuals who hold their feelings in and can't ask for what they need. These same individuals possibly also spend too much of their time trying to please others (this was termed "codependency" for some time, but the term has gone out of vogue). This kind of behavior can lead to inappropriate acting out in children and adolescents, and ulcers and other health conditions in adulthood. Similarly, a child who receives affectionate responsiveness only when he is ill may become skilled at developing illness and may practice this skill throughout life, even if it stops serving the initial purpose. Babies fed on schedules are left frustrated by their hunger between feedings, and as a result, they experience feeding as a way to relieve frustration. This could possibly be linked to eating disorders later on.

Eating disorders such as anorexia and bulimia are predominantly Western society disorders,[19] although they are now penetrating sectors of other countries where Western child care practices have become popular.[20] In France, responsiveness and other forms of affection are very high. Some point out that even though the French may worry about their appearance as much as Americans do, their eating disorder rates are much lower than ours, as are other psychological disorders.[21] A Minnesota survey of 30,000 adolescents found that eating disorders are related to "low family connectedness," as well as other insecure attachment signs.[22]

Nighttime is important too, comprising nearly half of an infant's life. Babies don't turn off at night, no matter how much we sometimes wish they would. They continue to have hunger, to grow, and to consolidate brain pathways. Their minds, feelings, and needs continue, and they continue to learn during their nighttime experiences, as much as at any other time. For babies, just as with mates, nighttime is a valuable time for catching up on the warmth and comfort of togetherness—this reassurance is available each time baby stirs. And when baby is close, little effort to wake up is required on the parents' part for providing protection, comfort, feeding, and support throughout the night.

Colic

Still, babies cry. It is normal. And some cry more than others. Sometimes parents who provide the very best response will have infants who frequently cry for long periods. So parents need to determine whether they believe an infant is in physical pain. Certainly, when an infant's inconsolable cries are signals of pain or disorder, parents should have their baby examined medically and should often get second opinions. Up until recently, for a large portion of these infants, no diagnosis was made, other than calling the problem "colic." Today, a new diagnosis is in vogue: gastric reflux or GERD. The popularity of this diagnosis soared with the introduction of a new drug designed for its treatment. While the actual presence of GERD is seldom established, the point is rather moot. It's no news that babies have weak sphincters between their esophagus (throat) and stomach. When something upsets a baby's tummy, reflux is a common result. Some parents are seeing mild to moderate decreases in colic with this drug and some see none. Either way, reflux is usually a symptom, rather than a significant abnormality in and of itself.

Studies comparing the acoustic values of cries during long bouts in "colicky" infants, versus their "normal" cries and the cries of "normal" infants, find higher acoustic frequency and other sharper acoustic measures during colic.[23,24] Yet, connected parents don't need much experience under their belts to detect these differences without fancy equipment. There is a different look and sound of pain or great distress. Intensive care nurses use the following scale to measure pain, listed in decreasing order: "fussiness, restlessness, grimacing, crying, increasing heart rate, increasing respiration, wiggling, rapid state changes, wrinkling of forehead, and clenching of fists."[25]

When an infant appears to be frequently in pain, and no diagnosis besides colic is made, there is in fact another diagnosis that will help the great majority of these infants. Doctors whose chief education about feeding difficulties comes from formula companies usually miss this simple solution. *Intestinal intolerance to cow's milk protein (not lactose) and other foods in mother's milk or in formula is the major cause of undiagnosed pain, usually called "colic."* Often other signs such as sleeplessness, waking with screams, abnormal stools, or rashes are part of this picture. This topic is covered extensively in the last few chapters of this book. Interestingly, cultures where colic is not a familiar condition are the same ones where infants do not receive cow's milk formulas and the mothers have very little dairy in their diets, if any at all. (Those studied include rural Japanese and Chinese, the Kenyans and !Kung San of Africa, the Balinese, the Samoans, and the Fore of New Guinea.)

I Hear Ya

When infants cry from physical pain, certainly we all wish to do anything we can to comfort them, just as we would wish to be comforted ourselves. Holding infants is very valuable. Rocking, providing something to suck on, or pacing the floors with them may provide additional comfort and pain relief.

Long periods of crying not related to pain also occur, frequently in some children. Who knows? Frightening thoughts or memories, confusion or bewilderment over their busy surroundings, recollection of frustrations, some say birth traumas—there are certainly many possibilities beyond pain or hunger that could cause an infant to cry, even in the arms of a responsive parent. Many caretakers observe that accumulated stimulation of random sights and noises and unfamiliar voices throughout the day may be a major factor in unappeasable crying, often referring to this as hyperstimulation. Crying may be a kind of emotional release from this accumulated stress, described well by psychologist Aletha Solter.[26] We must remember that infants may simply be crying to be heard—to express their feelings—even though they may not be able to reveal the source of their upset. It is advised that not all crying needs to be "fixed." When a child is apparently not hungry or in pain, but cannot be mollified with simple comforting, what they may need is simply an empathetic "I hear ya." Be there for them, meet their eyes if they look to you, tell them you understand they are hurting, and let them get it out. Children benefit from gentle comforting, mostly from empathy, but not from distraction or attempts to quiet them. Such attempts only invalidate their feelings. The goal is not to stop the crying; it is to let a child know that someone cares, to give him an outlet and a sounding board. The benefits from natural parental comforting are numerous.

According to psychologists, it is very important to acknowledge one's feelings. There may be damaging potential in telling a baby verbally or otherwise not to cry. "Stop crying," "don't cry," "it's not that bad," "you're all right," "that's enough," are ways of telling an infant his feelings are not valid. And, just as crying causes certain physical stresses, forced suppression of crying has been shown to cause undesirable increases in heart rate and blood pressure as well.[27] When adding the research findings on the damaging effects of prolonged crying to what psychologists say about healthy release of emotion, it appears likely that unanswered, frustrated crying would be very detrimental to health, but crying out your emotions, then knowing you are being validated, loved, and received, would be very beneficial, at least psychologically.

When children have a startle or a tumble, it is also best to hold, acknowledge, and comfort them, providing a safe place for empathy and protection. An exception to this, however, may be the child who experiences bouts of physical pain regularly; in this case it may be kind to attempt to distract them from their pain, which does not mean shushing them or plugging them. Distraction techniques are often taught in pain centers for adults who suffer chronic pain.

Of course, as parents we can only do so much, tolerate so much, and be there so much. When a child is occasionally left hungry for a time, or left to cry on his own, no major damage is done. The brain organization comes from the adding up of the many, many responses from the child's caretakers. We must also remember that sometimes it gets to the point where it is the parents who need to cry.

Infant Attention

Even in his latest (1998) book, Dr. Spock advised parents to be "hardhearted" toward their infants, because infants do not know what is good for them. If a mother has difficulty ignoring her infant, he suggests she make a schedule for herself that will keep her busy during most of the child's waking hours. When the infant becomes bored with his crib in the

> *And, just as crying causes certain physical stresses, forced suppression of crying has been shown to cause undesirable increases in heart rate and blood pressure as well.*

afternoon, she may move him to a playpen, and when bored with that, to a bouncing chair. He suggests the infant be hugged every hour or so, and mom should "play with him a bit at the end of the afternoon."[28]

In stark contrast to this kind of advice, it has been shown that a high level of attention to the infant creates good bonding, physical health, and social development. The stimulation of regular interaction leads to heightened brain and motor development, which will be discussed in the next chapter. Regular smiles, conversation, and play all constitute very important parts of nurturing. For this reason, infants have been designed so that it is difficult to take your eyes off them; the mere sight of them begs for illuminated facial responses, physical affection, and verbal engagement. On the one hand, Oxford researchers found that low levels of maternal play interaction are an important factor in the development of behavior problems in a child;[29] on the other hand, it has been shown that laughter stimulates the disease-fighting immune system in adults and infants.[30] It's even been shown that when a child in a stroller is facing mother, she will exhibit more laughing, a lower heart rate, and the ability to fall asleep more easily than when in a forward-facing buggy.[31] At the same time, regular contact with the child helps stimulate mother's maternal behavior.[32]

In Touch

Ashley Montagu wrote a venerable and timeless tome nearly 500 pages long, referencing over 900 studies, entirely devoted to the effects of touch between mother and infant and how this affects an infant's development.[33] He reminds us that "When a baby is born, a mother is also born." According to Dr. Montagu, it is a tragedy when "the two people who need each other at this time, more than they ever will at any other time in their lives," are separated from each other in their first days. He reminds us of simple lessons such as how the friendliness of pets depends upon the physical affection provided them during their infancy, and how many newborn animals die if they do not receive licking. He also recites some very early animal studies that demonstrated how young animals, given a choice between physical contact and obtaining milk, will prefer the close contact. Since his text was first published in 1971, research has rediscovered and confirmed his findings, repeatedly revealing the great value of contact for infants and the sad consequences when frequent affection is lacking.

Much of the human research into the effects of touch and other kinds of soothing and stimulation occurs with premature infants, for several reasons. First, these infants are in the hospital, available for study in a controlled environment; second, the effects of many stimuli may be greater in the youngest babies, or the differences produced more easily measured. Chiefly, however, typical preemie care is in such stark contrast to natural infant care that any positive intervention reveals its benefits readily. Even though these studies are performed on hospitalized premature infants, they provide a great deal of insight valuable for understanding all infants. A pair of Duke University researchers demonstrated that limited touching in infant rats leads to a decrease in the production of an important growth enzyme, reduced DNA replication, abnormal hormonal secretion patterns, and reduced response to growth hormone, prolactin, and to insulin (the hormone that regulates blood sugar). Their work led them to test the effects of touch on premature human infants in the United States, who are usually touch deprived. Their application of massage to these babies produced dramatic weight gain, enhanced behavioral development, and marked maturation of their hormonal regulation.[34] Similar trials using gentle stroking produced 47% more weight gain each day,[35] increased sleep states, and decreased stress hormones.[36] Preemie care nurses will tell you that these tiny beings consistently wriggle their way across their incubators to be in touch with a wall or at least have a foot against one side, instinctively seeking any kind of touch.

Massaging of preterm babies decreases the level of the stress hormone cortisol[37] and has also been shown to enhance the functioning of the immune system.[38] An investigation into "failure to thrive" infants discovered that the mothers of these infants provided much less touch and other kinds of stimulation to their infants than those of the normally growing infants in the study.[39] And an investigation into infants' attachment behaviors found the highest attachment rates in those with the most physical contact with their mothers.[40] German researchers, comparing maternal behaviors, reported that "experience of a direct sensual and physical contact was most important" for the continued loving relationship between mother and child.[41]

As with many other facets of child care, animal studies are valuable for studying the effects of touch and touch deprivation in infants, and they correlate strongly with human studies. One rat study found that the amount of physical affection received in infancy was a major determinant of adult stress control: the more licking and grooming received as an infant, the better stress control exhibited, both behaviorally and chemically.[42] These Canadian researchers also found *those who received the most affection displayed the highest levels of independence as adults.* They also demonstrated increased numbers of brain receptors for calming biochemicals. Interestingly, they noted that when mother rats needed to leave for short times to obtain food, they would groom the pups with enhanced vigor for a time after their return, as though they were making up for the reduction in affection. Another rat study found that depriving pups of physical sensory input leads to permanent deficits in the brain's ability to interpret touch sensations, in spite of months of training.[43]

> An investigation into "failure to thrive" infants discovered that the mothers of these infants provided much less touch and other kinds of stimulation to their infants than those of the normally growing infants in the study.

Untouched infants also become children and adults who don't touch. Compared to U.S. preschoolers, French preschoolers were not only touched much more by mothers and teachers, but they showed much physical affection toward their peers. The U.S. children displayed aggression toward their peers 29% of the time compared to 1% in the French youngsters. American children, who receive far less attention than most others around the world, displayed 3 times more attention-seeking behavior when compared to cultures that provide high infant contact such as those in Japan and Mexico.[44]

Caring by Carrying

Infants around the world are carried much of the day, either in the arms, in variously fashioned slings, or wrapped closely to the back as mother works in the field. Carrying provides stimulation through motion, known as "vestibular" stimulation, and allows babies and children to observe mother's activities and converse with her. Infant carrying also renders soothing through exposure to mother's odor, close body contact, body warmth, and body sounds, as well as with the motion.

When U.S. mothers in an experiment were given baby slings and instructed to increase infant carrying time, it was found that their infants were more securely attached to their mothers at 13 months of age than those who were simply given baby seats.[45] In another study that induced increased carrying for infants, the babies cried 43% less, fussed less, and ate more contentedly.[46] Yet, it has been shown that increased carrying may not reduce the crying in infants who have colic.[47] This refers to the colic with cries related to pain, as opposed to extended crying due to other reasons. If a food reaction or other disorder is occurring, carrying may provide support, but it does not make a painful problem go away.

Kangaroo Care

Standard care for Western newborns, for premature as well as full-term babies, is separation from mother. Full-term newborns remain in bassinet carts for most of the day. Preemies generally remain in incubators for their first weeks of extra-uterine life. Self-regulation of body temperature is weak in term newborns and very inadequate in preemies. Temperature, oxygen, and infection regulation are the chief purposes of incubators. Of course, breastmilk regulates infection too. It has been found that for all newborns, even very premature infants, placing them skin to skin on the chest of the mother or father provides superior temperature regulation[48] to that of an incubator. Measures of important energy conservation (oxygen consumption) in these infants are excellent as well.[49,50]

> *The U.S. children displayed aggression toward their peers 29% of the time compared to 1% in the French youngsters.*

The concept of kangaroo care was introduced in Colombia in 1978. Designed especially for small and preterm babies, the infant wears only a diaper and is placed upright inside the mother's clothing, in between her breasts. Here he can feed at will and can enjoy the comfort and gentle stimulation of continued contact with mother—her warmth, sounds, and odor. Almost no crying is heard this way, compared to the long pulses of "separation distress calls"[51] normally found in the nursery. This method of care has become standard in Scandinavian countries (where the infant death rate is half that of the United States) and has been adopted in other European countries for several hours per day. In the United States, in 1979, researchers demonstrated significant improvement in the recovery of newborns when affectionate treatment was given to them on cue. Not yet ready for allowing the mother in, this treatment was provided by nurses. Newborns were rocked, cuddled, and provided with verbal and visual stimulation, and they were allowed to suck on a pacifier as much as desired. In comparison with standard-care infants, these babies demonstrated superior temperature regulation and respiratory rate, far fewer heart murmurs were detected, fewer sucking and swallowing difficulties were seen, and almost no crying was found.[52] Over twenty years later, some in the United States are starting to seriously consider this kind of care.

Kangaroo care decreases newborn deaths, and these infants gain twice as much weight per day as incubator babies.[53,54] Kangaroo care also results in more sleep,[55] good oxygen saturation, less agitation, reduced stress hormone,[56] many fewer episodes of apnea (no breathing), and more stable heart rates.[57] A 1999 U.S. school of nursing study confirmed all these findings and reported that kangaroo care would be beneficial for newborns, beginning in the delivery room.[58] This care can also be used with preterm infants who require tube feeding; it even accelerates production of a hormone that stimulates secretion of digestive enzymes.[59] Even those on respirators can benefit from kangaroo care.[60]

Hospital procedures can be painful and taxing for preemies, causing stress hormone elevations and spending valuable energy resources. Several studies have confirmed that skin-to-skin care reduces the pain experienced by tiny babies.[61–63] Hospital stays are much shorter for preemies who receive this kind of attention. This early skin-to-skin care has also been shown to significantly improve mother's milk volume, a common challenge with preterm births,[64] and it improves mother's attachment and maternal behaviors.[65,66]

Certainly all the advantages of close contact and responsive care in newborns apply to older infants as well. Although it is difficult to study the individual effects of contact at different ages, the cumulative effects are apparent in attachment studies.

The Rock of Ages

In an infant, all six senses are developed by regular stimulation (yes, there are six senses). Vestibular information (the sense of position) is controlled by the semicircular canals in the inner ears that sense our position. Stimulating this sensory system helps develop the infant's balance and motor control, while also providing much soothing. Rocking an infant in a chair or while standing is a very popular form of vestibular, or kinesthetic, stimulation. The instinctive light bouncing commonly seen around the world, carrying, and playful "tossing" are all means of providing such input to the baby. Children love to swing, and various fashions of swings are found all around the world. Adults find rocking very soothing as well. Many rock themselves in their office chairs or during embraces. Grandma knew that soothing, pain relief, and brain stimulation could be found in her treasured rocker.

Although infants in Western societies were no longer carried much or slept with by the early twentieth century, they were comforted and stimulated with rocking in cradles for a few more decades, at least until twentieth-century advisors recommended that these comforting measures should also be thrown by the wayside. Today, many child experts still advise against anything that might provide comfort to an infant, for fear they may come to expect comfort, but they seem to have overlooked the new electric baby swings. These swings have found their way into most new Western families' homes. They are clearly beneficial in the absence of more natural means. Many people even take them along on family visits or vacations, or rent them, finding life with baby to be difficult without them.

> *Kangaroo care decreases newborn deaths, and these infants gain twice as much weight per day as incubator babies.*

Some authorities have suggested that rocking an infant can cause a self-rocking disorder; however, one study on self-rocking in (not retarded) youngsters found that self-rocking children displayed symptoms similar to those classified as poorly attached: hyperactivity or attention-deficit disorder.[67] This is not to suggest that children displaying such behavior are not well attached, but only to point out that the rocking of infants is not a likely cause of a psychological dysfunction. In fact, a study on developmentally delayed infants who exhibited self-rocking movements found that providing regular vestibular stimulation to them reduced this behavior and improved motor control.[68] Rocking has even been found to reduce spells of apnea in premature infants.[69]

A study of older infants who had life-threatening moments of apnea were found to have less than half as many episodes when they were rocked during sleep.[70] Infants also regulate their breathing more rhythmically with rocking,[71] and rocking relaxes infants' heart rates.[72] These studies suggest that sleeping in an electronically rocked cradle could be beneficial. These benefits are similar to the heart and breathing control benefits an infant receives by sleeping next to mother or father's body, another form of providing constant stimulation. However, these are not the only benefits of rocking.

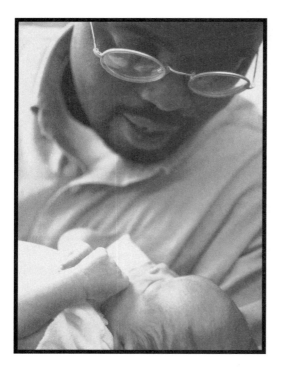

Vestibular stimulation such as rocking has been shown to improve the development of the cerebellum, which is in charge of motor control (coordination) and is still developing in the first 6 months of life.[73] Premature infants rocked for 15 minutes, 3 times per day for 2 weeks, demonstrated significant gains in motor control and muscle development as well as matured responses to auditory and visual stimuli. They also were more alert and had better defensive reflexes when compared to infants who were not rocked.[74] In another study, this same daytime rocking led to an improvement in preemies' sleep patterns.[75] One more similar study found improved neurological development and much higher scores on mental development tests.[76] A waterbed flotation study reported the same kind of benefits.[77]

In earlier chapters we noted that brain cell deaths occur in brain areas that the body deems unnecessary, in response to the parenting environment of the infant. A SIDS study found such brain cell deaths in the brain areas for vestibular control (and for facial sensation) in 76% of SIDS infants and none in infants who had died from other causes.[78] This suggests to me a great necessity for vestibular stimulation in infancy—that which is not stimulated in the brain is lost, in this case posing a threat to life.

Nursing and Nurturing

To all who know infants, it is apparent that infants are designed to nurse for the purpose of being soothed and for other benefits besides nutrition. Still, this form of comfort (called non-nutritive sucking) is discouraged by many once the meal is done, and parents are often encouraged to end all forms of sucking when their infants reach the age of 12 months.

Sucking at the breast increases EEG activity in areas of the brain that govern alertness and attention, as well as in areas that control the cycle of sleeping and waking. Bottle-feeding produces similar but lesser changes in brain patterns. Pacifier sucking has little effect,[79] but pacifier sucking has been shown to produce a valuable reduction in the heart rates of newborns, even much more than rocking.[80] Heart rates are lower still in breastfed infants compared to bottle-fed,[81] and this reduction continues during sleep.[82] Moreover, breastfeeding with skin-to-skin contact leads to far superior blood oxygenation in premature infants over standard breastfeeding (and the mothers were far more successful in continuing breastfeeding).[83] The dangerous reduction of oxygenation produced by crying in newborns who do not receive unrestricted breastfeeding can be prevented with pacifiers—the amount of crying is reduced and the oxygenation after crying is better than in those who do not receive non-nutritive sucking.[84]

Premature infants feed much better during inactive awake states, as opposed to excessive fatigue or fretful flailing. These calm states are associated with lower heart rates. It has been shown that pacifier sucking in preemies who are tube fed increases these beneficial behavioral states. When combined with rocking, significant improvement in feeding is found.[85]

In Holland, a country with low rates of nursing, it was found that babies who slept sucking on pacifiers had one-twentieth the chance of dying of SIDS.[86] In New Zealand infants who did not have the benefit of night nursing, a very significant reduction in SIDS rates correlated with pacifier use during sleep.[87]

Although sucking easily promotes sleep, many of those who make a living by treating infant sleep difficulties warn against allowing the infant to fall asleep through this natural means. Pediatrician Donald Shifrin of the University of Washington states that "Good sleepers are made, not born."[88] He advises that if an infant begins to look sleepy during feeding, you should stop and place the infant, now more awake, into his crib. This reverses all soothing, bonding, and brain and heart benefits, and leads to crying and the release of wakening stress hormones, which surely makes falling asleep much more difficult. He warns against any other natural soothing measures such as rocking, and he is against pacifier sucking as well. It's no wonder these babies now need harsh training and "expert" advice in order to sleep. Yet, nature has a wonderful plan that helps infants easily fall asleep. Breastfeeding, and to a lesser extent, bottle-feeding, lead naturally to sleep in an infant when sleep is needed. This is partly due to the natural comfort provided by sucking, partly due to hormone releases in the mother and infant due to sucking and body contact, and partly due to other factors in mother's milk. Even pacifier sucking can provide drowsiness. While Shifrin suggests promoting a bond with a stuffed animal containing mother's scent, the benefits to baby of bonding with real caretakers and receiving frequent comforting are far superior.

Breastfeeding is meant to be much more than just feeding—it is a time for nursing, a time to provide comfort and nurturing. This time is allotted for studying and memorizing each other's faces, for speaking or singing to the baby, and for developing nonverbal communications. When

> *Brain cell deaths occur in brain areas that the body deems unnecessary. A SIDS study found such brain cell deaths in the brain areas for vestibular control (and for facial sensation) in 76% of SIDS infants and none in infants who had died from other causes.*

allowed, comfort nursing often continues long after nutrition needs have been satiated, deepening the soothing, bonding, and educational relationship between parent and child. Bottle-fed babies can certainly be "nursed" as well.

The Downside of Pacifiers

Clearly, sucking a pacifier or a thumb helps infants when unrestricted breastfeeding is not available. Frequent sucking is very important to infants for many reasons, from reducing heart rate, stress, and SIDS, to increasing oxygenation and intelligence. While sucking on artificial nipples approximates some of the benefits of natural nursing, there are downsides to artificial sucking as well. The use of a thumb or pacifier after 2 years contributes to the development of crossbite,[89] whereas breastfeeding actually improves proper jaw development.[90] Pacifier use also increases the amount of bacteria and yeast in the mouth, which in turn increases the susceptibility to dental cavities. Using a bottle during the night, especially after age 2, causes a significant, but smaller, increase in tooth decay.[91] Using pacifiers or bottles during the first months of breastfeeding teaches improper sucking that can cause pain and infection in the mother and difficult nursing for the infant, reducing the chance of continued successful breastfeeding by half.[92,93] Thumb or pacifier use is high in those weaned prematurely from the bottle or the breast, and is generally minimal when there is extended on-cue breastfeeding.[94]

Safe Sleep and SIDS

Unlike most adults, when infants are tired they often become increasingly active, displaying restlessness, irritability, and crying. Also unlike adults, who sleep more deeply when stress is low, infants sleep more deeply when stressed. Stress is so fatiguing for the tiny energy-dependent body that nature uses deep sleep as a healing response. Infants delivered surgically, who miss out on many of the hormonal and other natural benefits of passing through the birth canal, and who often meet their mothers much later than those who are vaginally delivered, fall into longer sleep states for days after birth.[95] Although it was once thought that this deep sleep was desirable because it reduced an infant's requests for the comfort of his parents at night, and for food when his stomach was empty, we are now discovering that this once-coveted deep sleep has led to countless sudden infant deaths.

When bottle-feeding was successfully imposed on the majority of families early last century, the malady of severely sleep-deprived parents suddenly became commonplace. Babies had to sleep separately so that breastfeeding was not encouraged, although this was not the reason given. Other comforting measures were being taken away as well, one at a time. As a result, long and loud bouts of crying occurred throughout the night, and child care advisors had to search for measures that would promote long phases of deep sleep in infants to help parents get some rest. Because the unnatural position of sleeping prone (on the stomach) was found to deepen infant sleep states, it was promoted with vigor as a solution. Lying prone is unnatural for a young baby, in the sense that nursing is very difficult in this position, and it does not occur when mother and infant sleep together naturally—except when baby lies tummy-down on mom or dad's chest where the neck is less strained and a parent's heartbeat and respiration regulate baby's. Another motivation for the prone positioning was the unusual patterns of baldness developed by many highly frustrated and long-crying infants who flailed their heads left and right on their backs. Prone positioning in the crib also provided a solution for isolated infants who became withdrawn and developed flat spots on the back of their skulls from spending so much time lying motionless on their backs.

> *It's no wonder these babies now need harsh training and "expert" advice in order to sleep. Yet, nature has a wonderful plan that helps infants easily fall asleep. Breastfeeding is a time for nursing, a time to provide comfort and nurturing.*

It is now known that a baby lying prone has pressure on the brain stem (where sleep is controlled), partially occluding it. This is the likely reason such positioning produces deeper sleep, as well as why it is a factor in the escalation of SIDS. A gradual build-up of cell deaths in this region seems to occur, rendering the infant very fragile. Cellular destruction has been found in portions of the hippocampus that are very sensitive to reduced oxygen. In studies, this was seen in 44% of SIDS babies and in none of the controls, suggesting that *any additional reduction of oxygenation, such as from prolonged crying, would exacerbate the problem of infant deaths.*[96]

Now that prone sleeping has become greatly reduced, other statistical associations with SIDS are more easily found. For instance, a large New Zealand investigation found that, as compared to sharing a room with a non-smoking adult, sleeping alone in a separate room causes 5 times the risk of SIDS.[97] A later well-controlled study in England found sleeping outside of the parental room brought 10.5 times the risk of sleeping in the parents' room.[98] These studies came out only after another huge factor leading to SIDS had been revealed and adjusted for—smoking. A different New Zealand report had found that 26% of SIDS cases could be explained by the fact that babies were sharing beds with smoking mothers[99] (so they banned all infant bed-sharing for a time), while a later English study found that *full-sized infants cosleeping with a smoking parent showed 8 times the risk of SIDS* as those sleeping alongside non-smoking parents.[100] Even if a parent does not actually smoke in the bed or even in the bedroom, the particulate released from the smoker's lungs is released into the air and the nearby baby breathes it for hours. This ongoing release of tobacco combustion products from the lungs of smokers is well known in industry by those who work in clean rooms with semiconductors. After adjusting for smoking, researchers in England uncovered *a tripled risk of SIDS for formula-fed babies,*[101] a University of California study has reported the same results,[102] and a German study suggested nearly 8 times the risk for babies who are not breastfed.[103] Because sharing the bed promotes breastfeeding, and breastfeeding promotes sharing the bed, these two factors are intertwined in the protection against SIDS.[104] An Irish study comparing breast-feeding bed-sharers to non-breastfeeding bed-sharers found those breastfeeding had half the risk of SIDS.[105]

Now that crib-sleeping babies are being placed on their backs, new concerns over flattened skulls, called "positional pla-giocephaly," are arising. Large numbers of infants are now having to wear corrective

> *We are now discovering that the once-coveted deep sleep in infants has led to countless sudden infant deaths.*

helmets, and some are undergoing unnecessary tests and even operations. A cosleeping infant who nurses during the night spends much of its time on its side, and this position changes several times during the night as baby feeds and mother switches baby from one side to the other. This natural changing of back and side-lying positions creates a naturally, properly formed skull.

The circadian rhythms (daily cycle) for heart rate and blood pressure in the young infant are poorly developed.[106] Doctors at Baylor College of Medicine report that half the SIDS victims they studied had heartbeat irregularities a little beyond the norm.[107] Although only 1.5% of babies with such an irregularity will succumb to SIDS (compared to .037% without it), these researchers suggest all infants be screened and placed on beta-blocker drugs (which are not without serious side effects) when such an irregularity is found. Yet, numerous studies have shown that an infant in close contact with an adult has significantly better heart rhythms.

Significantly, *victims of SIDS spend longer intervals in deeper sleep and have very few arousal periods during the night (like those exhausted from crying or who are sleeping prone).*[108] This effect is most pronounced in the early morning hours when SIDS deaths most often occur.[109] On the other hand, cosleeping breastfed infants nurse most frequently during the early morning hours, thereby reducing the danger. Poor control of respiration rates, respiration reflexes, and poor arousal were also reported by Berkeley researchers looking into unexplained cases of infant deaths.[110] Remember that most of the infants studied were solitary sleeping infants because this has been the norm in the United States during the twentieth century. Ironically, for a time it was customary for some to instantly blame infant death in a cosleeping infant on parental suffocation. This notion is contradicted by research. James McKenna, PhD, and colleagues found that infants sleeping next to their mothers tend to synchronize their arousal from deeper to lighter stages of sleep on a minute-to-minute basis throughout the night.[111] Much sensory information is

> *A well-controlled study in England found sleeping outside of the parental room brought 10.5 times the risk of SIDS as sleeping in the parents' room.*

being exchanged between the two during the night. Additionally, such infants experience reductions in the deeper states of sleep (stages 3 and 4).[112] Their number of arousals (stages 1 and 2) is greatly increased, although actual wakefulness is not. The amount of REM (rapid eye movement) sleep was not affected.[113] English researchers have also suspected that prolonged periods of lone quiet sleep are a factor in SIDS.[114]

Infants sleeping close to a parent are physiologically regulated much like they are during rocking, tactile stimulation, and kangaroo care. They also do not suffer from the effects of crying and cortisol releases. Generally, they will frequently be nursing as well, therefore obtaining the sucking benefits as previously described. Heart rate and rhythm, respiration, and blood oxygenation are all improved in cosleeping babies, and apnea is reduced, thereby mitigating the influence of these harmful factors strongly associated with SIDS in Western families where babies sleep alone. In addition, when an infant has anxious or unusual moments, or a fever, they are rapidly noticed by a nearby parent, who can respond to difficulties that might have otherwise been missed. Some of these same benefits are experienced by infants who sleep in a bed near their parents. The odor and pheromones of the mother apparently play a regulatory role in ending spells of apnea.[115]

In cultures where sharing the bed with infants and nursing are the norm, SIDS rates have always been quite low. In England, this cultural difference was found to be responsible for the greatly lower sudden infant death rates among Asian populations,[116] and a Japanese study found sleeping alone to be a significant SIDS risk factor.[117] African Americans, who more often formula-feed, have high SIDS rates compared to the

After adjusting for smoking, researchers in England uncovered a tripled risk of SIDS for bottle-fed babies, a University of California study has reported the same results, and a German study suggested nearly 8 times the risk for babies who are not breastfed.

already high general American population,[118] yet Africans from the mostly breastfeeding and cosleeping peoples of Zimbabwe have a very low degree of SIDS,[119] one-fifth the rate of the United States. Taiwan is a nation that has been rapidly Westernized over the last decades. During the period from 1984 to 1993, the SIDS rate in this country more than doubled.[120]

Historically, in Europe, "overlying" on baby during the night was used as an excuse for "accidental" infant death in very poor families, when another baby meant too many mouths to feed (and when in reality, the mother purposely suffocated it). For this reason, bed-sharing was actually outlawed in some areas, giving cosleeping a dangerous reputation that still permeates the thinking of some today.[121] Such events still occur occasionally, and rumors of accidental suffocation due to cosleeping continue to circulate. There *is* a danger in cosleeping with a parent whose natural reflexes and awareness are greatly altered by drugs or alcohol, or with a neurologically compromised infant whose reflexes may be greatly impaired, who may not naturally turn his head, whimper, or move away if his air supply becomes compromised.

The U.S. Consumer Product Safety Commission reported in 1999 that there were 515 deaths of children up to age 2 sleeping in their parents' bed, over an 8-year period (about 64 per year).[122] Compare this to 7,000 U.S. SIDS deaths overall per year measured up to age 1. Many of the adult-bed deaths occurred when no parent was present in the room to monitor baby. One-quarter of these adult-bed deaths were reported as overlying of the child by a parent. I have addressed the factors associated with this verdict. The rest were reported as due to some kind of entrapment in the bed structure or bedding. Such entrapment deaths were extremely high in cribs for decades. In response to the recent CPSC report, the American Academy of Pediatrics released an advisory against children being placed in adult beds. Interestingly, it has never released any advisory about the 5 to 10 times higher risk of SIDS for babies sleeping alone in a separate bedroom. In contrast, when entrapment and suffocation dangers were found in cribs, recommendations were made to make cribs safer. Still, marketing of glamorous but potentially hazardous nursery bedding continues. Strangulation and suffocation still occur in infant furniture to this day. At the same time, countless infant lives are certainly being saved in numerous ways through sharing parental rooms and beds. Many more would be saved if more were not sleeping stressfully isolated from important comfort, bodily regulation, vigilance, and night nursing. Media reports of infant deaths from cosleeping are also often misleading, as some of these infants were not cosleeping at all. As mentioned, some were alone and unprotected in adult beds and other regular cosleepers were actually in their crib at the time of death. In addition, these reports do not distinguish between customary and impromptu cosleepers—the latter being at greater risk.

See the most recent cosleeping articles on my website at www. BabyReference.com for an examination of statistics and studies about

© 2001 Image Bank Anne Rippy

"SIDS Risk," a brief article in *Time* magazine, reported that "Babies who died from SIDS were found to have a much higher rate of *H. pylori* infection than other children. Manchester researchers theorize that the bug could be passed on to infants by parents' kissing them…" But the picture unwittingly attached to the blurb tells the actual tale. Babies either partly or fully formula-fed lack intestinal protection from dangerous microbes. *H. pylori* (the "ulcer" bacteria) is one of them. The chronic irritation that formula causes in many infant intestines leads to immune breakdown that allows this bacteria to take hold. Unless raised in a very sterile (and cold) environment, most babies (and most people) will be exposed to this common bacteria many times in their lives. With a healthy immune system, which during infancy requires mother's milk, exposure should help babies develop their normal balance of flora and their own protective mechanisms. Instead of never kissing your baby, I suggest smothering her with love, and providing her with the natural defenses of mother's milk.

cosleeping, SIDS, and safety. In addition to the factors mentioned previously, suggested risk factors in the parental bed include waterbeds, soft fluffy bedding, heavy bedding, pillow for baby, drugged or drunken bed-sharers, impromptu bed-sharing, and bed-sharing with an unrelated or unaccustomed partner, in addition to the possibility of the baby getting wedged between the mattress and headboard and unattended sleeping. Sofa sleeping poses a very high risk and other makeshift bedding can be dangerous. For the greatest infant survival, the answer is to make the parental bed safe, not to throw out the baby.

It appears that a combination of various factors comes into play in most cases of SIDS. In summary, these are some of the twentieth-century experiments in Western cultures that have led to the escalation of SIDS:

- Promoting artificial feeding
- Promoting isolated sleep
- Allowing babies to cry themselves to sleep
- Promoting the prone position in bed (seldom naturally seen in cosleeping, breastfeeding infants) to induce deeper sleep
- Discouraging pacifier use during sleep for those not nursing

There is a correlation between pertussis vaccinations and SIDS as well, as discussed in a later chapter, but one must consider that pertussis itself can occasionally cause episodes of oxygen deficit.[123] In either case, the safest place for a baby is in bed with or at least very near his parents where he can be monitored, his oxygenation can be regulated by his parents' rhythms, and he will spend less time in the deepest sleep states.

In addition, although about 7,000 U.S. infants die each year of SIDS, another 1,100 young children die each year in home fires[124] (mostly at night). Along with deaths from floods, storms, and other home disasters, how many may have been saved if they had been sleeping near their parents rather than in another part of the house?

Nurturing Sleep for Everyone

In the great majority of families around the world, throughout the millennia, and throughout most of the animal kingdom, babies sleep warmly and safely next to their mothers or a close family member. These cultures experience far fewer psychiatric problems, lower infant mortality rates, and much less SIDS. The same effects are found in the animal kingdom, when the health and survival of baby animals separated from their mothers is compared to that of those who are not. Among Westerners unfamiliar with this kind of sleeping arrangement, many often have some fear of "squishing" the baby. In fact, babies have strong instinctual protective reflexes that assure head turning, creeping (even in newborns), or whimpering if air availability becomes impaired. Adults also have a strong sense of orientation during the night, evidenced by the fact that few fall out of bed or even fall off their pillows. The roaming hormones of those affected by parenthood help to increase nighttime awareness. New mothers have practiced increased awareness during the night for many months because they have been arousing themselves to turn their large pregnant bodies during sleep.

Dr. Richard Ferber and others have demonstrated that allowing a child to cry alone at bedtime helps the child realize that its parents will not be there for them at night. Many children, however, will continue to cry themselves to sleep and will also cry during the night. Parents are encouraged to accept this situation as normal, not as a signal that baby needs something. Tine Thevenin, author of *The Family Bed*, put the possible consequences of such actions quite well: "Unfortunately, a suppressed need is not erased, although it may lie dormant within the person for many, many years."[125]

Forced isolation at bedtime is very stressful for infants. We know this from the almost universal fretful crying pleas against this abandonment. Cosleeping children exhibit lower stress hormone levels as well.[126] Some suggest that a person will never know how to fall asleep if not put through this traumatic nighttime ritual during infancy. However, throughout the cosleeping majority of the world, children, adolescents, and adults actually experience fewer sleeping difficulties than in the United States. Some studies suggest that cosleeping infants experience greater sleeping difficulties, but this is due to a definition of sleep difficulty that condemns the natural, more frequent (and possibly lifesaving) arousal to lighter stages of sleep, which are part of the infants' obvious enjoyment of having their parents near. We are told that forced isolation develops the autonomy that a child supposedly wants and needs; however, as soon as a child is able to climb out of the crib, she instinctively and most deliberately seeks out a warm, cuddly spot in her parents' bed. There are those who suggest that infants need to get the most sleep they possibly can and that isolated, cry-it-out, uncomforted sleep is the means to achieve this, even if it means they are actually sleeping off exhaustion from long crying and even if it means they are regularly entering prolonged deep sleep states that are associated with SIDS. It's difficult to agree that this practice is necessary for babies when, as I've shown, isolated sleep is associated with a 5 to 10 times increased risk of SIDS.

While cosleeping babies enjoy increased safety, bonding, and comfort, cosleeping parents usually get much more sleep as well, especially when nursing.[127] Gone are the startling, adrenaline-pumping awakenings to loud baby cries, the preparing of bottles, and the feeding in a chair, trying to stay awake, followed by trying to sneak away from the infant, now sleepy again, who hits the cold mattress and cries once more. Baby can have an open bar all night, with mother and child barely waking, and father often being entirely undisturbed. Since mothers' and infants' sleep levels tend to coincide, baby will nudge mother for nursing generally during mother's lighter sleep states. Then the hormones released from breastfeeding easily send mother and baby back to sleep. Neither parent need lie awake wondering whether the baby is all right, or spend the night peeking into the nursery for reassurance. Simply placing a hand on the baby's side reassures the parent that he is breathing. Many find that sharing the bed also helps make up for lost contact during a day spent away at work. Parents notice that baby finds a way to keep at least one foot in contact with at least one adult at all times during the night—revealing the child's constant innate need for security throughout the night and his constant awareness of his parents' presence. Nightmares and night terrors, common childhood dilemmas in today's society, are almost unknown in the bed-sharing youngster[128] (except for some special cases, such as with food allergies). Babies' daytime naps, if not on mother's back or in a sling, benefit from just being in the midst of daily activities—in the living room or somewhere close by—rather than stowed away in isolation. In fact, the sound of mother's voice produces healthy reductions in the infant's heart rate during sleep.[129] Lozoff has reported that when children fall asleep, the mere presence of an adult makes them less likely to suck their thumbs or use a regular attachment object—suggesting possibly more secure attachment to the parents.[130] When insomnia is present, even in a non-isolated infant, pain may be a component.[131] Intolerance of cow's milk proteins is, again, a major cause.[132,133]

> *Forced isolation at bedtime is very stressful for infants. We know this from the almost universal fretful crying pleas against this abandonment.*

What the World Needs Now...

Today there seems to be a race to get babies separated, off the bottle, toilet trained—to make "grown-ups" of them. But even under ideal conditions, being an infant is often painful and difficult, and babies grow up soon enough without any pushing at all. Possibly, many do not grow up in certain ways or to certain degrees because they have not fulfilled various stages or needs during the developmental years. While babies are designed to survive in the face of adversity, it may not be wise to intentionally create it. We should instead honor babyhood, rejoice in all the special cozy comforts parents are designed to provide, and shower our babies with unrestrained love.

5

Brighter Babies, Not Super Babies

As with many other aspects of a child's development, IQ can be greatly influenced by parenting choices and practices. Children and adults can be bright in many different ways—from artistic creativity, to a gift for reading human emotions, to physical or musical talent, to being able to achieve a high level of education. IQ tests try to measure how easily one can grasp or think through problems or concepts. While by no means the best measurement of success, IQ is often discussed instead of some other talents because it can be quantified and is therefore more easily researched. It's used here to compare brain development with regard to various environmental situations, such as diet and child care. But all the methods described below for enhancing IQ development are just as valuable for promoting any talent or potential brightness in a baby, so baby has the best chance of becoming a shining star in whatever direction calls her. These methods also promote healthier individuals who can build strong, lasting relationships and can lead honest and less stressful lives. To many, these skills may be the best measurement of success. Research into IQ development is designed to assist parents who desire to help their children achieve deeper educational experiences to expand their future possibilities.

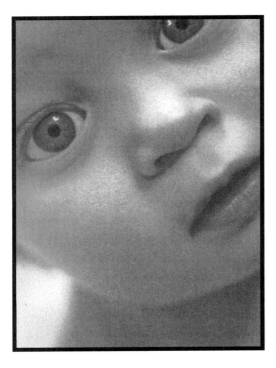

For a time there was quite a fad concerned with developing "super babies." Little intellectual develop- ment can take place when baby spends the waking hours in a pale-colored room staring at a white ceiling and the same little mobile day after day, so trendset- ters became enthralled with providing higher and higher levels of stimulation, then waited for the results. Fetuses were bathed with loud music and infants were bludgeoned with flash cards all day long. This was a valuable experi- ment for discovering the limits of intellectual development, although it may have produced some highly frustrated individuals as well. Soon researchers found that only a portion of the infants' great gains persisted throughout the school years, while other developmental elements may have been inadver- tently ignored during all the enthusiasm. In other children, the efforts didn't seem to work at all, and in some, they backfired.

We now know that regular stimulation throughout the day is valuable for baby's intellectual development, but there must be a wide variety of stimuli, and they must be within the limits of a child's attention and interest. We also know that breastmilk is important for brain development, and that without it, baby's IQ can fall well below his potential. Baby's brain does 80% of its (postnatal) growing during the first 2 years after birth, and during this time the body decides how big the brain should be and how many nerve cells will be retained in its various regions. Beyond genetics, the child's early environment may affect his intellectual potential by 15% or more.

Breastmilk for Brain Power

EEG activity in an infant's brain increases significantly during breastfeeding, but not during pacifier sucking. This increased activity leads to improved brain function.[1] As we will see later, only breastmilk contains the ultimate nutrition for the brain and body. Additionally, the neurological stimulation and emotional confidence gained through the ongoing breastfeeding relationship can provide an intellectual edge.

The 1990s brought a flurry of studies reporting greater intelligence in breastfed babies. A Spanish study showed that brain development in 2-year-olds was higher in breastfed than bottle-fed babies,[2] and an English investigation reported a "robust" statistical elevation of later intelligence in breastfed youngsters.[3] Following these, in the face of doubters, additional studies in the United States attempted to control for as many variables as possible, including maternal intelligence and environmental factors, and found a 5 point higher average IQ in 3-year-olds who had had any breastfeeding.[4] A more extensive U.K. study tested children at 8 years of age and found significantly higher IQs in those who had received human milk as premature infants.[5] This advantage was the same for infants who were fed with tubes and those who were nursed, laying most of the advantage on the milk itself. Additionally, preemies whose mothers chose to provide breastmilk, but failed, shared the same lower IQ as formula-fed infants, removing many confounding variables from the results and giving the credit to the breastmilk. British follow-up studies at 10 years of age revealed much higher vocabulary and intelligence

> Consistently, the longer the duration of breastfeeding, the greater the IQ advantage. Little benefit was found in those who received both formula and breastfeedings.

in children who had been exclusively breastfed.[6] A Dutch investigation reported similar findings, after adjusting for social and other factors.[7] More recently, a New Zealand study of over 1,000 children aged 8 to 18 years concluded that consistently, the longer the duration of breastfeeding, the greater the IQ advantage, as well as better reading comprehension, improved math and other scholastic abilities, and higher examination scores on national tests.[8]

A 2006 report led to big media announcements that breastfeeding does not improve intelligence after all.[9] This analysis of multiple earlier studies had at least two major flaws. First, the researchers randomly dismissed premature infants studies—whose intelligence margins are the greatest and most easily measured.

Second, this study provided no definition of what "breastfed" means. Multitudes of studies have shown that when breastmilk is supplemented with formula, juice, or other foods, the outcomes in all areas (such as illnesses, development, and survival) are much closer to that of fully formula-fed babies. The only meaningful measure is one of exclusive breastmilk early on versus exclusive formula, along with a measure of the continued duration of breastfeeding. In fact, the study itself reports that there were significantly higher test scores when comparing long durations of breastfeeding to short or none—demonstrating an intelligence benefit found that did not make it to the headline conclusion.

In 2008, a report was released on the largest breastfeeding study ever performed. This examination was designed to avoid or account for all issues of complaint by earlier IQ study critics and was performed on term babies. New mothers were assigned to either receive extra breastfeeding education and support, or standard treatment. There was a far greater percentage of exclusive and prolonged breastfeeding among those receiving breastfeeding-friendly support. At 6 years of age, a 6-point IQ advantage was robustly measured among those babies who breastfed more versus those cared for with standard feeding practices (usually some breastfeeding and a lot of formula).[10] Other advantages were reported as well. It can be assumed from these and other findings that a more distinct comparison of full breastfeeding to no breastmilk would reveal an even greater difference.

We can see that children who are allowed their natural diet for a more natural length of time are able to achieve what is likely their fullest potential, reaping the rewards throughout their maturation. Vision and neurological functioning benefit from breastmilk as well. A British study of 1,000 adults born in the 1920s found higher IQs in those who had been exclusively breastfed. As with most studies, little benefit was found in those who received both formula and breastfeeding.[11] This same investigation found pacifier use to be associated with lower IQ—most probably an indirect effect of other factors usually associated with prolonged pacifier use, specifically, the absence or reduction of breastfeeding. A Brazilian study discovered 40% fewer developmental delays in 1-year-olds nursed for over 9 months than in those nursed for less than 1 month.[12] Other studies have reported more activity in breastfed babies, especially arm movement[13] and greater "fluency of movement" in preschoolers who were breastfed as infants,[14] both indicating greater brain development.

Iron deficiency anemia is very common in infants who are not breastfed or who are supplemented or weaned early. This anemia is associated with lower IQs in children, regardless of oral iron supplementation upon diagnosis.[15] A rare cause of developmental mental retardation in children (1 in 12,000) is a genetic error in protein handling known as phenylketonuria. When diagnosed, this condition can be treated through dietary measures for nursing mother and baby. It has been found that phenylketonuric children who had been breastfed as babies score 14 points higher on IQ tests.[16] Those who had been breastfed before diagnosis fared far better than those on formula. These findings suggest that the protein levels in human milk are more appropriate for infants, thereby reducing brain damage before diagnosis; furthermore, other factors in breastmilk enhance intelligence after treatment has begun.

Caring for Cognition

Studies show that the sensitivity with which parents care for an infant, such as frequent affection and interaction and quick response to cries, is strongly correlated with intellectual development[17] and is the best predictor of school performance.[18] On the other hand, harsh discipline and low motherly warmth are associated with a 12-point lower IQ.[19] Also, high levels of stress hormones in infancy—seen in those often separated from mother, frequently left to cry, and comforted less—are associated with nerve cell alterations that are linked to reduced intellect and memory.[20,21] There is a linear relationship: Those with the most cortisol have the lowest scores on mental and motor ability tests.[22] Brain development advantages have been measured in premature infants receiving kangaroo care as well.[23]

In addition to high levels of parental response, other child management practices have been found to powerfully promote intellect, language, and problem-solving development in children. Psychologists suggest that more dialog and presentation of consequences, and less authoritarian control of behavior may be beneficial. These parental behaviors have twice the impact on a child's intellectual development as mother's education level and birth problems combined.[24] Another group of researchers focused on the mother's ability to accurately understand her small infant's cues, an ability developed through strong bonding practices. They found a significant correlation between this and positive language and intellectual measures at 18 months of age.[25]

Mother's frequent stimulation of her infant is a key factor. In an early study, Belsky confirmed a relationship between mother's attention-focusing conversations with baby and the growing baby's attention span and exploratory interests.[26] Fortunately, after some time, Tufts University researchers decided to focus on father's contribution as well. Their recent, large study of low-birth-weight babies found that infant IQs averaged 6 points higher in those with highly involved fathers compared to those with detached fathers.[27] Many studies have shown that increased social interaction with caregivers during infancy significantly improves mental development later on.[28]

An infant's interest in novel stimuli, the eagerness to continually embrace the unknown, strongly predicts later intelligence.[29] In those who are not so self-motivated (hence demanding less attention), other research indicates that frequent introduction to novel situations will likely produce a similar end result (or else clutter the mind of a potential Plato). According to professors Todd Risley and Betty Hart, the amount of speech a baby hears will strongly determine future intellectual development and social success.[30]

Others have found that maternal attention has especially significant effects on preterm infants.[31] Apparently, preterm babies have a broader range of possible outcomes than full-term infants. Those with highly stimulating environments seem to be able to catch up and overcome delayed intellectual development while those without much stimulation seem to decline further below their potential.[32] Researchers found a specific pattern in many preemie EEG tracings, referred to as "407-Trace Alternant," that was strongly correlated with later IQ levels.[33] Low levels of this particular trace were linked to lower IQs that persisted through the end of the study, which was to age 8. The researchers noted an exception to this pattern, however, in babies who were raised in "consistently attentive, responsive environments." By age 2, these children had higher IQs, equal to those who initially had more promising EEG tracings. On the average, preterm infants and low-birth-weight babies demonstrate an average IQ that is 5 points lower. Yet, studies on preemies show that high language involvement from mother can raise this by 8 points, a positive, warm home environment by 5 points more, and preschool attendance by another 5 points.[34] As mentioned in the previous chapter, preterm infants are often more available or more interesting to study. Most findings on their brain development in response to various environments should certainly provide insight pertinent to all babies.

At 2 years of age, preterm infants who were regularly exposed to rocking and heartbeat sounds (a synthetic comforting mother of sorts) during their hospital stays scored significantly higher on mental development tests.[35] Another similar experiment using rocking alone found increased auditory and visual interpretation and increased alertness.[36] Also, increased cognitive abilities result from massage therapy.[37] One study even demonstrated that vaginal delivery can provide an edge for developing a higher IQ. Compared to surgically delivered babies, these infants had preferable lower respiration rates during sleep, even at 6 months. Lower respiration correlates with higher mental scores at 1 year of age.[38]

From all these studies one can see that, while IQ may be largely determined genetically, parental practices can influence it; some studies suggest by as much as 10 to 15%, or approximately 10 to 15 points on the IQ scale. As found in the above study and others, premature infant IQs can be influenced even more—nearly 20%—with institutionalized babies showing even greater variations, at least with regard to ability to function intellectually.[39]

Animal Models

Psychology researchers P. A. Ferchmin and V. A. Eterovic first reported on the effects of genetics and early environment on rat brain development in 1970. Then in 1980, they reported on experiments with rats bred to be genetically learning deficient (low IQ). They found that providing highly stimulating environments to these rats, including increased physical, visual, auditory, and touch stimuli, produced animals that could outperform genetically superior rats that were left in normal environments during early development.[40] Fourteen years later, these same researchers measured the brain's uptake of a specific sugar used in the laboratory to reflect brain activity, suggesting development. They found evidence of significantly higher levels of brain growth in rats raised in "enriching" environments compared to those raised in "impoverished" ones similar to the environment of infants left in their cribs for much of the day.[41]

Womb Lessons

There was a time in my life when I was extremely aware of a physical condition I had—I was pregnant. I was also assured by everyone that one day I was going to have a baby. I took care of myself in this condition, taking proper measures not to pollute the tiny group of cells growing inside me. At the same time, I made preparations for the eventual arrival of a child. When my own infant was a few weeks old, I met some tiny preemies and I suddenly realized that I had "had" a baby for quite some time: There had been a thinking, feeling human being inside of me. Somehow, this reality never quite sank in until I got to know him on the outside. As we struggled through his 8 P.M. crying and fussing session every evening, I realized that the kicking tummy we had reacted to each evening by poking, calling to, and shining in flashlights was actually this little tiny person feeling some kind of distress.

As the super baby movement correctly declared a while back, a child's intellectual development begins inside the womb, and parental behaviors impact the fetal brain. Researchers have found that the emotions and stress levels of pregnant mothers have significant effects on the brain development of the fetus.[42] Lower blood flow to the fetal brain is found in women with higher anxiety levels,[43] and increased levels of stress hormones in the mother will alter the development of the fetal brain.[44]

The fetus begins to produce detectable responses to sound by 23 to 28 weeks of gestation.[45] The noises that reach him are those that are louder than his background environment of heartbeat, respiration, and digestion. Mother's voice is most prominently available to him, both as sound and vibration.

Investigations have found that mother's voice and low sounds are actually enhanced by the uterine environment, but outside voices (which have a higher pitch) are somewhat subdued.[46] Many classical and behavioral conditioning experiments have demonstrated that fetuses can learn, yet there's no evidence that providing anything beyond the voices and sounds that naturally occur will provide any intellectual edge.[47] In response to reports from researchers, there was a time when many parents were bathing their wombs with the music of Mozart in effort to enhance their child's intelligence. These findings later came into question, and the playing of classical music to fetuses has gone out of vogue. Responses to music are certain however[48], and it appears that the fetus forms memories of distinct voices and musical sounds.[49] Scientists are convinced that language acquisition begins in the womb.[50]

Electronic Teachers

A variety of stimulation provides enhanced brain development and education to youngsters. Our new age has brought many declines in the stimulation of infants. They have much less exposure to bugs and butterflies, gibbering squirrels, rustling leaves, and falling rain. Moreover, most do not have the ever-present neighbors and extended family members conversing, working, and playing about them, and paying attention to them.

In the place of this, we have electronics. While human interactions are the best, we unfortunately live highly isolated lives (partly as a result of television). I have seen households where adults or other children are seldom available to stimulate baby, yet television shows or battery operated toys are felt to be stunting, so baby's exposure to these are limited. Instead these youngsters lie or sit alone with a few bland toys and four pale walls around them, their brains wasting away. While the occasional Waldorf school provides wonderful natural environments to nurture youngsters, our electronics are not all bad. Growing up in the modern world, children will constantly use and depend on computer technology and other electronic devices. Teaching is one way we introduce the young to society's collective knowledge and belief systems: morals, daily living skills, culture, arts, language, science, and trade skills. Computers and other electronics are intimately entwined with many of these.

Our education needs to go beyond growing or catching our food and contending with the elements—a vast amount of brain training and knowledge is needed to obtain an average college degree today or even just to enjoy some of what our technology has to offer. The incredible amount of stimulation and education available through educational television cannot be discounted.[51] Neither can the significant brain developing effects of some video and computer games and electronic toys. Psychologist Patricia Greenfield of UCLA describes how playing video games can quickly improve scores on tests of spatial relations.[52] Others tout the improved concentration, social development, and imagination children get from watching good preschool television shows.[53] In moderate amounts, media can be used in controlled contexts for intellectual and other benefits to children of all ages.

However, there is little doubt about several negative qualities of the media. The extreme amount of violence that can be seen on TV when it is not vigilantly monitored is often associated with violent acts in children and adolescents.[54] In fact, *introducing television broadcasts to previously remote areas has resulted in a more than 50% increase in murder rates 10 to 15 years later.*[55] Even cartoons, Disney movies, and other shows designed for our youngest children parade large amounts of weaponry, violent acts, and cruelty toward innocents—as if this were acceptable in everyday life (possibly helping to make it a reality). TV viewing ratings do not help to screen this either. Our society finds weapon-toting warriors an important theme for children's shows and baby toys, but the sight of life-providing vessels of baby nourishment (breasts) is vehemently guarded. Another drawback of television is that time spent with other valuable activities is reduced when much time is spent with television and other electronic entertainment.

> *Our society finds weapon-toting warriors an important theme for children's shows and baby toys, but the sight of life-providing vessels of baby nourishment (breasts) is vehemently guarded.*

Got Fatty Acids?

Visual function as well as many other brain functions are improved in breastfed infants compared to formula-fed babies, and in direct correlation to the duration of breastfeeding.[56] Various fatty acids thought responsible for some of the brain development attributed to breastmilk have not been found in formulas until very recently. Most U.S. formulas now have moderate added amounts of two of these found to be quite important: ARA (an omega-6 fatty acid) and DHA (an omega-3 fatty acid). Another known important omega-3 fatty acid, EPA, is not being added to any.

The facts that more DHA has been found in the brains of breastfed compared with formula-fed infants, and that DHA is found in human milk but not in formulas, suggest that DHA comes to babies directly from their diet. Recently, it has been confirmed that infants can convert certain fatty acids in their diet into other important fatty acids that are building blocks of the brain. It is for this reason that infants have survived with formulas at all. Yet this research also demonstrates that fatty acid availability in formula is not complete enough for the optimal development seen with breastmilk. Early researchers' attempts to fortify formulas with DHA, however, did not lead to any hoped-for benefits.[57] A later investigation attempted fortification with DHA as well as another fatty acid, ARA, but this effort did not produce breastfeeding standards of development either.[58] Others tested four different concentrations of fatty acids hoping to raise DHA and ARA levels. They were successful in raising DHA levels in infants, but ARA disappointingly decreased and the sought-after visual improvement did not occur. Also, infant growth was reduced below desirable levels.[59] Still more attempts yielded similar results,[60] and it is currently found that, while infant blood levels of DHA are being raised, no developmental advantage is being gained by the supplementation.[61–63]

The addition of these fatty acids is used heavily as a marketing tool today, calling these formulas the "closest ever" to breastmilk. Yet, many lactation professionals are reporting findings of diarrhea in infants fed formulas with these added where these same infants were fine with non-supplemented versions. As with many other efforts to make formula "behave" like breastmilk, so far, all efforts to fortify formulas with various combinations of fatty acids have failed to produce the level of eye and brain development that breastfeeding and only breastfeeding can provide. It's clear that breastmilk is far more complex than a set of simple nutrients.

A comparison of the spectrum of fatty acids between breastmilk and today's formulas reveals many differences, including low or missing palmitoleic and gadoleic fatty acids. The effects of all these differences are unknown. Even when human levels or ratios of certain fatty acids are well matched by a formula, results are not as desired. Why? First, there seem to be too many fatty acids in human milk to attempt to match them all. Second, other brain factors are certainly missing in formula as well. Third, colostrum, premature breastmilk, newborn breastmilk, mature baby milk, and toddler age breastmilk all differ in their lipid concentrations—providing exactly what is right for each stage of development. Hundreds of components of human milk, as well as the hormones and other factors connected with the act of nursing, all operate in concert, in ways we will likely never be able to synthesize or even understand. We are only beginning to learn the many implications of these crude imitations.

We have all heard of omega-3 fatty acids and their great health benefits by now. Walnuts, flax seed, and canola oil are some popular foods that are high in ALA, which can be converted in the body to DHA and EPA. The conversion process is variable, however, and direct intake of DHA and EPA provide far superior results. Fatty fish and fish oil supplements are the main source for these. An algae-derived version is available for vegans.

There are common warnings that consuming fish during pregnancy can be a concern in terms of mercury levels. A study was performed on heavy fish consuming women of the Seychelles Islands to determine the gravity of such consumption. Instead of discovering adverse effects, the children were actually found to have developmental advantages.[64] It could be, however, that lower mercury exposure with equal fatty acid availability could provide even superior results.

Consuming fish oil supplements during pregnancy and while breastfeeding is shown to provide a mental advantage for children.[65] Based on the various studies available, a cumulative of 2 grams of DHA plus EPA per day may be a good, effective dosage.

Autism is a multi-cause set of behavioral symptoms related to neurodevelopmental irregularities. A large survey from the University of California found that children who were fed formula, rather than being exclusively breastfed (no formula or solids) for 6 months, had a much higher rate of autism.[66] The greatest difference was seen where those fed formula without DHA/ARA were many times more likely to exhibit autism with regression in development as those breastfed exclusively.

Avoiding all hydrogenated vegetable oils (trans fats) is very important for all children and mothers. These artificial fats were created to replace saturated fats in packaged foods. Like so many things we've discussed, these too are a very unnatural experiment gone bad. These fats replace healthy useful fats in the membranes of nerve cells in the brain as well as other cells in the body. While they are linked to heart disease and other ill health, the effects on the brain are as of yet unknown.

Brighter Times

The quest for super babies is no different from many other sincerely motivated but somewhat misguided attempts to control our children's behavior and destiny. Some important research was initiated by this fad, but in the long run, what we really learned was that good attentiveness, warmth, and natural feeding makes for the healthiest children. The evidence is overwhelming that breastfeeding and plenty of attention give a child the best opportunity for success. At this point in time, research is showing us in bits and pieces that following your instincts and holding dearly to Mother Nature's course is usually the first choice in child care. True super babies are those with high self-esteem and high bonding ability; everything else follows from the parenting techniques that create these—including higher IQ, good health, and just about any other talent you would like your child to have.

6

Immune Protection Matters

INFANTS ARE BORN WITH ACTIVE IMMUNE SYSTEMS, BUT THESE SYSTEMS ARE
not mature, so babies are very vulnerable to illness and infection. Luckily,
babies receive a lasting immune boost from mom during labor, if labor is
allowed. Then, mother's milk, if it is available, adds the remaining protection that is needed. Still, a child's health is often challenged, and the
parents' behavior can either help or hinder the child's immune battles. As
with many other facets of baby's well-being, parenting choices influence
to what extent a child develops infection and illness. Every day more
and more information comes to light that calls into question many of the
practices followed during the previous decades. I feel that the only way an
individual family can truly make informed choices is understanding the most

debated issues and the current research findings about them. First, however, it is necessary to have some background about how babies function and the role of human milk in baby development.

Without Protection

Studies from various parts of the world report that the infant death rate for infants missing human milk is anywhere from 2 to 13 times that in babies breastfed for one year, even after controlling for many confounding factors—and usually without even considering whether the breastfeeding is exclusive or not.[1-6] Such studies are almost solely performed in developing nations, chiefly because their mortality rates are higher than developing countries, with problems of poverty and poor sanitation affecting all babies, no matter how they are fed. Industry lobbying and lack of available funding are two more reasons that industrialized nations are not under the same scrutiny. I am quite interested in one such mortality study, performed in Malaysia, because the overall infant death rate there is barely above our own. This study reports a doubled infant death rate for formula-fed infants.[7] Studies in industrialized nations reveal that, for formula-fed children, the rates for most illnesses are doubled and tripled, there are much higher rates for some predominant diseases, and illnesses are usually prolonged as well. It follows that deaths from these maladies would be proportional to their occurrence (and severity). Even conditions such as congenital defects and complications during pregnancy and birth sometimes lead to lower survival rates when the babies do not receive breastmilk from birth. SIDS deaths are on the average (weighted average of industrialized nation studies) quadrupled. In response to critics, breastfeeding studies attempt to compensate statistically for factors such as smoking, socioeconomic status, and education level of the mother. Nearly every subsequent study takes into account more factors that may confound its findings. While for many reasons it is

In industrialized countries, even in the United States, the infant death rate in formula-fed infants is twice that of exclusively breastfed babies.

unpopular to mention an increased mortality rate from formula feeding in the United States, I have amassed and examined a large amount of the available evidence, which has led me to conclude that *in industrialized countries, even in the United States, the infant death rate in formula-fed infants is twice that of exclusively breastfed babies.* All documentation can be found on my website at www.BabyReference.com. Since the United States has an infant death rate of 6.5 per 1,000, and a breastfeeding rate that drops quickly from under 70% to 30% in the first 3 months, one could deduce that there are at least 3 extra infant deaths per 1,000 due to the absence of breastmilk. Nations with much higher breastfeeding rates have only half or less than half of our infant mortality rate. Statistically, the longer the breastfeeding, the better the protection; hence, a portion of breastfed babies who die are likely those who were weaned very early. As already noted in the previous chapter, SIDS is less often a problem in naturally fed babies. Breathing and heart regulation provided by mother's proximity accounts for part of the protection. At the same time, the stress of infant separation can contribute to SIDS. Undetected infections resulting from reduced immune protection in those not receiving mother's milk contribute to SIDS as well. Nutrition, brain development, and allergies are also responsible for some of the difference in SIDS rates.

> A significantly higher risk of childhood cancer exists for those who never received human milk, compared to those who nursed exclusively and for extended periods.

Beyond the elusive SIDS deaths, infections account for most of the difference in mortality rates between those who receive mother's milk and those who do not. The greatest danger is death from intestinal infections and diarrhea. While the risk of death from diarrhea in developing nations may be 14 times higher or more without exclusive mother's milk,[8] the risk in industrialized nations is at least double. One predominant form is up to 20 times more frequent.[9] As usual, those who receive a mixture of human milk and formula fall somewhere in between, but much closer to formula-fed rates.

The increased threat to the lives of artificially fed children persists

> *While mixing breastmilk with formula partially protects children, this protection is minimal for common illnesses when compared to exclusive breastfeeding.*

beyond the age of formula and nursing. A significantly higher risk of childhood cancer exists for those who never received human milk, compared to those who nursed exclusively and for extended periods.[10,11] Clearly, breastmilk should be considered an important part of the child's immune system.[12]

Infection Protection

Not only does formula feeding increase infant and child mortality, but the number of infant illnesses such as respiratory infections, ear infections, intestinal infections, pneumonia, and influenza doubles to quadruples in industrialized nations, as does the need for health care.[13–18] The duration of most illness is significantly longer as well. While mixing breastmilk with formula partially protects children from mortality and some non-fatal illnesses, the largest study to date, performed by the University of Michigan School of Nursing, suggests this protection is minimal for common illnesses when compared to exclusive breastfeeding.[19] This finding is consistent throughout studies comparing exclusive to supplemented breastfeeding. Regardless, a positive relationship between the increased duration of breastfeeding and reduced illness remains strong in all studies.[20]

Lasting Protection

In 1998, in light of emerging findings, Dr. M.K. Davis of the CDC (Centers for Disease Control and Prevention) confirmed that *breastmilk plays a role in the long-term development of the immune system and the prevention of disease, well beyond the time of breastfeeding.*[21] At the same time others reached similar conclusions,[22,23] and for the first time suggested the chemical pathways[24] for breastmilk's apparent role in encouraging heightened immune system development in the child.

Baby's First Defenses

An infant is generally born "sterile," meaning without any bacteria or other germs in his body. Never having been exposed to any kind of microorganism, newborns haven't built up any antibodies to resist the germs that are all around us. Without any defenses, newborns would have to develop hundreds of different antibodies to fend off hundreds of infections in the first days of life. The energy consumption for this battle would be trying for a young infant who already has so much growing and neurological development to orchestrate. But, by design, a baby doesn't have to fend for itself. In addition to its own immature immune system, there are two other key sources of immunity for defense against disease—antibodies from mother's placenta *and* the antibodies and many other immune factors in mother's milk.

In the immune system, antibodies are created specifically for each kind of invading microorganism or foreign protein that threatens the body—each specific type of invader causes the creation of specific antibodies. The body can then copy these by the millions to mount a counterattack. Creating a tailor-made antibody can take from a day to over a week. The cells that create these antibodies are not fully mature until a few weeks after a full-term birth,[25] and the reliable development of antibodies does not occur for many more months.

Another immune system defense includes the gobbling up of invaders and damaged cells by immune cells called "phagocytes." A newborn has a limited ability to develop new phagocytes, and as a result, large or prolonged battles are difficult for her to wage. Additionally, immature phagocytes have reduced ability to go to the part of the body where they are needed.[26] But baby's immune system may be somewhat limited by design. During the huge influx of microbes in the first hours and days of life, the newborn could be overwhelmed with inflammation resulting from immune battles. Filling in for baby's limitations, mother's milk also supplies anti-inflammatory agents, while it provides less-damaging ways to fight infection.

Placental Transfer

Baby receives certain antibodies from mother during the last weeks in the womb, especially during labor. These help fight the thousands of microorganisms

> Infants born via low-risk elective (meaning non-necessary) cesareans have a tripled death rate in the first month of life versus vaginal births.

that mother has already developed resistance to, including polio, measles, and pertussis. Although I say "thousands" of microbes, this does not mean that mother has been ill thousands of times. Only 1% of all bacteria cause disease in a normal healthy human being. A weakened immune system may be susceptible to double this amount. In general, immunity is acquired to many of the microbes that lead to the well-known diseases without noticeable illness. Most of the antibodies obtained from mother while in the womb remain abundant in the infant's body for about 6 months after birth, with some lingering on several months more.

The transfer of antibodies is greatly reduced when a baby is born without labor (planned C-section),[27] which reduces his infection-fighting abilities over the next several months. This is likely part of the reason that infants born via low-risk elective (meaning non-necessary) cesareans have a tripled death rate in the first month of life versus vaginal births.[28] Commonly delayed breastfeeding after C-sections and the absence of other features of the normal birth process also account for some of the elevated risk of death. Incidentally, the mother's risk of death from an elective cesarean is also 3 times the risk of a vaginal birth, although still very low.[29] Premature infants are born with many fewer of mother's antibodies—the earlier, the fewer. Also, the earlier the birth, the less mature baby's immune system is. Thus, the protection provided in mother's milk is all the more valuable for premature babies.

Some antibodies seem to transfer to the fetus better than others. Furthermore, when mother's immunity to a disease such as measles is from vaccination rather than through natural exposure, the immunity passed on is often very slight or absent.[30] As a result, now that most mothers have received vaccinations before they developed natural immunity to many diseases, vaccinating infants at more and more delicate ages is deemed necessary. All these vaccines need to be repeated at the usual intervals as well, because the young infant is unable to develop an adequate amount of antibodies after early vaccination to build any significant resistance. Moreover, the levels of antibodies from mother are unknown at the time of vaccination, and any existing antibodies from mother will prevent the infant from developing immunity upon vaccination.

Breastmilk Completes Baby's Protection

While the placenta provides many antibodies, breastmilk contains more kinds of antibodies, plus a multitude of other infection-fighting, healing, and growth factors. These not only provide multiple means to fight disease, but these antibodies and other factors also fight infections for which few or no antibodies are received before birth. Few if any cow's milk antibodies are pertinent to the human infant since different animal species are susceptible to different microbes. A majority of the immune factors in human milk are not found in cow's milk at all. Some factors do exist in fresh cow's milk, but few are known to be effective in humans and these are only minimally found in formulas.

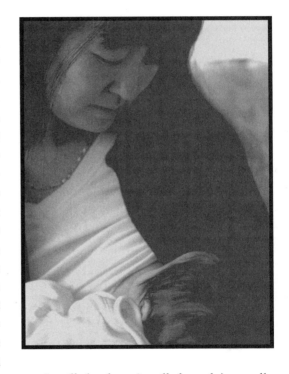

Certain antibodies in cow's milk (and cow's milk formula) actually pose problems for human infants, sometimes leading to disease.

Complimenting placental antibodies, mother's milk is most helpful in the gastrointestinal tract from the mouth to the end of the intestines, where it is introduced and travels. Most microbes enter the body this way as well. Even microbes that enter through the nose meet mother's milk defenses in the back of the throat.[31] The throat openings to the ear tubes are protected as well, preventing ear infections.[32] In addition, certain milk factors also pass through the walls of the intestine to aid other areas of the body. This can occur because of the special properties of milk and the young intestines.

Breastmilk antibodies offer a much broader spectrum of protection than those from the placenta. In addition, antibodies to new organisms that mother and child are both exposed to can be developed by mother and furnished to baby through mother's milk. Beneficially, mother's milk provides protection without causing inflammation.[33] Breastmilk can also be provided long after placental antibodies are gone.

Protective Factors in Mother's Milk

One unique ability of the antibodies in mother's milk is interfering with many microorganisms' ability to attach to the mucous membranes lining the throat and intestines, including those that can cause middle ear infections.[34] Factors associated with the fat globules of breastmilk also augment this protection. For instance, one factor protects against a dangerous form of E. coli, at least in the mouth,[35] and another limits an E. coli that causes bloody diarrhea.[36] Still another binds with an intestinal virus, rotavirus, to prevent infection.[37] Rotavirus and E. coli are responsible for most cases of infectious diarrhea in infants. One million and five million annual infant deaths, respectively, are attributed to these worldwide.[38] Another factor, called "90K," stimulates maturation of the infant's immune system, reducing respiratory and other infections.[39]

Oligosaccharides are non-digestible complex carbohydrates (fiber) with immune properties. Oligosaccharides are found in abundance in human milk (making up one-third of the solids), but almost never found in the milk of other animals—there are very few in cow's milk and they are less complex than those in human milk. The levels of these important factors in mother's milk vary with the maturity of the newborn at the time of birth and with the age of the child, in concordance with the child's need. One function of oligosaccharides is to act as "prebiotics," or food for healthy flora that are known as probiotics. They only feed one very specific friendly, protective bacteria, Bifidobacteria infantis.[40] Oligosaccharides are known to prevent dangerous invaders, such as E. coli, Streptococcus pneumoniae, and a host of others, from adhering to the walls of the intestine and causing infection. Over 200 in number, they belong to a larger family of milk components known as glycans.

Along with glycoproteins, glycolipids, and other milk glycans, these represent thousands of immune-providing components in human milk.[41] Along with their general protective actions, many have been found to act against specific microbes.[42] As example, one has been found that blocks the first step in infection by HIV (the virus that causes AIDS).[43] Chondroitin sulphate has antibacterial and antiviral activities.[44]

The whey proteins of human milk consist mostly of lactalbumin and lactoferrin, important components of immune protection. The chief whey protein of cow's milk is beta-lactoglobulin, which is actually a problem protein for humans in terms of digestion and allergy. It may also induce diabetes. Lactoferrin provides antibacterial, antiviral, and antifungal protection in several ways,[45] but *infant formula actually encourages the growth of many dangerous bacteria, including* E. coli, *salmonella, and shigella.*[46,47] A human curd protein, kappacasein, acts against *Helicobacter pylori*, a factor in ulcer formation,[48] and possibly SIDS.

Lactose is a special sugar designed only for babies and found only in the food of baby mammals—mother's milk. Lactose itself provides immune protection by encouraging the growth of only certain friendly bacteria.

Necrotizing enterocolitis is a serious inflammation of the intestines that involves destruction of the cells used for nutritional absorption. It generally occurs during the first days after birth, although it is seen at up to 3 months of age. Five to ten percent of premature infants are affected, as are over 1% of full-term infants. One-quarter of those affected die. This disease is rare among exclusively breastfed infants. Mixed breastmilk and formula tube feeding is common for very premature infants. An infant receiving at least 50% breastmilk has only one-sixth the risk of necrotizing enterocolitis as those receiving less, and the more breastmilk an infant receives, the lower her chances of contracting this deadly disease.[49,50] One could almost say that formula feeding "causes" this deadly disease. Of those breastmilk-fed infants who are affected, most are in hospital care units where babies develop less natural early protective intestinal flora due to lack of exposure to mother's breast itself. While imbalance of flora contributes to this disease,[51] human milk also contains an enzyme that prevents tissue destruction. This enzyme is more prevalent in breastmilk when an infant is born prematurely, and its level continues to rise over the next weeks to protect against necrotizing enterocolitis.[52]

These are only a few of the disease-fighting factors in mother's milk; to cover them all would require a book in itself. Pasteurization of breastmilk, as is performed on donor milk, reduces its antibacterial capacity by possibly one-fourth to nearly half.[53] Fresh milk refrigerated for 2 days or less, or frozen, tends to maintain most of its antibacterial power[54] though antioxidant strength is gradually lost over time in the freezer.[55] Adding formula or solid foods to the breastmilk diet dilutes all of the immune factors and directly interferes with the actions of at least several of these. While full protection from exclusive breastmilk is optimal for the infant in his early months, much of the protection from breastmilk goes on as long as it is fed to the child in any amount. Nearly all the important factors are absent or poorly functional in formulas, including the following:

- White blood cells (immune system cells), including neutrophils, macrophages (phagocytes), and lymphocytes (including B cells and T cells) known to be active and mobile within the infant's system[56]

- Prostaglandin E2, plasminogen activator, and complement, produced by the macrophages to help to orchestrate immune reactions

- Many different cytokines, including several chemokines and colony-stimulating factors, which stimulate immune functions[57]

- Lactadherin, which promotes intestinal repair[58]

- Products of human milk fat digestion, which have antibacterial, antiviral, and antiprotozoan action.

- Bile-salt-dependent lipase and peroxidase that kill bacteria

- Antiproteases to protect valuable immune proteins of mother's milk from digestion[59]

- Neuraminic acid and linoleic acid, which have antibacterial actions, found in higher concentrations in human milk than in cow's[60]

- Superior levels of iron, zinc, and selenium absorption to aid the fight against disease

- Higher levels of arginine, glutamine, and nucleotides to assist intestinal adaptation

- Interferon with powerful antiviral properties

- Lysozyme, which degrades undesirable microbes

- Probiotics, friendly bacteria for protective colonization of the intestines, and prebiotics, including many of the complex carbohydrates, to feed and foster beneficial flora[61]

- Growth factors, including nucleotides,[62] polyamines,[63] and hormones, that encourage maturation of the various immune defenses in the intestines

- Antioxidants, including multiple forms of vitamins C, E, and A, along with cysteine, to protect against oxidation damage of the immature immune system[64]

- Tumor necrosis factor receptors and interleukin receptors, which have anti-inflammatory consequences[65]

Adding formula or solid foods to the breastmilk diet dilutes all of these and directly interferes with the actions of at least several of these. While full protection from exclusive breastmilk is optimal for the infant in his early months, much of the protection from breastmilk goes on as long as it is fed to the child. Around 6 months of age, just as the effects of the original IgG antibodies from mother's placenta are wearing off, infants become less able to pass immune blood cells and other breastmilk factors into their bloodstream. As solid foods are introduced, other immune factors are becoming somewhat less effective as well. Luckily, by this time, the lysozyme in mother's milk has increased to 10 times its level when the infant was 2 weeks old, in a sense to make up the difference. Other immune factors in her milk change with the increasing age of the child as well.

Interestingly, various studies compare the amount of infection in infants to the levels of 90K, lactadherin, and other components found in their mothers' milk. Reduced numbers of certain infections are seen in infants when higher levels of certain components are in their mother's milk. We can only hope that future research will investigate how a mother can influence the levels of various immune factors in her milk, although it is already known that the levels of most of these do not reflect the levels in mother's blood.[66]

We also know that when mothers stay close to baby and are exposed to baby's saliva via kisses and stools during diaper changes, this helps mother provide appropriate immune factors to baby through her milk. The "entero-mammary pathway" is the name given to the process by which mother supplies specific immune factors in her milk according to what she has been exposed to. Baby even passes cells directly into mother's breast while nursing.[67] When premature infants receive mother's milk in neonatal centers, they receive much better immune assistance when mother is in intimate contact with the infant.[68] *High levels of sanitation between the nursing mother and her infant can prevent this valuable transaction from occurring.*[69]

Colostrum, the name for mother's first milk, is especially high in antibodies, immune cells, lactoferrin, and other factors, but levels drop off over a few weeks' time. Lysozyme levels are also high and drop significantly in the first weeks; however, they rise again by a factor of 10 around 6 months of age,[70] just when placental antibodies are wearing off.

Breastfed infants have less need for vaccinations than formula-fed infants. Nevertheless, breastfed infants produce a superior immune response, creating better and longer-lasting immunities.[71]

The thymus gland in the upper chest is an immune system organ that typically shrinks during puberty and then shrinks more with advanced age, leaving the elderly system low on defenses. It is important for fighting disease, especially for creating T cells to fight viruses. Recently, *researchers found that starting from birth the thymus gland shrinks much more in formula-fed infants compared to breastfed babies.*[72] At the age of 4 months, the thymus of the artificially fed infant is only half the size of a breastfed baby's gland, most likely accounting for some of the increased susceptibility to disease that accompanies formula feeding. The breastfed baby's thymus gradually reduces in size after weaning. Apparently, breastmilk provides some unknown stimulant that maintains a large thymus capable of supplying more T cells during the first years of life, when these cells are immature and slow to respond, or the stress of formula feeding causes the thymus to shrink. Stress-related cortisol releases cause this gland to shrink, but this can be reversed by relieving stress.[73] We have already discussed the fact that infants who frequently suffer from separation and inattentiveness have higher cortisol levels throughout much of their lives, and that these infants may develop health problems and may succumb to early aging. The thymus gland's sensitivity to stress is certainly one source of these reported results.

Other Immune System Defenses

Adding to the body's arsenal of defenses against microbes is fever, a powerful disease-fighting tool. Fever not only indicates the presence of infection, but also fights it; in fact, that is its purpose. Today, parents have been programmed by advertisers as well as the medical community to reduce fever whenever present, even in light of the side effects of fever-reducing medications. Fever should not be routinely reduced;[74] in fact, it has been shown that *in most infections, illness and death increase when fevers are reduced.*[75,76] A cold washcloth over the forehead can reduce any dizziness, hallucinations, or seizures the child may have. These symptoms are not considered to be damaging[77] but can be disturbing to parent and child. Many even believe that recovery from infection is swifter when a fever is raised with warm baths, warm fluids, covering warmly, or raising the house temperature. Fevers are thought to be dangerously high however somewhere beyond 106° F (41° C), at which point reduction through medication or a cool bath should be considered to prevent possible brain damage (thought to occur around 108° F, 42° C). Natural illnesses should never cause a fever beyond 106° but poisoning or heat stroke could.[78]

> We also know that when mothers stay close to baby and are exposed to baby's saliva via kisses and stools during diaper changes, this helps mother provide appropriate immune factors to baby through her milk.

A child under 3 months of age with high fever must be medically examined. By blocking certain elements of the immune system, common fever-reducing drugs such as aspirin and ibuprofen (Motrin) interfere with disease fighting, and healing as well. Using ibuprofen with chicken pox greatly increases the chance of developing a necrotizing fasciitis (flesh-eating bacteria) infection,[79] since it reduces a child's immune defenses. Some other drugs cause this as well. Aspirin or acetaminophen (Tylenol) use with influenza, chicken pox, and some other viruses can lead to dangerous Reye's syndrome. Acetaminophen prolongs chicken pox,[80] among other illnesses, and poses liver risks.

Other symptoms in ill children can generally be respected as well. If they are tired, they should rest, if they are energetic, they can probably play. If they have no appetite, this may be the body's way to concentrate on the infection. Food should be in sight, but not forced, although one may wish to provide vitamin supplements. On the other hand, fluid intake is always important and should usually include electrolytes (Infalyte, Pedialyte) when no breastmilk or other nutrition is being consumed. Infant formula can be irritating when diarrhea is present, but breastmilk is helpful. It is rare for an ill child to stop nursing.

Other Issues of Immunity and Health

The human immune system is far more complicated and powerful than anything medicine will ever develop to fight disease. For this reason, protecting and boosting the immune system often makes the most sense in the face of illness. Antibiotics are wonder drugs that can kill dangerous, life-threatening bacterial infections. Many are borrowed from the chemical defenses of fungi that must fight bacterial foes just as we do. But our bodies are able to discriminate between friend and foe when they attack bacteria, whereas antibiotics don't. This often creates imbalances in the normal flora, creating susceptibility to other normally unexpected infections. Vaccines also come to mind in the saga of science versus disease. They do not in themselves prevent disease; they are intended to encourage the body's own immune system to develop antibodies against the introduced, weakened version of the disease. In theory, this facilitation of the body's own immune system seems ideal.

The infant's strong desire to orally sample everything in the environment, starting tentatively with more familiar objects such as the parents' fingers and noses, then gradually graduating to small and then greater amounts of dirt and other matter, *is an important facet of developing the child's immune system.* This is a natural vaccination practice whereby the youngster slowly ingests tiny samples of the environment, subsequently developing antibodies to introduced microbes. This occurs while the thymus gland is large and additional infection fighting power is supplied via mother's milk. Another function of the thymus gland is to catalog which proteins and other elements are "self," and therefore should not be attacked by antibodies, and which represent foreign matter. The environmental sampling aids this endeavor while the thymus is at its peak. In children where this practice has been strongly discouraged, far fewer antibodies are developed to protect against infection.

The safety of this sampling process has a limit, however. When large populations of people live closely together, increased exposure to dangerous microbes becomes a problem, especially due to sewage, rats, and some other major hazards, hence the value of modern sanitation.

> *Fever should not be routinely reduced; in fact, it has been shown that in most infections illness and death increase when fevers are reduced.*

The Vaccination Question

With major sanitation problems resolved in most industrialized nations, many epidemic diseases were subdued even before the advent of vaccines. Likewise, in regions of the world where sewage sanitation is not adequate, new epidemics occur frequently, even though polio and other diseases may be controlled through vaccination programs. Interestingly, when polio was epidemic in the United States in the mid 1900s, it was not those from impoverished areas who were affected the most, but those from affluent urban locales. Most likely, people in these areas acquired less immunity during infancy from natural environmental exposure. It has been suggested that improvements in water treatment and sewage handling in the late 1800s and increased sanitation in the early 1900s may have caused the polio epidemic. As exposure to human waste diminished, so did natural immunities, leaving vulnerable communities.[81] As outbreaks occurred, community immunities again grew, and the epidemic naturally subsided, as most do. Now, rightfully reluctant to reverse sanitation practices, only one other option exists to prevent further epidemic cycles of this paralyzing disease—developing immunity through vaccination, which is a more controlled means as well. There is hope that the strains of poliovirus for which widespread vaccination occurs will entirely disappear from the planet, as smallpox has.

Vietnam still suffers from inadequate sewage handling in most of its communities. This nation also frequently suffers from epidemics. Formula feeding is quite uncommon in this country, but solid foods are introduced at a very early age, so the ratio of solid food to breastmilk quickly becomes very high, even though some nursing generally occurs for extended periods.[82] Hence, in addition to poor sanitation, the infants here are generally not receiving the exclusive breastfeeding that is most important for early disease protection and extended immune system development. Most likely both of these factors contribute to the continuing suffering from disease in Vietnam.

As the rates of serious infectious disease drop in the industrialized nations, and the memories of these maladies fade, the occasional, unfortunate adverse effects of vaccinations become a clear target of criticism. However, some real questions do exist, and there is a real potential for future difficulties. It is best for the public to remain informed in order to keep vaccine manufacturers and policy makers vigilant.

In light of many issues surrounding vaccination programs, many now question immunization of their children. Those wishing to find true information come across some highly sensational anti-vaccination literature, as well as much pro-vaccination literature that tends to wear rose-colored glasses. Without digging deeply into volumes of literature, there is no way to make an educated choice.

A review of the literature shows that while some claims in anti-vaccination books are inflated, and some prove to be untraceable, there is a growing body of valid information presented. Fortunately, concern over some of the issues has led to further studies, such as a 1988 vaccine trial that suggested an increased rate of bacterial infections in vaccinated children compared to children receiving placebo.[83] A 1992 report reviewed nearly 65,000 vaccinated children and found no such correlation.[84] Some vaccine information websites are becoming quite valuable as supposed facts can usually be checked on the Web through the CDC and other websites and exaggerations and flaws in arguments are pointed out by others.

Without a doubt, vaccination programs have been scarred by many unfortunate errors. While we need to look at today and the future, only the near past can give us insight into the handling and validity of the vaccination program and their claims. The most valid popular questions and objections about vaccinations and what seems to be the most reliable information about these issues are listed below. Many more valid issues exist, but most are similar to these:

- Antibiotic therapy reduces the risk of death from many diseases.

    True, but antibiotics are already being overused, causing the development of more serious microbes and more serious diseases. Antibiotics are also not without side effects. Yet, the availability of antibiotics does tremendously reduce the death rate of most currently vaccinated-for diseases—either directly or by reducing dangerous secondary infections.

- Many epidemics are already prevented through sanitation in industrialized nations.

    Yes, but as described above, regions eventually lose their natural immunities and become vulnerable to rapid spread of disease, especially in the face of today's high-speed world travel.

- There is a high correlation between many epidemics and malnutrition from blights, droughts, and high grain prices.

    Yes, the above factors of sanitation and malnutrition play definite roles in epidemic cycles—both prior to the introduction of vaccinations as well as during immunization programs. Both need to continuously improve in all populations. Still, significant drops in disease correlate with introducing or improving vaccination programs and rates of previously ameliorated disease often increase sharply when vaccinations wane or are discontinued.[85]

- New epidemics from microbes for which there is no vaccination persist and grow in the absence of sanitation,[86-89] *including 3,333 strains of polio-like viruses,*[90] leading one to wonder whether vaccine money could be better spent elsewhere.

    Japanese encephalitis virus has nearly been eradicated in Japan due to sanitary control measures,[91] although it continues to be bothersome in other nations. Unfortunately, not all diseases can be controlled like encephalitis; it depends on the disease's mode of transmission.

- Many sometimes devastating accidents of vaccination programs have occurred, including the probable introduction of HIV into the human population through the use of infected monkey serum in an African polio vaccine.[92,93] For every study that denounces this claim, another arises with further evidence to rekindle the notion. This is an important issue, although this was apparently not the first or only introduction of HIV to mankind. Monkey virus, SV40, was found in polio vaccines prepared in the 1960s and 70s, after regulations were set to prevent such infection, likely explaining some geographic clusters of rare SV40-related tumors found in humans.[94]

Many of the same techniques that have caused such accidents continue to be used today.[95] In fact, polio vaccine was recently recalled by Britain's Medical Control Agency due to suspected mad cow disease contamination, where fetal calf serum was being used. So-called stealth viruses are being found today in some chronic fatigue and brain-disordered patients, the likely result of other monkey viruses obtained through polio vaccines.[96] These monkey viruses have shown the ability to spread from human to human, as seen in a 1996 burst of neurological illnesses in the Mohave Valley,[97] with the potential to create a brand-new epidemic.

In addition to the stealth viruses, well-known evidence reveals that genetic mutation and recombination of vaccine-acquired polio viruses cause a wide spectrum of neurological symptoms.[98] Known strains are rare, but one must remember that polio strains are seldom looked for in patients with neurological disease.

• Questions often arise about the legality of the absolute immunity from lawsuit that the United States has granted vaccine companies.

The logic seems to be that, while unfortunate effects are expected, more damage may be expected without the vaccines, and vaccine companies could not afford to do their research if constantly sued. This is a radically different approach to the Hippocratic "First do no harm."

• Occasional neurological damage has been found to have statistically significant correlation to pertussis vaccines[99–101] and, although less provable, a possible link to SIDS.

Pertussis itself can cause the episodes of stopped breathing (apnea) that are associated with SIDS.[102] SIDS rates increased in response to increases in pertussis rates in Sweden after pertussis vaccination ceased.[103]

Although pertussis immunity is not permanent—either from vaccination or natural exposure[104]—well over 99% of pertussis exposures probably go unnoticed in adults, leaving many with ongoing protective antibodies.[105] However, more than half of the young children in Sweden contracted pertussis after vaccination was terminated in 1979.[106] Dangerous complications of this respiratory disease include pneumonia and brain involvement.

A Swedish study compared an acellular form of pertussis vaccine to the whole cell form (chiefly used in the United States until the end of the 90s, and still used in other countries today) to DT vaccination with no pertussis serum, for control, in nearly 10,000 infants. The study found "significantly higher" rates of adverse effects in those receiving the whole cell vaccine compared to either of the other two.[107]

Fever and pain at the site of the injection are expected from many vaccines, the fever resulting from the body's efforts to build immunity to the introduced germs. Seizures, shock, cyanosis (turning blue due to lack of oxygen, a precursor to SIDS), encephalitis (inflammation of the brain), and persistent high-pitched crying are more serious consequences consistently associated with whole cell pertussis vaccines. This alarming cry occurred with 1 in every 113 doses of whole cell vaccine as well as 1 in 500 acellular injections.[108] The whole cell vaccine led to 4 times as many convulsions as did the acellular. Apparently both vaccines can potentially cause damage, but it took the United States far longer than other nations to begin recommending the less-damaging acellular version.

A large workshop in the United States concluded that these seizures following pertussis vaccination were not simply a result of vaccine-related fevers, and are therefore a cause for concern.[109] Brain damage is observed in a significant, although small, number of children after this crying. When these reactions do occur, they are often not reported by MDs, preventing good statistical analysis of whether there is real causation or just coincidence. Brain damage related to birth defects often becomes apparent around vaccination age, argue vaccine supporters, although pertussis vaccines are given at 3 different ages in the first 6 months. This workshop was able to ascertain that seizures occur in 2% of actual pertussis cases, brain involvement (encephalitis) in .3%, and death in 2 to 3 out of 1,000 reported cases (only serious cases are reported, which is only a fraction of all cases)—significant numbers for parents to consider should they pass on the vaccine.

A University of California experiment was designed to establish the accuracy of determining vaccine efficiency rates through reporting. Here, it was concluded that observer bias probably plays a large role in efficacy trials, and that actual infection most likely occurs in considerably more (even twice as many) vaccinated individuals than reported, leading to inflated accounts of vaccine effectiveness.[110] From this trial and a Swedish report, one may conclude that the efficacy of pertussis vaccines may be only 40 to 50%.[111] Many reports in the medical literature suggest that the whole cell vaccine is superior while other reports applaud the acellular vaccine. Physicians' assumptions and mind-set lead to far greater underreporting of adverse results after vaccination than so-called controlled trials suggest. The tragedy is that inaccurate and greatly limited reporting of adverse reactions make it impossible to calculate the statistical advantage of vaccinations, especially in the case of the pertussis. Pertussis is not a disease that can be eradicated through vaccinations as smallpox was, because it is spread by respiratory means.[112]

- There is increasing risk of Guillain-Barré Syndrome (a nervous system disorder) resulting from any vaccination as the number of vaccines provided per child escalates.[113]

    This real but slight risk is lower than the risk of serious disease to the unvaccinated.[114,115]

- In 1998, Dr. A. J. Wakefield reported a correlation between measles vaccination and inflammatory bowel diseases and autism;[116] a contention that has sparked much controversy. In 2006, Dr. Stephen Walker reproduced the findings of vaccine-associated measles viruses found in the guts of autistic children and not healthy children, giving further credence to the continued allegations by Wakefield and others.

There are many who denounce this theory, yet the debate continues. There is also other evidence of a link between autism and the measles virus in the MMR vaccine.

• There are strong concerns expressed by many researchers about links between mercury (thimerosal) regularly used in vaccines and the development of autism and other attention deficit disorders. While decrying any accusations, the United States has called for thimerosal-free vaccines, at the same time strengthening protections for vaccine manufacturers against lawsuits. Veterinarians removed thimerosal from their vaccines a decade earlier, based on concerns over scientific findings. It is known that the ethylmercury (thimerosal) level injected into many infants exceeds the EPA limits and that this mercury passes the blood-brain barrier to go into the brain, residing there for many days at more than 3 times the concentration found in the blood.[117]

A large multidisciplinary workshop in the United States reviewed all available data and concluded that these seizures following pertussis vaccination were not simply a result of vaccine-related fevers, and are therefore a cause for concern.

Again, the CDC argues that the age of vaccination happens to be the age when the symptoms of autism and other brain damage normally appear, but this argument is used in response to pertussis/neurological links as well as MMR/neurological links when pertussis vaccination occurs around 2, 4, 6, and 15 months and MMR vaccination around 12 months and 4 years.

There have been widely promoted concerns about mercury consumption from eating fish. Currently, even dentists are encouraging the FDA to call for a consideration of limiting mercury amalgam filling usage in young children until more research is done.

Perhaps the most damning evidence of a vaccination link to

autism came out in 2008 when the courts conceded to a lawsuit for vaccine damages in the case of Hannah Poling. After receiving 5 vaccines at one time, she reacted violently and turned into a permanently changed girl. She was eventually diagnosed with autism. Her father is a neurologist and PhD and her mother is a nurse and a lawyer. While most parents' stories are put off, these parents were difficult to ignore. It was found that Hannah had a cell disorder that made her especially vulnerable to react in this manner. Many similar lawsuits are awaiting trial while the exact cause of the vaccine-related damage is unknown. While this mitochondrial disorder is rather rare, it's been found in 7% of children with autism.

There are other links between vaccines and autism besides the mercury link, so the removal of mercury does not end all concerns. The live measles virus in the MMR vaccine poses one such separate threat. The use of acetaminophen to relieve discomfort after the MMR vaccine has been linked to the development of autism.[118] Clearly, combinations of multiple genetic and direct exposures combine to create the larger picture and confuse the determinations of cause and effect.

With mercury being removed, the use of another metal has grown immensely. The growing use of an aluminum adjuvant sparks many concerns in those who are familiar with its chemistry and history. For starters, it's been linked to Gulf War illness and has been shown to cause nerve cell deaths in mice and rabbits.[119, 120]

• There are human rights issues about mandatory introduction of foreign proteins into one's body.

Yet the first few known AIDS victims were not quarantined, leading to countless suffering and deaths, due to human rights issues.

• Risks of allergic response to vaccines exist.

These risks are reportedly slight, and known allergic individuals can avoid vaccinations. On the other hand, many food allergy sufferers report that their symptoms began or increased with a vaccination—many vaccines do contain dairy, corn, egg, and other potentially allergy-causing residues not intended for direct entry into the bloodstream. Such substances are routinely injected into rats in order to create allergies in them for study.

- Infant vaccination programs cause late-life occurrences of diseases because weak, unnatural immunity wanes later in life (although adolescent and adult boosters would prevent this).

Vaccinations create weaker immunity compared to the immunity developed through natural exposure (whether illness occurs with such exposure or not). As a result, one must consider the substantial danger of diseases such as measles and mumps that can be far more devastating when they infect adults. Measles had a death or disability rate of 1 per million in France before widespread vaccination.[121] This would involve chiefly childhood cases. The risk of death or disability would be higher in adults.

- Less immunity is passed on to infants from vaccinated mothers than from those who were naturally exposed to a disease.

Older adults with reduced immunity due to vaccination develop diseases and then pass them on to the very young who have not yet been vaccinated.[122] The very young exposed to these adults also have less protection of their own because their mothers had childhood vaccinations and thus may be passing on weak or no antibodies through the placenta and breastmilk. Increased disease, including measles and pertussis, are now being seen in these two most delicate groups.

Because of the weaker immunity that results from vaccines, the danger of contracting diseases in adulthood, and the danger that these adults will then infect infants before vaccination, an immense increase in the number of vaccinations is suggested: vaccination right after birth, revaccination according to today's childhood schedules, revaccination in adolescence, and then once or more for each vaccine type during later adulthood. Additionally, there are suggestions about vaccinating before birth through vaccination of pregnant mothers. One small study suggests a startling rate of neurological damage to fetuses from MMR vaccination prior to or during pregnancy, also finding autism complications in breastfed babies of mothers who were vaccinated after birth.[123] Again, mercury is not the concern here. The virus in the vaccine is suspect. Others as well are finding this increase in infantile onset autism while autism related to vaccination of children is known as a "regressive" autism that appears later after birth. While the CDC and AAP are aware of these year 2000 findings, and similar reports continue to arrive, purposeful vaccination of pregnant women continues to occur. Others are vaccinated without knowing their pregnancy status and studies show that vaccination even months before a pregnancy can pose a risk to the child. Nearly all vaccines need boosters throughout life to remain preventive. Unfortunately, the risk of serious side effects from a vaccine multiplies as the number of vaccinations goes up (and as new vaccines continue to emerge).

• Some vaccines may be pushed before adequate safety testing has been performed.

   Rotavirus was responsible for fewer than 100 deaths in the United States each year, before vaccination, but the Advisory Committee on Immunization Practices suggested in 1998 that every child in the United States should receive a high-dose vaccination for this diarrheal disease,[124] which is generally milder in and occurs much less often in exclusively breastfed infants. Only four months later, this recommendation was then rescinded by the CDC based on reports of dangerous bowel obstructions occurring after vaccinations.[125]

   It wasn't until 2009 that the cause was discovered for a large cluster of extreme respiratory reactions to an earlier RV vaccine in the late 1960s.[126] This complicated science may also explain some serious illnesses that are reported to occur after other vaccines that do not contain actual live viruses, known as inactivated vaccines. The scientists claim they now understand how to make such vaccines safe.

• Widespread chicken pox vaccination may leave both our oldest and youngest populations at greater risk.

   Chicken pox vaccination was introduced in the United States in 1995. Chicken pox deaths in the United States have dropped since then from 100 or 150 per year (about half of these occurring in children) to 66 per year or fewer. A five-year study in France from 1991 to 1995 revealed that no deaths due to chicken pox occurred in that nation, even though no vaccination was used there.[127] Their population is one-fifth of ours. Complications occurred in 2% of reported French cases, all with complete recovery. They may have used less medication in treating cases there, as medication is a major cause of chicken pox deaths. By 2005, over 25,000 adverse events had been reported in the United States in relation to the chicken pox vaccine. Five percent of these were considered serious reactions,[128] including a number of deaths. The number of permanent injuries is unknown. The FDA advises that typically fewer than 10% of serious adverse reactions to vaccines are actually reported.

It used to be expected that every child would obtain chicken pox exposure or infection, as well as mumps and measles, and then have life-time immunity to these diseases. Deaths from chicken pox are most often associated with the use of steroids, antibiotics, or fever reducers such as aspirin, acetaminophen, or ibuprofen, and even here, mortality rates are incredibly low. Yet, at the time of introduction of the vaccine for chicken pox, articles and advertisements suddenly flourished about the serious dangers of chicken pox. I saw a magazine ad that said, "40 (U.S.) children died this year from chicken pox." On the very next page was a formula ad, which did not happen to mention that 1.5 million deaths could likely be prevented worldwide each year by exclusive breastfeeding.[129] These ads also referred to the economic burden of treating ill children—read economic profit from selling vaccinations. Exposure to the wild chicken pox virus usually gives lifelong immunity, whether one

> I saw a magazine ad that said, "40 children died this year from chicken pox." On the very next page was a formula ad, which did not mention that 1.5 million deaths worldwide could likely be prevented each year by exclusive breastfeeding.

becomes ill from exposure or not, but with enough waning in late life to sometimes allow the development of shingles. Shingles can be very painful and long lasting. It develops from a reactivation of the chicken pox virus in the body (the virus comes from natural exposure or vaccination), creating not chicken pox but a different set of painful symptoms. Regular exposure to chicken pox in the community reduced this risk greatly. Without becoming ill again, the immune system's response to the exposure creates a boosting of immunity that prevents shingles development in later life. With this natural, regular opportunity for immune boosting gone, the development of shingles in the older population is much more immanent. The results of this scenario are already beginning to emerge, with a significant increase in older adult shingles cases measured since 2001.[130] Chicken pox vaccine does not impart lifelong immunity. Boosters are needed every 10 to 20 years. Chicken pox is a very serious disease in teens or adults. Since vaccination wears off by this time, our adult population will soon be at risk (routine chicken pox vaccination began in 1995). The same is true for measles.

Most vaccinations, if the decision is made to give them, should be repeated throughout teen and adult years, although currently they seldom are. Many medical experts assert that with an active childhood vaccination program for chicken pox, there is a strong possibility that many younger adults will soon be developing shingles due to their waning immunity.

Finally, this scenario puts our youngest infants at the greatest risk. Pregnant mothers who were vaccinated as children rather than acquiring natural immunity will be at an increased risk of developing chicken pox during pregnancy. More cases of serious damage to fetuses will occur because of the vaccine program. With these same mothers passing on little or no antibody protection during birth or breastfeeding, and with tiny infants barely able to mount any defenses on their own in response to either vaccination or infection, many more dire cases of this disease will develop in our most vulnerable population. We will be only just approaching the threshold for this widespread occurrence some years after 2010.

• Is disease load always reduced by vaccination?

Haemophilus influenzae type b (Hib) is a bacteria that can cause meningitis, with a high risk of death or permanent damage. There were around 600 deaths per year from Hib-related meningitis before the Hib vaccination program began in 1987. The number of Hib meningitis deaths is now reduced to a handful a year. Meningitis deaths from all causes dropped dramatically decades ago with the introduction of antibiotics, though the death rate from such infections is still uncomfortably high. While the Hib vaccination program is considered to be among the most successful, with drastic reduction in this disease, it turns out that meningitis cases and deaths overall are not reduced. There has merely been a shift in which organisms are causing meningitis infections.[131] Hib was once a very common "natural" flora in human nasal passageways, possibly keeping down the activity of more dangerous microbes. Now that this competing organism is no longer commonly harbored, other microbes have simply taken its place, some being antibiotic-resistant bacteria. When an individual is vulnerable to developing meningitis due to some illness, different bacteria now step up for the job. More new vaccines are being developed to defeat all the new prominent bacterial strains.

• How many more vaccines will be required for infants?

Hepatitis B vaccination, which is not without complications, is now provided regularly to tiny infants, even though disease risk occurs only after needle sharing, receiving blood, sexual promiscuity, or through transmission from an infected mother during birth. A mother can have herself tested for hepatitis B prior to delivery, as she could be a carrier without symptoms. Some non-infected mothers choose to delay this vaccination for their newborn if the infant is not going to be hospitalized. Along with increasing numbers of booster shots, many new vaccines for other maladies are on the horizon for compulsory use as well.

Many parents question the wisdom of vaccinating their children, and there are valid concerns. Some feel most comfortable in at least delaying some vaccinations until an infant is older and stronger, as long as they know she has obtained good antibodies during labor and is receiving ongoing protection from exclusive breastfeeding, and even then being selective about which they feel to be most appropriate. The hope of vaccine supporters, and all of us, is that the level of suffering, disease, and mortality caused by immunization is outweighed by the reduction of the same due to disease itself. It should be recognized that this equation will be different in different regions of the world as well as in different individual situations.

Antibiotics

In cases where the immune response lags behind a bacterial infection that is dangerously decimating the body, the advent of antibiotic medications (introduced 1950 to 1960) has miraculously saved the lives of millions of people who would have otherwise succumbed. However, the massive overzealous use of these wonder drugs has now created a new realm of powerful diseases we are unable to fight with existing antibiotics.[132] Once a resistant bacteria has been created in response to antibiotic therapy, it has the power to transfer its resistance to other microbes, developing new resistant strains.[133] This has been an especially significant issue for the young, who have been chief targets for antibiotic misuse, because they are more susceptible to infections, and infections are more worrisome in them. It is now recognized that these powerful resistant strains spread easily around daycare centers.

The excitement over antibiotics has led to reduced hygiene in hospitals. Sanitation peaked decades ago when its importance was first widely recognized. Now 10% of the patients in hospitals acquire infections; a large portion of these infections are resistant to antibiotic treatment due to its expansive use in hospitals. Three percent of these patients die from their infections.[134] TB and pneumonia were once conquered with antibiotics, but we are now threatened again by tuberculosis epidemics and increased pneumonia deaths.

In addition to the burgeoning strains resistant to antibiotics, more invasive forms of bacteria are also being created by widespread antibiotic therapy.[135] Some strep strains have recently become more aggressive and can produce infections that rapidly destroy skin. These often fatal "flesh-eating" strep (chiefly) infections occur especially often in people who have previously been on antibiotics or other therapies that alter the immune balance. Even scarlet fever, another strain of strep, seems to be reemerging, and a new antibiotic resistant infection called MRSA (methicillin-resistant *Staphylococcus aureus*) caused an estimated 18,650 U.S. deaths in 2005.[136]

Antibiotics have many possible side effects. Diarrhea, malabsorption, cramping, yeast infection, agitation, rashes, and blood disorders are a few of these. By wiping out much of the normal flora throughout the body, they leave the child, especially, far more vulnerable to other infection such as thrush (oral candida) or dangerous intestinal microbes that cause diarrhea. Infectious diarrhea follows most antibiotics at a rate of 5 to 39%, depending on the drug.[137] The most common intestinal infection caused by antibiotics is colitis from clostridium infection, which has a 3.5% mortality rate.[138]

With all of this in mind, much evidence suggests that common casual antibiotic use in children is ineffective. A controlled study of antibiotic therapy for sinus infections showed that antibiotics had no influence on recovery or on the occurrence of relapse (and that X-rays were not useful in treatment decisions).[139] Significantly, antibiotics are generally inappropriate for treating ear infections as well. They have no effect on viruses and are certainly inappropriate for colds and flus, where they can lead to secondary infection. Yet, the majority of children visiting physicians with these complaints will receive antibiotic prescriptions. This is unfortunate because, most of the time, children are better off left to fight illness with their own immune systems, while the parents and physician provide careful monitoring.

Delaying antibiotic treatment of strep throat for 2 days after the child is seen by the doctor greatly reduces the number of recurrences,[140] probably because the body is allowed to develop its own defenses. This delay also allows time to obtain laboratory culture results, leading to more accurate treatment as well. Valid concerns about heart disease (rheumatic fever) lead most to recommend antibiotics in the case of strep infection, although most strong immune systems will conquer strep very well on their own, especially if fever-reducing drugs are not used.

The medical community is not entirely to blame for overuse of medications. Many parents bring their children in to their doctors at the first sign of a cold and demand medication. For many doctors, antibiotics and fever reducers have become an obligatory prescription. Moreover, excessive antibiotic therapy in humans is not the only source of new, dangerous, resistant strains. Regular prophylactic treating of animals creates resistant strains that can pose problems to humans. As we are increasingly exposed to antibiotics in meat, poultry, and cow's milk, we may often be developing resistant strains inside our bodies.

Ear Infections

The now highly prevalent middle ear infections in children illustrate the parameters of wise antibiotic use and its abuse, while at the same time revealing the effects of breastfeeding and formula. Middle ear infections (otitis media) have been on the rise throughout the twentieth century, increasing 175% between 1975 to 1990 alone.[141] The major source of these infections is threefold: the withholding of protective mother's milk, antibiotic treatment for mild, non-bacterial ear conditions, and the inflammatory reactions to certain foods, particularly cow's milk, as covered in the last chapters of this book.

The middle ear is the part of the ear that is enclosed behind the eardrum. There is a tiny tube, called the eustachian tube, intended to drain any fluids from the middle ear into the throat. Colds and episodes of allergic runny nose, due to airborne allergens or cow's milk or other food allergens, block this eustachian tube with mucus and inflammation. When this tiny mucous-membrane-lined canal is closed off, inflammatory fluids build up in the middle ear cavity (serous otitis media), sometimes referred to as effusion. Over time, passage of nasal and throat bacteria into this tube, especially when a child is lying on his back, can seed the middle ear; then the bacteria can multiply to large numbers in the friendly fluid-filled middle ear environment, creating painful infection and fever (acute otitis media).

> There is a higher rate of returning acute ear infection seen in those who receive antibiotic therapy, and the return of serous otitis is 2 to 6 times higher in those treated with antibiotics.

The occurrence of otitis media was found to be 19% lower in breastfed infants, with 80% fewer prolonged episodes.[142] The risk of otitis remains at this reduced level for 4 months after weaning, but by 12 months after weaning, the risk is the same as in those who were never breast-fed.[143] In addition to general immunities afforded the infant through breast-milk, there are specific antibodies that prevent otitis-causing bacteria from attaching to the mucous walls of the middle ear. Pacifier sucking increases the risk of ear infections.[144]

The presence of fluid in the middle ear from chronic or acute conditions reduces the child's capacity to hear. This fluid muffles sounds, but does not cause damage to the hearing mechanism, so hearing returns once the fluid is gone. *While permanent hearing damage does not occur from acute or chronic otitis,* chronic interference with hearing can delay language development.

In some cases of acute infection, treated or not, the eardrum may rupture, allowing the pus to drain, most likely resolving the infection. The eardrum will then heal with some scar tissue, just as it would have after

> *A controlled study of antibiotic therapy for sinus infections showed that antibiotics had no influence on recovery or on the occurrence of relapse.*

tube insertion. Once healed, hearing is affected very minimally or not at all by this scar tissue found in many an eardrum. (Drainage from an ear can also be an outer ear infection. This is common after swimming and responds to ear drops. Drainage from the ear for more than 2 days, especially associated with hearing loss, requires prompt medical attention.)

The major concern with ear infections is that infection will develop in the mastoid air cells behind the ear. This is called mastoiditis and is of concern because of the proximity to the brain. Mastoiditis, seen as redness behind the ear and protrusion of the outer ear, can occasionally lead to brain damage as well as to permanent hearing loss. Although claims are made that the incidence of mastoiditis has been greatly reduced since the introduction of antibiotics, this is not clear from a review of the literature. After the advent of antibiotics and CT scans, however, it is apparent that serious complications of acute mastoiditis have been reduced, and that the number of mastoid removals (mastoidectomies) has been reduced as well. In fact, antibiotic therapy for cases of mastoiditis appears to be valuable for preventing surgery in 86% of cases.[145]

Just over half of all mastoiditis cases occur following bouts of acute otitis media; other cases appear due to other causes, but less than 4% of the rare deaths from mastoiditis complications occur in cases that originated as ear infections.[146] Some mastoiditis is blamed on poor antibiotic treatment of ear infections; however, some is blamed on antibiotic therapy itself. At the 1998 American Academy of Otolaryngology meeting, it was reported that serious cases of mastoiditis are currently on the rise as a direct result of strongly resistant bacteria developed through the common use of antibiotic therapy for ear infections.[147] Additionally, "masked mastoiditis" is a highly worrisome, occasionally seen condition that is directly caused by antibiotic treatment of ear infections. The behavior of the bacteria that promote this condition makes it very difficult to discover, and the condition has a high rate of dangerous complications.[148]

Standard treatment for acute middle ear infections is antibiotic therapy. Antibiotics are also prescribed very often when fluid buildup is present by itself, without infection, although the parent is generally told infection exists, chiefly because it is often impossible to know for sure without puncturing the eardrum and taking a sample. At times the eardrum can appear very red just from crying or fever of other origin or allergies, causing suspicion of infection and prescription of drugs. One-third of ear infections are viral and the distinction cannot be made upon examination.[149] Antibiotics do not kill viruses, but can make viral infections worse by wiping out competing bacterial flora and encouraging secondary bacterial infections of resistant strains. Although seldom recognized, a number of chronic ear infections are actually fungal (candida), produced when multiple courses of antibiotics disrupt the normal floral balance and encourage fungal growth.[150] Many large studies have shown that antibiotic treatment provides only a small benefit over no treatment for short-term resolution of ear infections. A large 1994 analysis found that spontaneous recovery without medical treatment occurred in 81% of acute cases, and that short-term recovery with antibiotics occurred 95% of the time.[151] A 2004 review found antibiotic treatment to be only 7% more effective than non-treatment, leading to no fewer complications.[152] Still, 98% of ear infections in the United States are treated with antibiotics. Side effects are experienced by at least one-third of the children on antibiotics. Although short-term resolution is slightly improved, long-term benefit from antibiotic therapy is not seen: Medicated children demonstrate no less otitis 4 weeks after treatment than those on placebos.[153] In fact, there is a higher rate of returning acute ear infection seen in those who receive antibiotic therapy, and the return of serous otitis is 2 to 6 times higher in those treated with antibiotics.[154]

There is much discussion as to the value of surgical insertion of tubes through the eardrum as there are risks involved, and there is a much greater return of infection once the tubes are gone.[155]

The most sensible modern recommendation regarding ear infection treatment is to use antibiotic therapy only in acute infections that do not resolve on their own within a few days.[156] This regimen is currently followed in several European countries with positive results; it also reduces the development of bacterial strains resistant to antibiotics. A heating pad over the ear affords some relief, and many feel that warm garlic or tea tree oil drops in the outer ear speeds recovery. Favorite antimicrobial supplements such as goldenseal or grapeseed extract may provide benefit. Fever should not be reduced.

> *Permanent hearing damage does not occur from acute or chronic otitis.*

In conclusion, medical treatments not only complicate the picture of middle ear infections, but they also don't provide long-term benefits. Removing the chief causes of middle ear infections should be the preferred goal, which can be achieved by providing breastmilk, avoiding overuse of antibiotics, and recognizing, treating, and avoiding exposure to allergens, especially food allergens.

Natural Immune Assistance

Herbal remedies have been used in health care as far back as we can trace human history. There is no question about their power—a large portion of today's modern medications are made of or fashioned after natural extracts from plants, molds, and fungi, including aspirin, antibiotics, migraine medicines, and heart medications. The exciting thing about time-tested herbal remedies is that a very large portion of them have now been formally researched at least to some degree; many of them thoroughly. Formal medicine sometimes refuses these remedies because "we don't know how they work" or "there's no control over concentration or dosage." All of that is rapidly changing as well. Medicine did not understand the chemical actions of aspirin during the first decades of its medical use, and many pharmaceuticals are used today whose mechanisms are poorly understood. Today, when an herb or other food is proven to have therapeutic benefits, medicine will try using a one-ingredient extract of it, often with little success. Sometimes such an effort is even followed up by a report that the original herb may have no effect after all. In the case of Red Rice Yeast, the sale of the original yeast was banned once it was determined to be highly effective,[157] probably because it competes so strongly with cholesterol reducing drugs, and because those at pharmaceutical companies are hopeful of using extracts of the yeast profitably. Although there are many valuable nutritional supplements being used today, it has been and will be proven over and over again that whole foods and herbs work much more effectively than one-ingredient extracts. On the other hand, we also need to remember that just because something is "natural," this does not necessarily mean it is without side effects. Use of lavender oil, a common topical remedy also added to shampoos and lotions, has recently been found to occasionally cause breast growth in young boys.

Many parents are finding valuable help for their children through various physical treatments such as acupuncture and chiropractic approaches, as well as attaining valuable herbal and nutritional advice from these and other natural practitioners.

A Road Less Traveled

Medical intervention sometimes interferes with the body's natural and powerful processes of fighting infection and developing immunity. Unfortunately, at this point in time, the long-term benefit-to-harm ratio of interventions such as vaccination and antibiotic therapy is less than certain. By the same token, there are strident critics of this medical care who apparently are more aware of the dangers of treatment than of the harrowing consequences of some diseases.

Advances in sanitation and wonder drugs have miraculously all but eliminated many diseases of horrific consequence that many of parenting age know little about. The wise parent will keep this in mind when they search for middle ground. Further doses of pertussis vaccine should be seriously questioned if any dose leads to piercing cries. Chicken pox vaccines are of questionable benefit because the disease is mild in children, and vaccinated immunity likely wanes during adulthood, leading to more dangerous adult disease and the endangerment of fetuses and newborns whose mothers lack immunity. Yet, with dwindling opportunities to gain natural immunity in childhood, vaccination may become the only means of protecting adults who fear exposure.

In cases of apparent ear, sinus, or throat infection, antibiotics should be withheld for a few days instead of routinely applied, to allow some natural immunity to develop and to confirm bacterial infection. After confirmation, antibiotic use may be beneficial when bacterial infection causes great illness for days. Sometimes antibiotics can be lifesaving, as in the case of rheumatic fever. On the other hand, for ear and sinus infections antibiotic use is often misguided, especially in light of the effectiveness of proper diet and other supportive therapies.

Make decisions cautiously; the body is wise, but it is not all-powerful. Treatment can be dangerous, but disease can be even more so. Above all, remember that many fewer difficult decisions have to be made by parents who choose to give their children all the advantages of breastfeeding (the biggest vaccine), a more natural birth, appropriate hygiene, and a nutritious diet free of allergenic foods.

1

Digestion Matters

NATURALLY, PARENTS WILL TAKE MEASURES TO PROTECT THEIR BABIES FROM disease, and they will seek the best possible nutrition for their development. Furthermore, parents will take measures to prevent future disease, to promote lifelong health for their children. But, in order to do this, they must have the correct information. Unfortunately, misinformed parents with the best intentions can unintentionally have a negative impact on their children's health.

As we go on, we will see, as we have seen so far, that what is natural is usually best for baby. In order to understand the significance of intestinal symptoms such as colic, diarrhea, and gas, and have a better grasp of infant nutrition and immunity, a good understanding of the unique mechanisms of infant and childhood digestion is necessary. Only then can we understand the ramifications of feeding cow's milk and formulas to young children, instead of human milk.

Several attempts to improve the survival of prematurely born infants and questions about the early introduction of solid foods have spurred new research about how the digestive system develops from birth throughout childhood. It is apparent that although many digestive functions are intact at birth, the maturation of numerous digestive processes goes on for years. In addition, the immunological workings of the newly formed digestive tract are unlike the adult system and differ considerably between breastfed and bottle-fed babies.

In many countries, people are keenly aware of how valuable good digestive functioning is to overall health and energy. They monitor the appearance and characteristics of each stool passed for clues about their state of health and the adequacy of their diet. Even in the United States, parents of a newborn often adopt this practice for their baby and will have many a conversation on the subject.

Baby's Digestive System

The villi of formula-fed infants are slightly shortened, and multiple large "holes" are found.

The digestive tract begins with the mouth. Food or liquid is swallowed and travels down a tube (the esophagus) to the stomach. Here, some acids are released and some initial digestion occurs. From the stomach, materials pass through the small intestine for more digestion and for absorption of nutrients. Eventually the rest goes on into the large intestine, the colon, for a little more work, until it is finally eliminated. The average length of the small intestine in a fetus at 20 weeks of gestation is 4 feet. At 30 weeks it has grown considerably to 6.5 feet long. A full-term (40-week) infant has approximately 9 feet of small intestine.[1] This rapid growth rate toward the end of gestation creates some of the nutritional difficulties faced by preterm infants, because their short intestines have little surface area for digestion and absorption. The inside walls of the digestive tract are lined with mucous membrane, like in your mouth. In the intestines, the walls are covered with small finger-like projections called "villi" that are the surfaces that absorb nutrition.

In the newborn, these villi are relatively undeveloped. They grow rapidly over the next several months with the aid of an insulin-like human growth factor from mother's milk, and other factors such as nucleotides and polyamines from breastmilk.[2-5] Lacking these growth factors, the villi of formula-fed infants are slightly shortened, and multiple large "holes" are found.[6] It has been shown in formula-fed rabbits that these holes allow bacteria to be transported directly into the bloodstream, a process that can lead to illness.[7]

The Digestive Process

Hunger starts the digestive process going, and enzymes are released in the stomach and small intestine. If one eats or is fed when not hungry, these enzymes are not present, and indigestion can occur. Therefore, when infants are fed on a schedule rather than when hunger is expressed, poor digestion and painful indigestion might be the result.

Stomach enzymes continue to work on food until it enters the small intestine. Then, in this intestine, enzymes perform most of the digestion. Most nutrients are absorbed through the walls of the small intestine into the bloodstream to become available to the body. The unabsorbed portions are then passed on to the colon. Bacteria living in the first portions of the colon further degrade waste, using it for their own nutrition, while also manufacturing some vitamins. Water is absorbed along the entire intestinal tract.

Unique to Infants

The digestive system of the newborn infant is not at all equipped to handle solid foods or digest anything but mother's milk. Human infants, like all other mammals, are designed to survive on nutrition made by the mammary glands of the mother, just as they were previously supported by her placenta. This arrangement provides many survival advantages because it ensures parental protection, loving social contact, and controlled, optimal nutrition.

Whereas digestion in the older child or adult begins in the mouth, *the infant is wisely born with a protective tongue-thrust reflex that pushes foods not obtained through nursing out of the mouth.* Likewise, infants are born without teeth and without coordinated tongue and swallowing movements to help keep out foods they cannot handle. These reflexes make it obvious that young infants should not be fed solid foods, yet various forms are frequently promoted and encouraged for babies only weeks or months old, only to block much of breastmilk's immune-providing powers. Compared to the mature digestive system, infants' systems produce only a very small amount of digestive enzymes. This helps them to use important components of mother's milk. By design, breastmilk is so easily digestible that few digestive enzymes are needed. Notably, lactase, the enzyme for lactose digestion, is quite plentiful. The infant's large intestine is rather "leaky" to larger molecules, which allows valuable immune factors from mother's milk to pass through its membrane into the bloodstream and causes problems when foreign proteins from cow's milk or soy are introduced. The immune functioning of the digestive system is also diminished in several ways. For instance, baby's own immune cells meant to protect against allergic reactions to foreign foods are not highly present until around 7 months of age and increase throughout the first several years of life. This is another important reason to take caution with solid food or formula for babies. Not only is the newborn system not yet fully equipped with adult levels of digestive enzymes, but newborns have some unique digestive mechanisms that they will lose later on.

The infant's nourishment system is designed to achieve maximum benefit with minimal work. This savings of energy and effort is possible because mother's system is expending extra energy to create a special food, which is why this ideal arrangement (for baby) cannot go on indefinitely. Luckily, mother's milk makes up for all the shortcomings of the infant's system. The composition of her milk even changes as the infant grows.

Lactose: The Mommy Sugar

The amount of sugar (or carbohydrate), mostly in the form of lactose, in the milk of any given mammal is generally directly proportional to the size of that creature's adult forebrain, humans therefore having the greatest proportion of sugar in their milk.[8] (An exception to this rule is the sea lion, whose pups rely solely on fat and protein to grow.) The access to sugar, as well as a great number of other nutrients in proper proportions, is essential for proper brain development in infants. Infant sugar (carbohydrate) digestion is designed mainly for the unique sugar of mother's milk, lactose, and this special sugar helps to maintain the friendly flora found in an exclusively breastfed (no solids or formula) infant's gut. Lactose is also found in cow and all other mammal milks (except for sea lions) and exists in most milk-based formulas. In order to be utilized, lactose must be broken down by lactase, an enzyme found in infants and young children. This enzyme *normally* begins to diminish around the age of 2 and disappears somewhere between the ages of 6 and 15.[9,10]

Descendants of northern Europeans are an evolutionary exception to this situation.[11] Left with little to eat in the winters, early people migrating to colder northern climates learned they could depend on cows to turn tiny tufts of grass into consumable nutrition for them: milk. Initially, unable to digest lactose, very few of these people would have stayed healthy on this winter diet long enough to reproduce. Those who did were the ones who retained the lactase enzyme for longer periods. (Inuits are cold climate people who did not depend on lactase persistence; instead, they survived on the meat and blubber of seals.) As these lactase-persistent adults reproduced, and as their lactase-persistent offspring did so as well, a huge population of adults developed who could digest milk at later and later ages. These European descendants account for a significant percentage of U.S. citizens today, but are a small segment of the world population.

Nearly all infants are born with the lactase enzyme. From an evolutionary standpoint, we realize that an infant without lactase couldn't survive on mother's milk; therefore, this genetic condition would never be passed on. Such an infant would quickly suffer brain retardation from lack of sugar in the system, and would die of diarrhea within weeks. Interestingly, there is a small pocket of this recessive gene disorder in Finland.[12]

One would assume this kind of persistent gene mutation would have been a rather recent phenomenon, because an infant couldn't survive unless the problem was understood within a few days of birth and a formidable nutritional substitute for milk was supplied. Of course, today we have lactose-free formulas with an alternate sugar for this extremely rare situation (most likely much rarer than the 1 in 23,000 fructose intolerant mentioned below). Many infants sensitive to cow's milk proteins are incorrectly labeled as lactase deficient. Although many with diarrhea may be diagnosed as lactose intolerant with lactose intolerance tests, they will continue to have difficulties with lactose-free formulas based on cow's milk. By contrast, even though mother's milk is full of lactose, these infants will have no difficulty tolerating human milk after a couple days of recovery—if the breastmilk comes from a mother who doesn't drink cow's milk, that is!

Digestion of Other Sugars

Oligosaccharides are complex sugars in human milk that are not digested in the small intestine. They are meant to be preserved so they can provide immune functions. They also serve as nutrition specifically for *Bifidobacterium infantis,* friendly protective bacteria found in high quantities in the large intestines of breastfed infants.

Corn solids and sucrose, commonly found in formulas, are fairly well digested in infants, even though they are not considered ideal sugars for brain development and calcium absorption.

> Many infants sensitive
>
> to cow's milk proteins
>
> are incorrectly labeled as
>
> lactase deficient.

Occasionally, one hears of sugar intolerance in children. Just as a very few children are born without the lactase enzyme, in rare instances a liver enzyme is deficient, leading to a hereditary absolute inability to digest fructose, thought to occur in 1 in 23,000 children.[13] On the other hand, it's been found that around two-thirds of children and adults actually have poor digestion and absorption of fructose, called fructose malabsorption.[14,15] Child-to-child differences are more a matter of dosage while about half of those malabsorbing have no symptoms. Fruits contain small amounts of fructose and should not pose a problem. The large amount of fructose in a can of soda is above the average intolerance dosage. Corn syrup is not high in fructose until it is altered with enzymes to create "high fructose corn syrup." More is being learned every day about negative effects this artificially created sugar has on the liver where it's processed, and on the rest of the body. Fructose malabsorption can also lead to anemia. Honey is high in fructose but few use this healing nectar in anywhere near the doses of HFCS found in sweet foods and drinks and it's a natural form. Some children who react to both kinds of corn syrup will be found to also react to whole corn and these are corn allergics rather than fructose malabsorbers; also a common finding.

In the United States, 99.9% of all candy and other sweets are sweetened with sugars that have been derived from corn such as corn syrup, fructose, glucose, dextrose, maltitol, sorbitol, and "hydrolyzed starch."

Indigestible and unabsorbed carbohydrates are broken down by normal bacterial flora in the large intestine; this occurs more efficiently in the breast-fed infant and is important for taking advantage of certain nutrients in mother's milk. When in excess, the fermentation of undigested and unabsorbed materials in the large intestine can create uncomfortable gas. In infants and young children, colic and other behavior fluctuations accompany the gas.

Protein Digestion

In adults, protein digestion begins with enzymes in the stomach, which is very acidic. The infant stomach maintains a much less acidic state and digestion occurs here only minimally. This protective mechanism ensures that immune factors,[16] live immune cells, and beneficial bacteria from mother's milk survive to be used in and even passed through the infant intestines. Undesirable components of cow's milk are also protected by the infant's lack of stomach acid. In infants, protein digestion occurs predominantly in the small intestine, and even here, infant digestion is weak compared to adults. Unfortunately, this reduced ability to metabolize protein in infants will leave many of the larger cow's milk proteins undigested, whether they come from formula or from a mother who drinks cow's milk. Other undesirable components of cow's milk (formula) are protected in this way, and cow's milk itself has factors that protect its bovine hormones and other substances from early destruction. As a result, these are able to pass through the unusually leaky colon walls of infants, allowing allergic sensitization and other possible consequences.[17]

In the small intestines of adults, the acidic content from the stomach is quickly neutralized until it becomes alkaline. The intestinal environment of the breastfed infant stays closer to neutral (neither acidic nor alkaline) than a formula-fed infant's (whose is alkaline).[18] The neutral state in breastfed infants better resists colonization by some unwanted bacteria and prevents the destruction of lysozyme from mother's milk,[19] which helps the infant destroy unwanted bacteria.

Fat Digestion

Lipase is the key enzyme for breaking down fats into important elements that are used for brain and body nourishment. For the first several months, stomach lipase is twice as effective at breaking down the fat in breastmilk than

This reduced ability to metabolize protein in infants will leave many of the larger cow's milk proteins undigested, whether they come from formula or from a mother who drinks cow's milk.

the fats in formulas.[20] As a result, breastfed infants are likely receiving superior brain food. Mother's milk also contains a form of lipase (found only in humans and gorillas[21]) that is activated in the small intestine. This makes up for the normally low amounts of lipase available in infant intestines, so that breastmilk fats completely break down and the resulting fatty acids are readily available for optimum brain development. Various breakdown products of breastmilk fats also provide specific immune protective functions. Formula manufacturers are currently researching and improving the fatty acid contents in some formulas, although they are not yet able to approach the quality of breastmilk.

Closure

Compared to adult absorption, whole proteins pass easily across the newborn's colon membrane and into the bloodstream. This is by design, so that certain factors in mother's colostrum and milk can leak into the infant's bloodstream and provide immune protection throughout the infant's entire system, most noticeable in the first few weeks after birth.

Eventually, the membrane barrier of the large intestine becomes more adult-like, disallowing most protein leaking. This process, called "closure," is pronounced by around 3 months of age, but may not be complete until around 5 years.[22] Closure occurs more slowly in artificially fed infants than in breastfed.[23] In addition to the gradual closure, many of the newborn's low or absent enzymes begin appearing in higher quantities around 5 or 6 months of age. Waiting for at least 6 months of age to add solid foods to the breastmilk diet, as recommended by the American Academy of Pediatrics (AAP) in 2005, allows the infant to achieve a good level of closure, as well as more adequate levels of digestive enzymes and the infant's own antibodies, before any formula or other foods are introduced.

Calcium Absorption

Calcium absorption is promoted by vitamins C and D, among other factors. While breastmilk is low in vitamin D and contains much less calcium than formulas, the calcium in mother's milk is extremely available for absorption in the small intestine. Lactose greatly increases calcium absorption; it is prevalent in mother's milk and is often less present in artificial feeds. The sugars such as sucrose and corn syrup that are commonly added to formula do not aid calcium absorption. Formulas also contain 2 to 4 times the amount of phosphorous as mother's milk (and cow's milk has 8 times the amount). This is not good because phosphorous competes with calcium for absorption. Therefore, when there is too much phosphorus, calcium isn't used to build bones. Phosphorus also binds to calcium, forming salts that can't be used by the body in the presence of the alkaline milk, thereby further reducing the amount of available calcium and hardening the stool. However, by adding extra calcium and vitamin D and by altering some other factors, formula manufacturers have created formulas that prevent the rickets that was rampant when feeds based on cow's milk became popular in the early 1900s.[24] This leg-bowing disorder, a result of calcium deficiency, is no longer a risk in modern formula-fed infants.

Beyond the differences in available calcium between breastmilk and formula, calcium is less of a concern for those who do not consume large quantities of cow's milk. In contrast to the claims of the dairy industry, epidemiological studies demonstrate sufficient or improved calcium bone density in nations with lower milk and calcium intake, in general, than in the United States. Vegetables apparently prevent osteoporosis (insufficient bone strength) better than cow's milk, because vegetarians who don't drink milk (vegans) have lower intakes of calcium, but have higher bone density than the average American.[25] It is now known that the reduced bone density prevalent in the United States and some other industrialized nations is not so much the result of inadequate calcium intake, but rather is the result of high calcium loss into the urine associated with high phosphorous and animal protein intake (meat and dairy consumption),[26,27] as well as insufficient intake of magnesium (the high dairy diet is magnesium deficient), other bone-building nutrients, and possibly other factors. (*This is covered more completely in Chapter 11.*)

Iron Absorption

Iron behaves differently than most vitamins or minerals in that it is used over and over again in the body. Generally, only a very small amount of ingested iron is absorbed. The need for added iron is greater when there is growth, as is the case with all children.

Lactoferrin, a protein that is abundant in human milk, aids iron absorption in the infant intestine and is carried through the intestinal wall to regulate cell iron levels throughout the body. Lactoferrin is also found in very small amounts in cow's milk, but is inactive in formulas. Attempts to fortify formulas with added lactoferrin have not yet successfully increased formula-fed infant blood iron levels to those of the breastfed, until after 90 days of life.[28]

Extra iron is also needed when there is blood loss, as with the *common intestinal blood loss in infants fed formulas based on cow's milk*, which is any formula with whey or casein, or cow's milk itself.[29] For this reason, iron is added to formulas at values that are very high when compared to human milk, enough to prevent anemia in a majority of infants. Iron deficiency anemia is a condition where the red blood cells do not contain enough iron and hence cannot carry enough oxygen throughout the body. Various other factors in breastmilk besides lactoferrin also help to make its iron highly absorbable.

Generally, infants absorb 50% of the iron in human milk, but only about 4% of that in formula. When there is intestinal reaction to cow's milk derivatives, as most eczema and often diarrhea or constipation suggest in infants, the cells at the tips of the villi, where the iron is being slowly absorbed, become destroyed, and consequently iron is lost. Beyond this stage, *dark tarry stools are a sign of significant blood loss—often labeled as a normal infant reaction to milk products, but in my opinion, a signal to change the infant's formula.* Just because this occurrence is somewhat common does not mean it is healthy.

Copper is 5 times more concentrated in human milk than in cow's milk and helps make iron available to the blood after absorption. Formulas generally add copper to nearly human levels. Vitamin C is also important for absorption of iron. While the vitamin C in cow's milk is only one-fifth that in human milk, formulas are supplemented to human levels of this vitamin.

Living with Bugs

Although newborn infants are born sterile, within hours they are inhabited by vast numbers of bacteria. Within days, infants not on antibiotic therapy will develop large colonies of friendly normal flora in the mouth, throat, stomach, and small and large intestines. Normal flora assist digestion and form certain vitamins. They compete with undesirable microbes to help prevent colonization that could lead to illness. The normal flora in infants is quite different from that of adults, becoming more and more adult-like as solid foods start to predominate in the diet. Eventually, there are over 5,000 different bacterial species in the normal intestine,[30] including *E. coli*, enterococci, and lactobacillus. Also, the flora of formula-fed infants is very different from that of breastfed babies. Where do these bacteria come from? This necessary invasion of flora comes primarily from the food in our diet. The very first infestations come from mother's milk, formula, the normal flora on the skin of mother's nipples, kisses from mom and dad, sucked-on fingers, and the air. Remember, the stomach and intestines in newborns are rather neutral (neither very acidic nor alkaline), allowing these bacteria to survive and flourish. No, you do not want to prevent this from occurring. This is a necessary part of life and good health, unless you wish your child to live in a sterile plastic bubble, untouched by human hands.

Remember, only 1% of all bacterial species cause disease in humans.

The natural defense systems developing in the infant, the temporary immunity gained from mother's placenta during labor, and the broad and continuous immunity derived from mother's milk all help to vanquish incompatible microbes, preferentially allowing compatible ones to flourish. The sooner infants can go through this process, the sooner their natural immunity to undesirable organisms will develop, making them less susceptible to infection and illness. The infant cared for in a highly sterile fashion will have less immunity. The flora double in number once to twice every day and make up one-third the weight of eliminated stools.

Establishing flora has been shown to occur more quickly in infants who "room-in" with their mothers after birth, thereby reducing their early rates of infectious diarrhea and other diseases.[31]

Normal Flora

The colon of a breastfed infant is almost entirely inhabited by odorless bifidobacteria. This helps protect the young system from infection and illness caused by more potent bacteria, many of which will eventually, but gradually, become a part of the flora as solid foods are gradually introduced at an older age, when the immune system is stronger. Lysozyme from mother's milk helps to break bifidobacteria down in order to release usable proteins for the colon flora and for absorption.[32] Also seen in the colon of the breastfed infant are some lactobacilli and some friendly staphylococci (staph). Normal breastfed infant stools are very light in scent, soft to loose, and mustard in color. In contrast, the formula-fed infant is colonized chiefly by bacteroides and (foul-smelling) *Escherichia coli*, better known as *E. coli*, which predominate in adult systems. Accordingly, their stools are the same brown color (and odor) as adult stools. *E. coli*, as well as some strains of bacteroides, can cause diarrhea in the very young infant whose immune system is not yet strong enough to tolerate this challenge. Certain strains of *E. coli* are more dangerous than others. Some of these are the ones heard about in the news. While many strains are tolerated around us and in us, the news stories are related chiefly to *E. coli* from the intestines of feedlot-raised cows (via contaminated meat or apples fallen on the ground where cow's manure has been used). Children and adults can also become ill from strains of *E. coli* from other parts of the world, because people only maintain immunity to the strains from the region where they live.

Significant numbers of other potentially dangerous bacteria are found in the artificially fed infant. Diarrhea or antibiotics can wipe out much of the weaker flora, allowing some mighty nasty bugs to grow in abundance. Once they reach a critical density, these microbes release their harmful toxins, causing diarrhea, abdominal cramping, and fever. Clostridium infection has been indicated in a "modest proportion" of crib deaths in formula-fed babies.[33]

Some good news is that many studies are demonstrating good immune and digestive benefits to formula-fed infants, or infants on frequent antibiotic therapy, through the oral supplementation of high doses of friendly bifidus, lactobacilli,[34] and S. boulardii. These can be found in health food stores in various forms.

Vitamins in the Colon

In formula-fed infants, E. coli and streptococcus are 10 times more prevalent than in breastfed infants. These bacteria produce B vitamins[35] and vitamin K_2 (a factor in blood clotting), and possibly some others. Much higher amounts of vitamins K_1 and K_2 are found in the colons of formula-fed infants, and their blood concentrations of K_1 are higher, meaning their absorption of this nutrient is good. However, K_2 is found only in the blood of breastfed babies.[36] Apparently some factor in human milk provides for its absorption. We do not yet know what the effects of insufficient K_2 in formula-fed children may be, but K_2 is known to be an important factor in maintaining bone density. Children beyond formula and breastmilk feeding are at risk for vitamin K deficiency when on prolonged antibiotics, because vitamin K-forming E. coli are destroyed by many antibiotics, so they lose this intestinal source, and their diets may not be high in vitamin K_1-containing dark green vegetables.

More Bugs

Candida albicans normally cannot grow inside the intestine with well-established natural flora because they cannot compete with the resident bacteria. Found everywhere in our food and environment, external candida overgrowth is responsible for many diaper rashes. It colonizes in the intestine as a result of other infection, antibiotic use, or intestine-damaging food sensitivity reactions (or does its colonization cause some sensitivities to develop?). Commonly known as "yeast," candida can become established in the intestines, bringing harmful changes in digestive functioning.

Streptococcus mutans in the mouth is the chief bug involved in childhood cavities. It lives on sugars, such as those in fruit juices, sweetened beverages, and sweetened treats, as well as any sweeteners added to formulas other than lactose. Generally this bacteria is not found in an infant's mouth until there are teeth to live on and these sweet foods have entered the diet.[37] Cavities are significantly less frequent in children breastfed for more than 3 months.[38]

Lactoferrin

Lactoferrin, the breastmilk protein that aids iron absorption, acts somewhat selectively against undesirable bacteria in the infant's digestive tract, killing them by binding with their iron. In the laboratory, lactoferrin derived from cow's milk will kill bacteria also, but attempts to supplement formulas with this ingredient have failed to achieve this benefit inside the human infant.[39] In breastfed babies, the infant's own lactotransferrin apparently can attack strains of *E. coli* that mother's milk does not. This ability to inhibit *E. coli* is not seen in bottle-fed babies or even in bottle-supplemented breastfed babies.[40] This is one of the many poorly understood deficiencies of formula feeding.

If a breastfed infant is supplemented with iron, infant formula, or much solid food, the free iron in these will bind with the lactoferrin in mother's milk and prevent it from being able to maintain the infection-resistant flora found only in exclusively breastfed infant intestines. Low-iron formulas may be a better option for short-term or low-volume supplementation. When possible, providing no supplementation is the healthier answer.

Abdominal Pain

Studies on the sources of pain in the intestines have suggested that pain is caused chiefly by distension of the bowel, from the bloating associated with gas, infection, and diarrhea, or from the build-up of material with constipation. Pain may also arise from spasms in the stomach and intestinal wall muscles. In general, the rhythmic waves of normal intestinal contractions that flow regularly along the intestines (peristaltic waves) are not felt, although they may be associated with hunger pangs. "Colicky pain" is the name given to abdominal pains that build and diminish rather cyclically with the on-and-off nature of peristaltic waves, most likely secondary to bloating. The term "colic," when associated with infants, describes this condition, but the frequency and duration of the infant's crying is generally the reason for using this term, whether or not the crying spells are colicky, and whether or not the condition is associated with abdominal difficulties.

Gas

Gas is normally created in every intestine every day, much of it by bacterial fermentation of underdigested or unabsorbed foods. Generally, most gas created in the intestines is absorbed into the bloodstream; then part of it is filtered out by the liver, and part is expelled through the lungs. Excess gas that is not absorbed will be passed. Prior to solid foods, the breastfed infant who is not reacting to any foods in his mother's diet should pass very little gas. More gas is produced when a child is fed when not hungry, when the child is fed harder-to-digest infant formulas or early solid foods, when digestion and absorption are reduced by food sensitivity reactions, and when undigested milk lactose is passed into the large intestine in the much older children whose lactase enzymes are no longer sufficient. Broccoli and cauliflower in the nursing mother's diet cause gas in many a tiny infant, as may onions and garlic. Certain foods, especially beans, are rich in indigestible complex carbohydrates that can create great increases in gas production when consumed directly by the child, especially when not eaten regularly. Excess gas trapped inside stools is generally the

If a breastfed infant is supplemented with iron, infant formula, or much solid food, the free iron in these will bind with the lactoferrin in mother's milk and prevent it from providing important immune protection.

cause of floating stools. Plenty of jiggling helps infants to move gas through and out of their systems.

Diarrhea

When certain elements, such as undigested lactose, become very highly concentrated in the colon, relative to their concentrations in the colon's blood circulation, this difference can cause fluids to flow into the colon from the bloodstream, causing loose or watery stools. High concentrations of acids produced by fermentation of undigested materials cause diarrhea as well, as can chemicals released by intestinal allergic reactions to milk proteins, or toxins released by overgrowing, unfriendly microorganisms. Additionally, loose stools may have portions of very bright green color. This is bile that has gone quickly through the system and is a sign that baby has not had much time to digest and absorb nutrients from his diet. Sometimes parents' complaints of diarrhea in their infant are only answered with the suggestion that they misunderstand the term. Strictly defined, diarrhea is the frequent passage of loose or watery stools. Since a normal infant can pass several stools per day, or 1 every 3 days, the term "frequent" is relative. The consistency and color of the stools are truly the more important factors. No matter the definition, one must recognize that there is a reason for any change in stool habits. Minor changes can result from variations in diet. Generally, however, if an infant normally has one stool of medium firmness per day, but then has a couple loose stools in a day, or even just one watery stool, this is significant. An infant can even withhold stool for several days, followed by an explosion of loose stool.

Diarrhea causes digestive enzymes to be flushed through the system too quickly to be used well. The irritation sometimes leads to reduced production of enzymes as well, including lactase. These two factors lead to positive lactose intolerance tests when an infant has diarrhea, often leading to the improper diagnosis of lactose intolerance. Normal flora can be flushed out also. Clearly the child can quickly become nutritionally deficient. Probiotics such as lactobacilli (L. acidophilus, L. sporogens, and Lactobacillus GG, to name a few), bifidus (bifidobacteria), and the yeast S. boulardii are often beneficial in reestablishing normal flora and normal intestinal function in infants with diarrhea. It is customary for hospitals to advise that breastfeeding should be discontinued for 2 days when there is diarrhea or dehydration, but this advice is quite contrary to what is best for the infant, and only follows from what is best for formula-fed babies. Breastfed infants with diarrhea of any cause should continue to nurse to their desire. On the other hand, formula is difficult for any infant to handle, and diarrhea reduces the child's digestive enzymes, making it more difficult to handle formula. Additionally, the breaks in the defenses of the mucosal walls can allow undigested proteins to enter the child's system to a much greater degree. If large quantities of foreign milk or soy proteins enter the bloodstream, allergic reactions can develop. Even the child with no previous intolerance to formula can now become intolerant. Bottle-fed infants with diarrhea, even when caused by antibiotic use, sometimes do better with only electrolyte solution such as Infalyte (a Pedialyte type drink which contains no corn products) for a couple of days. Alternatively, a well hydrolyzed formula, such as Alimentum, may be well tolerated and provides good nutrition as well.

Constipation

As with diarrhea, many definitions of constipation may meet with resistance from some quarters. There are babies, especially breastfed babies, who will not pass stools for 7 and even 10 days. If their stools are not hard and are not particularly painful or difficult to pass, and there are not intermittent loose, watery stools in between, this may just be baby's happy normal. On the other hand, 1 movement in 1 or 2 days is suspicious in an infant who normally moves her bowels 5 times a day. Regardless of frequency, a movement that is unusually prolonged, hard, painful, difficult to pass, or causes rectal bleeding should cause concern and should be considered constipation. Constipation is more common in formula-fed infants.

The exclusively breastfed infant has

It is customary for hospitals to advise that breastfeeding should be discontinued for 2 days when there is diarrhea or dehydration, but this advice is quite contrary to what is best for the infant, and only follows from what is best for bottle-fed babies.

little waste from her diet and will have fewer and smaller bowel movements than those fed formula or solid foods. There is a considerable amount of indigestible or unabsorbable matter in formula. The usual stools of formula-fed infants are much firmer and darker than those of breastfed babies. Bottle-fed infants have very high amounts of minerals and fats lost in their stools. These form calcium–fatty acid soaps and mineral salts that cause their stools to be harder. These soaps are responsible for the frequent intestinal obstructions seen in formula-fed preterm babies.[41]

Studies have found that 78% of infant and child constipation cases resolve with the removal of cow's milk proteins from their diets.[42,43] Often other food allergy symptoms exist in these children, helping to confirm the suspicion of allergy. It was long thought that negative symptoms associated with constipation arose from the toxins absorbed during the long stay of material in the colon. It is now generally accepted that potential toxins released in the colon are chiefly dealt with by the liver before they can reach the blood circulation. Sluggish symptoms sometimes associated with constipation are thought to be caused simply by the distention and irritation of the bowel. They may also be associated with a food allergy reaction that is causing the constipation.

What Does It All Mean?

Baby's system is designed to take advantage of mother's milk in many ways. Mother's milk meets all of baby's nutritional and immunity needs so baby can conserve energy and have time to develop his own digestive system and immune defenses after birth. During the transition period from placenta feeding, tiny infants are not at all equipped to handle solid foods. Formula falls into this solid food category: It is difficult to digest and obtain nutrients from, and it allows dangerous flora to develop.

Studies have found that 78% of infant and child constipation cases resolve with the removal of cow's milk proteins from their diets.

It takes years for the immune system to become fully developed. Digestive enzymes appear only very gradually with maturation.

The lactase enzyme is normally lost in the middle of the first decade of life, and intestinal closure occurs in this same time frame. A child's drive for sucking, when allowed, will last for years, whether on a bottle, nipple, thumb, pacifier, or sippy cup; therefore, it could be surmised that the human system is designed to benefit from breastmilk for several years. Further support for this contention will be presented in later chapters.

8

In the Womb and the First Few Days

A CHILD IS AT GREATEST RISK WHILE DEVELOPING INSIDE MOTHER, during delivery, and during the first days outside the uterus. During this time the parents' actions can impact the likelihood they will have a healthy baby. We must remember that the pregnant mother's world, including her diet, is the fetus's world as well, and that her behavior can definitely affect the developing little person. Infants born too early or too tiny are most in need of their parents' care and must be given very special consideration. Often parents of preemies need to be proactive to achieve the best results. Healthcare providers are learning how to help parents in most of these areas, but educated parents can help to speed this positive progression along.

Stressed Before Birth

When mom is under stress during pregnancy, her stress hormone levels become elevated even though pregnancy hormones are designed to have a calming effect on the mother-to-be. Stress hormones disrupt some of the protection induced by the hormonal state of maternity. Increased levels of these stress hormones increase the chances of a preterm delivery.[1] The stress regulation systems of a fetus subjected to this hormonal environment are disrupted as well,[2] just as the hormonal balance is altered in infants living in stressful home environments. Exposure to loud noise during uterine life, such as a mother working in noisy surroundings, has been shown to reduce the newborn's protective immune system,[3] possibly due to stress.

And After Birth

We have already discussed the physical and psychological stress a newborn experiences when separated from mother. This separation has a tremendous impact, reducing the chances for prolonged breastfeeding, mother-child attachment, health, and survival. There is evidence that intense noise surrounding newborns in the hospital after birth may be stressful to the newborn as well. Tiny nervous systems are much more sensitive to various sources of stress than adult systems, and noise levels safe for infants' hearing may be well below those considered safe for adults.[4] Abrupt noises such as rapidly closing incubator doors are potentially worse than background noises such as the hum of the incubator motor. When it comes to nursing, some infants do not seem to mind a flood of loving attention from friends, relatives, and lactation nurses, while others need quiet peace and solitude and the familiar sound of mother's heartbeat if they are to nurse comfortably in the beginning.

Dangerous Foods for the Fetus

Many new potential dangers to a developing fetus have been recognized in the last decade, but this information has barely made its way into maternity care. More than 15,000 (of a total of more than 70,000) man-made chemicals are used in significant quantities in our environment today, most of them introduced within the last 60 years. More than half of these remain untested for their toxicity,[5] and many may mimic or block the action of reproductive hormones (estrogens and androgens). When they have the potential to disrupt the normal functioning of hormones inside the body, they are called "endocrine disrupters" and are a focus of concern. The newborn and the developing fetus are most vulnerable to possible adverse effects from these environmental pollutants.

These chemicals include PCBs, dioxins, pesticides, and plasticizers. We have not yet witnessed their effects on an entire generation exposed to them from conception to death, but medical studies are already uncovering evidence suggesting significant reductions in fetal development and increased rates of malformation. We also know that each successive generation of men has a lower sperm count than the one before, and we suspect that man-made chemicals are at least part of the problem. These environmental pollutants are suspect with regard to increased cancer rates as well.

Chemicals make their way into our food chain when air and water pollutants come into contact with fruits and vegetables (even organic vegetables), as well as when pesticides are used directly on crops. Non-organic peaches and apples have the highest levels of added pesticides,[6] but the level on most fruits and vegetables is low compared to the levels in foodstuffs further up the chain. Livestock are fed on these crops and are also exposed to chemicals in the air and water. Additionally, they are fed other overmedicated livestock deemed unfit for human consumption. Drug-tainted milk unfit for commercial sale is fed to calves, adding further to their lifetime toxic buildup. As a result, toxins become concentrated in the fat tissues of livestock until a lifetime of toxins is contained in a few servings of meat. These chemicals also become concentrated in the fat portions of cow's milk. Thus, eating meat and dairy fats introduces significantly higher quantities of endocrine-mimicking toxins, and humans accumulate these chemicals in their own tissues. Milk fats make up an especially large portion of the typical American diet (cheese, ice cream, butter, sour cream, whole and low-fat milk), and dairy consumption has the most impact on statistical risk estimates of potentially harmful effects.[7] It is believed that endocrine disrupters have mild effects on all ages of people, as well as on many animals, but the greatest potential danger by far is to the developing fetus. Young children have the next highest risk, and sperm-producing tissues in males of any age can be affected.

Incidence of hypospadias, a defect in the placement of the penile urethra, or urinary outlet of males, has doubled during the 70s and 80s[8] and has likely continued to increase since then. The severity of these cases has risen considerably as well. Most agree that fetal exposure to chemicals that disrupt the sex hormones appears to be the chief cause. In 1993, this defect alone was seen in 1 out of every 100 newborn boys. The rise in various cancers, especially testicular and breast cancer, lymphatic cancers, and leukemia, is being linked to hormone mimics in the environment, and partial responsibility is being assessed. Subtle, generally permanent effects that can only be measured by large population studies also include mild reductions in brain and motor function, reduced sperm quality, and reduced immune function. Apparently, vitamin K deficiencies can result from these toxins as well. Subtle birth abnormalities are now found in 10% of newborns in the high meat- and dairy-consuming Netherlands.[9]

Several key problems plague attempts to correlate endocrine disrupters to birth defects. First, few of these chemicals leave detectable fingerprints at their low levels. Second, there is a huge variety of chemicals and modes of exposure in the environment. Also, many are thought to have an additive effect on each other, increasing the impact through accumulated exposure. As far as anyone can tell, there is no threshold quantity for endocrine mimics to be dangerous, below which they could be considered safe.[10] It appears that even very tiny amounts of various chemicals can accumulate or complement each other to produce small effects (such as reduced sperm counts). Hence, setting government controls is difficult, and it is now clear that the Environmental Protection Agency's (EPA) guidelines for testing chemicals prior to 1998 were inadequate. Now, safety testing for all chemicals, such as multigenerational reproduction studies on animals, needs to be performed again under the newer guidelines.[11]

Animal studies can reveal the potentially toxic consequences of these chemicals. Suspicions are then confirmed by epidemiological studies such as reviews of infants born to agricultural workers. The rates of nervous system abnormalities, oral clefts such as a cleft lip and cleft palate, male genital malformations, and other anomalies are considerably higher in children born to mothers (but not fathers) who work in gardening or farming occupations, with high exposure to many endocrine disrupters.[12,13]

Although studies suggest that many chemicals accumulate in the mother's body over many years, they also suggest that the rate of occupational exposure during and just before pregnancy is highly important. Hence, while women planning to have children should reduce their exposures to man-made environmental chemicals many years before conception, mothers-to-be can make some difference in the risk of malformation or miscarriage through preventive measures during the pregnancy as well. Using mostly lean organic meats and dairy products in small amounts, consuming filtered water and organic fruits and vegetables (non-organic grains are fairly safe), and avoiding solvents such as fingernail polish remover and paint thinner or foods heated in plastics may be reasonable measures to take.

BPA, or bisphenol A, is an estrogen-mimicking chemical that leaches from most plastics such as plastic food wraps, baby bottles, dental sealants, plastics that line infant formula and other food cans, those that create that "new car" smell, and from new furnishings made with particle board (which contains formaldehyde) or covered with fabric guards. The longer food is in contact with plastic, or when it is heated in plastic, the greater the absorption of BPA. When doses of BPA estimated to be similar to human exposure levels are fed to pregnant mice, the males demonstrate mild altera-tions of their reproductive organs, and the young mice grow larger and enter puberty earlier.[14,15]

DEHP is another chemical recently raising serious concern, especially for high exposure to the early fetus. Found in soft vinyl plastics such as IV bags, some toys and teething rings, and respiratory care products, only a few pregnant mothers may have enough exposure to pose a risk of reproductive organ abnormalities or other birth defects. Many plastic bottles and contain-ers have a recycle number on the bottom inside a triangle. The numbers 3, 6, and some with 7 (Nalgene) are considered unsafe plastics. There are mixed messages about the others.

Dioxins come into our air and onto our foods from burning of municipal waste, factory pesticide production, industrial paper production, chlorinating processes, and steel mills. They have an elimination half-life of 7 to 11 years inside humans,[16] which means that after about a decade, only half the amount of a consumed chemical remains in the body. Infants can be exposed to these during their critical development periods inside mother's womb. Dioxins also concentrate in mother's milk, and the breastfed child is exposed to these during nursing. Most formulas have the cow's milk fat removed, reducing dioxin levels, but many are stored in plastic-lined cans or packages, which would cause BPA leaching. When milk or formula is stored or warmed in plastic bottles, significant levels of BPAs can leach into the formula as well.

Dairy products contribute nearly 50% of the accumulated PCB and dioxin found in toddlers. Breastfeeding for 6 months contributes 13% to the levels accumulated in one's body by age 25.[17] (Tripling the breastfeeding time, however, increases, but does not triple, the levels attributable to breastfeeding. Typically, a child who is weaned early consumes meats and dairy fats so their continued exposure is the same or higher than from breastfeeding.) Intrauterine exposures to these environmental toxins lowers the IQ several points in those with higher exposures, while breastfeeding has shown no such correlation.[18] By reducing animal fats and eating organic, mother can reduce the amount of toxins she passes to her fetus, and later to her baby through her milk.

One More

Another reason for pregnant mothers to limit dairy is a finding that pregnant women who drink 3 or more glasses of milk a day are found to have a doubled risk of developing preeclampsia,[19] a dangerous pregnancy disorder that includes high blood pressure and risks to the mother and fetus. While these researchers did not compare whole milk intake to nonfat, they suspect milk fat may be the culprit. A more current study measured a 25% increase in eclampsia risk for every serving of milk.[20] Still another, 2008 study, reporting a decreased risk of eclampsia with higher fiber intake,[21] measured a 50% increase in eclampsia for more than 2 servings of milk per day but did not publish the finding. It is known that high levels of milk protein intake reduce one's calcium retention, and calcium is known to reduce high blood pressure. In fact, calcium supplementation (of nondairy sources) during pregnancy actually reduces blood pressure and incidence of preeclampsia.[22] I suspect that milk proteins, or hormones, which are found in the milk fat, may be part of the problem in some preeclampsia.

Dangerous Fumes for the Fetus

Cigarette smoke contains scores of toxins. The connection between maternal smoking and underweight newborns, which reduces survival rates, has been known for some time. Blood flow to the infant becomes constricted as a result of nicotine, thereby limiting nutrition. A 1997 review estimated that 46,000 cases of low birth weight and 2,800 cases of miscarriage and newborn deaths per year can be attributed to parental smoking.[23] In fact, infants of smoking mothers are born abnormally small nearly twice as often as those of non-smoking mothers.[24] Connections between maternal exposure to cigarette smoke and childhood cancers are only being proven recently.

Researchers investigated samples of cord blood that had been passed from mother to fetus in mothers who were exposed to passive cigarette smoke only. When compared to those not so exposed, they found a significant number of genetic mutations in blood cells: the type that generally are associated with blood cancers such as leukemia or lymphatic cancers.[25] It has also been discovered recently that some smoke, from mother or anyone smoking around the mother, gets to the fetus directly through the birth canal, giving him direct exposure to the carcinogens of tobacco smoke. This passage of toxins to the developing fetus carries a much higher risk for cancer than was previously thought possible.[26] While secondhand smoke from father can damage a developing fetus, smoking by the father prior to conception of an infant, even with a non-smoking mother, has been shown to more than quadruple the child's chance for leukemia or lymphatic cancer.[27] It is expected that this may be due to tobacco-induced genetic damage to the sperm.

In addition to cancer risks and reduced birth weight, significant alterations in prolactin and growth hormone have been discovered in pregnant smoking mothers. These same alterations are found in their newborns.[28] This demonstrates that cigarette exposure disturbs an infant's hormonal balance, including those for dealing with stress. This may explain another researcher's finding that most newborns will be calm and peaceful if laid upon their mother right after birth, but those born to heavily smoking mothers continue to cry and behave anxiously.[29]

Vitamin K: To Inject or Not

Newborn infants routinely receive an injection of vitamin K after birth in order to prevent (or slow) a rare problem of bleeding into the brain weeks after birth. Vitamin K promotes blood clotting. The fetus has low levels of vitamin K as well as other factors needed in clotting. The body maintains these levels very precisely.[30] Supplementation of vitamin K to the pregnant mother does not change the K status of the fetus, confirming the importance of its specific levels. Toward the end of gestation, the fetus begins developing some of the other clotting factors, developing two key factors just before term birth.[31] It has recently been shown that this tight regulation of vitamin K levels helps control the rate of rapid cell division during fetal development. Apparently, high levels of vitamin K can allow cell division to get out of hand, leading to cancer.

There are some bleeding problems that can occur within the first week after birth from the naturally low clotting ability, such as excessive bleeding of a circumcision. Though this is named "early haemorrhagic disease of the newborn" (early HDN), it's not really a disease, rather a natural state that is inconvenient when certain procedures are required. Late HDN is the real concern, more recently called vitamin K deficiency bleeding (VKDB). This problem of bleeding into the brain occurs mainly from 3 to 7 weeks after birth in just over 5 out of 100,000 births (without vitamin K injections); 90% of those cases are breastfed infants,[32] because formulas are supplemented with unnaturally high levels of vitamin K and the *E. coli* in formula-fed intestines makes vitamin K. Forty percent of affected infants suffer permanent brain damage or death. The cause of this bleeding trauma is some form of liver disorder that has not been detected until the bleeding occurs. Most cases are a blocked bile duct that will require surgical repair for the infant to survive. Bile is required for good absorption of vitamin K so infants become deficient when this duct is blocked and this deficiency allows bleeding into the brain. Infants exposed to drugs or alcohol through any means are especially at risk, and those from mothers on anti-epileptic medications are at very high risk and need special attention.

It has recently been shown that this tight regulation of vitamin K levels helps control the rate of rapid cell division during fetal development. Apparently, high levels of vitamin K can allow cell division to get out of hand, leading to cancer.

This rare but tragic bleeding into the brain has been found to be highly preventable by a large-dose injection of vitamin K at birth. *The downside of this practice, however, is an increased risk of developing childhood leukemia.* While a few studies have refuted this suggestion, several tightly controlled studies have shown this correlation to be most likely.[33,34] A 2002 review of all available studies concluded there was no significant risk[35] although every one of their calculated rates showed a small increased risk. Apparently, the cell division that continues to be quite rapid after birth continues to depend on precise amounts of vitamin K to proceed at the proper rate. Introduction of levels that are 20,000 times the newborn level, the amount usually injected, can have devastating consequences.

Nursing raises the infant's vitamin K levels very gradually after birth so that no disregulation occurs that would encourage leukemia development. Additionally, the clotting system of the healthy newborn is well planned, and healthy breastfed infants do not typically suffer bleeding complications, even without any supplementation.[36] While breastfed infants demonstrate lower blood levels of vitamin K than the "recommended" amount, they show no signs of vitamin K deficiency (leading one to wonder where the "recommended" level for infants came from). But with vitamin K injections at birth, harmful consequences of some rare disorders can often (but not always) be averted.

Infant formulas are supplemented with high levels of vitamin K, generally sufficient to prevent intracranial bleeding in the case of a liver disorder and in some other rare bleeding disorders. Although formula feeding increases overall childhood cancer rates by 80%, this is likely not related to the added vitamin K.

Extracting data from available literature reveals that there are 1.5 extra cases of leukemia per 100,000 children due to vitamin K injections, and 1.8 more permanent injuries or deaths per 100,000 due to brain bleeding without injections. Adding the risk of infection or damage from the injections, including a local skin disease called "scleroderma" that is seen rarely with K injections,[37] and even adding the low possibility of healthy survival from leukemia, the scales remain tipped toward breastfed infants receiving a prophylactic vitamin K supplementation. Injections are shown to be very painful and stressful for newborns though breastfeeding during the procedure can reduce the pain. There are possibly better options than the 1 milligram injections typically given to newborns.

Infants can receive oral doses of vitamin K after birth. The dosage that has been recommended over the last decade has been found not to be adequately preventive. Investigation of a large study group of Danish and Dutch infants with blocked or absent bile ducts has provided valuable information on what dose is optimal. The provision of 1 oral milligram per week to the infant for 4 weeks has been shown to provide as much protection as an initial injection of 2 milligrams (which is twice the injection dose used in the United States).[38] Alternatively, the nursing mother can take vitamin K supplements to increase the amount she delivers in her breastmilk.[39] (Supplementation of the pregnant mother does not alter fetal levels but supplementation of the nursing mother does increase breastmilk and infant levels.) This mode was not tested in the recent large study, but maternal supplementation of 2.5 milligrams per day, recommended by one author, provides a higher level of vitamin K through breastmilk than does formula[40] and is the highest among such recommendations. Formula provides 10 times the U.S. recommended daily allowance, and this RDA is about 2 times the level in unsupplemented human milk. If a breastfeeding mother takes this amount for 10 weeks, it is shown that she will provide a cumulative extra 2.5 milligrams to her infant over the important period. Neither mother nor infant require supplementation if the infant is injected at birth.[41]

There is no overwhelming reason to discontinue this routine prophylactic injection for breastfed infants. Providing information about alternatives to allow informed parents to refuse would be reasonable. These parents may then decide to provide some gradual supplementation, or, for an entirely healthy term infant, some choose to simply provide diligent watchfulness for any signs of jaundice (yellowing of eyes or skin) or easy bleeding. There appears to be no harm in supplementing this vitamin in a gradual manner, however, and early signs of liver disorder are often missed.

One more curious finding about childhood leukemia is that when any nation lowers its rate of infant deaths, its rate of childhood leukemia increases.[42] Vitamin K injections may be responsible for some part of this number, but other factors are surely involved, about which we can only speculate.

The Unkind Cut

Once considered a cure for maladies from diphtheria to insanity to paralysis, male circumcision is chiefly a phenomenon in the United States, practiced very rarely in Western Europe and most of the rest of the world.[43] Even among European Jews it is only considered necessary among those who are Orthodox. By the turn of the twentieth century, circumcision became a symbol of social class, of being delivered by a doctor in a hospital.

There is no medical reason for routine painful and damaging circumcision of male newborns. Many reasons are given for this surgical removal of a large, sexually sensitive portion of the male genitalia. It has been shown that circumcised male infants experience about two-thirds fewer urinary tract infections,[44] although these are generally easily treatable and without complications. These are also reduced with bathing and timely diaper changing. In fact, greater complications arise from the surgical procedure itself, up to 10%, including infections (rather common), excess scar tissue formation (leading to deformity and reduced sensitivity), granuloma (precancer) formation, frequent removal of the most sensitive fornix portion, narrowing of the urinary outlet, hemorrhage, accidental partial amputation, need for total amputation after death of penile tissues, denudation (falling off of the skin), childhood penile cancer, and rarely death.[45-53] The cruelty of the great pain imposed upon newborn males by this surgery has recently been recognized; still, less than half of all U.S. doctors use anesthesia,[54] which has some occasional complications as well. Researchers from the University of Toronto performed an experiment on a hunch about the reason male infants seemed to respond more painfully to vaccinations than females. They found that circumcised males showed significantly greater pain responses than intact males, representing, in their eyes, a memory of the pain of circumcision.[55]

It has also been argued by some that penile cancers are reduced by circumcisions. This rare disease has actually been shown to occur up to 3 times more often in intact males.[56] This disease of the elderly has a high long-term survival rate of over 70%. In Finland, a nation where circumcisions are uncommon, 1 in 1,000,000 men die of penile cancer each year.[57] Possibly more than twice the number of cancers occur in similar female genitalia,[58] with similar survival rates,[59] suggesting utility in female circumcision by the same token. Female circumcision is widely considered dangerous by those in industrialized nations, yet the chief complications of this procedure arise from uncleanly techniques, and uncleanly male circumcisions pose similar risks.[60] Incidentally, cancers of female external genitalia occur at the lowest rates by far in Asia and Africa,[61] where female circumcisions are chiefly performed. And, by the same male circumcision argument, we could point out that the much more common disease of breast cancer would likely be

incredibly high reduction of HIV transmission as well as many other sexually transmitted diseases and pregnancy. One will need responsibility and protection regardless.

The Canadian Pediatric Society, the British Medical Association, and the Australian College of Pediatrics all hold firm that routine male circumcision should not be practiced. The American Academy of Pediatrics fluctuates in its opinion from year to year, but the latest policy statement in 1999 does not recommend routine circumcision,[69] especially since the American Cancer Society stated it wished the AAP would stop promoting routine circumcision as a prevention of cancer, calling it a mistaken belief.[70] Still, circumcision is performed on 56% of males in the United States.[71] In 2008, there were moves by several British parliamentary parties to propose a ban of infant male circumcisions, as they have on females. Their opinion was that males can make the decision for themselves when they come of age.

Feeding the Premature Infant

The premature infant, as well as a term infant born too small, presents a very special and delicate case nutritionally. They are designed to be fed totally digested nutrients in mother's blood through the umbilical cord; their digestive systems are not well developed, and some may be too weak to suck. Many are given various feeds through tubes, bottles, or through needles directly into their veins, even though in other countries all but the tiniest of these infants have been successfully fed by using mother's milk exclusively.[72] When the infant is too tiny or weak for breastfeeding, mother can express her milk for spoon or cup feeding, or for tube feeding if necessary. Artificial nipple (bottle) feeding should not be used in an infant intended for breastfeeding because it has been shown to reduce the success of an infant's continued breastfeeding by nearly two-thirds (known as nipple confusion).[73] Not only does the opioid reward of food intake and sucking help to bond the infant to

The American Cancer Society stated that they wished the AAP would stop promoting routine circumcision as a prevention of cancer, calling it a mistaken belief.

the artificial nipple instead of to mother's, but the latching technique, sucking pattern, and the use of tongue and mouth muscles are very different for
bottle nipples and real nipples. The tiniest infants are generally fed intravenous sugar, fats, and protein pieces, but can take breastmilk by mouth even
on day one. At least a small amount of colostrum should be given. Although
seldom practiced in the United States, these infants should be fed on nothing but breastmilk as soon as possible, within a few weeks at most.

Nearly all kinds of infections are significantly elevated when premature
infants are fed artificial formulas instead of breastmilk, including urinary
tract infections and diarrheal diseases.[74] Among the tiniest preemies, there
are far more serious infections in those exclusively fed formula (*see Figures
8-1 and 8-2*).[75] Infections are highly challenging for preemies and many
result in death. The statistical benefits of breastmilk in these studies are

Human Milk versus Formula in Preterm Infants[76-80]		
Author and Year	**Study**	**Human Milk versus Formula**
Meinzen-Derr 2009	1272 preterm infants	Lower chance of death and NEC the more human milk given
Sisk 2007	202 preterm infants	6 times lower chance of NEC with greater than 50% human milk
Vohr 2006	1035 preterm infants	Lower chance of hospitalization Greater neurodevelopment
Ronnestad 2005	462 preterm infants	Lower chance of sepsis
McGuire 2003	4 small '80s trials	4 times lower chance of NEC
Hylander 1998	212 preterm infants	2.3 times fewer infections 2.1 times less sepsis and meningitis
Contreras-Lemus 1992	118 preterm infants	Lower chance of NEC Fewer urinary tract infections Lower chance of infectious diarrhea

Figure 8-1 Studies comparing illness rates when preterm infants are fed human milk
versus formulas.

NEC: Necrotizing enterocolitis, a serious intestinal inflammation with a 25% death rate
Sepsis: A life-threatening whole-body inflammatory response to infection

reduced by some of the various types of breastmilk used (stored, pasteurized, term or preterm milk) and the various forms of supplementation or fortification of breastmilk.

It has been found that the breakdown of fats in the diet of the preemie fed mother's milk is twice as efficient as in formula-fed, making the appropriate fat products more accessible for use.[81] Of course, other nutrients are more available in mother's milk as well. Many studies on breastfeeding preterm and low-birth-weight babies complain that the nutrients in breastmilk are lower than in chemically derived milks, and breastfed preemies usually gain weight more slowly during their stay in the hospital. However, follow-up studies to age 2 or 3 show there is no difference in the size between naturally or artificially fed babies.[82] Additionally, studies suggest the breastfed preemie's growth rate is similar to that inside the uterus.[83] In fact, the bone mineral content is greater in childhood follow-ups in direct proportion to the amount of human milk received.[84] The growth of head circumference, an indicator of brain development, is not lower during premature hospitalization in infants fed human milk, even when the breastfed infant weighs less.[85] Preterm infants who are fed breastmilk grow up with higher intelligence scores, and other neurological development parameters are better as well (*these are discussed in Chapter 5*). Also remember that permanent long-term immune development is superior in those who receive breastmilk. *Breastmilk-fed preterm and low-weight infants have higher survival rates, lower illness rates, stronger bones (eventually), greater intelligence, and superior neurological development; hence, weight gain comparisons are not highly relevant.*

> *Breastmilk-fed preterm and low-weight infants have higher survival rates, lower illness rates, stronger bones (eventually), greater intelligence, and superior neurological development; hence, weight gain comparisons are not highly relevant.*

A big difference in the health of tiny hospitalized infants can be induced by caring for them via kangaroo care and other nurturing measures, as presented earlier. Oxygenation, temperature control, and respiration are all superior when these infants are directly breastfed. Additionally, they have fewer sucking and swallowing problems, they tolerate their oral feedings earlier, and their breastmilk feedings are greater when received directly at the breast or in another nurturing manner. When these measures are added, weight gain is faster than for those in standard care. Thus, although a small infant fed breastmilk through a tube will have a higher chance of healthy survival than one fed formula by tube, any infant who is fed directly at the breast or who is otherwise fed breastmilk with warm body contact and affectionate care will have the best chance for success.

Unfortunately, kangaroo care and exclusive breastfeeding are almost seldom seen in U.S. neonatal intensive care units (NICU). Breastfeeding at any level is not always encouraged, and sometimes not even allowed. I heard of a mother who was laughed out of the NICU when carrying in 1 or 2 tiny ounces of her first colostrum, which is actually liquid gold. I must reiterate that infant mortality rates (up to age 1 year) in the United States are higher than in 45 other industrialized and developing nations who record and report statistics.[86] The restricted availability of premature feeding formulas and supplies, incubators, and other equipment in less affluent nations cause premature infants to be more often held and breastfed—hence, they more often survive. Additionally, it has been shown that early discharge of low-weight infants (at 4 pounds or less) leads to faster weight increases as well as longer breastfeeding with no decline in health or survival rates.[87] In the Philippines, where an infant born at home will generally stay at home regardless of birth weight, low-birth-weight infants were breastfed far longer when born at home than when born in hospitals.[88]

Mothers of underdeveloped infants need to be proactive in order to improve the outcome for their children. Mother has to be as close as possible to her preemie from the very start to encourage her milk development. Just hearing the infant cry will help to promote milk production.[89] When some kind of breastfeeding attempt is made within the first 6 hours after birth, prolactin levels are much higher than when the first attempts are 3 days later.[90] Mother needs to take measures to maintain elevated prolactin levels. If breastfeeding attempts are infrequent or weak, the possibilities include kangaroo care, maintaining nearness to the infant, hearing and responding emotionally to baby's cries, having the infant attempt to suck or at least

Comparing Mother's Own Milk, Donor Milk, and Formula in Preterm Infants

Author and Year	Study	Mother's Own Milk	Donor Milk	Formula
Boyd 2007	7 trials reviewed		Lower chance of NEC than with formula	Faster growth
Quigley 2007	8 trials reviewed		2.5 times lower chance of NEC than with formula	Faster growth
Schanler 2005	234 preterm infants	Lower chance of sepsis Lower chance of NEC Fewer cultured organisms in blood Shorter hospital stay	No benefit over formula	Faster growth

Figure 8-2 Studies comparing illness rates when preterm infants are fed their mother's own milk, donor milk, or cow's milk-derived formulas.[91-93]

NEC: Necrotizing enterocolitis, a serious intestinal inflammation with a 25% death rate
Sepsis: A life-threatening whole-body inflammatory response to infection

nuzzle, and regularly attempting to manually express or pump milk (which is beneficial even though only drops may come the first days). Every time the infant receives food other than mother's milk, mother's milk production is impaired. Thus, she should express milk each time such a feeding occurs.

As mentioned before, many kinds of breastmilk are fed to low-weight infants. Pooled donor milk, which is a collection of stored milk from multiple donor mothers, can be of two types: from mothers of term infants, or from mothers of premature infants. Mother's milk after premature birth is much higher in many nutrients and studies show superior growth and head circumference in low-weight infants fed milk from preterm baby mothers.[94] Important fat absorption is greater when pooled milk is not sterilized,[95] and antibiotic power is reduced by pasteurization. Growth is shown to be even better when mother's own milk is used, rather than donor milk,[96] likely because it is fresher and unprocessed, naturally customized to the maturity of the infant, and because mother's exposure to the infant allows her to create customized antibodies in response to the microbes in the infant's body and environment.

Researchers have just discovered (to their admitted surprise) that when preemies are being bottle-fed or spoon-fed, these infants, when allowed, quickly become able to self-regulate their caloric intake when fed in response to hunger and to satisfaction.[97] As suggested in earlier chapters, there are many advantages to on-cue feeding, especially less frustration and better digestion. In all likelihood baby knows best, yet scheduled feeding of prescribed doses continues to be the norm in hospitals, likely because they are easier to monitor in this kind of setting.

Fortify Mother's Milk?

Attempts to fortify human milk for preemies are very common. Calcium and phosphorous are often added in an attempt to improve early bone mineralization.[98] Protein is added in an attempt to increase growth rate. Other vitamins and minerals are often added as well. It all sounds great, but there are many problems associated with fortification.

One study analyzed the feeding of a high-protein formula that contained 3 times the protein of human milk, comparing this feed to mother's milk in low-weight babies.[99] The growth rates were similar, but the high-protein infants had high levels of toxins from protein breakdown in their blood (urea and creatinine). Additionally, two amino acids (components of protein), phenylalanine and tyrosine, were found to be too high in the formula-fed infants' blood. In excessive amounts, these hinder nervous system development. Another study reviewed protein utilization in a formula with extra cow's milk protein added, compared with human milk with extra human milk protein added.[100] The human protein fortified infants gained more weight and had better protein balance. A more recent examination of non-human protein enrichment of mother's milk found more severe illnesses and a reduced duration of "full" breastfeeding while a greater duration of full breastfeeding was associated with better growth scores.[101]

Most breastmilk fortification contains cow's milk proteins. These are not desirable with breastmilk or in preemie formulas (although they are in nearly all formulas). A few of the problems with these dairy proteins are the high incidence of bovine protein intolerance associated with intestinal inflammation, bleeding, and diarrhea; the slow breakdown of these large proteins in the tiny system, preventing additional formula feedings as early as they are needed for proper caloric intake; and the increased risk of developing childhood diabetes—the risk being greater the earlier cow's milk proteins are introduced (*all of these topics are addressed elsewhere in this book*).

It has been shown that breastmilk fortified with any cow's milk products, which includes nearly any preemie or infant formula or milk fortification powder, reduces the immune protective properties of mother's milk. A higher rate of infection is seen in infants fed fortified breastmilk versus those fed only human milk,[102,103] though more studies are needed using exclusive mother's milk versus fortified milk. Studies in the previous and following charts are from industrialized nations. Some fortification studies in countries with poorer nutrition show benefits to fortification. The immune protection from mother can be reduced by fortification in part because *E. coli* bacterial growth in the intestine increases, which mother's milk alone hinders. This bacterial flora sets the stage for many diarrheal illnesses. Non-iron-containing soy-derived products do not promote *E. coli* and lead to a lesser increase in infection overall; however, soy can also cause allergic intolerance.

Various researchers are interested in supplementing elements such as sodium, phosphorous, calcium, and vitamins to the breastfed preemie. These can all be provided without dairy products or iron. Iron supplements will feed *E. coli* and other challenging bacteria, blocking much of breastmilk's infection protection, and is not needed in most cases. Vitamins shouldn't be harmful in low quantities according to the research to date, and vitamin D may enhance bone building when neither mother nor infant is obtaining much sun exposure.

In a German study, half of the preterm infants receiving medium or high levels of calcium supplementation were found to have dangerous calcification in their kidneys, and many suffered abdominal distension as well.[104] We have already seen that breastfed preemies eventually show very good bone mineralization with no supplementation. Another study suggests that bone mineralization in breastfed preemies is as high as in formula-fed preemies by just a few months after birth,[105] but the concern continues about the light bone mineral content early on for breastfed low-birth-weight infants. While it seems a little backward to use formula-fed infants as the gold standard, comparisons to intrauterine growth are used as well. Breastfed preemies' bones may lag behind formula-fed preemies in this arena. While a very low level of calcium and phosphorous supplementation

> *A higher rate of infection is seen in infants fed fortified breastmilk versus those fed only human milk.*

Comparing Human Milk plus Cow's Milk-Derived Fortifier versus Human Milk Alone or versus Formula in Preterm Infants[106–109]

Author and Year	Study	Fortified Human Milk versus Human Milk Alone	Fortified Mother's Milk versus Formula
Funkquist 2006	52 preterm infants	Longer hospital stay	
Mead-Johnson 2004	181 preterm infants	Same sepsis or NEC than typically reported for human milk alone (formula company study)	
Schanler 1999	108 preterm infants		Lower chance of NEC and lower chance of sepsis than with formula
Lucas 1996	275 preterm infants	More infections than with mother's milk alone	

Figure 8-3 Studies comparing illness rates when preterm infants are fed human milk plus cow's milk-derived fortifiers (called human milk fortifiers) versus human milk alone or versus formulas.

NEC: Necrotizing enterocolitis, a serious intestinal inflammation with a 25% death rate

Sepsis: A life-threatening whole-body inflammatory response to infection

to the breastfed preemie does not appear harmful, the latest review of studies is unable to confirm an advantage.[110] There are some indications that added vitamin D may help these to be absorbed. If protein fortification is desired, it should come from a human or possibly soy source. Much more research is needed in this area. Vitamin fortifications appear to have little downside, as opposed to minerals, proteins, or other components.

IV Feeding of Preemies

Parents should know about a potential, but preventable danger to the tiny newborn who is receiving nutrition parenterally, that is, not by mouth but directly into the bloodstream. This feeding is known as TPN for "total parenteral nutrition." It seems that vitamin E, which is typically a beneficial antioxidant, can actually become a harmful oxidant, a pro-oxidant, when exposed to light, especially phototherapy lights, throughout the day.[111] This causes the fats in the parenteral formula to quickly become rancid. This infusion into the bloodstream of rancid fats, which are toxic and can even be cancer causing, may add to the many difficulties encountered in these tiny infants. This oxidization can be prevented by covering the liquid with aluminum foil or by adding vitamin C to the solution at time of use, although this is not always practiced.

TPN solutions can be lifesaving when they are truly needed, but these formulas are far from perfect nutrition and are not yet truly safe. Liver damage is very common in tiny infants receiving TPN.[112] Although this damage is generally reversible in adults, it can be more permanent in infants and can lead to lifelong illness or early death.[113] A recent study has found that the addition of fish oils to the TPN solution can reverse TPN-caused liver damage in children,[114] and one would assume it could also help prevent it. This procedure is not yet in practice. Finally, this liquid sits for long periods in plastic bags and tubing, allowing dangerous leaching of DEHP into the IV fluid as most of these bags and tubes are PVC plastics.

Oral feeding of breastmilk is tolerated much sooner than formula by mouth.[115] Moreover, early introduction of formula increases the chance an

Tests on Milk Samples[116-118]

Author and Year	Study	Human Milk	Human Milk plus Cow's Milk-Derived Fortifier
Chan 2007	10 human milk samples	Strong antimicrobial activity with human milk alone and with human milk-derived fortifier	Blocked antimicrobial activity
Ovali 2006	28 human milk samples	Strong antimicrobial activity	Low iron fortifier does not change effect but addition of iron lowers antimicrobial activity
Quan 1994	22 human milk samples	Strong antimicrobial activity	Lower antimicrobial activity

Figure 8-4

infant will develop life-threatening necrotizing enterocolitis.[119] This condition is rarely seen in infants receiving no formula by mouth even if they received parenteral nutrition. Human milk proteins and lipids are more easily absorbed than formula components, and human milk speeds the maturation of the digestive system. Hence, feeding of breastmilk by mouth to the infant who is on intravenous feeding will reduce the total amount of parenteral solution needed, reducing the possible negative consequences.

Robbing Antioxidants

Oxygen therapy, direct or through an incubator, causes many harmful oxidizing reactions in infants.[120] This creates toxicity and predisposes them to cancer. Furthermore, this oxidation uses up the infant's supply of antioxidants, including selenium and vitamin E. Low levels of selenium and vitamin E predispose an infant to more infections. Supplementing these elements as well as vitamins A and C may help to reduce this, but the infant's ability to absorb these is limited. When these supplements are added to mother's milk, they are absorbed more readily than with formula. In addition, kangaroo care can provide superior oxygenation, reducing the need for artificial oxygen supplementation.

Regardless of oxygen therapy, parenteral nutrition preemies develop very low selenium levels within weeks.[121] Selenium levels decline in formula-fed infants as well. This decline is likely due to oxidative breakdown in these feeds as well as other stresses caused by the feeds and feeding methods. Supplementation does not adequately compensate. On the other hand, those fed mainly breastmilk maintain healthy selenium levels (except with the highest levels of oxygen therapy).

Feeding the Term Infant

The newborn should feed at mother's breast within the first hour after birth. Those who feed early and stay close to their mothers in the hospital have a doubled chance of continuing to breastfeed exclusively.[122] Spinal anesthesia (which keeps mother awake) for cesarean birth aids early initiation of breastfeeding. Breastfeeding in the first weeks, and especially in the first hour, also helps to contract mother's uterus to expel the placenta and allow the uterus to return to normal size (due to oxytocin release). When the newborn is given sugar water during the first days, as continues to be common practice in some hospitals, breastfeeding for mother and infant is disrupted. As a result, the infant will be less likely to receive exclusive breastfeeding afterward and statistically will lose her breastfeeding opportunities entirely at a younger age. Infants who do not receive sugar water do not display hypoglycemic (low sugar) symptoms,[123] which reveals that there is little justification for this practice. The rare very low sugar newborn is thought to result at times from living long hours inside a mother who has been prevented from eating during an extended labor and delivery.

Breastmilk Jaundice?

Jaundice, a slight yellow coloration to the eyes and skin, develops in the first days and weeks after birth in about 15% of babies; mostly breastfed babies, leading to the unfortunate term, "breastmilk jaundice." This symptom results from higher than normal levels of bilirubin in the blood. Bilirubin is a product of red blood cell breakdown. Babies are born with more red blood cells than they will keep. These help provide extra iron stores. Because excessively high levels of bilirubin are known to cause brain damage (higher than the levels most often seen in jaundiced newborns), doctors have long been heavy-handed in treating this common occurrence. The problem is that their interventions jeopardize optimal breastfeeding—the one best treatment for jaundice and prevention of serious consequences.

One "treatment" doctors use is the provision of formula bottles for a day or two. Because of its unabsorbable fats and other excess ingredients, formula causes greater amounts of stool loss. This speeds up the elimination of bilirubin through the stools. Of course, the free iron in formula allows challenging bacteria to develop in the newborn's intestinal environment, getting baby off to an unhealthy start. This unhealthy bacteria also breaks down bilirubin well. Exclusively breastmilk-fed flora allows the body to re-uptake some of the bilirubin, keeping blood levels higher. But, formula feeding at this point greatly jeopardizes the successful establishment of full breastfeeding. Typical poor breastfeeding advice given to new mothers, of scheduled feedings every 3 to 4 hours, slows initial stooling and increases the number of babies showing jaundice to begin with.

Another treatment for jaundice is phototherapy, where the infant is placed in an incubator under special blue phototherapy lights. Blue light causes the skin to rapidly breakdown bilirubin. However, a baby in a plastic bassinet is not snuggled up next to mother establishing breastfeeding, creating bonding hormones, and keeping stress hormones low. A third treatment effort for less prominent jaundice is giving bottles of sugar water. This too reduces the amount of breastmilk received and slows the establishment of a good milk supply. This practice has been shown to often make jaundice worse. A few babies are given drugs to lower bilirubin.

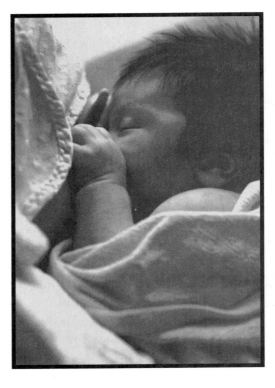

It doesn't make sense that around 15% of naturally fed babies would develop some kind of harmful condition that requires artificial baby milk, unhealthy flora establishment, and separation from mother. Well, it turns out that bilirubin is about the strongest antioxidant available to the human body and no harm has been shown from these commonly high bilirubin levels when not extreme. Rare, exceptionally high levels typically signal some kind of liver disorder, or very poor feeding, and do need immediate attention.

While this beneficial potential of bilirubin was reported as early as 1987,[124] and reiterated by other scientists over the next decades, this information has been ignored medically. Commonly elevated bilirubin is known not to be harmful and the science shows that it's actually very protective. Bilirubin has been shown to prevent retinopathy of prematurity,[125] a common overgrowth of blood vessels in the eyes of preemies that threatens vision. Premature infants are exposed to many threatening oxidation exposures and the anti-oxidation from bilirubin could be very health protecting. It's also been shown to be neuroprotective, preventing brain damage.[126] This strong antioxidant can offer many immune-providing benefits as well.

By design, there is little breastmilk available to just-born infants. The breasts provide colostrum in the first days after birth with powerful immune protective, digestion maturing, and stool clearing factors. New mothers should have baby at breast at least every 2 hours to provide regular amounts of colostrum, get the stools moving, and program the breasts to create milk. With this proper stimulus, full milk usually comes in within 2 to 4 days. In the absence of a liver disorder, good feeding should keep jaundice appearance low or absent.

When a baby does exhibit much jaundice, watchful monitoring of bilirubin is all that should be needed medically. Blood does not need to be drawn often as there is a mechanism available to measure bilirubin right through the skin. Slightly brown urine may signify a problem. (Salmon-colored urine is a common finding that might signal a little dehydration.) A consult with a non-hospital-associated lactation specialist can assure that the infant has a good latch and that feeding is going well. Jaundiced babies (and those medicated during birth) may be extra sleepy and need to be awakened to nurse. If doctors want bilirubin levels to be lowered more quickly, there's a wonderful natural resource that's often available, the sun. It can be summer or winter as blue light is part of sunlight year-round. Of course, sunburn in the peak of summer and chilling in the cold of winter provide challenges, but actually, blue light goes right through the window (all the colors combine to create the white light we see coming in the window), while very little UV light does. One can warm up the room, strip down the baby, and nurse in a sunny window. For more extreme needs, there is a phototherapy blanket that can be used at home while the infant snuggles and nurses. It works as well as the phototherapy in the hospital.

A Kinder, Gentler Relationship

Rooming in with mother is where the newborn belongs, if at all possible. If not, the parents can room in with the baby as often as possible. This way the infant's protective natural flora develop more quickly, breastfeeding becomes more successful, and establishing an early connection between mother and infant generally leads to a longer duration of healthy practices overall. Reducing medical procedures applied to the delicate newborn, increasing intimacy, reducing noise, and providing natural feeding lead to more survivals as well as to healthier, less-stressed babies. The birth of a child should not be viewed as a medical procedure, but as the beginning of a family. The parents and the dynamics of the family unit will benefit from promoting togetherness from the start.

9

Baby's Nutritional Beginnings

WE CAN BE IMMENSELY GRATEFUL THAT RESEARCH HAS DEVELOPED AN
artificial substitute for mother's milk that can keep most infants alive when
mother's milk is unavailable for some reason. Although wet-nursing was
likely commonplace for millennia, feeding with the milk of mother goats,
cows, and other animals has largely usurped this practice in recent centuries.
The younger the infant, the lower the chance of survival on these animal
milks, with few likely to survive if this substitute is implemented exclusively
at birth. Today's infant formulas generally begin with cow's milk, but an
enormous amount of processing, extracting, and supplementing is done to
make it adequate for consumption by infants.

Many like to point out that formulas have higher levels of many
nutrients than mother's milk, thereby implying that natural human milk is

deficient by comparison. But it is the poor digestion, absorption, and availability of nutrients in formula that necessitate these higher levels—and nutrients are still deficient in formula feeds. A more important distinction is the large array of immune factors, enzymes, hormones, and growth factors found in breastmilk, which are not available in formulas. Because the interplay between all the elements within any food is extremely delicate, attempts to provide the correct balance of many factors in formula usually fall short.

It is known that in the absence of interventions in the natural birth process, when birth mothers are given ample assistance, around 99% of those who so desire can breastfeed their infants. Yet, as a result of an extremely successful worldwide marketing campaign, this does not happen. In fact, by only 3 months of age, fewer than 30% of U.S. babies receive any breastmilk at all. Sometimes the choice is not so much whether or not to breastfeed, but whether and when to supplement with formula, when to provide solid foods, or how soon to wean from the breast. A good understanding of the nutritional dynamics of both formula and breastmilk should help parents make the decisions best for their family situation.

Fat Intake and Fat-Soluble Vitamins

Milk fat is removed from cow's milk as it's being adapted for infant feeds. This is just as well since fat contains the most residue from pesticides, drugs, and other contaminants. Unfortunately, fat-soluble vitamins, A, D, E, and K are removed along with it. There is an inadequate supply of these fat-soluble vitamins in cow's milk for formula anyway, so they are added as supplements. Only one form of each of these vitamins is added back, even though we now know that there are at least 4 kinds of vitamin E and 5 kinds of vitamin A, all having slightly different benefits, and all found in mother's milk.

It has been customary to use the least expensive oils in place of the milk fat, but the balance of fatty acids is getting more attention today. Still, the ratios of the various kinds of fats in formula are very different from those in human milk. Each formula is very different from the others as well, depending on the combination of fats chosen. One commonly used oil of concern is palm oil. The palmitic acid in this oil is largely unusable—very different from the palmitic acid beneficially found in breastmilk. Palm oil fat combines with available calcium to form soaps that are passed in the stool. Thus, both fat absorption and calcium absorption by the infant are decreased when this palm oil is present.[1]

Human milk has a broader spectrum of monounsaturated and polyunsaturated fats and mono-, di-, and triglycerides than butter fat or any of the oil combinations used in formulas. Possibly the most important of these are the omega-3 fatty acids, which are considered heart protective. One of these still often missing in formulas is DHA, recently found to be very important in brain development. Even more recently it has been decided that other fats missing in formulas are important as well. DHA and the omega-6 fatty acid ARA are being added to more expensive formulas to levels matching average American breastmilk levels. Study results are mixed as to whether they allow for brain development closer to that of breastfed infants or not. EPA is another important omega-3 fatty acid that is not yet being added to formulas. Average Western breastmilk levels of these fatty acids are not optimal either. Studies have been performed with nursing mothers attaining up to 6 grams per day (and 1 to 4 grams in most studies) of DHA and EPA combined, with measurably greater brain developmental results the greater the amount consumed. Pregnant and lactating mothers not eating oily fish regularly should supplement their diets with 2 or more grams per day of combined DHA and EPA from marine sources. Vegetable sources of omega-3s provide only precursors (ALA) and are not consistently converted to important DHA and EPA and do not lead to the most optimal levels being provided for the baby. Vegan algae sources of DHA and EPA are now available.

Many difficult-to-use fatty acids contained in infant formulas bind with the formula's calcium, forming soaps and making the stools hard.

As mentioned previously, attempts to more closely match the ratios of fats, especially fatty acids, to those in human milk have not led to successful absorption of the correct ratios by the infant. It is assumed that an infant can manufacture the non-essential fatty acids, but with formula feeding this ability relies on an ample supply of the essential fatty acids, linoleic, linolenic, and arachidonic, as well as other nutrients such as the vitamin E needed to alter them. It appears that this manufacture of fatty acids by the formula-fed infant does not occur to the optimal extent. Additionally, many fats in human milk considered non-essential confer many special benefits. Their variety and ratios appear to aid absorption of other nutrients. On the other hand, the poor digestibility and improper ratios of fatty acids in formulas cause competition that decreases their utilization by the body. Debate continues among researchers about which fats and what ratios of these should be in formulas.

Since there is no longer animal fat in most formulas, there is little to no cholesterol. (Small amounts remain in the nonfat milk.) In ample supply in mother's milk, cholesterol is an important building block for many hormones. The level of cholesterol in the mother's diet does not impact the cholesterol level in her milk, indicating that the body maintains a close watch over the level of this ingredient supplied to the baby. It is likely that a formula-fed infant without liver impairment is able to manufacture at least his minimum requirement of cholesterol, however.

Even from mothers with average diets, breastfed infants have higher levels of long-chain fatty acids in their blood and tissues, including DHA. Their muscles have higher percentages of them as well. The impact on muscles is not well known, but researchers have found that children who incorporate these lipids in their early muscle development maintain lower blood-sugar levels and may be less prone to developing diseases such as diabetes.[2]

Calcium

Many difficult-to-use fatty acids contained in infant formulas bind with the formula's calcium, forming soaps and making the stools hard.[3] Because this reduces the amount of calcium available, formulas need to have extra calcium. Manufacturers need to be careful how much they allow, however, as calcium can compete with iron for absorption, and iron absorption is already a problem. Breastfed infants have ample calcium. Beyond any preterm period, children have the same bone mineral compositions whether they were breast- or formula-fed.

Adequate Iron

Iron deficiency is a potential problem in formula-fed infants. The chief causes are the frequently seen intestinal bleeding caused by cow's milk formulas,[4] and the very poor absorption of iron from infant formulas, despite high levels of this mineral being added to these formulas. Feeding whole cow's milk instead of formula before many other high iron foods are in an infant's diet leads to the worst iron deficiency of any diet. Cautions against this practice are common but not always heeded. The pale appearance of anemia is not observable until iron deficiency is rather pronounced. The earlier signs of irritability, weight loss, and poor appetite are difficult to recognize. In addition to low energy and slow growth, the chief concerns associated with iron deficiency anemia in infants are reduced neurological development of mental and motor capacities,[5] and increased incidence of mild and moderate mental retardation.[6] The proteins from both cow's milk and formula bind quickly with iron and most iron (96%) is passed unused into the diaper.[7] Soy protein also inhibits iron absorption.

When an infant is formula-fed, his stores of iron received from mother prior to birth help maintain adequate iron until 4 to 6 months of age. After this time, those not receiving high-iron cereals or other iron-containing solid foods are at risk of anemia. Those receiving cow's milk as part of their diets more often become anemic. In fact, research suggests the milk in a non-breastfed infant's diet should be formula rather than cow's milk for at least 18 months. Higher mental and motor functioning has been found in inner city infants fed this way; moreover, 2% of these infants were anemic compared to 33% of those consuming cow's milk.[8]

As stated, most infant formulas are supplemented with very high levels of iron compared to the level in mother's milk. This is to compensate for blood loss and poor absorption. Although iron supplementation definitely reduces anemia in formula-fed infants, there are downsides to this supplementation as well. The more iron an infant receives in his formula, the higher the level and the greater the variety of potential illness-causing bacteria in his intestines.[9] Also, the more iron there is in infant formula, the harder the infant's stools are, sometimes leading to constipation and to local blood loss where this hard stool passes. Low-iron infant formulas were chiefly introduced because of perceptions that high iron sometimes causes infectious diarrhea. Higher levels of undesirable bacteria suggest that these infants should be more susceptible to infectious diarrhea, and a small difference has been found, but it is very slight compared to the high diarrhea rates from formula feeding in general, as compared to exclusive breastmilk feeding. Iron in great excess can potentially become an oxidizing agent as well, which increases susceptibility to cancer. Also, the more iron supplemented, the lower the infant's absorption of copper and selenium[10] and possibly other trace minerals.

The so-called low-iron formulas on shelves in the United States are still supplemented with iron. In fact, the levels of iron in some of these (Similac: .7 milligrams per 100 calories, which is equivalent to .14 milligrams/ounce) are comparable to levels found to be quite acceptable as standard iron levels in formula in other countries,[11] while others are lower (such as Wyeth). There is a very delicate balance to be sought to achieve optimal iron supplementation in infant formulas. European iron-fortified formulas contain half the iron of those in the United States. Infants drinking iron-fortified formulas in the United States take in (but do not absorb) nearly 100 times more iron each day than breastfed infants do. Some suggest an iron level between our high-iron and low-iron formulas may be the best choice.[12] University of California, Davis researchers suggest that .6 milligrams per 100 calories is ample.[13]

> Iron deficiency is a potential problem in formula-fed infants. The chief causes are the frequently seen intestinal bleeding caused by cow's milk formulas, and the very poor absorption of iron from infant formulas.

Mother's milk contains lactoferrin, which carries iron directly into the infant's system, providing a very high percentage of absorption. Efforts to supplement formulas with lactoferrin concentrated from cow's milk found higher iron absorption in infants only occurred after a few months. Since iron-fortified solid foods can be started soon after that, it has been decided that it is not worth the cost to add this ingredient to formulas.

Children who are exclusively breastfed for long periods sometimes demonstrate little or no extra iron *storage* on blood testing (ferritin), allowing formula promoters to label them iron deficient even though they are robust and do not display iron-deficiency anemia (low hemoglobin).[14,15] In fact, breastfed babies' chief blood iron indicators are more often than not superior to formula-fed infants' (red blood cells have very good iron levels). Nonetheless, doctors often insist on providing these infants with iron supplements because of low stores. When a breastfed infant is supplemented with iron, this binds up the remaining lactoferrin and prevents it from performing its other chief duty—providing immune protection. When a nursing mother is given high iron supplements, the level of iron in her milk does not change,[16] indicating that the body tries to precisely control iron levels for optimum infant health.

Just as formula-fed infants develop more undesirable intestinal flora with increasing doses of iron in their formula, when a breastfed infant is given iron supplementation or iron-supplemented formula, he develops more dangerous fecal flora as well. The Centers for Disease Control found that breastfed infants receiving higher-iron-fortified formula supplements developed diarrhea 6% more often than those receiving low-iron formula, who develop it much more often than those receiving no supplemental formula.[17] Why supplement for iron, however, when those feeding exclusively on mother's milk to even 9 months of age do not demonstrate anemia?[18]

Some infants receiving mother's milk as well as formula become more iron-deficient than those fed exclusively on either. Adding formula or baby food to a breastfed infant's diet significantly decreases the absorption of iron from mother's milk.[19] While the formula prevents mother's iron from being absorbed, and its own iron is poorly absorbed, it also may introduce some bleeding that reduces iron stores. Researchers from Iowa tried providing iron supplements to breastfed infants from 1 month of age to 6 months, allowing solid foods at 4 months, and found no increase in iron status,[20] suggesting that mother's plan is a determined, well-designed mechanism. These same authors reviewed a number of other studies and summarized that anemia occurs in about 3% of unsupplemented breastfed infants in the first 6 months after birth. It is found that while iron status cannot be increased with supplements when infants are not actually anemic, iron supplementation does work for those who are anemic. A 2008 Canadian study confirms the common finding that exclusively breastfed infants have many fewer intestinal infections than those receiving formula supplements or full formula feeding;[21] one of the important reasons not to supplement unnecessarily. This study also confirms that exclusive breastfeeding may lead to lower iron stores, but not to iron deficiency anemia. Another study of breastfed infants of various ages who began receiving foods not fortified with iron (and no cow's milk) showed that the longer the infants were exclusively breastfed, the better their iron status was. Forty-three percent of these infants whose exclusive breastfeeding lasted less than half a year became anemic, while none whose breastfeeding was exclusive for 7 months showed anemia at either 7, 12, or 24 months.[22] *The longer the exclusive breastfeeding, the less chance for developing anemia* (as studied up through 9 months).

Once one decides to be committed to solid foods, beyond tests and tastes, plenty of high-iron foods should probably be used in the first few months. Those supplementing breastmilk with formula feeds may want to introduce iron-fortified cereal between 4 and 6 months.

These breastfed iron guidelines pertain chiefly to term children of well-nourished mothers. Some studies suggest that breastfed infants of anemic mothers experience more anemia and other studies do not. It appears that the main component involved is mother's full nutritional status. Among other nutrients, vitamins A, B12, and C, and folic acid, are important for iron absorption. Mothers who are poorly nourished overall will have milk that does not provide optimal nutrition, and their children will likely have been born with lower nutrient stores to begin with.

There are other risk factors for anemia besides those already mentioned. One factor associated with reduced iron stores in both breastmilk and formula-fed infants is rapid clamping of the cord at birth. When this standard procedure occurs, baby does not receive her fully intended dose of iron-rich blood. Prematurely born infants have not had a full opportunity to develop iron reserves and may not be absorbing iron well in their first weeks after birth, providing them with less cushioning against any extra iron demands. Any surgical procedure or bleeding disorder will place extra demands on iron stores. Additionally, heavy use of reflux medication reduces iron absorption as does chronic diarrhea.

When at least one element of either poor diet, early introduction of formula supplements or solid foods, intestinal bleeding reaction to dairy in breastfeeding mother's diet or to milk formula, antacid usage, diarrhea, or intervention in the natural birth process exists in the vast majority of mother-infant pairs around the world, standard recommendations of starting children on high-iron foods at 6 months make sense; possibly a little earlier for those receiving formula. When a mother is working to optimize her own nutritional status and that of her infant, and other factors are favorable, delaying solids beyond 6 months for a child that is not overly eager, makes more sense. Because there are dangers associated with anemia as well as negative side effects of unneeded iron supplementation (including iron-fortified cereal), measuring infant iron status at some point between 6 and 9 months may be a good option in many situations.

Zinc and Selenium Concerns

Although infant formulas are supplemented with triple the amount of zinc found in human milk, formula-fed infants have blood zinc levels that are half the

> *The longer the infants were exclusively breastfed, the better their iron status was.*

level found in breastfed infants, when measured at 3 months of age.[23] One cause for poor zinc absorption in formula-fed infants is the high levels of competing iron in formulas. Women who consume double the recommended level of iron during pregnancy and lactation have significantly lower zinc levels in their milk, due to this same competition.[24] Balanced nutrients are just as important as ample nutrients.

Only as recently as 1980 did formula companies decide that some formula-fed infants were not obtaining enough zinc, leading to supplementation of this mineral. Then, it wasn't until about 1990 that researchers suggested some formulas needed more selenium, a mineral that was highly variable in formula. Selenium levels vary in human milks also, depending on mother's intake, and can be low when mother lives in a region with low selenium soils (although more foods come from distant regions today) or selects a selenium-poor diet. Zinc is important for good vision and fighting infection. Selenium is important for blood vessel integrity and immunity, and it is an antioxidant.

Fluoride, Teeth, and Bones

Fluoride, like selenium, is a trace element that varies in its availability in the soil and water in different areas of the world. Dental researchers have found that higher levels of fluoride slightly reduce the incidence of cavities in children's baby teeth. For this reason, many public water systems around the country and around the world have added fluoride to the drinking water in an attempt to reduce dental caries. Fluoride is added to most toothpaste and is applied in some dental treatments as well. Believing breastmilk to be low in fluoride, many pediatricians and dentists are recommending fluoride supplements to breastfed babies. However, since the installation of water fluoridation and other measures beginning around 1950, the results of excess fluoride have revealed themselves.

Today, fluoridation is all around us, in 50% of U.S. drinking water, in 50% of bottled drinks, and it gets into cow's milk and soy and thus infant formulas. Although human milk appears unaffected by the amount of fluoride ingested, concentrations of fluoride in cow's milk can be 20 to 70 times the level found in breastmilk, depending on the level of fluoride contamination from fertilizers and pesticides a cow is exposed to.[25] This fluoride is concentrated in the milk for formulas as a result of dehydration, and then more is added with the water used for rehydration. Now nearly a quarter of all our children are showing some signs of excess fluoride, or fluorosis.[26,27] An early sign is altered formation and discoloration of teeth, or little white spots on teeth. Fluorosis is marked in 5% of these children and very notable in some of those.

It is becoming increasingly apparent that high fluoride levels damage bones.[28] In Morocco, a nation with rich fluoride levels in its soil and water, fluorosis is common. Skeletal defects, such as knock knees and joint pains and teeth abnormalities are commonly seen.[29] This damage can include a wearing down of the teeth, as well as deviation of teeth and eventually cavities.

Moderate fluorosis, seen in some heavy drinkers of fluoridated water, juice, or soda, is associated with mild teeth and bone malformations, possible nervous system alterations, osteoporosis, and eventually kyphosis, a humped upper back. Gastrointestinal pain and damage can occur with established fluorosis as well.[30] Severe fluorosis leads to misshapen major bones and other bony defects, along with neurological problems. Development of severe fluorosis is not likely except in children who especially like to swallow toothpaste and have other high fluoride sources as well.

Excess fluoride, at the level considered beneficial to teeth, causes detrimental changes in the mineralization of bones.[31] Fluoride replaces magnesium in bones, making them harder. This hardness is partly desirable in teeth, giving them extra defense against destructive cavity-causing bacteria. But excess fluoride combines with available calcium, and they leave the body together, leaving less calcium for bone strength and density. Thus, bones become hard in the sense of brittle, and at the same time there is deficient bone calcium (osteoporosis), which leads to easy fractures.

The latest studies suggest the benefit to children's teeth from ingested fluoride (water or supplements) is very small.[32] The greatest benefits seem to result from situations when fluoride comes into direct contact with teeth, suggesting that using a small amount of fluoridated toothpaste, without swallowing any, would be the best choice for cavity reduction.

Fluoride supplementation for children is strongly associated with increased risk of fluorosis.[33] *Beyond supplementation, the major risk factors for fluorosis are formula feeding, weaning before 9 months of age, and swallowing toothpaste.*[34] Breastfeeding to at least 6 months may even protect against fluorosis in the permanent teeth.[35] Breastfed infants are not drinking fluoridated water, and mother's milk provides a very consistent level of fluoride regardless of the amount the mother ingests.[36] A large body of evidence suggests that one should not supplement fluoride for breastfed or other babies or older children, and it is no longer recommended by researchers, even when levels in water are low.[37] Unfortunately, many doctors continue to recommend it for breastfed kids although the American Dental Association came out in 2006 with an advisement that fluoridated water (which is 100 times the level found in breastmilk) should not be given infants nor mixed into their infant feeds. With unresolved concerns about increased bone fracture rates and other complications, flouridation of entire city water systems doesn't make sense.

> *Nearly a quarter of all our children are showing some signs of excess fluoride, or fluorosis.*

Vitamin D

Vitamin D deficiency rarely occurs in breastfed children—only when a child and mother get little sun and the mother's stores are low. This can happen when one child quickly follows another (depleting mother's stores), when either mother or child has darker skin pigmentation, and when the family lives in northern latitudes. Vitamin D is manufactured by skin when exposed to sunlight, and is then stored. So, preventing vitamin D shortage in an infant requires either the breastfeeding mother or the infant to be exposed to some sun each week. The further north, the closer to December, or the darker the skin, the longer this exposure needs to be. Supplementing vitamin D to mother or child (as in infant formulas) is a fine alternative to sun exposure for breastfed babies.[38] Except for these easily preventable cases, breastfed infants show excellent bone mineralization, which depends in part on vitamin D, even though typical mother's milk has been labeled as low in vitamin D.[39] As a backlash from ever-declining outdoor activity and ever-growing sun protective practices, vitamin D deficiency is growing, and additionally, experts are deciding that larger doses of vitamin D than previously recommended can bring cancer protection and other health benefits.

> *Excess fluoride, at the level considered beneficial to teeth, causes detrimental changes in the mineralization of bones. Bones become hard, in the sense of brittle, and at the same time there is deficient bone calcium (osteoporosis).*

Nucleotides and More

Free nucleotides (building blocks of RNA) are highly beneficial factors in mother's milk that promote iron absorption, fatty acid digestion, the presence of healthy flora, and intestinal and possibly liver growth.[40] Any benefits from supplementing formula with nucleotides appear limited so far. In some cases, supplementation helps growth-retarded newborns catch up in their growth.[41] U.S. manufacturers have been adding these to some of their formulas for several years now. Research is also under way not only to better determine optimal levels of many nutrients in infant formulas but also to shed light on the need for adding many other factors known to be absent, such as prebiotics, probiotics, factors known as glycomacropeptides and TGF-beta, and various human milk-derived proteins. Some of these will be the most valuable for premature infants. The future of infant formulas may hold certain enzymes, growth factors, and immunoglobulins as well.

Protein Ratios Are Important

Free amino acids (protein building blocks) are abundant in human milk at 4 times the level found in cow's milk.[42] Levels vary during lactation in a predictable pattern, independent of mother's diet, and glutamate remains the predominant amino acid.[43] Attempts to supplement amino acids in formula have not matched breastfed baby blood levels in formula-fed infants.[44] Even with high glutamate in formula, phenylalanine is found to be high in the blood of formula-fed infants. This is the amino acid that causes mental retardation when in very high levels due to the rare disorder called phenylketonuria (PKU).

Milk proteins are divided into casein proteins and whey proteins. The casein in bovine milk comes in large units that are difficult for humans to digest. The chief whey of cow's milk is another large protein that is not found in human milk at all. Mother's whey is predominantly lactoferrin, good for providing immunity. Forty percent of mother's whey is alpha-lactalbumin. Only 3% of bovine protein is similar to this.[45] Bovine milk is 20% whey and 80% casein. The ratio of whey to casein in formula significantly affects the availability of other nutrients and the digestibility of the formula. Both bovine whey and casein interfere with iron absorption in humans. Many formulas add whey to achieve a 60:40 whey to casein ratio, which is the average found in mother's milk. However, both portions are very different from their human counterparts, both are problematic, and each interferes with absorption of various nutrients. Hence, there are advantages and disadvantages to any ratio found in a formula. Formulas vary this ratio considerably in either direction. Human milk starts out with an 80:20 ratio of these protein fractions (the opposite of cow's milk) and gradually moves to 60:40 whey to casein over several months. A 50:50 ratio is found in milk of mothers who nurse for extended periods.[46]

Tolerance of Formula and Mother's Milk

Intolerance of formula made from cow's milk is very common in infants. This intolerance is to the unusual bovine proteins, not to lactose (*see Chapters 7 and 10*). Colic, frequent fussiness, poor sleep, waking with screams, frequent spitting up, vomiting, diarrhea, constipation, painful gas, blood in the stools, green stools, eczema and other rashes, including many diaper rashes, ear infections, chronically stuffy nose, and failure to thrive are among the most common reactions. These same symptoms often occur in breastfed infants who are reacting to foods in their mother's diet, especially dairy. Continuing to allow a child to experience these symptoms means continuing to allow damaging inflammatory reactions to go on inside their growing intestines, as well as decreased absorption of nutrients. For breastfed infants, mother simply changes her diet. Initial relief may be found for artificially fed infants through use of soy formula, although many infants eventually develop sensitivity to the corn or soy in these. Hydrolyzed milk protein formula works for many, but a small amount of intact bovine protein remains, often enough to continue to aggravate a sensitive child. Solutions to these symptoms and problems are presented in the last chapters of this book.

Soy Formulas

The fact that soy is used as a base for an alternative formula stems from an over-abundance of soybeans, not from research on what would provide the best alternative in the case of a milk formula intolerance. Soy, in fact, is among the most commonly reported allergens (as is corn, which is added to many formulas in the form of cornstarch, corn syrup solids, corn-derived dextrose, or corn oil). Actually, formulas based on lamb meat (some have existed in Europe) or possibly rice would likely be better alternatives.

Phytate (or phytic acid) is a plant acid found in high concentration in soy formulas. Unfortunately, this ingredient causes greatly reduced absorption of zinc, copper, iron, and other minerals from the formula.[47] The high fraction of protein in soy formula further reduces mineral absorption.[48] Additionally, the protein of soy formula is difficult to digest, and the available amino acids are in the wrong proportions, thus requiring twice as much protein to be put into soy formula than is in mother's milk, in an attempt to compensate. Researchers suggest that reduction of the phytate and partial hydrolysis (chemical breakdown to aid digestion) of the soy protein could reduce the problems of poor absorption and digestibility.[49] Hopefully, these alterations will be found in soy formulas on grocery shelves in the future.

Soy formula also contains high levels of phytoestrogens, estrogen mimics that behave as mild estrogens in a woman low in them (reducing symptoms of menopause), but that compete with natural estrogens when they are prevalent (reducing chances of breast cancer, for instance). The effect of these on infants eating nothing but soy formula is not known. An infant fed soy formula receives more than 7,000 times the amount of phytoestrogens as the infant fed mother's milk, leading to blood levels 13,000 to 22,000 times that of their own natural estrogens.[50] Some researchers predict these phytoestrogens may provide powerful cancer prevention to those who begin life on soy formula;[51] others express concern over possible toxicity from this tremendous dose.[52] Slight reproductive system effects have been measured in adults who were raised on soy formula from birth. If the effects were large, they would have shown up already, as soy formulas have been available for over 75 years. While dairy formula, if tolerated, is preferable to soy, overall the risks of soy and dairy formulas, or simply the risk of missing breastmilk, appear to be comparable, if slightly different.

Soy formula does not naturally contain the milk sugar lactose. I have found none with this ingredient added, although it should be. Lactose, in the milk of almost all mammals, greatly augments calcium absorption. Hence, soy formulas need to add more calcium than do milk formulas. The galactose produced from lactose digestion and barely found in any other food in the diet makes valuable contributions to rapid brain development.[53] In all probability, lactose, which is truly baby sugar, is not added to soy formulas since they are designed for those who cannot tolerate bovine formulas, and the misconception that lactose intolerance causes this sensitivity is promulgated by many.

Dynamic Mother's Milk

In contrast to the nutritional constraints of formulas, breastmilk is dynamic in its nutritional makeup. Mother's earliest milk is exceptionally dense in certain nutrients and many immune factors. When comparing mature milk at various stages of lactation, protein levels are highest early on when the infant is growing most rapidly. Protein levels drop 30% by 6 months and remain around this level during the rest of lactation.[54] Lactose levels increase somewhat over the first months; but oligosaccharides, the immune and fiber-providing complex carbohydrates, begin higher and decrease slightly over this same time.[55] Immune-providing zinc levels are also higher in the first months, dropping to a new level by 6 months. Magnesium levels plateau at 3 months. Calcium levels increase over the first month and remain high during the next 4 months, during the time of greatest bone growth.[56] After this time, calcium levels gradually decrease by 25% to a level at 12 months that remains steady throughout the rest of lactation.[57] Vitamin K levels increase gradually over the first weeks after delivery,[58] matching a newborn's need for tight control over K levels. Overall, fat levels and calories do not change as the baby gets older.

There can be nutritional variances in each successive child. On one hand, the second fetus and breastfed child receives fewer toxins from mother's body than does the first. On the other hand, mother's stores of iron, vitamin D, B12, and other elements can become reduced through her first pregnancy and nursing, and a second child can be born with lower stores of certain vitamins and minerals than the first, more so with each successive child. Of course, good diet and supplementation on behalf of the mother will prevent this.

While many studies reveal that supplementing mother's diet with certain nutrients does not affect the levels in her milk, this is not exactly the case for very malnourished mothers. And for some nutrients, especially the B vitamins, as well as omega-3s and even healthy probiotic bacteria, mother's intake does affect her milk levels. This suggests that all nursing mothers, as well as pregnant mothers, need to maintain their own health in order to provide the best nutrition to their infants. Many pregnant mothers take multivitamin and mineral supplements, beneficially. Mega-dosing of any nutrients can cause imbalances. Certainly, in the same way, maternal supplements can be beneficial to mother and infant during breastfeeding as well, although it does not appear to be highly necessary in a mother who eats a good diet high in vegetables, legumes, dark-colored fruits, and fish or other DHA source. Any supplements given directly to a breastfed infant should first be researched and well thought through.

A Weighty Issue

Breastfed infants gain weight more slowly than do formula-fed babies, especially after the third month. Their head circumferences and lengths are the same however,[59] and health, activity, and brain and motor development are superior in breastfed infants. All indications show that the weight difference between breastfed and formula-fed infants is fat.[60] This excess fat in formula-fed babies is an artificially developed characteristic, and fat infants are nearly twice as likely to become obese adults.[61] Although adults who gained excess weight only during adulthood are able to control high blood pressure with diet, large adults who were obese in early childhood are not able to reduce high blood pressure in this way.[62] Excess fat provides no health advantage for the infant except in the case of starvation, as occurs during prolonged bouts of formula-induced diarrhea. Hence, we should more accurately say that *formula-fed infants generally become overweight after 3 months of age*.

Formula-drinking infants consume 20% more formula each day than the amount of milk a breastfeeding infant drinks, although these milks have similar calories per ounce.[63] Even though most formulas have less fat than mother's milk, formula-fed infants still put on more fat weight than do breastfed ones. The protein in formula is harder to absorb, and certain unusable fatty acids combine with calcium to form soaps that are lost in the stool. Well-absorbed carbohydrates (sugars) are converted and stored as body fat in formula-fed infants, which causes the unnecessary weight gain. Their bodies know how much protein, fat, and particular nutrients they need, and they have to consume more calories in order to acquire them.

At least two other factors play a role in the disproportionate weight gain in formula-fed infants. Breastmilk becomes higher in fat the longer an infant nurses on a breast,[64] providing greater satiation of hunger and preventing the nursing infant from overfeeding. Breastmilk also contains leptin, which signals fullness and may help prevent overeating.[65]

Formula researchers recently tested a formula made with reduced protein to match the same protein-to-calories ratio as human milk, wondering whether this more "natural" concoction would be beneficial. They found that infants consumed considerably more calories, most likely in an attempt to acquire enough usable protein for their bodies.[66] While their length was not different, they gained considerably more weight in the form of fat. The conclusion was that this formula is not safe. But more importantly, this study is another indication that *the higher weights of formula-fed infants is not a good sign, but rather a sign of malnutrition*. Reducing the available nutrition increases total consumption. Excess fat is the result.

While some have suggested that breastfed infants are lighter because of "low" protein intake (compared to cow's milk), researchers have shown that supplementing breastfed infants' diets with added concentrated protein (and vitamins and minerals) does not increase their weight gain compared to non-supplemented infants.[67] Nor does the amount of fat or calories in individual mothers' breastmilk have any impact on the weight gain of their infants.[68] Neither the weight of the mother nor her nutritional status (beyond severe malnutrition) impacts the growth rate of a breastfed baby,[69] nor does the size of her breasts.

Formula companies developed weight charts in the early 1900s based on the weight gain of formula-fed infants. They provided these in baby-weighing stations they set up around the world in order to sell their products. With these, they could often convince breastfeeding mothers that they were suffering from insufficient milk, and that their "malnourished" infants needed supplements of their new "scientific" milk formulas.[70] Of course, formula only replaces mother's milk so mother makes less and less milk until the child eventually becomes totally formula-fed. As medical doctors were invited to attend these weigh-ins, these weigh stations gradually evolved into well-baby medical office visits, and the pediatrician was born. Formula companies continue to provide these charts to pediatricians today and encourage them to advise formula supplementation for infants whose growth is "faltering." These charts now reflect the average of all U.S. babies. Most of the statistics for these were gathered in the 1970s and 80s when a very tiny percentage of U.S. infants were exclusively breast-fed beyond a few months; even fewer than today. Hence these charts simply portray formula-fed patterns. By definition, nearly half of all breastfed infants will fall below this so-called average weight even during the first 2 months when their weights are similar to those who are bottle-fed. Then after the second month, many more will fall into the "below average" range on these charts. The World Health Organization (WHO) released new weight charts in 2006 based on healthy breastfed babies, and there are hopes that these are more useful, although, as of yet, these charts aren't appearing in many pediatric offices.

Weight gain *is* an issue. One needs to know that an infant is growing in order to know that they have no serious digestive disorders or other problems and to be certain that they are indeed taking in nutrition. There is concern that slow weight gain can retard brain growth and this should be the most important concern. However, a large 2008 Boston study determined that a slow weight gain in a term baby does not lead to reduced neurodevelopment.[71] But just because grandma likes fat babies doesn't mean parents should attempt to alter a lean and active baby. Should they try, the desired result is unlikely. By the same token, of course, plump babies should not be dieting. In many cases, you would simply find that one or both parents were pudgy-cheeked babies themselves. What is important is that an infant continues to gain weight (after the natural initial drop in the first week). Do not be concerned about the rate of gain or the child's weight. These are greatly governed by heredity (especially in the naturally fed infant), as is final height.

Babies exclusively breastfed for 3 to 5 months have been shown to have only half the chance of being obese as children. Those breastfed for more than 1 year develop childhood obesity only 17% as often as formula-fed babies.[72] Other studies show a very high correlation between childhood obesity and adult obesity. Obesity very often means the development of diabetes, heart disease, and cancer.

Much more important than weight is neurological development, which is evidenced by reaching various developmental milestones. Although these vary widely even in very healthy children, one might wish to look for some milestones being reached a littler early, while others are normally reached late. Slower rates are expected for prematurely born infants. The intuition of experienced parents and doctors goes a long way here and is usually far more valuable than any growth chart. Among breastfed infants, even those with the slowest growth rates show no differences in their average rates of neurological development or of illness.[73] Dozens of studies have suggested that separate growth charts need to be made for naturally fed infants. Still, they are hard to find. Interestingly, a London psychologist's study on the impact of growth rate versus intellectual and motor development suggested that the first few months pose a "sensitive period," beyond which there is no relation between growth rate and mental development. One-third of the differences in intellectual and motor development of 15-month-olds could be explained by growth rates that occurred between birth and 3 months of age.[74] These researchers did not discriminate between those who were formula-fed or breastfed. Since the slightly brighter infants, on the average, would eventually be the smaller infants for the most part (breastfed), it is not surprising that this 3-month critical period showed up in their study, and that a slightly negative relationship between weight and intelligence eventually revealed itself beyond that age.

Beginning Solid Foods

It may be important to supply formula-fed infants with the appropriate weaning foods at 4 to 6 months of age in order to provide relief from many of the negative effects of formula, one of those being iron loss. Their bodies are especially getting eager for certain other minerals, fiber, and antioxidants by this time, and in those receiving formula, there is no issue of bursting the immune-protective bubble of sorts, as formula-fed infants are essentially already eating "solid" foods, i.e., non-human-milk nutrients that test the digestive system and establish mature, more-challenging flora. At the same time, formula feeding should be continued in lieu of straight cow's milk, well beyond a year. The growth rate of formula-fed infants does not vary whether solid foods are introduced at 3 months or at 6 months of age.[75] The majority of formula-fed infants tend to lose their excess fat by 15 months. The formula-fed infant starting on solids experiences catch-up growth from nutritional deficiencies at about the same rate that they lose fat. Solid food introduction at 4 to 6 months is not for faltering physical growth, but for improving nutrition in formula-fed children. Formula-fed infants who are smaller due to intolerance of bovine milk proteins will gain weight faster only after most of these are removed from their diets.

> *This study is another indication that the higher weights of formula-fed infants is not a good sign, but rather a sign of malnutrition. Reducing the available nutrition increases total consumption. Excess fat is the result.*

In contrast, for naturally fed infants, based on iron studies, as well as on bone density, immunity, allergy, cancer, intelligence, motor development, and other studies presented throughout this book, it is apparent that *the longer the duration of exclusive breastfeeding (no supplements or solid foods), the better*—with at least 6 to 9 months being a good goal. Most nutritional studies on exclusive breastfeeding have gone as far as 9 months, finding that these infants have no nutritional deficiencies by that age.[76]

Breastfed infants who received complementary foods by 2 to 3 months were shown to have "significantly lower" *length* for their age within weeks, as well as lower weight for length.[77] They then continued with steady growth rates from this lower level. *Breastfed babies begun on solids at 4 to 5 months showed drop-offs in their weight gains as well.* Thus, early attempts to plump up breastfed infants are counterproductive. Those complemented with solid food at 6 to 7 months showed no difference in growth from those continuing to be predominantly breastfed. The World Bank reports problems in breastfed infants if supplements or solids are not started by 3 months (formula companies are part of the World Bank support), based on their studies of African women. But independent studies in Zimbabwe find quite the opposite,[78] as have other studies.[79] Occasional suggestions that one or two nutrients, such as zinc, become insufficient in babies with prolonged breastfeeding come from studies performed in world regions where maternal malnutrition is common. Zinc, calcium, and protein deficiencies are all suggested quandries for the infant not receiving solid foods by 6 months, but there are no actual cases of such deficiencies where mothers are not severely malnourished. The amount of protein actually absorbed by toddlers receiving the recommended protein percentages in their solid food diets happens to be the same amount that is absorbed from human milk.

> While there is no need to restrict solid food intake in breastfed infants after 6 months, neither is there reason to strongly encourage it at or before this time, regardless of advertising or common pediatrician and family pressures.

While there is no need to restrict solid food intake in breastfed infants after 6 months, neither is there reason to strongly encourage it at or before this time, regardless of advertising or common pediatrician and family pressures. Scientific evidence does not support this early feeding practice. A large and highly detailed study of mothers and infants in the West African nation of Cameroon suggests a gradual diminishing of the benefits of exclusive breastfeeding over partial breastfeeding beginning between 8 and 12 months of age.[80] After 1 year of age, the lifesaving benefits of full or partial breastfeeding appeared to be about equal until the data suggest a sure advantage to starting solid foods by 2 years of age. Basically, introducing solid foods to breastfed infants under age 1 only replaces the more nutritious and otherwise highly beneficial mother's milk with inferior calories. Baby likely knows best, and each will vary in his own natural timing of ingesting solid foods, based on the readiness of his digestive system and his motor interests in straying from mother, as well as genetic and other factors. Infants with food sensitivities naturally tend to want fewer solid foods, especially after reacting to a few.

Most infants will show interest in foods around 4 to 6 months of age, but observation usually reveals that this is chiefly curiosity and a search for teething comfort. It generally takes effort to get much down a baby at this age, unless the food happens to bring them some physical relief from an all dairy diet. While the age of curiosity presents a beneficial window for important solid food introduction in those who are formula-fed, it may be best to keep it to a play-and-taste level for breastfed infants. Urges to chew and swallow (different from teething on anything available) come a few months later. Potentially allergy-causing high carbohydrate cereals from refined grains may not be an optimal choice for starting foods. Neither are the nutritionally poor puddings, fruit sauces, and pale overcooked squashes with added starch often given as first foods.

> *Potentially allergy-causing high carbohydrate cereals from refined grains may not be an optimal choice for starting foods.*

When any infant stubbornly avoids certain foods (especially dairy, wheat, corn, tomatoes, or citrus), he is probably sensitive to these and his cues to this fact should be heeded. Keeping foods in the diet that cause diarrhea, fussing, rashes, or other symptoms only reduces nutritional absorption in the intestines. In the last chapters of this book, information is provided about how to recognize the symptoms of food allergy and intolerance, and how to diagnose, avoid, and treat these. These steps should be initiated in nearly all infants starting on solid food.

Fatty Thinking

Even with all of today's information about increasing insulin resistance (risking diabetes) when weight gain is rapid, increasing adult obesity, and cancer and heart disease risks as well, there are still those who encourage mothers to try to fatten up their babies, often through addition of fats to their diets. Fats as a whole represent a spectrum of fatty acids all with distinct and valu-

able qualities. Selectively adding one kind of fat to the breastfeeding child's diet only imposes an imbalance of these and leads the child to feel full sooner, diluting the amount of all other nutrients the child receives. It is already known through studies that higher fat in mother's milk does not produce a fatter child, nor does higher fat in infant formulas. All attempts to fatten up a baby with its own genetic determinations lead only to less-optimal circumstances.

On the other hand, some believe that daily doses of one-eighth of a teaspoon of cod liver oil or partial egg yolks from DHA-supplemented hens might provide a healthy addition of important fatty acids and fat-soluble vitamins to a formula-fed infant's diet because the fats offered in formulas are limited in variety and value.

Babies are born with mechanisms to control their nutrient consumption and regulate their weight gain so they can meet their genetic targets throughout life. While attempts at force-feeding infants and young children seldom have much impact on weight initially, these practices do serve to disrupt natural controls. Babies consistently encouraged to finish their bottles against their better instincts later become children with poor appetite control and excessive weight gain. Avoid encouraging children to eat before they are hungry, and don't encourage continued consumption after they are full. Children can learn, as many of us have, to consume calories for reasons other than hunger, such as pleasing others and enjoying calorie-dense rewards. Once natural weight control is gone, obesity, and the health challenges that go with it, is a possibility.[81]

No Cigar

Since the end of the nineteenth century, child rearing in the Western world has been characterized by attempts to improve on Mother Nature's fine-tuned, million-year plan for developing healthy babies. Many of these attempts have been characterized as "scientific," although I believe that the information in this book shows that much of it was not scientific at all, but rather the product of culturally expedient programs promoted by doctors and industries. Out of this melee, however, the groundwork was laid for true scientific investigation and debate.

Formula sustains the lives of many infants and is a valuable substitute when breastmilk is not available (although banked milk is still a better alternative). It has taken a huge effort to convince the public that breast and bottle-feeding are similar choices, but this is not even close to being true.

10

Baby Feeding: Facts and Fallacies

"To ensure that all segments of society, in particular parents and children, are informed, have access to education, and are supported in the use of basic knowledge of child health and nutrition, the advantages of breastfeeding..."
—United Nations Convention on the Rights of the Child

THE UNITED STATES AND SOMALIA ARE THE ONLY NATIONS IN THE WORLD that have not ratified the Convention on the Rights of the Child, which was enacted in 1990. Books provide access to information, but the only prominent advice in the United States promoting the advantages of breastfeeding is the required little statement for formula ads, "Breast is Best," which is not very informative. As for education about the advantages of breastfeeding, I had no pamphlets given me, no statements from my obstetrician or pediatrician, no suggestions by hospital staff. I saw no posters or TV public service announcements. I did receive formula samples and coupons from my obstetrician's office, from the hospital, and in the mail.

Insufficient Milk Syndrome: A Fallacy Becomes Reality

One of the biggest fallacies surrounding breastfeeding is that it can provide insufficient amounts of milk. This fallacy was purposely created by formula manufacturers. The fact is, mother's breasts are designed to produce as much milk as baby desires, whenever natural feeding is allowed. Careful studies demonstrate that mothers who initially complain of insufficient milk are usually in fact producing adequate quantities, and their babies are growing normally.[1] The faulty perception of insufficiency can be made a reality, however, with scheduled feedings, mothers made to feel nervous about their adequacy, and with formula supplementation,[2] especially in the beginning. A few studies suggest that 1% of women around the world are unable to breastfeed adequately for various physical reasons, yet the percent of women in the United States who find themselves unable to fully breastfeed is more like 15%. Lost social wisdom and misinformed guidance, lack of adequate support for the new mother, stress-related hormonal imbalances and other stress factors, hormonal treatments and possibly hormone-mimicking pollutants, other drug usages during pregnancy, birth, and immediately after, induced births, scheduled C-sections, other interruptions in the natural birth process, keeping mother and baby separated after birth, highly sterile early parenting practices blocking pheromonal signals, and emotional inhibitions stemming from social cues are likely some of the other causes for the unfortunate high rate of breastfeeding failure in the United States.

Regular, frequent stimulation of oxytocin and prolactin by the act of breastfeeding is required to keep milk levels flowing. When a baby cries with hunger, but a schedule prevents feeding, mother's body still responds to the cries with oxytocin release. But when the milk is not taken, prolactin is not produced; thus, there is no milk production when suckling does not occur. Just as a dog will stop responding to your call when no reward is given, hormone and milk production decrease when the body perceives that the need is less. Then when formula supplements are provided to an infant, the amount she takes from the breast is further reduced, again decreasing the amount the breast believes it should produce.

If milk production is suspected to be inadequate, the last thing to do is to provide a supplement to baby. The first thing to do is to increase nursing time and frequency and make sure the mother is not dehydrated. The milk supply can be quickly renewed within a few days in this way if supplementation or infrequent feedings have caused decreased milk production. The next thing to do is to seek the advice of a wise lactation consultant.

In addition to self-serving marketing, poor medical advice, and misinformed family advisors, another reason many mothers feel they have inadequate milk is that a few days after birth, and then for several weeks more, there is a sensation of engorgement. This sensation is natural in the beginning and is probably designed to guide mother's behavior to get breastfeeding established. After a while, as the breasts "figure out" the milk levels required, and hormone levels adjust, this engorged sensation lessens or disappears and breasts remain less full, producing most milk only on demand. As this breast filling reduces, some mothers wait for prolonged intervals to feed until they feel their breasts are engorged. Every time this happens, the breasts fill more and more slowly and produce milk with less fervor. Hence, a natural process turns into a true problem. Trying to maintain an engorged sensation can also lead to mastitis, an inflammation of breast ducts due to pooling of bacteria or candida. At this point, certain ducts do not produce normally. Slower, but not inadequate, milk production is the result.

The production of any notable quantity of milk does not occur until 2 to 4 days after birth. This, too, is by design. If formula supplements are given during the period when there should be frequent suckling and taking of colostrum, the stimulation of milk production will be inadequate. In fact, the success of breastfeeding is dangerously impaired by early formula supplementation.[3] Supplements will only serve to allow undesirable bacteria to become established in the gut, putting baby's health at risk and reversing much of the benefit of early breastfeeding. The first few days of colostrum provide a high degree of important immune protection during this most vulnerable period. At the same time, with minimal fluid intake and little to digest, the infant's system rids itself of excess fluid and develops balanced kidney control, clears intestine-clogging meconium, and ramps up for its first attempts at digestion, with the help of some initial growth-promoting factors received from the colostrum. At birth, the system is not instantly ready to begin full digestive and elimination duties, but needs a few days of "priming." This is well known for premature infants but not always remembered in term newborns.

Any time mother's milk production has diminished or disappears, which occurs during restricted access to a preterm baby in intensive care (which should not occur), re-lactation usually can be induced with frequent pumping and suckling, and sometimes with drugs and hormonal supplements. By this same means, adopted babies can often be breastfed as well.[4]

Sleep Aids

The belief that feeding cereal to infants before bedtime will prolong their sleep has been perpetuated for a long time. It is interesting that this practice is recommended at the ages of 4 weeks and 4 months, ages when most infants adopt less fussy, longer sleeping on their own. Controlled studies do not confirm increased sleeping with cereal feedings,[5] although one study did find an undesirable reduction in the infants' calcium levels.[6] Another study found no increase in sleep or decrease in crying with thickened bedtime formula, but reported a dangerous sevenfold increase in the bacteria level in stools, which were harder as well.[7] Some parents report improved sleep when their formula-fed infant with highly problematic reflux is given thickened formula before bedtime. Reflux is a common cause of colic seen especially when baby is in a reclined position. Merely reducing the liquid in the stomach reduces the amount returned to the esophagus but does not eliminate the cause of the problem. These days, reflux is regularly blamed solely on a weak gastroesophageal sphincter, although this is actually the norm for young infants except in extreme cases. Allergy to formula or the nursing mother's diet generally causes this reflux. Young infants are designed to fall asleep nursing, and the desire to feed during the night is natural and important for tiny, rapidly growing infants who can consume, digest, absorb, and assimilate only so much food at a time.

The Lactose Fallacy, the Protein Reality

Mother's milk is full of lactose. Lactose is a sugar designed especially for the babies of mammals, like us. This sugar aids calcium absorption, ensures sugar is released at the proper time, nourishes healthy flora, and supplies carbohydrates important for infant brain development. "Lactose-intolerance" has become a household term, alluding to an inadequate presence of lactase, the enzyme needed to digest lactose. As mentioned before, babies unable to digest lactose would quickly suffer brain damage and die unless there was quick and appropriate substitute feeding. The loss of the lactase enzyme is

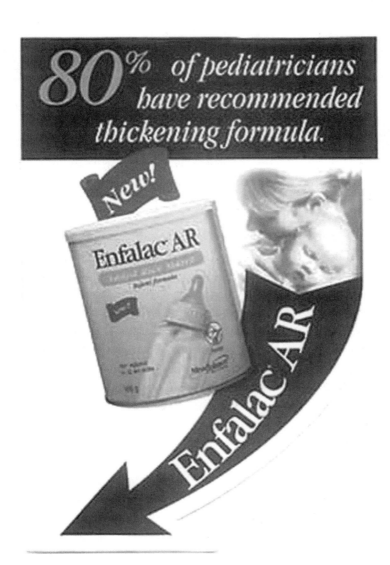

Figure 10-1 Apparently 80% of pediatricians have not read the research. This formula contains nonfat milk solids, lactose, and rice starch, which is added carbohydrate, for thickening. In all, it has a little more carbohydrate and protein and a little less fat than standard formula. Taken from *INFACT Canada,* "Enfalac ARGGG..." www.infactcanada, summer 1998 newsletter.

a natural part of growing older, but a deficiency of this lactose-digesting enzyme at birth could never have persisted during our evolutionary history, because lactase-deficient babies would never have lived to pass on their genes, until recently. Lactose-free formulas have only been available for a few decades. Other animals' milks contain lactose as well and would not sustain a lactase-deficient infant. Genetic mutations or rare genes can produce such an infant, but quite rarely.

Still, lactose-free formulas are highly promoted. Why? Because many babies have difficulty digesting cow's milk proteins in formulas or have allergic reactions to these proteins. Additionally, formula-fed infants have frequent problems with diarrhea: both infectious diarrhea due to a lack of immune protection from mother and non-infectious diarrhea from digestive and allergic intolerance to cow's milk proteins. When these illnesses and reactions occur, the resultant inflammatory process and rapid transit of intestinal contents cause many digestive enzymes, including lactase, to become depleted in the digestive tract. In advertising to the public and to pediatricians, formula manufacturers recommend lactose-free formulas when babies appear to have digestive problems from their milk formulas. Lactose digestion tests are sometimes performed and serve to confirm this recommendation. These tests will often suggest a lactase enzyme deficiency, but this is not the source of the problem. Lactose-free formula will likely provide little improvement in the infant unless it contains partially hydrolyzed milk proteins, which some do, in the hope that these proteins will be better tolerated.

The dairy industry appears to be careful to prevent widespread recognition of dairy protein intolerance. Instead, the public's awareness is focused on lactose intolerance. Milk, formula, and dairy products with the lactose removed or with added lactase enzyme (for predigesting lactose, the milk sugar) can be easily sold, with little added expense. The positive reputation of dairy products is strongly based on their protein content, so it is in the dairy industry's best interest to keep this reputation intact. Predigested (hydrolyzed) protein products are expensive and poor tasting. Even infants don't accept the taste of hydrolyzed milk formulas well.

When are lactose-free formulas appropriate? When formula-fed infants have had diarrhea, they may produce less gas due to undigested lactose if they are given lactose-free formula. In this situation, however, the infant is vulnerable to developing an allergic reaction to cow's milk proteins, because these poorly digested proteins easily leak through the damaged intestinal walls. Hydrolyzed formula or elemental formula (both are lactose-free) are the appropriate choice after diarrhea or for formula intolerance, if the infant must be fed formula. Breastmilk-fed infants do not need a reduction in lactose after diarrhea. Their feeding patterns are much more gradual and intestinal recovery of enzymes will be quick once the offending agent is gone.

Feeding and Cavities

Breastfed children have far fewer dental cavities than those who are bottle-fed.[8–10] This includes nursing caries as well as other cavities. The unfortunate term "nursing caries" refers to a typical pattern of dental decay seen when food, such as juice or formula, sits in the mouth frequently for extended periods. Nighttime snacks are highly cavity causing because saliva is not very mobile during sleep, leaving baby without this rinsing and antibacterial protection. Juice bottles by far promote the greatest number of what is now referred to as early childhood caries (ECC).[11] Many studies performed in the 90s report no link between prolonged breastfeeding and ECC though nighttime formula bottles are definitely linked, especially in those who have nighttime bottles at older ages. A 2008 review of several newer studies comes to the same conclusion,[12] and an even more recent study confirms that even nighttime breastfeeding does not cause ECC.[13] Among breastfed infants who do develop ECC, most are those who have frequent snacking and sugary foods or juices in their diets.[14,15]

In cavity-prone families, or when any evidence of decay has been detected in an infant, night bottle practices can be gently reduced (not necessarily eliminated) once several teeth are present. If night nursing causes worry when caries are present, a squirt of water into the mouth or stirring the child enough to cause some extra swallowing after nursing will help to clear the mouth of milk. Juice bottles should never be given at night. Still, genetic tendencies and other unknown factors make some children susceptible to bacterial presence and destruction in their mouths no matter what measures are taken.[16] Good dental hygiene in the parents' mouths will reduce baby's risk of developing cavities. Although damage to baby teeth does not affect adult teeth, a strong tendency for decay will likely carry over to adult teeth. Caries in baby teeth can serve as a warning that good preventive measures must be taken with permanent teeth.

Mother's milk has immune factors that reduce the presence of unfriendly bacteria, and laboratory tests show human milk does not encourage cavities.[17] On the other hand, formula is definitely cavity promoting.[18] Formulas with sugars other than lactose are the worst.[19] Although *Streptococcus mutans* bacteria are generally thought to be the chief cause of dental decay, the candida yeast that builds up on pacifiers has been found to promote cavity formation to a great degree.[20] Because of this candida and the occasional incidence of nursing caries from bottles or nighttime breastfeeding, dentists and pediatricians commonly recommend throwing out bottles and pacifiers at 12 months of age and weaning breastfed infants prematurely. But we must remember that permanent teeth are not harmed by baby teeth cavities.

> *While dental treatments on infants are certainly traumatic, the mere possibility of infant caries (about a 14% chance) is not enough of a worry that I would withhold or withdraw important feeding and comforting from any infant, especially before any such symptoms have occurred.*

Babies naturally experience hunger and need comforting during the night. Withholding response to these needs can possibly be more harmful to a child than any risk of damage to temporary teeth, although your dentist may feel that teeth are the primary concern. Certainly, the known health benefits of extended breastfeeding outweigh any perceived (and unfounded) challenges to temporary teeth. While dental treatments on infants are certainly traumatic, the mere possibility of infant caries (about a 14% chance) is not enough of a worry that I would withhold or withdraw important feeding and comforting from any infant, especially before any such symptoms have occurred. Feeding and comforting practices can be modified when needed to protect teeth, without blunt, drastic weaning measures.

Avocados, carrots, raspberries, strawberries, yellow plums, and chocolate have all been found to contain anti-cavity ingredients. Likely many more fruits and vegetables do as well. There are many herbs that fight caries, such as cloves, mint, thyme, and savory. In cheese, the lactose sugar is pre-digested. The milk protein left in cheese has been shown to be anti-cavity. Once baby is eating solids regularly, it would be a great practice to end a meal with any of these foods or to choose them as snacks.

Nursing mothers may be prone to cavities related to nursing (maybe these are the true "nursing caries"). Especially during the first months of breastfeeding, nursing mothers often find a need for midnight snacks. This food sitting against the teeth in a sleeping mom may cause some cavities in her teeth, which have mildly reduced calcium content (no matter how much calcium she supplements) until after the end of lactation. Preventive measures should be taken in a cavity-prone mom.

More on Teeth

"Did you know that according to the American Association of Orthodontists, two out of three children need braces?" cants an orthodontic ad in my local paper. As mentioned in the chapter entitled "Crying and Caring," prolonged bottle-feeding, pacifier use, or thumb-sucking (found chiefly in bottle-fed, schedule-fed, or prematurely weaned children) cause dental malocclusion and crossbite (buckteeth) that lead to the recommendation of correction with dental braces. Breastfeeding does not. Beyond the issue of baby's milk, today's soft diets of ground beef, French fries, juices, sodas, apple sauce, and dairy products do not provide the natural chewing needed for normal jaw development.

A Breastfeeding Effect in Mother

Breastfeeding mothers often experience about a 5% reduction in bone density. This is not rightfully referred to as osteoporosis because this level of reduction does not lead to bone fractures. This effect is seemingly harmless for mom (except possibly to teeth), and this bone loss is not prevented or reduced by calcium supplements[21] or by exercise.[22] Bone density returns to normal after weaning, with some return beginning during lactation at around 9 months.[23] The return of density after weaning is only slightly augmented by calcium supplementation. Reduced estrogen is most likely responsible for the reduced retention of calcium in mother's bone, just as it is after menopause.

This period of low estrogen is also responsible for the reduction in breast and ovarian cancers in women who breastfeed. This period of lower bone calcium should cause no concern about osteoporosis since it has been shown that women who have breastfed suffer fewer hip fractures in old age (indicating less osteoporosis).[24]

The amount of calcium available to baby through mother's milk is just right and is also unaffected by calcium supplementation to mother (including cow's milk). Incidentally, research suggests that vitamin A, not calcium, may be the most important supplement for increasing baby's bone growth when there is an undernourished mother.[25]

Breast and Nipple Pain: The Unrecognized Reality

Painful breasts, itchy or painful nipples, cracking, bleeding, and scabbing of nipples, and mastitis are problems for some breastfeeding women. In general, little help or information is available. Nipple pain and sometimes scabbing may be common in the first 2 weeks of nursing. When latch-on is correct and the problem persists beyond that time, candida is generally the cause. Will you hear this from your doctor? Probably not. Medical practitioners receive little or no breastfeeding education; in fact, this information has only begun to penetrate La Leche League and the realms of other lactation specialists within the last several years. The earliest medical reference to this problem I found was 1990, with one 1980 citation coming close to an understanding. Although the source of the problem is not that difficult to ascertain with a little research, it apparently was not a matter of concern in the once male-dominated medical field (just as PMS and other female maladies were often written off).

Candida is normal flora. This may be recited to you when complaining to your doctor. Trust me, painful overgrowth of candida is not normal. When "alternative health" proponents began diagnosing, and then over-diagnosing, some yeast problems that medicine was ignoring, the issue of yeast overgrowth, especially when chronic and other than vaginal, became a bit of a joke in the medical community. This has led physicians to ignore these complaints even today. Secondary overgrowth of common bacteria often compounds this candida nipple problem, especially when there is cracking or fissuring.[26] Why would nature do this to us? Nature did not. Candida cannot grow if nipples aren't frequently confined in a warm moist environment. In addition, antibiotic use will encourage candida growth in many parts of the body. Any antibiotic use or yeast infection in the months before birth or during lactation can lead to chronic "nipple thrush," as it is often called.[27] The usual recommended moist care for episiotomies and tears also provides an excellent environment for yeast to become established in the body. On the other hand, exposure to UV radiation from the sun kills candida and other microbes. The answer? Certain climates and job situations preclude going topless, but growth of candida can be limited in other ways.

First, recognize the problem. Nipples that are bright red and persistently sore and possibly itchy are likely infected with candida. Candida has a way of changing its own environment to be more amenable to future habitation. Sometimes little white spots will be seen inside the mouth of the infant. Mother and infant often share a candida problem and pass it back and forth.

Painful let-down (filling with milk during nursing) or deep shooting or radiating pain is likely infection in the ducts, often termed "chronic mastitis." This might be candida, but it is more likely bacterial.[28] Frequent (and prolonged if the nipples are not too sore) nursing will reduce the pooling of flora in the ducts that encourages flora to establish and overgrow. Application of heat will help mobilize the microbes out of the area. Also determine the source of the microbes—an infected nipple, baby's mouth, or associated vaginal or even colon infection (mom gets a little "diaper rash" or itchy bottom)—and treat the source. When painful, hardened areas of the breast or bright red branching over portions of the breast occur, eventually with fever, "acute mastitis" is the appropriate term. Pay prompt attention to acute mastitis. Treat it immediately and regularly with heat, massage, increased nursing frequency or pumping, and possibly taking healthy probiotic bacteria, lecithin, and your favorite antimicrobial supplements such as goldenseal and grapeseed extract so that a need for antibiotics might be prevented. There are small microwaveable hot packs that will fit right into the bra, which can be pre-charged for use away from home. The baby is not harmed by any increased levels of bacteria in the milk. By design, normal flora are always present in mother's milk, helping maintain baby's normal flora balance. Breastmilk contains factors that prevent these from getting out of control. (Today's cow's milk has higher microbe counts, and not always of the friendliest kinds—even after pasteurization.) If antibiotics are needed, only a very small percentage (generally much less than 1% of mother's dose) goes into baby, so minimal if any side effects result (possibly a bit of diarrhea, diaper rash, or thrush).[29] When antibiotics are prescribed, candida growth is encouraged due to lack of competition, and a twofold medical approach may be needed. Again, taking acidophilus and other probiotics may help mom or baby deal with primary candida infections or reduce candida overgrowth associated with antibiotics.

For nipples, frequent washing with warm water and drying well, followed by applying moisturizing cream with some vitamin E, aloe, or other friendly ingredients is helpful, at least for starters. Yes, candida likes moist places to grow, but it also establishes well in any skin that is irritated—not entirely intact. When even microscopic skin breaks occur, candida and bacteria find deeper and better homes. Hence, nipples need to be dry but moisturized, not dry and chapped, as with alcohol or some other preparations. Some mothers find help from applying over-the-counter anti-fungal creams (sold for vaginal yeast infections) to the nipples, while many others do better with Neosporin (helping when there is also bacterial growth). These should be applied right after nursing so they have time to soak in before nursing again. Used gingerly, there is no need to wash these off before nursing. Some do well with diluted gentian violet application (a messy fungus-killing dye), but these are terribly drying for the skin and may produce more cracking and irritation, thus creating the very environment where more candida and then bacteria can thrive. Treat baby, too, if mother's condition is stubborn. Treat any vaginal infection (or even suspected yeast overgrowth) quickly and re-treat mother if an infant has any oral thrush or candida-induced diaper rash.[30]

Breastfeeding Benefits to Mother

Breastfeeding for more than 2 years cuts a premenopausal woman's chances of breast cancer in half.[31] Recent reports suggest there is considerable postmenopausal benefit from prolonged breastfeeding.[32] Currently, nearly 4% of all women die of breast cancer, one-quarter of these before the age of 55.[33] Ovarian cancer is reduced by breastfeeding as well.[34] Also, a breastfeeding mother's stress responses are significantly restrained by the associated hormonal changes, with healthy results.[35] Mothers who breastfeed exclusively have much greater levels of oxytocin and prolactin than those who provide supplements,[36] and certainly much higher than those who do not nurse at all.

Sustained elevation of oxytocin provides for reduced blood pressure, a benefit that lasts long after breastfeeding ends.[37]

Breastfeeding is a wonderful way to lose the excess weight of pregnancy—which was gained to supply energy for making breastmilk—provided a woman eats according to her hunger and does not pad her diet for some reason (such as the unfortunate recommendation to consume 4 to 5 servings of dairy a day). When nursing on cue, menses generally do not return for a year or two, allowing mother to have more regular energy and the patience to care for a young infant without the stress of PMS.

Formulation

Dr. Naomi Baumslag and Dia Michels present an in-depth history of formula in their enlightening book *Milk, Money, and Madness: The Culture and Politics of Breastfeeding.*[38] Boiled condensed milks were introduced in the late nineteenth century, eliminating some of the problems of contamination and spoilage associated with fresh cow's milk, and making milk suddenly highly available to many. Soon after came powdered milk. Even as infant deaths were declining as a result of public sanitation advances, infant death rates rose against this trend due to the new popularity of artificial feeds in the early twentieth century. It was later learned that many nutrients were destroyed during sterilization, leading to rickets, scurvy, blindness, anemia, and beri beri, and several contamination issues continued. The sale of these products was so profitable, however, that large-scale advertising expanded worldwide. Occasional improvements or additions to the formulas were made. A large advertising campaign was also required to get the public to accept rubber nipples, which didn't become widespread until decades into the 1900s. Infant weighing stations were created around the world to promote the newly invented "problem" of breastfeeding: "insufficient milk syndrome." It became rampant. More and more babies were switched to the artificial concoctions, and infant death rates around the world soared from diarrhea, failure to thrive due to malnutrition and intolerance, and increases in many other illnesses due to lack of immune protection. Newborns could rarely survive on these early renditions. Every year another important missing element was discovered or some other improvement to the recipe was made. Only in the last several decades have young infants survived rather well on artificial formulas. Of course, reduced survival, health, and intelligence continue around the world from formula feedings today.

Without the natural birth spacing provided by breastfeeding, *birth rates around the world have climbed since artificial feeding became popular*, further reducing infant survival. Close spacing of children poses a high risk to their survival for multiple reasons, including shortened breastfeeding, decreased parental attention, limited food and parental resources, and decreased nutritional stores in the mother.[39,40] Mother's system can easily become depleted of nutrients when infants are born within 1 or 2 years of each other, especially after two children. The newborn's nutrient stores are then depleted as well.

Incidentally, pediatric medical schools and their continuing education seminars are highly funded by formula manufacturers and dairy associations. Even some of the vaccination literature (and research) that keeps babies coming in regularly is funded by these groups. Although the American Academy of Pediatrics (AAP) has broken some ties with the American Medical Association, due chiefly to cow's milk issues, most pediatric offices continue to push formula and dairy.

Promotional and Pediatric Practices and Policies

The World Health Organization (WHO) has long known that marketing from formula companies greatly influences mothers' breastfeeding decisions. In 1981, in an attempt to reduce the severe diarrhea, malnutrition, and deaths caused by formula use around the world, WHO/UNICEF developed a code to restrict the mass marketing campaigns of breastmilk substitutes. But many people now believe that formula companies attempt to influence choices without appearing to break the code, providing a wide array of breastfeeding pamphlets and videos that convey carefully worded but misleading information with strong subliminal messages. Few if any of these truly meet the criteria of the code.[41] "Follow-up" formulas are another way to violate the code without appearing to do so. The marketing verbiage for these products proclaims that the breast is best, as is now required, but indirectly implies that several steps of breastmilk supplements or substitutes become appropriate to achieve adequate nutrition. Additionally, while the code bans using pictures of babies or glamorized formula bottles on "breastmilk substitutes," pictures of babies with sippy cups containing white liquid appear on follow-up formulas. The front of one such product says, rather unspecifically, "better than milk."

In addition to the many methods used to skirt the code, direct violations are rampant around the world.[42] According to some sources, more than half of all new mothers in the United States illegally receive free formula samples, coupons, or gifts from formula manufacturers either through direct mail or through baby "welcome" packages passed out in hospitals, in return for generous gifts given to the healthcare workers. This occurs to varying degrees around the world as well. These have a proven negative impact on the duration of breastfeeding.[43] Posters, calendars, promotional booklets, and other supplies end up prominently used or displayed in hospitals. Additionally, in my city, La Leche League brochures mysteriously disappear in the hospitals shortly after being put out. Women, Infants and Children (WIC) programs and food banks strongly (albeit indirectly) promote formula feeding with strong encouragement from formula companies, using funds from the government. Over half of all formula sold in the United States is distributed through the WIC program, and the rate of breastfeeding among WIC recipients is consequently only half the national average.[44]

> Infant weighing stations were created around the world to promote the newly invented "problem" of breastfeeding: "insufficient milk syndrome."

Impoverished mothers around the world are the chief targets of formula manufacturers and the dairy and baby food industries. As these companies obtain much wealth from government and charity funds, the plight of the women is increased, and the future of their children is impaired. Nestlé always has been considered the biggest offender under this code, as well as earlier codes and rulings. For this reason, grassroot efforts to boycott all Nestlé products have survived since 1974. Women originally from areas that are isolated from or highly resistant to formula promotions are often swayed by formula-promoting influences once they have come to the United States in pursuit of the American dream, equating artificial feeding with an elite and superior lifestyle. For example, although 97% of the Indo-Chinese breastfeed in their native lands, in a recent survey only 4% of pregnant Indo-Chinese migrants from Cambodia and Laos living in the United

States expressed the intention to breast-feed their babies.[45]

Pediatric medical school education on breastfeeding goes little beyond information provided by the formula companies. A recent large (AAP) survey found that 42% of pediatricians do not believe that the benefits of breastfeeding outweigh the challenges.[46] A survey was made comparing the knowledge of pediatric practitioners with 3 to 5 years of practice to that of early pediatric students, in an attempt to reveal the amount of accurate breast-feeding information obtained in current education. The difference between these two groups was found to be quite small, indicating little education is being provided. Sixty-four percent of practitioners versus 52% of residents were aware that providing supplements in the first weeks of life can lead to breastfeeding failure.[47] More than one-fourth of both groups felt that exclusive breastfeeding was not the best feed for infants. Of course, this lack of education and abundance of misinformation percolates into the nursing staff as well. Breastfeeding failure is extremely common for premature infants being held in U.S. neonatal intensive care units (NICU), and most nurses seem to accept that this is the only possible outcome. But a breastfeeding intervention force concentrated efforts in a Chicago NICU with the result of eliminating breastfeeding failures completely.[48] One investigator attempted to add up the cost of formula use in the United States. She estimated that in 1999, the healthcare costs of excess cases of diarrhea, middle ear infections, respiratory viruses, and diabetes totaled a billion dollars annually.[49] Of course, neither the cost to society of widespread lowered intelligence nor the loss of lives can be measured in dollars. While formula companies have failed to gain any increase in the numbers of U.S. women who *initially* use formula over the last three decades (actually dropping from 50% to 26%), the companies' success is growing, as the average duration of breastfeeding is now even shorter than it was in the 80s.[50] While much of the United States' low ranking as forty-sixth among world nations for infant survival (under age 1)[51] is certainly attributable to low breastfeeding levels, lack of extended breastfeeding in the United States may be partially responsible for the

> Pediatric medical education on breastfeeding goes little beyond that provided by the formula companies.

country's childhood death rate (under age 5) being higher than 39 other nations (rank according to UNICEF).[52]

Convenience?

Where is the convenience of having to buy formula weekly at the store (and pay for it), carry it home, store it, wash, sterilize, and maintain bottles and nipples, crawl out of bed in the middle of the night to mix formula to the sound of hunger cries, warm it to just the right temperature, hold the bottle in the infant's mouth while trying to stay awake, try to figure out and keep track of how much the infant has had and will need, carry formula and all associated tools wherever you go, always have extra with you in case of emergency, keep formula cold while out and find ways to warm it away from home, and tote all the empty cans to the recycle station? A breastfeeding mother has warm, perfectly mixed, fresh milk available immediately upon request, anytime, anyplace, with no spoilage, no fuss, no mess, and no waste. She can even feed in her sleep, and the milk is much cheaper, too. With far less spitting up from breastmilk than formula, clothes and carpets look better and last longer. Then there are the diapers. While breastfed

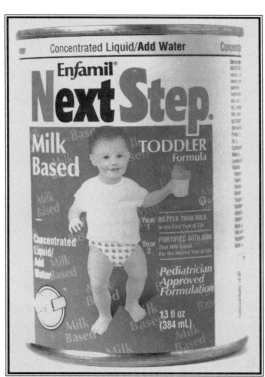

Figure 10-2 Skirting the WHO code.

stools have a familiar, almost sweet odor, and much less stool is passed due to the high absorbability of breastmilk, formula-fed stools are full of unusable and undigested materials and offensive smelling bacteria; these stools are quite foul and frequent. Nothing cute or convenient about that, except for

Shugrue Photography

knowing quite well when it's time for a diaper change. Their urine is more odiferous as well.

Controlled?

Still, some assert ingrained propaganda such as "How can you know how much a breastfed infant is getting?" There is a simple way to find out—weigh before and after. However, there is no need to take such measures as long as the infant is being allowed to feed as much as she desires. Infants have growth spurts and slow periods. While babies know the amount of milk they need, how does a formula-feeder know when it is time to provide more formula for a spurt, or to stop pushing the bottle during a slow period?

Civilized?

Highly successful marketing has elevated the perception of an infant sucking on a rubber and plastic breast device, even in public, to that of adorable. To accomplish this, baby bottles were supplied early on to toy manufacturers to go with every doll and thus every doll ad. Billboards, posters, and magazine ads of babies with bottles were seen everywhere until the WHO's advertising code restricted this practice in connection with sales of artificial baby feeds. So, these images had to be worked into TV shows in other ways. Then came wrapping paper, greeting cards, shower gifts, and sundry other items. In my state, where cigarette smoking has been outlawed in public places, the appearance of one sucking on such a smelly thing has lost much of its once enjoyed glamour and has become quite distasteful for many. The sight of a pregnant mother in public was once considered very embarrassing and distasteful. Certainly, the appearance of an infant discreetly and peacefully cozied up against her mother's breast could regain an image of civility or dignity, even of health and beauty.

What Is Natural?

Several times, when people were trying to find a nice way to tell me that a, say, 7-month-old baby was too old to be nursing, I heard things like, "I think it's natural for a baby to wean when their teeth start coming in." Of course, since an infant, or even a toddler, is too young to chew, digest, and survive on solid foods alone, especially before food processors were invented (although pre-chewed food has been used), these people are actually suggesting that it is natural for babies to be weaned onto the highly processed milk of another very different species, onto a plastic bottle with a rubber nipple— not exactly "natural" in my eyes. Most baby mammals nurse with their milk teeth in place (hence the name), and cross-species nursing is not observed in nature. The milk of each mammal is very specific to that species and few could likely survive on the milk of another. Human milk appears to be the most complicated and sophisticated of all milks by far, along with the development of the most sophisticated species. Still, it is not appropriate for other young animals.

The appearance of certain enamel defects in first teeth has been found to correlate with stress on a developing child. On ancient finds, these are chiefly associated with the stress of weaning, which includes altered nutrition and increased infection. Anthropologists can "read" the dental records throughout history to surmise at what age weaning was begun, and when it was well under way or nearing completion. Anthropological reports on prehistoric populations from Illinois around A.D. 1000 reveal that weaning (meaning adding solid foods) was likely begun by the age of 2 years

Lack of extended breastfeeding in the United States may be partially responsible for the country's childhood death rate (under age 5) being higher than 39 other nations.

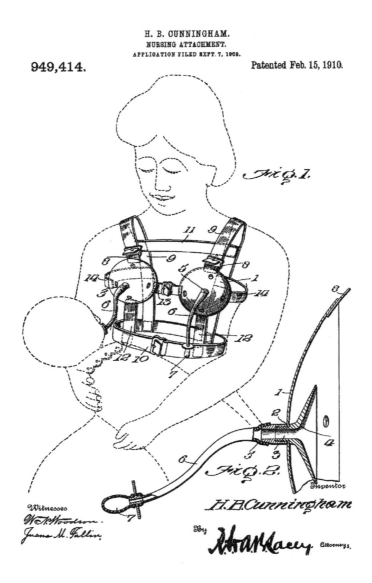

Figure 10-3 This public breastfeeding device was invented in 1910 to be worn under the clothing, with a nipple attached to a tube that comes out from the bottom of the shirt, in order to "avoid unpleasant and embarrassing situations" of "exposure of the breast in suckling the child." No explanation was made in the patent as to how the milk was to be released from the breast.

and was well under way by the age of 4.[53] Studies of children's teeth from Guatemala coming from 700 B.C. to A.D. 1500 similarly suggest that corn foods were started here before the age of 2, but nursing lasted for several more years.[54] Studies on nineteenth-century Americans found heightened peak stress levels between 2.5 and 4 years of age.[55] This research suggested that these samples revealed an earlier final weaning age compared to prehistoric finds that point to age 6. Evidence was also found that children in this industrialized society had inferior health during this more abrupt weaning, compared to that of earlier agricultural societies. Researchers in Italy also reported 2 to 4 years as the peak stress in a nineteenth-century northern Italian village, suggesting this stress was greater and somewhat earlier than some other populations observed for the same time period.[56] Chimpanzees live much shorter lives than we do, but they nurse until nearly the age of 5.[57] One can find that children in remote areas around the world nurse until near this age or longer.

When not strictly prevented, most children have a desire to suck for several years, indicating an instinctual need to breastfeed. Pacifiers or thumbs are often seen in mouths to this age and beyond when not countered. Over 40% of U.S. children still receive bottles at 2 years and 8% are still using them at the age of 4.[58] These numbers would be much higher if this practice were not generally restricted out of dental and social concerns. The passion for sippy cups demonstrates a continuance of this sucking desire as well.

All agree that children need milk for multiple nutritional reasons for at least 2 or 3 years. Children are born with a unique enzyme, lactase, to digest their unique milk baby-sugar, lactose. Normally, this enzyme begins to decline after age 2 and lasts in the child for 8 to 15 years, except in people of northern European descent whose lactase persistence was evolutionarily selected for during 2,000 years or so of cattle domestication. The digestive system takes several years to mature before it can obtain optimal nutrition without easy-to-digest, nutrient-packed mother's milk. Similarly, it takes many years before a child's immune system matures and can provide immune protection equal to that supplied by mother's milk. The immune system also depends on long-lasting influences from mother's milk to maintain top functioning well beyond the nursing years. Baby's best motor, intellectual, visual, and other neurological development depends on extended breastfeeding, as does parental bonding with baby. Assuring parental resources through spacing between children also depends on prolonged nursing. Human infants are quite helpless and have ongoing needs to be close to mom for protection. This need gradually reduces after the age of 3 or so. *Clearly, it is natural to nurse for several years and highly beneficial to nurse for at least 2.* It is also natural for nursing practices to vary from pair to pair, according to the needs of mother and child.

The Bottom Line

When you decide to begin weaning foods, and then to totally wean your child, keep clearly in mind what your reasons are—who you are trying to appease or please, and who is important.

Some feel that we have become "scientific" and have "evolved" above the "animal behavior" of nursing. Any science or supposed modern evolution that precludes a parent's desire to provide the best nutrition, protection, bonding, and development for her child is no step forward to me. Even if we one day develop means to entirely replicate mother's milk, hormones, immune factors and all, there would be no reason for it to replace nursing. Of course, the womb is the next target. I heard a neighbor describe a medication she now gives her dog to alleviate his separation anxiety. Already the widespread use of Ritalin and anti-depressants sometimes substitutes for lost parenting and compensates for allergenic, mood-altering artificial feeding. I still personally lean toward the irreplaceable joys and rewards of total motherhood and the sense that babies have an inalienable right to natural babyhood.

11

The Dangers of Cow's Milk

WE HAVE DISCUSSED THE MANY DOWNFALLS OF INFANT FORMULA. IT reduces nutrition, bonding, immune protection, and intellectual development, and increases the death rate. The story does not stop here. We haven't even gotten to the core of the dangers of dairy products. Cow's milk and formula consumption lead to increased risk of childhood diabetes, bowel disease, osteoporosis, heart disease, cataracts, leukemia, and bowel and reproductive organ cancers. And that's not all. Intolerance reactions to bovine proteins in formula or breastmilk of moms who drink cow's milk lead to higher incidence of colic, ear infections, and attention-deficit disorder.

While there are literally thousands of research studies, each revealing at least one of milk's hazards, the dairy industry goes to great lengths to stifle any damaging information. Blanket statements, such as, "There is simply no scientific research to back up these claims," are easily made. With a long and successful history of dairy promotion, these are readily accepted by the public. *More people need to go to the real research and learn the truth for themselves.* They should be suspicious of these unnatural foods being pushed on their children. They should question motives as well as possible outcomes. Although some of the dangers of cow's milk consumption relate more to adults than to children, I touch on these topics since early childhood is when lifelong habits are formed. Yet, maybe the most vivid, immediate reason to question bovine milk consumption for children is that *40% of young children experience intestinal bleeding from cow's milk consumption.* That just doesn't sound healthy. Bleeding from dairy formula is almost this high though some formulas are partially altered in an attempt to somewhat reduce this occurrence. Nestlé's own scientists admit to this bleeding,[1] though they claim it ends right at 12 months, while other researchers know differently.

The harmful components of cow's milk include all the major parts of it, as well as some more minor elements. Lactose is a sugar meant for babies, but it's generally harmful to adults. The proteins in cow's milk are different from human milk proteins and cause problems of digestion, intolerance, impaired absorption of other nutrients, and autoimmune reactions. Few of the proteins meant for baby cows are found naturally in human mother's milk, and none are found in any "natural" adult human food. Even the high protein content in cow's milk creates problems. Human babies need the saturated fats and cholesterol in mother's milk. There is less health benefit from these fats after early childhood. Cow hormones are not meant for humans, and older children and adults are not meant to consume hormones. And, cows have been selectively bred over time to create high levels of these hormones—those being the cows that grow the fastest and produce the greatest amount of milk. As discussed earlier, cows also concentrate pesticides and pollutants into their milk fat, from high dietary food and water requirements. The drugs now given to cows adds to this chemical soup. But we need milk to build strong bones, don't we? Sorry, heavy milk consumption leads to increased osteoporosis.

Milk Proteins and Diabetes

Although one highly promoted 1996 study contradicted the American Academy of Pediatrics (AAP) 1994 announcement of a link between cow's milk consumption in infants and development of diabetes,[2] many well-conducted studies have since left little doubt that the great increase seen in childhood diabetes mellitus is caused largely by early exposure to dairy products.[3-8]

The methodology of the study that found no correlation between milk and diabetes was flawed because it was based on the type of feed the infants reportedly received, breastmilk versus milk formula, without regard to whether the breastfeeding mothers were consuming cow's milk and passing it along to baby. A more recent study again finding no links between diabetes and early milk consumption had the same design flaw.[9] Breastfed babies often receive significant exposure to cow's milk proteins when dairy is a part of their mothers' diets.[10,11] Both negative studies were performed in nations with high dairy consumption (United States and Austria), so that the difference in bovine protein exposure between the formula-fed and breastfed groups was not significant enough to show up statistically. Studies performed on populations such as the Arizona Pima Indians and people in a rural part of Chile, where adult dairy consumption was minimal at the time the studied children were born, did indeed find a higher incidence of diabetes in formula-fed versus breastfed children.[12,13]

> In fact, the rate of childhood diabetes in dairy-consuming, formula-using nations is up to 35 times that in nondairy nations.

The first indications of a relationship between childhood diabetes mellitus and dairy were discovered by correlating diabetes rates with the total dairy consumption by nation. A 95% correlation was found.[14] In fact, the rate of childhood diabetes in dairy-consuming, formula-using nations is up to 35 times that in nondairy nations.[15] In the United States, 1.8 children per 1,000 under the age of 19 currently have diabetes[16] and the CDC estimates the overall rate of diabetes will triple between 2005 and 2050.[17]

Diabetes associated with dairy exposure is thought to stem at least partly from infant hypersensitivity or allergic-like reactions to bovine proteins. Studies more accurately investigating the relationship between cow's milk proteins and childhood diabetes measure the amount of anti-bovine antibodies found in diabetic children's systems versus those found in healthy infants. Now, a firm relationship between cow's milk exposure and the development of diabetes has become clear.[18,19] A recent study suggests that exposure to cow's milk proteins before the age of 2 years has the strongest effect on development of diabetes.[20]

Large dairy proteins, which are quite foreign to our bodies and difficult for young infants to handle, often lead to immune or allergic attacks in the infants' bodies, but not all infants are prone to these reactions. Whether they react to certain food proteins or not depends in part on heredity. However, one cannot determine in advance whether such a reaction will occur in any given newborn. The earlier the age of exposure, the greater the number of infants who react.

> *When an infant sensitive to cow's milk fills up with destructive immune antibodies in response to milk exposure, the islet cells of the pancreas become subject to destruction at the same time.*

Diabetes is a reduced ability to maintain proper sugar levels in the blood due to decreased sugar-clearing insulin, or reduced response to it, allowing blood sugar levels to become harmfully high. Insulin is manufactured in the islet cells of the pancreas beta cells. There seems to be a similarity between these beta cells and the beta-lactoglobulin or betacasein proteins in cow's milk. Thus, when an infant sensitive to cow's milk fills up with destructive immune antibodies in response to milk exposure, the islet cells of the pancreas become subject to destruction at the same time.[21,22]

Additionally, the bovine insulin in cow's milk is different from human insulin by only 3 amino acids. Some infants create antibodies against this foreign bovine insulin.[23] It is believed that regular consumption of the high amounts of insulin in cow's milk causes sensitive infants to become immune to the effects of their own insulin. Hence, we have at least two routes that can lead to diabetes. First, insulin production is reduced due to the destruction of insulin-producing cells. This creates what is known as childhood-onset or type 1 diabetes. Second, there is a diminished ability to respond to one's own insulin, having become "immune" to it. This is type 2 diabetes, which has traditionally been referred to as adult-onset diabetes, but this name is being dropped as the rate of insulin resistance has been seen in children at alarming rates over the past decades in formula and dairy-consuming regions.

A Swedish researcher suggests, based on twin and other epidemiological studies, that genetic risk factors play a role, but that environment interacts with this suscepti-bility to cause the disease.[24,25] The environ-mental factors she noted, in addition to early exposure to cow's milk proteins, were a cold environment, a fast growth rate, a high rate of infections, preeclampsia, and stressful life events. Interestingly, all these other factors mentioned are associ-ated with dairy consumption as well. Dairy consumption in general is higher in north-ern climates. Formula feeding leads to a greater number of infections, faster weight gains, and possibly greater infant stress from receiving propped bottles rather than affectionate nursing. Preeclampsia, or toxemia in the mother, is associated with high dairy consumption during pregnancy. Not only is *early* exposure to cow's milk proteins a risk factor for childhood diabetes, but *3 or more glasses of milk per day during childhood leads to a quadrupled risk of diabetes.*[26]

Not only is early exposure to cow's milk proteins a risk factor for childhood diabetes, but 3 or more glasses of milk per day during childhood leads to a quadrupled risk of diabetes.

Soy formula substitution may not be the ideal alternative to dairy for-mula. Early exposure to soy protein (and wheat protein) has been associated with some increased incidence of diabetes as well, thought to be another allergic mechanism,[27] although it may be simply the lack of something from breastmilk.

Interestingly, although formula companies deny links between early formula consumption and childhood diabetes, they are conducting several trials of potential alterations to formula in the hope of reducing diabetic development. One of these performed in Finland looked at removal of the bovine insulin hormone from infant formula. Finland has not only the highest dairy consumption in the world but also the highest incidence of diabetes in the world. The formula company apparently did not want the public to be aware of the potential damage that standard formulas could be causing, as it was accused, and found guilty, of performing trials on Finnish infants without the informed consent of parents.[28] Another such trial in Israel involves adding human insulin to infant formula. It is known that human insulin in breastmilk promotes intestinal maturity in the infant. The theory is that this may help prevent diabetes.[29]

Not only does diabetes force a child to have blood and urine tests frequently, and possibly to have insulin injections daily, but it can cause painful nerve irritations, sores that do not heal, and eventually loss of extremities, kidney and heart damage, and blindness. Additionally, diabetes is the seventh leading cause of death in the United States today. A few have pondered whether someone with early diabetes should eliminate dairy from their diet, since the pancreas should have regenerative powers like other organs in the body, and it may be possible that insulin generation could gradually return to normal.

Multiple Sclerosis

Researchers have noticed a strong correlation between milk consumption and multiple sclerosis.[30–32] Multiple sclerosis is a disorder in which, for some reason, the body attacks the protective covering (myelin) on nerves. Just as milk protein antibodies attack similar proteins in the pancreas, causing diabetes, a comparable autoimmune reaction has been suggested in the case of multiple sclerosis. It is known that while the correlation between milk consumption and multiple sclerosis development is strong, the link to milk fat is weak and there is no link to cheese (in which milk proteins are broken down by bacteria). Similar abnormal immune reactions to certain cow's milk proteins have been found in M.S. patients and those with diabetes.[33,34] Filling in the picture, it has been discovered that a certain cow's milk protein mimics a nerve myelin protein, and antibody reactions to these are seen to cross-react inside the central nervous system of mice with multiple sclerosis. Hence, antibody reactions to milk proteins may destroy similar proteins in nerve cells, leading to the development of M.S.[35–37]

Milk and Heart Disease

Elevated levels of oxytocin and reduced levels of cortisol from positive attachment behaviors such as nursing and nurturing responsiveness can cut heart disease risks for the nurturing parent, as well as for the adult who was nursed in such a fashion as an infant (*see Chapter 3*). In fact, it has been shown that 7-year-old children who were raised on formula have significantly higher blood pressure than those who were breastfed,[38] although addition of fatty acids DHA and ARA to infant formulas may counteract some of this effect.[39] The consumption of cow's milk at all ages has strong ties to heart disease. Although not all reasons are known for the ever-growing rates of heart disease, one common denominator keeps showing up: milk consumption.

While it is currently understood that higher calcium intake reduces blood pressure and heart disease, this finding does not hold true when milk is the chief source of calcium.[40] A study from India found significantly higher rates of coronary artery disease with higher milk and butter intake.[41] Since dairy can be a large source of dietary fat consumption, and high animal fat intakes are linked to heart disease, some assume that milk fat is the chief assailant. An epidemiological study looking at Asian and Mediterranean countries suggested that high dairy fat (but not high "good" fat) consumption increased heart disease.[42] An earlier analysis of 21 countries reported that milk proteins and milk fats had strong statistical ties to coronary artery disease.[43] While milk fat is clearly a problem, a more recent 32-country study reported the strongest dietary connections with heart disease to be *nonfat* milk and lactose.[44] An even newer 20-country study found a strong correlation between milk protein consumption and the development of heart disease.[45] Such results are consistent with findings (*see Chapter 13*) that antigen-antibody complexes formed through allergic reactions to cow's milk proteins can deposit in the artery walls, leading to plaque formation and heart disease.

> It has been shown that 7-year-old children who were raised on formula have significantly higher blood pressure than those who were breastfed.

Another study reviewed many of the links to milk and the heart, confirming that rates of consumption and timing of increasing consumption in regions all around the world correlate with development of heart disease. The study also confirmed that the presence of a suspicious antibody reaction to a certain milk component (milk fat-globule membrane) is correlated with deaths from coronary heart disease. These United Kingdom researchers surmised that lactose and the high calcium to magnesium ratio of milk both also exhibit strong links to coronary artery damage (with proposed biochemical pathways). It may actually be the combination of these three harmful aspects of milk that make it such a strongly linked agent.[46] Generally, fermented milk products (where lactose and major proteins are pre-digested by bacteria) such as yogurt and cheese are not implicated in coronary artery damage.

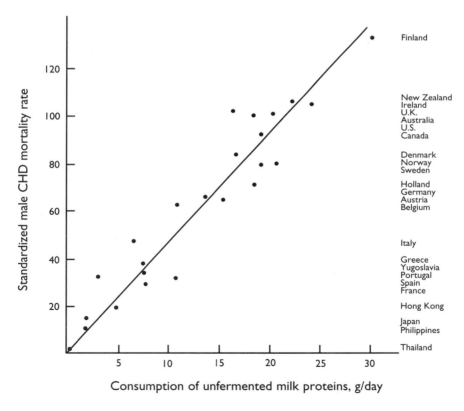

Figure 11-1 Rate of deaths from coronary heart disease (CHD) in relation to amount of milk consumption, for 24 countries.[47] Reproduced by permission of the publisher, Churchill Livingstone.

Lactose and Pain

There are two chief problems with post-childhood consumption of the baby sugar, lactose. One is that most adults around the world are unable to digest this sugar since the infant enzyme lactase is normally lost after childhood. Many Americans are of Northern and Western European descent, so they carry genes for lactase enzyme persistence developed over millennia. Yet a growing number of Americans come from the rest of the world where lactase enzyme and therefore the ability to digest lactose is naturally lost in late childhood: 80% of Native Americans, 75% of African Americans, 100% of native Asians and Africans, and 50% of all Hispanics.[48] These percentages correlate with the amount of non-European heritage. The result is fermentation of this sugar in the large intestine, causing painful bloating and gas, and often diarrhea. Although cheeses are well tolerated, and yogurt is partially tolerated, any significant amount of milk leads to misery. We will see that this trait, if it leads to avoiding dairy products, has provided health benefits such as reduced osteoporosis to those who are not lactase persistent. Unfortunately, dairy is added and often hidden in more and more prepared foods and restaurant meals, and free milk is given to school children around the nation.

We will see that this trait of inability to digest lactose, if it leads to avoiding dairy products, has provided health benefits such as reduced osteoporosis.

A report by the National Dairy Council (NDC) wants us all to know that "many people erroneously believe they are lactose intolerant…psychological factors can contribute to gastrointestinal symptoms that mimic lactose intolerance."[49] It is true that many who have painful intestinal problems after dairy consumption are not lactose intolerant; rather, they are bovine protein intolerant. But the NDC won't tell you that. Many who *are* lactose intolerant are protein intolerant as well. This is why many who eat cheese (where lactose is consumed by the bacteria) or who use lactase enzyme additives still experience discomfort. Furthermore, protein intolerance reactions often lead to transiently reduced lactase enzyme. The dairy council adds to its report that people with low levels of lactase can consume "2 servings of milk per day in divided doses." The report includes suggestions that "porous bones" and hypertension can result if one does not do so. This report attempts to shame, embarrass, and frighten people into continuing to consume dairy regularly, no matter how much it hurts, while the document's supporting arguments are contrary to what science shows today. And, anything that causes diarrhea does nothing to contribute to nutrition.

Lactose and Cataracts

Lactose consumption produces more permanent, long-term effects in those who *are* able to break it down to its component sugars, glucose, and galactose. When older adults drink milk, and *do* break down lactose into galactose, they can develop high levels of galactose in their blood. A high rate of cataract formation is seen in older adults who are lactose digesters (lactase-persistent), and galactose from milk is believed to be the cause.[50] Damage is caused by the elevated levels of galactose sugar circulating in the blood. Adults often gradually lose the enzyme that breaks down galactose. According to gynecologist Daniel Cramer, 10% of Americans are unable to digest galactose, and one does not know whether they are digesting galactose or not, since there are no noticeable immediate symptoms for inability to digest it as there are with lactose.[51]

In nature, this would not be a problem for adults, as just about the only source of galactose in the diet is from milk sugar—a baby food. An infant born with a rare inability to break down galactose (found in 1 in 18,000 infants) develops mental retardation and cataracts, which often become pronounced before a diagnosis can be made.[52] Mice experimentally subjected to regular galactose exposure show the kind of brain deterioration seen in humans who develop Alzheimer's disease.[53]

Milk and Leukemia

Bovine leukemia virus is widespread in commercial dairy herds.[54] This leukemia virus is a member of the human leukemia group of retroviruses and is known to infect human cells in the laboratory. Pasteurization kills this virus in cow's milk rather efficiently, although accidents certainly happen. Pasteurization errors are documented to have caused other diseases. Such incidents may be responsible for the occasional geographical

THE DANGERS OF COW'S MILK

pockets of leukemia cases identified. Raw milk is certainly dangerous to drink if not from a well-trusted source. It has been established that dairy farmers have higher leukemia rates.[55] In the late 70s it was also determined that geographic areas of high cow's milk consumption have higher leukemia rates than areas of low consumption.[56] Iowa, a major dairy-producing state, has a high rate of leukemia, and these cases tend to concentrate around counties with the highest rates of leukemia in the cows.[57] Recent studies comparing the diets of leukemia patients with those of healthy patients in Italy and Poland both came up with heavy milk consumption as the strongest risk factor.[58,59] The Polish study points out that the drinking of milk from one's own cows (which would be very fresh and unpasteurized) poses a great risk.

The most worrisome aspect of this situation is the U.S. dairy farmer's attitude toward this possible danger. A Swedish study on this problem reported that their dairy industry was striving to eradicate this infection in their herds.[60] By contrast, U.S. dairy farmers have noted that milk production goes up when a cow is infected with this leukemia virus, so they promote ways to take advantage of this situation. While the "genetic potential for milk production was significantly greater in seropositive cows (those with the leukemia virus)...milk fat percentage was significantly reduced" when cows developed full-blown disease. The recommendation?—"These results suggest a need to reevaluate the economic impact of bovine leukemia virus infection on the dairy industry."[61] Yes, you heard right, the *economic* impact. It is also known that cows infected but not extremely ill with leukemia virus actually live longer.[62] University of Illinois researchers discovered a way to save the dairy industry the estimated $42 million dollars each year that was lost due to full-blown infection in these desirable leukemic cows. The researchers found a gene that allows cows to maintain their infection without converting to the full-blown stage.[63]

> *U.S. dairy farmers have noted that milk production goes up when a cow is infected with this leukemia virus, so they promote ways to take advantage of this situation.*

Unfortunately, a cow with the leukemia virus does not need to be in the full-blown stage in order to spread the virus to other mammals, like humans. Another link between milk and leukemia will be discussed a bit later.

Lung Cancer

While the role of diet in highly fatal lung cancer is weak when compared to that of smoking, recent studies have looked for such links since smoking rates have decreased faster than lung cancer rates have, and nonsmoker lung cancer cases are going up. A U.S. study found a dietary connection between saturated fat consumption (meaning dairy and meat) and increased lung cancer risk.[64] An Uruguay study found that a saturated fat effect from fried meats, which creates a different kind of carcinogen, only affected current smokers, but dairy products affected both current and past smokers. Dairy fat is different from other fats due to its concentration of hormones. A Norwegian study reported that whole milk has twice the risk as skim milk, while no association was found for other saturated fats or cholesterol intake.[65] Two separate Swedish studies mentioned milk as the only dietary risk, high intake leading to double the number of lung cancers as found in low-dairy consumers.[66,67]

Milk and Prostate Cancer

A study of nearly 26,000 Norwegian men found nonfat milk to be the most significant dietary link to prostate cancer.[68] A smaller Italian study also reported milk, but not milk fat, to be a risk factor, and a strong factor with 2 or more glasses of milk per day.[69] Most recently, a 1999 epidemiological study of 41 countries found the strongest association between diet and prostate cancer to be the nonfat portion of milk.[70] Some continue to suggest that genetic differences associated with race are the key to the wide variations in this disease rate around the world. However, when Asians and Africans from regions with very low prostate cancer rates migrate to the United States, their rates rise dramatically with each generation or with the amount of time spent in this nation.[71] Prostate cancer has traditionally been very rare in Japan, but rates have soared since Western formula supplementation and adult dairy consumption were introduced.[72] Prostate cancers in the African nation of Nigeria, much of which was hit early and hard by milk formula campaigns and followed by promotion of milk consumption for children and adults, have climbed rapidly over each of the last 4 decades.[73] These cancers remain rare in African populations with prolonged breastfeeding and non-dairy diets.[74] A study spanning 42 nations finds strong associations of cheese and milk with testicular cancers as well as prostate.[75] Prostate cancer attacks U.S. men in their 50s and 60s and is the second leading cancer killer in U.S. men (now number 1 in Nigeria). The exact role of milk has yet to be determined, but its estrogen is one suspect.

Milk and Ovarian Cancer

Female milk drinkers face 2 to 3 times the risk of developing ovarian cancer.[76,77] While dairy products contain much fat, and fat consumption is known to be linked with ovarian cancer, the milk connection proves to be much more powerful than just this. Traditionally, ovarian cancer has been considered a disease of societies with lactase enzyme persistence, and links to lactose have been hypothesized.[78,79] However, as dairy has been pushed into more areas around the world, even where adults do not retain lactase enzyme, ovarian cancer rates have increased parallel to per capita milk consumption. Increases are also being seen in the United States, England, and Canada in lactose-intolerant subpopulations where ovarian cancer was once low, seemingly because lactose-intolerant people have been encouraged to eat cheese, yogurt, and milk with Lactaid, increasing their dairy exposure. Contemplating their findings of strong

A 1999 epidemiological study of 41 countries found the strongest association between diet and prostate cancer to be the nonfat portion of milk. Prostate cancers have climbed rapidly over each of the last 4 decades.

links between milk, cheese, and ovarian cancer, Japanese researchers suggest the connection may be the high levels of estrogen and progesterone found in cow's milk over the last many decades.[80] Humans now drink the milk of pregnant cows—something new to our diets since the mid-twentieth century. This milk has considerably higher levels of female bovine hormones compared to traditional cow's milk. The 5-year survival rate for ovarian cancer is less than 40% and 8 in every 100,000 American women die of this cancer.

> *Female milk drinkers face 3 times the risk of developing ovarian cancer, and 8 in every 100,000 American women die of this cancer.*

Milk and Infertility

Increasingly younger infertility ages have also been linked to the harmful effects of dairy consumption with increasing milk consumption per capita.[81]

Puberty and Breast Cancer

In some portions of the world, and in some peoples, puberty is arriving at earlier and earlier ages. These regions and peoples are the ones with the highest rates of formula feeding and childhood dairy consumption. These same children are also approaching their mature heights sooner. This phenomenon has been ascribed to improved nutrition. Dairy products are responsible for much of the perception that improved nutrition is being supplied, as well as for many of the consequences being recorded. In fact, regions that do not meet the accelerated growth expectations of large dairy-consuming populations are labeled deficient and malnourished, as are vegans (who consume no dairy), even though dairy consumption and its effects are not natural. There is no basis for assuming the results are superior or desirable. The actual effects are shocking. Two percent of U.S. girls are beginning pubic hair growth or breast development at the age of 3! Faster growth may sound appealing, however, not only does early puberty lead to increased teen pregnancies and sexually transmitted diseases, but *accelerated growth means cancer*, and the statistics are bearing this out.

In 1988, Japanese researchers noticed a high correlation between early puberty and higher milk consumption.[82] Milk is not the only factor associated with early onset of menstruation; higher consumption of animal fats is also linked,[83] but milk is a major contributor to the total animal fat in diets. We have already discussed the connection between low parental responsiveness, which is sometimes connected with formula feeding, and early puberty. Another strong link to early puberty is a decreased response to insulin which leads to elevated blood insulin levels along with increases in an insulin-like growth factor.[84] Remember, early and extensive dairy consumption is strongly linked to this pre-diabetic condition.

Ages of puberty among specific populations in the United States and around the world correlate with the history and volume of childhood dairy consumption. African Americans receive formula from birth more often than the rest of the American population. At age 8, 15% of white girls and nearly 50% of African American girls are showing pubic hair or breast development.[85] The average age of menstrual onset for U.S. black girls is just over 12 and for whites is just before 13. Compare this with girls studied in the African country of Cameroon who began menses after the age of 14 when living in highly breastfeeding rural areas,[86] but where the age of menarche dropped toward 13 the closer the children lived to the breastfeeding but formula-supplementing urban center of Yaounde.

> Ages of puberty among specific populations in the United States and around the world correlate with the history and volume of childhood dairy consumption. Early puberty is strongly associated with developing breast cancer.

In nearby Senegal, with nearly universal breastfeeding and minimal dairy exposure, average menarche is at age 16. Mexico and Cuba are strong breastfeeding countries. But the breastfeeding rate for immigrants from these countries living in the United States drops for each successive generation. Recent measures show 45% of Hispanic American girls, 42% of Caucasians, and 80% of African Americans are developing breasts at 9 years of age.[87] In Mexico, the average age of menstrual onset was reported to be 14.25 years in rural areas in 1977, and 12.65 in urban centers where formula supplementing was widespread.[88] Japan has been seeing reductions in puberty ages following years of increased dairy consumption as well, along with the attendant accelerations in attaining mature height.[89] Norwegians, who have long been moderate dairy consumers and who have maintained very high breastfeeding rates, have seen little change in their average puberty age over the last century.[90]

Early puberty is strongly associated with developing breast cancer.[91–94] The increased growth factors involved and the earlier estrogen surges are in large part responsible for the accelerated cellular reproduction in the breasts that is associated with cancer development.[95]

Breast cancer is the second leading cause of cancer deaths for U.S. women. This disease rose by more than 50% from 1950 to 1990.[96] This corresponds with the rise in formula-feeding decades earlier when these women were infants. Many studies reveal that breast cancer rates correlate directly with levels of milk consumption in childhood and adulthood,[97–99] while more current studies fail to find a relationship with adult consumption levels. Two studies specifically point out that a failure to receive breastmilk correlates with a 35% increase in breast cancer risk.[100, 101] Let's return for a moment to Cameroon. While formula supplements are infiltrating urban regions, the nation's overall rate and duration of breastfeeding is much higher than that in the United States, and adult dairy consumption is relatively new. Cameroon's overall breast cancer rate is estimated at 10 per 100,000 citizens (corrected for under-diagnosis),[102] while that of the United States is 110 per 100,000[103]—11 times higher. The French authors (from a very formula- and dairy-oriented country) of the Cameroon puberty study suggest that the reduced age for menstrual initiation in the city girls demonstrates improved nutrition (which would mostly be from formula and milk). Another French study similarly interprets data on girls in another West African country. Peoples of rural Senegal have maintained nearly universal breastfeeding for long periods. Researchers report "stunted" growth before puberty, and menarche that is "delayed" to age 16.[104] Their studies then report that boys and girls experience "catch-up growth" after puberty. The final attained heights in adulthood in all such studies appear to be the same, with some conflicts in Asian reports.

By way of comparison, the "early growth stunted" people of Senegal suffer one-fiftieth as much colon cancer as is seen in the United States.[105] Overall cancer rates in Cameroon are one-fifth that in the United States, and Senegal's rates are even lower. As with early puberty (and diabetes, heart disease, bowel disease, osteoporosis, and several other cancers), breast

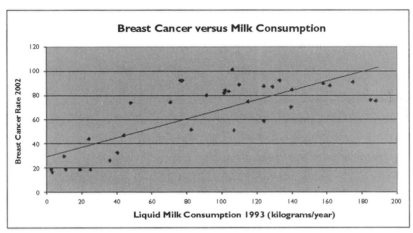

Figure 11-2 Palmer, 2009. 2002 breast cancer rates per 100,000 people versus 1993 liquid milk consumption for 34 countries from left to right: China, Thailand, Cameroon, India, Senegal, Chili, Uganda (1997), Mexico, Japan, Philippines, Argentina, Italy, Belgium, France, Greece, Germany, Switzerland, Canada, Australia, United States, Spain, Denmark, Norway, Czechoslovakia, United Kingdom, Netherlands, New Zealand, Austria, Finland, Iceland, Sweden, Israel, Malta, Ireland. [106–110]

cancer rates around the world correlate strongly with dairy consumption, trailing dairy increases by 2 or 3 decades.

Cow Hormones and Cancer

All cow's milk contains a protein called "bovine insulin-like growth factor-1." This factor is identical to human IGF-1.[111] This growth-promoting hormone is named for its structural similarity to insulin. Insulin also plays a role in growth regulation. We have already seen how cow's milk is connected to either too much insulin from decreased recognition of it by the body, or too little insulin, due to the body's autoimmune destruction of insulin-producing pancreatic cells. Human IGF-1 exists in mother's milk and is an important factor in the growth of infants. However, beyond childhood we have no reason to consume growth hormones. This growth hormone may be partly responsible for the accelerated growth seen in dairy-consuming children. Remember, rapid growth, especially when controls are out of balance, leads to cancer. Adults often harbor multiple benign tumors (cell overgrowths that are not out of control) in their bodies. Influenced by high doses or prolonged exposures to growth-accelerating factors, these can become malignant, meaning cancerous. Infants or young children should not have such precancerous growths in their bodies, and thus the growth hormones needed for rapid development don't promote tumor growth. As mentioned earlier, vitamin K injections at birth may be one source of loss of control over cell growth leading to early precancerous conditions in children, which could then be susceptible to the effects of growth hormones, leading to malignancies in children, such as leukemia. Human growth hormones naturally peak during puberty and drop gradually throughout maturity. There is a protective reason for this drop after growth is completed. Excess IGF-1 is strongly implicated in many kinds of cancers. Besides promoting cell division, IGF-1 protects cells from their normal preprogrammed cell deaths, creating a further cancer risk.[112]

> Breast cancer is the second leading cause of cancer deaths for U.S. women. Studies reveal that breast cancer rates correlate directly with levels of milk consumption in childhood and adulthood.

A large percentage of the IGF-1 in dairy foods is protected from digestive enzymes by the casein protein and milk's buffering effects. Human, cow, and all mammal milks are designed this way in order to make important hormones, proteins, antibodies, and many other milk factors available to the baby. As shown in Chapter 13, infants and others who have intolerance reactions to bovine proteins suffer intermittent drops in digestive enzymes and develop "leaky guts" that allow even greater concentrations of various undigested proteins into the bloodstream.

Greek medical researchers studying childhood leukemia recently confirmed that excess quantities of IGF-1 might play an important role in developing this devastating cancer that has become increasingly prevalent throughout the twentieth century.[113] These researchers also answered one of the common rebuttals to the IGF cancer reports. Dairy supporters suggest that the levels of IGF-1 in milk are infinitesimally small. However, the effective level of this growth hormone normally active in the human body, even in childhood, is also very small. Although the average level of IGF-1 in cow's milk is around 30 nanograms (.00000003 grams) per milliliter, growth promoting effects are seen in response to 1 nanogram per milliliter.[114] San Francisco researchers showed that addition of IGF-1 alone was enough to stimulate the kind of accelerated white blood cell growth connected with leukemia.[115]

Some naysayers suggest that growth hormones are digested before having any effect. Again, milk is purposefully designed to deliver these hormones. It is proven that IGF-1 from milk is absorbed by rats and pigs, and high dairy intake is associated with high blood levels of IGF-1 in humans.[116]

Prostate cancer also has strong ties to high IGF-1 levels.[117,118] Breast cancer researchers from Baltimore reiterate that insulin-like growth factors are potent promoters of malignant cell production, and they specifically indict IGF-1.[119] Others have drawn the same conclusion.[120,121] Similarly, IGF-1 is implicated in ovarian cancer, which has risen in the United States by 18% in the last 20 years alone.[122-124] Brain tumors, gastrointestinal cancers, and childhood bone cancers are also associated with IGF-1.[125-127]

Other hormones and factors in cow's milk remain after pasteurization and have the potential to promote cancer as well. These include free estrogens, at a level similar to that in human milk,[128] and prostate-specific antigen, in high levels compared to that in male blood.[129] Other naturally occurring growth factors and hormones and estrogen mimics from concentrated pesticides and other environmental pollutants are suspected as well. Although the growth factor picture is very complicated and direct links to that from cow's milk are not entirely proven, IGF-1 attracts special attention for many reasons. One is the play of events to follow.

An Udder Conspiracy

As if cow's milk weren't bad enough in and of itself, now one-third of all U.S. cows are being injected with a synthetic bovine growth hormone (BST or rBGH). This hormone is used to increase milk production by about 15%. It also raises the IGF-1 levels in milk by 2 to 10 times.[130] This additional growth hormone is much more potent because much of it is "free," rather than bound to milk proteins. Additionally, it has been learned that pasteurization actually increases its potency, according to a 1990 Food and Drug

Administration (FDA) report. Concerns have been raised by many scientists over rBGH use since 1985 when the FDA approved widespread experimentation with this hormone in commercial milk production. In 1993, the agency completely approved commercial usage. Its approval was based on safety studies provided by Monsanto, the manufacturer of the hormone.

Robert Cohen, in his highly revealing book, *Milk, The Deadly Poison*, presents a large amount of detailed documentation about how Monsanto's top scientist was hired by the FDA to review her own research.[131] Monsanto's attorney was hired by the FDA to write regulations for the rBGH approval. Using this hormone in cows causes a large increase in udder infections, and thus a large increase in the use of antibiotics. This attorney also helped make sure that the regulations for antibiotic levels in milk were revamped (i.e. loosened) at the same time. He then was hired by the USDA where he implemented related protocols. These ties go on and on. The Dairy Coalition conducted a large seminar on rBGH safety for medical doctors, then a coalition doctor and a Monsanto-paid doctor wrote the key paper for the *Journal of the American Medical Association*, expounding on the safety of rBGH and the need for milk to promote health. The AMA and American Dietician's Association received large sums of money from Monsanto as well. A U.S. Congress bill to mandate labeling of milk products with rBGH in them was never voted on; four congressmen on the committee had received monetary gifts from Monsanto. Monsanto now tries to sue anyone who attempts to label any milk-based product as "rBGH free." Ben and Jerry's Ice Cream won the first lawsuit.

Monsanto's research paper presented to the FDA was never released for public or outside scientific review; instead, Monsanto provided the FDA with summaries of the company's own experiments. When the case was brought before the Canadian government, however, the Canadian Health Protection Branch scrutinized the evidence and discovered that this hormone was absorbed into the bloodstream of 25% of the study rats, even though the paper's conclusion claimed otherwise. The Canadian researchers also noticed that some rats developed dangerous indications in their thyroid and prostate glands in this short trial. Canadian scientists caused a serious setback for Monsanto when they revealed Monsanto's bribery attempts. Canada has banned the use of this synthetic growth hormone, as have Europe, Australia, New Zealand, and Japan.

When investigative reporters for a Fox-owned TV station in Tampa,

Florida, tried to release the story, their report was stopped by Fox under pressure from Monsanto. They were asked to report a false rendition of the story, but they refused. Ensuing struggles by these reporters and their refusal to accept Fox's monetary offers finally led to their firing. The details of the lawsuit they won can be found on the Internet.[132] There is no absolute proof of danger to humans from consuming this hormonally enhanced milk; no human studies have been done. Instead, the research is going on today in your baby's body and your own. The results will not show up for two or three decades, but since the milks are not labeled, the evidence will be impossible to assemble.

Osteoporosis

But doesn't my child need the calcium? While the National Osteoporosis Foundation tells us we need more calcium, especially from cow's milk, in order to build stronger bones, the scientific evidence does not support this.

The Chinese University of Hong Kong performed successive studies in the 90s analyzing milk and calcium intake as related to the growth of children. This was an ideal place and time for such an investigation because cow's milk was just making its way into popular use in that country, and the traditional diet was not high in calcium. The first study looked at children from birth to 5 years of age. With 90% of the study children drinking milk, their average calcium intake was 550 milligrams.[133] In the second study, 7-year-old children were given calcium supplements to bring their daily calcium intakes up to 800 milligrams. Over 18 months, no increases were seen in height or arm or leg bone density beyond those not supplemented, although some improvement in spinal bone density was seen.[134] At ages 12 to 13, calcium intake did not correlate to bone mineral content, except that the girls who consumed the higher levels of calcium had *lower* bone density in their arms.[135] In all these studies, higher weight and greater physical activity were strongly associated with higher bone mineral content. By adolescence, neither calcium intake nor physical activity had any more influence on bone mineral improvement.[136]

In a widely quoted study by a British hospital, researchers provided an extra glass of cow's milk to adolescent girls' diets, comparing their growth to those who drank an average of just over one-half cup per day. Total daily calcium intake at the beginning of the study was 750 milligrams; the extra milk group increased to 1,100 milligrams. The researchers reported about 10% greater bone growth rate for those with the extra milk.[137] These children also gained a little more weight, but not height. The reported extra bone density could not be validated by any changes in the blood enzyme markers that typically reflect bone growth and bone reabsorption. Insulin-like growth factor was found to be higher in the extra-milk group. Several experts wrote replies to this study, which had been paid for by the U.K. dairy industry. One group suggested that *their* math found the milk group to actually have a slightly lower average total bone mineral content at the end of the study.[138]

Scientific and dairy industry studies on childhood milk consumption come and go frequently. While marketing success keeps the milk mantra alive, there have been large reviews of the most well-designed studies concluding that there is no benefit toward encouraging any level of milk consumption by children. The journal *Pediatrics* published a 2005 medical review of 58 studies on calcium consumption in children and reported: "neither increased consumption of dairy products, specifically, nor total dietary calcium consumption has shown even a modestly consistent benefit for child or young adult bone health."[139] In 2006, an Australian team selected only the most controlled of studies and found a one-tenth of 1% increase in bone mineral content (bone hardness) for children with higher amounts of calcium from diet or supplements.[140]

While dairy promotions include praise for the protein in milk, this protein may be more of a problem in osteoporosis than calcium, a solution. The animal proteins of meat and dairy products cause calcium loss.[141] The level of calcium needed in the diet depends greatly on animal protein intake.[142] For many Americans with high animal protein diets, it may not be possible to consume enough calcium to compensate for the amount lost to these high-acid proteins.[143] For this reason, Americans have among the highest osteoporosis rates in the world. Doubled animal protein causes 50% more calcium loss. Yet, when a high-protein intake is soy based, a positive calcium balance can be maintained with only 450 milligrams of calcium per day.[144]

> The animal proteins of meat and dairy products cause calcium loss. Americans have among the highest osteoporosis rates in the world.

The chief concern over bone density is that bone density gradually declines with maturity. At a certain point of bone loss, the term "osteoporosis" is used. This is a level where low-trauma bone fractures become more frequent. Spinal fractures are a problem, as are hip and arm fractures. The highest level of bone density attained in young adulthood correlates with the bone density maintained in later decades. What is not entirely understood is how much impact dietary factors have on these events. Studies do not reveal any benefit from childhood milk consumption.

At the same time that diabetes, cancer, and other concerns may limit the amount of dairy that should be given a child, after childhood bone protection is no reason to establish a dairy habit in children. In 1986 a Harvard researcher produced the following graph, which demonstrates a nearly direct relationship between calcium intake and hip fractures,[145] i.e., the more calcium consumed, the more likely are hip fractures. A 1987 study of 106 adult

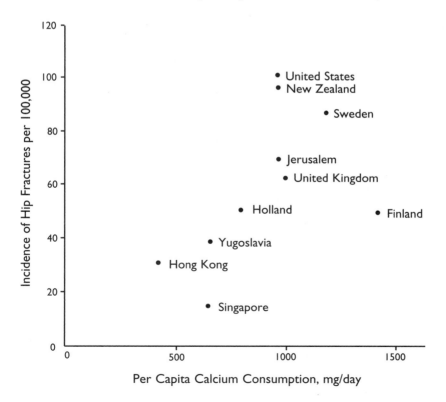

Figure 11-3 Rate of hip fractures occurring (signifying osteoporosis) in relation to the calcium consumption of several nations. Hegsted, 1986.[146]

women suggested that calcium intake between 500 and 1,400 milligrams per day led to no difference in bone mineral densities.[147] A larger Italian study found that in women who consumed between 440 and 1,025 milligrams of calcium per day, a slightly increased number of hip fractures occurred with higher milk intakes.[148] *A more recent study of 78,000 nurses found that women who drank more than 1 glass of milk per day had a 45% greater chance of hip fractures*, compared to those who drank far less.[149] Those who took in the same amount of calcium from nondairy sources saw no such increase, nor a decrease in fractures. Since many studies are performed on women only—they do suffer more osteoporosis—Harvard researchers decided to look at men. They found that those who drank 3 or more glasses of milk per day, compared to 1 or less per week, had very slightly fewer hip fractures, but these were balanced by slightly more arm fractures.[150] The highest calcium intakes from food and supplements together produced an increase in fractures overall.

The rate of hip fractures in the United States for people of many races and ethnic origins is exactly inverse to their rates of lactose intolerance. In other words, those who are likely avoiding milk as adults have the fewest fractures. Non-Hispanic white women have 139 per 100,000, Mexican Americans have 67 per 100,000, and African Americans average 55 per 100,000.[151] The indigenous people of South Africa have not traditionally been dairy consumers. Their consumption is still very low, although formula is making great inroads. Those of osteoporosis age today, however, would not have been raised on formula. Typically, South Africans consume only 200 milligrams of calcium per day, but their rate of fractures is extremely low—fewer than 7 per 100,000 people per year.[152] Compare this to their dairy-exposed American counterparts. The milk-drinking (and higher calcium intake) populations around the world are the ones who have osteoporosis as a major problem.[153] These rates are increasing in typically low fracture areas around the world as these regions adopt Western practices.

> *A recent study of 78,000 nurses found that women who drank more than 1 glass of milk per day had a 45% greater chance of hip fractures, compared to those who drank far less.*

In Japan, as with many other non-Caucasian populations, dairy intake has traditionally been minimal and calcium intakes have been low—and hip fracture rates are low, but have been growing recently,[154] as is the portion of adults who were raised on dairy. While industrialization also brings reduced physical exercise, there is a much more consistent common denominator seen in the timing and geographic regions of these bone problems—cow's milk. While we feel our nutrition is superior today than centuries past, archeological research has shown that Caucasian post-menopausal bone loss in the eighteenth and nineteenth centuries was less than that seen today.[155] Clearly, high calcium intake, and certainly high dairy intake, are not the way to prevent osteoporosis.

Milky Messages

Why the conflicts between the bulk of research findings and the recommendations of the National Osteoporosis Foundation (NOF)? It could be because much of NOF funding comes from corporations such as Kellogg's Cereal Company and Dairy Farmers of Maitland, Florida. Other funding comes from small and large private donations, with some from the federal government.[156] Another big supporter of the National Osteoporosis Foundation is Bozell Worldwide, the marketing firm that created the huge milk mustache campaign for the dairy industry. Only 2% of the NOF's funding has gone to osteoporosis research.

Good, Bad, and Curious Solutions

Other common foods that are excellent sources of calcium, listed in order of highest amount per calorie, are molasses, dark salad greens, cabbage, broccoli, green beans, cucumber, peas, soybeans, squash, most types of beans (including cocoa), figs, kiwi, almonds, real maple syrup, brown sugar, and tomatoes. In addition to this list is, of course, human milk. Calcium may also be added to corn tortillas and some orange juice, apple juice, and rice and soy milks. When these foods are the major source of calcium, and meat intake is not high, USRDA levels are likely in great excess of needs.

The World Health Organization suggests that 400 to 500 milligrams of calcium per day is appropriate for adults. The United States RDA for calcium is 800 milligrams for most people 1 year of age and over and 1,200 milligrams for teens and pregnant and lactating mothers. The United States' is the highest recommendation in the world. Beyond these earlier set standards, the U.S. National Institutes of Health (NIH) has gradually raised its recommendations for calcium: for children 6 to 10 years old, 800 to 1,200 milligrams; 11 to 24 years, pregnant, or nursing, 1,200 to 1,500 milligrams; over 65, 1,500 milligrams. These new recommendations were based chiefly on increasing osteoporosis problems. At the Development Conference on Optimal Calcium Intake, the NIH stated, "The preferred source of calcium is through calcium-rich foods such as dairy products."[157] The NIH reinforced vitamin D intake, too, which is added to milk and naturally derived from sun exposure or eating fish. The NIH does not, however, mention any of the other nutritional factors that are important for bone development—those that are inadequate in milk. At the same time, the report makes taking calcium supplements sound very complicated. Boron, copper, magnesium, manganese, zinc, and vitamins C and K are just as important as calcium for optimal bone growth. None of these are high in cow's milk, so none of these are advertised as important for bones. Phosphorous is important for bone development as well, but cow's milk has too much of this, causing decreased calcium availability. This is apparently why phosphorous is not mentioned either. Nor does NIH mention that reduced animal protein consumption would help calcium levels. (Remember that the beef industry is the other end of the dairy industry.) Deep in the text, the authors mention some other foods naturally high in calcium, but only in reference to vegans who do not drink milk. This list is rather inaccurate and exclusive, sounding quite distasteful. They also emphasize that a little pain and gas should not prevent the lactose intolerant from having at least 2 servings of milk per day.

> The milk-drinking (and higher calcium intake) populations around the world are the ones who have osteoporosis as a major problem.

As more problems become apparent with milk, and people buy less, greater measures are taken to encourage milk drinking. The motto for the government's Healthy People 2000 initiative was, "at least 3 cups of milk every day" for "every body." The NIH, whose initial intentions are often better than its final reported conclusions, funded half of the huge 1997 study that showed that nurses have more fractures when consuming more milk. To date, however, the agency has not changed its recommendations about milk consumption. All the while, the American Dietetic Association, with grants from the dairy industry, continues to publish reports such as "Many Asian American elderly consume an inadequate amount of dietary calcium."[158] Its conclusions were based on their milk consumption, not their bones. It's obvious what the recommended solution was. A year 2000 dairy commercial shows young men playing basketball (exercising), while outside (soaking up vitamin D), two great ways to build stronger bones. A milk carton stands alongside urging them to go inside, sit down, and have some milk for their bones.

Dutch dairy researchers have come up with a new milk product designed to be better for bone health. They increased the calcium content and lowered the protein, phosphorus, and fat content—in other words, they lowered the dairy content. Not surprisingly, elderly people taking this new low-milk calcium supplement lost less calcium each day than those drinking normal milk.[159]

Raw Milk and Goat's Milk

Today's raw milk supporters assert that all of these studies on cow's milk are relevant only to the consumption of modern pasteurized, homogenized milk, not raw milk, proclaiming raw milk to be the true manna that was once attributed to this drink. However, some of the populations in these studies actually do drink raw milk. There are few studies performed specifically on raw milk, and cancer and other health links have not been measured.

Pasteurization of milk is a quick and low-temperature process that destroys few of the main components of milk. It doesn't even destroy all of the bacteria (its intended purpose). Pasteurization does reduce some of the immune-providing and absorption-aiding components of cow's milk, although far fewer of these exist compared to human milk. Bovine hormones, known to be problematic to humans, would only be more active in raw milk, if anything. Raw and pasteurized milk contain similar excesses of calcium, phosphorous, and protein, and have similar tendencies to cause anemia and relative magnesium deficiency, although it is possible that there's a trivial increase in absorbability of iron through lactoferrin in raw milk. Lactose content is the same in raw and pasteurized milk, and the major proteins do not become more or less easily digested by the application of low heat. I've heard it said that raw milk contains enzymes to break down lactose, but this is simply not true. Raw milk does contain bacteria that, over time, will digest both the lactose and proteins (as in cheese or yogurt). This is souring and soured milk is more digestible (the Maasai know this). Refrigeration retards this process greatly.

Allergenic potential remains,[160, 161] and I have seen this effect personally, although there are unexplained claims that raw milk does not cause the same allergic reaction as pasteurized milk. One may gain immune system boosts from the greater spectrum of bacteria in raw versus pasteurized milk. When the raw milk comes from conscientious organic dairy farms, these bacteria are nonthreatening and the milk is safer than commercial milk in terms of historic contamination accidents. There is talk of immune stimulating properties of the whey protein beta-lactoglobulin from raw milk, but one laboratory study of this claim found that the immune stimulation was actually caused by endotoxins[162]—a substance released by bacteria. Homogenization of milk fats may cause harmful health effects just as once seemingly innocent hydrogenation of vegetable oils has, but there are no reports of this in the scientific literature. Goat's milk, raw or processed, has many of the same issues as cow's milk. The proteins are shown to be similarly difficult to digest and almost as frequently allergenic, in spite of claims to the contrary.[163] It has the same lactose, of course, similar IGF-1 and other hormones concentrated in similar fat portions, excessive phosphorous, etc.

There is a small trend today toward creating homemade infant formulas from raw cow's or goat's milk. I have examined the ratios of the major components in these and find them to be startlingly different from human milk or even formula. For starters, the protein/carbohydrate/fat ratios are incredibly important and are not being mimicked. A study on providing bovine colostrum to tiny infants, as some are trying, shows,

> Boron, copper, magnesium, manganese, zinc, and vitamins C and K are just as important as calcium for optimal bone growth. None of these are high in cow's milk, so none of these are advertised as important for bones.

unfortunately, that a baby mounts an adverse inflammatory reaction to it, outweighing any potential benefits.[164] Looking at the efforts of oodles of scientists working for over 100 years at multiple infant formula laboratories to optimize nutritional viability of formulas—and the continual discoveries of imbalanced or lacking nutrients hindering the health and development of babies to this day—it's extremely risky to try experimenting with homemade formula on one's very precious newborn. On the other hand, I have evaluated the amounts of all major nutrients in a recipe by the Weston Price Foundation and find it to be rather complete for an artificial baby milk. I see some trying to reduce the sugar amounts in recipes they find and this is most dangerous. Human milk is nearly 50% carbohydrates, and this sugar is important for brain development. Organic formulas (and possibly the provision of one-eighth teaspoon daily of cod liver oil) may be a preferable option to standard or homemade formula, but it's hard for any substitute to measure up to the proven benefits of breastmilk.

Deflating Dairy

The norms promoted as desirable for childhood growth rates and puberty are based on those who consume bovine growth hormones early and regularly, not those who are raised on natural foods. While the same height is achieved in the end, with obesity more common on the side of dairy consumers,[165] those with the so-called superior nutrition experience a traumatic increase in cancer, heart disease, diabetes, and many other diseases.

The highly promoted idea that milk builds strong bones refers to attempts to prevent osteoporosis. Decades of effort to demonstrate that high calcium diets chiefly derived from dairy products build strong bones have failed to prove any such correlation. In fact, the opposite seems to be true.[166] It appears that high calcium intake before puberty, and especially in young childhood, may have some slight positive effect on bones, but a high dairy diet is not the answer. A balanced intake of all the bone minerals, along with adequate vitamins A, C, D, and K, is what is truly needed. A balanced intake of minerals cannot occur when the diet emphasizes dairy. Dairy's high calcium causes relative deficiencies in magnesium and other bone-building minerals, and its high phosphorus and animal protein reduce calcium availability. Physical activity has the greatest benefit—the body efficiently uses what is available to build strong bones when it senses the need. Human milk and vegetable sources are superior to dairy for calcium and other nutrients in many ways. There are fewer nutritional or other health advantages to giving cow's milk to children than is generally believed, while there are certainly many risks.

If you pay attention to health research announcements in the news, you will notice that almost every day another finding is made about the benefits of whole grains, soy, a serving of vegetables, two fruits per day, cashews, legumes, fish, or some other food, and their connection to a reduced risk of heart disease, breast cancer, stroke, diabetes, or other disease. Milk is conspicuously absent from this list. While recent tests in the lab have supposedly revealed certain minute elements of milk that have beneficial actions, these petrie dish findings are relatively meaningless in light of actual population studies that tell a different story. This is because cow's milk and its derivatives today make up one-third of the adult diet and half to two-thirds of caloric intake in children, thus replacing so much other important, nutritious food needed in the diet. This leads to insufficient intake of some important vitamins, several minerals, healthy fiber, and fatty acids. Cancer-preventing antioxidants in foods are low in this milk diet as well. While a valuable form of antioxidant vitamin A is found in milk fat, and is added to nonfat milk (but not all dairy products), the full complement of vitamin A precursors and associated enzymes, found in vegetables and other foods, is required for cancer prevention. Many, many more kinds of antioxidants are found in vegetables, legumes, fruits, and grains.

No other animal in the animal kingdom drinks milk beyond childhood. No other animal suffers from osteoporosis, except the occasional pet raised on human meals.

If there remains a desire to provide milk to a child who has no diarrhea, rashes, or other intolerance reactions, organic, possibly raw milk would be the best choice. In organic milk there are fewer antibiotic residues, no added hormones, and cows are given better feeds. Nonfat means fewer hormones and less chemical residue, although some believe in the positive effects of consuming the retinol form of vitamin A found in milk fat.

Goat's milk is considered by many to be superior in many ways. Much less documented information is available about goat's milk; however, there is no evidence that it is any more like human milk, or more human-friendly than cow's milk. It is claimed that the proteins are less problematic for digestion, although this is not recognized in studies. Allergic intolerance is just as likely, although babies would be less likely to be initially sensitized to goat's milk if their mother did not drink it during pregnancy or breastfeeding. Issues of lactose, hormones, and nutritional shortcomings remain, although, to date, goats apparently are not injected with extra growth hormone.

Although it was apparent from day one that formula was a health risk for infants, back when it was first promoted, cow's milk for older children appeared to be a nutritional manna. And with 1 or 2 fresh glasses a day from a healthy, range-fed animal, it likely was a beneficial addition to a good diet. Since this time, however, the quality of dairy has plummeted while its consumption has exploded…with a little advertising help. The evidence suggesting that the early faith in milk was misplaced has been building for decades. The dairy industry has had to take increasingly extreme efforts to keep this information out of public awareness.

I have only touched on the tip of the existing evidence against the health claims of milk industry promoters. Since our childhood, the dairy industry has worked hard to have dairy products enshrined in a food group of their own. Even though dairy products were given their own space in the new Eating Right food pyramid, they were placed in a small upper portion, prompting industry lobbyists to move to have the pyramid withdrawn.[167] Many nutrition experts such as Harvard's Dr. Walter Willett[168]

Figure 11-4 "Each year, LP&M (advertising agency) helps the American Dairy Association execute its national milk theme in elementary and junior high schools throughout the Northeast. The goal is to increase the consumption of milk by students during their school time meals."

—Latorra, Paul & McCann Advertising

suggest dairy products should not be a featured group in the pyramid at all. The dairy industry has also successfully convinced many vegetarians that milk from cows is a vegetarian food. Since few substantiated health claims can be made anymore, the milk industry's most recent promotion has been to simply show milk on the upper lip of celebrities of all kinds, even those who are dairy allergic (Bill Clinton), and even on those who are too young to be consuming whole milk (the Rugrats). Before this promo it was simply "got milk?" While an ever-growing preponderance of scientific information points to the dangers of cow's milk, favorable public and even mainstream medical opinion about dairy products has been very successfully maintained.

> My mother insists that we take him off dairy to see if that stops
> the ear infections. I have resisted because I have seen nothing
> in the literature to indicate that milk causes ear infections in a
> toddler. To be honest, he doesn't drink much milk or eat much
> cheese anyway. Should I take Mom's advice?

I won't repeat the answer this mother received, except to say that I
believe a simple dietary experiment has less potential for harm than a surgery
under anesthesia.

The most likely cause of this child's problem is obvious; the mother
provided multiple clues. First of all, this child had eczema—a condition
strongly correlated with food allergies. Secondly, at 17 months this child
apparently had no symptoms of an ear infection—no pain, fever, ear tugging,
complaining, or fussiness; therefore, in order for him to be diagnosed with
an ear infection, his doctor must have seen fluid in the child's ear. Mucus
production in the sinuses and inflammation of the mucous membrane tube
leading to the middle ear (the eustachian tube) prevents normal drainage,
allowing fluids produced in the middle ear to build up. Acute blockage can
occur with a cold or flu, but these were not mentioned, and the problem was
chronic. Chronic inflammation of the eustachian tube occurs as a result of
food or airborne allergic reactions. In this case, it appears that the normal
balance of flora in the middle ear was disrupted by multiple courses of antibiotics, until the child finally developed a true, painful infection. The third
clue is that the boy avoids dairy products. Finally, the grandmother must
have made some observations of her own, based on her suggestion.

My recommendation to the inquirer: Follow your mother's advice.

Colic, fussiness, sleeplessness, waking with screams, "owie" tummies,
spitting up, constipation, diarrhea, green stools, blood in stools, red anal
ring, pustules in the diaper area, eczema and other rashes, asthma, tantrums,
hyperactivity, malaise, ear infections, chronic stuffiness or nose picking,
bedwetting, and more: These are many of the maladies of infancy and childhood that are frequently associated with allergies and food sensitivities, and
thus are mostly avoidable. All of these symptoms have increased dramatically
in our children over the better part of the last century. Not only have we lost
much of the wisdom of our foremothers and polluted our surroundings with
countless chemicals, but we have drastically altered the diets of our babies and
children—not always with the best results.

How Common Are Allergies and Sensitivities?

During the early twentieth century, the introduction of cow's milk formulas and the push for nursing mothers to drink cow's milk saw a concurrent rise in eczema, diarrhea,* colic, ear infections, behavior problems, and other complaints in children. Today, chiefly because of cow's milk, food reactions and other allergies are at an all-time high. For decades, the average number of allergic individuals in the United States was accepted to be 15% of the population. Studies after the 1920s started to report increasingly larger numbers.

An allergy reaction is a set of symptoms resulting from the body's response to something that most healthy systems would not respond to. Infants most commonly display food allergies, and later these same children may display more airborne allergies. What is the rate of allergies in children today? It tends to boil down to a matter of semantics. Allergists typically like to speak only of reactions that can be measured by one kind of blood test for one kind of antibody, known as IgE antibody. There are all other kinds of immune system reactions to foods and environmental exposures, however (such as IgG, reduced IgA, various T-cell responses, and factors known as IL-10, TNF, and TGFß), and many of

In the United States, estimates are that well over 50% of children suffer some kind of hypersensitivity to foods, additives, or factors in the environment.

these reactors are not easily detected by common laboratory tests. Whether one wishes to call it allergy, intolerance, sensitivity, or enteropathy, the key should be whether certain normal foods or environmental substances make a child feel bad or break out in rashes. Those adhering to strict definitions, whereby their blood or scratch tests define whether one is allowed to claim they have negative reactions to a substance, report ranges of food allergy in

---

* Infectious diarrhea increased greatly, due to formula feeding, before the popularity of refrigeration and sterile bottle measures. Even now with good sanitation, infectious diarrhea rates are much higher because fewer infants are gaining disease protection from mother's breastmilk. Non-infectious diarrhea, related to food sensitivity reactions—which are discussed here—also increased considerably with the popularization of dairy products.

young children between 4 and 15% and total allergies up to 25%. By more encompassing, symptom/relief diagnosis, in 1993, Poland reported that 39% of its infants suffered from allergic disease.[1] A 1996 Health Survey for England reported 45% of children suffered from some form of allergy. As high as these numbers seem, they may not account for many delayed reactions that are poorly understood by the mainstream medical community. Today in the United States, estimates are that well over 50% of children suffer some kind of hypersensitivity to foods, additives, or something in their environment.[2]

How Often Is Food Sensitivity Found with Colic?

Colic, affecting at least 10 to 30% of babies,[3] is often one of the first signs of food sensitivities. Colic is characterized by inconsolable bouts of crying, gassiness, fussiness, poor sleep, and the appearance of being in pain. For those who are formula fed, removing cow's milk protein from the diet (using soy formula) leads to substantial improvement in many cases. With soy removed from the diet as well (using hydrolyzed protein formulas), relief is seen in 68 to 95% of infants.[4-7] Breastfed babies have a somewhat lower incidence of colic and food sensitivities (to foods in mother's diet) in general. Studies find 30 to 50% of breastfed colicky babies improve with removal of cow's milk and possibly a few other common allergens from mother's diet. Appropriate, complete elimination diets would reveal all problem foods, to relieve a much higher percentage of babies.

How about Food Sensitivity with Other Symptoms?

According to the Centers for Disease Control, nearly 20 million acute ear infections occurred in U.S. children in 1994. Allergist Tala Nsouli found food allergies in 78% of children with chronic ear infections.[8] In studies, food allergy has been found to be the cause in most cases of colitis in infants.[9-11] When milk and other allergenic foods were removed from these infants' diets, not only did symptoms disappear, but intestinal biopsies revealed great improvement in the intestinal walls, which had been damaged.

Gluten sensitivity, or celiac disease, generally beginning in infancy or childhood, is the only intestinal reaction that has long been medically recognized as a food intolerance. In this case, the gluten protein found in wheat and other grains instigates the destructive inflammatory reactions. The damage seen in this syndrome is very similar to that seen in milk sensitivity and other intestinal sensitivities.[12] It is well known that dietary management is the way to prevent the symptoms of celiac disease as well as the intestinal damage, and this has almost always been the recommended treatment. Unfortunately, most cases of celiac are missed, or misdiagnosed. Mood swings are reported in at least 37% of celiac children. It is now known that gluten and dairy sensitivity often go hand in hand.

Depending on the study, 80 to nearly 100% of Crohn's sufferers can maintain remission of symptoms and damage through food elimination diets.[13–15] The success of the study is usually dependent on the conscientiousness of the participants in following the diet. Significant elevations in IgA, IgG, or IgM antibodies to cow's milk particularly have been found in those diagnosed with Crohn's disease or ulcerative colitis.[16] These are diseases where inflammation and ulcers occur in the intestinal linings. Abdominal pain and diarrhea, sometimes bloody, are the chief symptoms. Eighty-seven percent of children suffering with the abdominal pain and diarrhea of irritable bowel syndrome recover through dietary management as well.[17]

In one study, migraine headaches may have been relieved in nearly 90% of children by eliminating the offending allergenic foods.[18] Other studies have produced similar results. In this migraine study, half of the children were found to have behavioral disorders, and 90% of those showed improved behavior on non-allergenic diets.

Elimination of cow's milk and other discovered allergens led to significant improvement in 73% of attention-deficit hyperactivity disordered (ADHD) children in a 1994 double-blind study.[19] Another study of behavioral disorders showed relief in more than half of those studied with the elimination of cow's milk alone.[20] A study that mapped electrical brain activities during food trials supports these conclusions.[21] The behavior that is diagnosed as ADHD in school-age children may stem from the same cause as great fussiness and irritability in infants, and bouts of wild and contrary behavior in preschoolers.

A high percentage of bedwetting children are found to be cured by eliminating allergenic foods.[22] Interestingly, a study of ADHD children found that they suffer day-wetting or bedwetting problems 4.5 times more often than other children.[23]

Food or other allergic reactions have been suggested as the cause for some cases of SIDS,[24] although the few small studies performed to date give weak, or absent, correlation.

Most cases of infant eczema are associated with food sensitivities. Skin rashes can be seen with the unaided eye, and thus, whether or not there are symptoms is less subject to interpretation (frequently, the validity of complaints of abdominal pain is questioned). For this reason, infant eczema seems to have become the most highly investigated manifestation of food allergy. While skin rashes are relatively minor compared to the other problems a child could have, it is rather rare to have eczema without any other signs of food sensitivity. The potential value of eczema observation is that it reveals to the unaided eye what may be occurring insidiously in more vital and more vulnerable organs inside the body—about which one should truly be concerned.

> *Elimination of cow's milk and other discovered allergens led to significant improvement in 73% of attention-deficit hyperactivity disordered (ADHD) children in a 1994 double-blind study.*

Combination and Progression of Symptoms

Generally, when more than one, especially more than two, symptoms are seen chronically without an obvious explanation, the chances that they are related to an allergy (and thus at least partially avoidable) are high.

A study by Italian doctors documented the evolution of allergic symptoms in some growing infants who couldn't tolerate cow's milk protein, the most common food sensitivity.[25] They found that the earliest symptoms were chiefly gastrointestinal, including colic, diarrhea or constipation, gas, abdominal pains, and vomiting. Around 5 years of age, the same children presented more wheezing (asthma) and constipation (although I see diarrhea at this stage just as often), and their reactions were more delayed. More often, children with persistent cow's milk protein intolerance presented multiple food intolerances and had parents with allergic symptoms. Many of those with persistent intolerance also have what is called "atopic disease," which is asthma, eczema, and rhinitis (runny nose), while very few of the children with short-term intolerance demonstrated these conditions. Another 1998 study, this time performed in Spain, reported a natural progression from food sensitivity, to respiratory allergy, to (not so surprising at this point) medication allergies.[26] Food sensitivities are also retained into late childhood and adulthood by many, but often to a milder or at least less symptomatic degree than in infancy.

Abdominal Pain

Abdominal pain can arise from dozens of disorders that originate everywhere, from the throat to the genitals. When any behavior in a child seems out of the ordinary to a parent, even when a child with frequent abdominal symptoms suddenly presents these symptoms differently, more severely, or they just arouse concern in any way, the parent may certainly wish to have the child examined for disease or disorder. In young infants, most chronic abdominal pain presents itself as colic.

Usually, abdominal discomfort in children is related in some way to food. Infants can have abdominal distress when they are hungry or when they have overeaten. A child whose diet varies widely can also have indigestion when his digestive enzymes are not accustomed to certain kinds of foods. It has been shown that levels of certain digestive enzymes take a few days to adapt to a change from the usual amounts of certain dietary constituents.

In a small infant, abdominal pains can sometimes be suspected when crying is accompanied by arching backward (often off the bed onto head and heels), refusing to lie on the stomach, or drawing the knees up over the abdomen. An infant in pain may kick, flail tight fists, and appear to be in despair. Parents learn to recognize their own infant's signs. All of these actions are certainly common in many infants. Possible allergic connections should be investigated when these behaviors occur frequently with no (or very slight) fever, when the parent derives a sense that the child is in frequent discomfort, and especially when other allergy symptoms are present as well. As an infant gets older, this same kind of pain may elicit more fussiness and crabbiness than crying.

Unless the child is throwing up and starting to swell minutes after consuming a food, delayed reaction is usually the more common but less recognized type of reaction. Abdominal pain will begin anywhere from an hour to two days after the offending food has been ingested—most often beginning

1 to 12 hours after ingestion. The pain may then continue on and off for a couple of days. Most bouts of abdominal pain in food-intolerant children usually coincide with other digestive symptoms such as passing gas, spitting up, vomiting, diarrhea, constipation, and rather varied stool appearance, including signs of undigested materials.

Acid Reflux or GERD

Pain that occurs 10 to 40 minutes after eating, especially pain felt while lying down, could be associated with gastric reflux. Gastric reflux is stomach acid spilling upward out of a weak gastroesophageal sphincter at the junction of the esophagus and stomach. A weak sphincter is actually normal in infants, with 60% of infants exhibiting some degree of gastroesophageal reflux, or GER, but they should not be in frequent pain from this. Rightfully, only rare, extreme cases of reflux should be diagnosed as gastroesophageal reflux *disease*, or GERD, and treated as such, but since the introduction of a new drug for reflux, suddenly most fussy, colicky babies are being diagnosed with GERD. Interestingly, these new, widely prescribed, proton pump inhibitors (such as omeprazole or Prilosec) admittedly do not improve colic.[27] They reduce measurable acid but seldom alter the course of the infant's symptoms. Reflux, which may or may not carry the pain of acid burning with it, is typically a secondary symptom resultant from foods consumed. If not caused by overeating or unusual diet, the source is usually a sensitivity reaction to the diet. One study found 42% of infants with gastric reflux were sensitive to cow's milk proteins.[28] If looking for all offending foods, and using food challenge methods (*see Chapter 14*), the relationship between food intolerance and GER would be found to be very high. Hiatal hernia might mimic reflux. A hiatal hernia is a condition in which the upper portion of the stomach is able to roll up through a weakened hole in the diaphragm. Even when this condition is found, if not extreme, it's not prudent to blame all of the child's symptoms on it.

"Allergy Ring" and Diaper Rash

Many food-sensitive infants will display an "allergy ring" many hours or up to 1 or 2 days after allergenic food consumption, providing a clue to his parents that he is suffering. Allergy ring is the popular name for a round area of bright redness (1 or 2 inches in diameter) around the anus. This bright redness of the skin surrounding the anus indicates an inflammatory reaction going on deep inside—in the colon. Sometimes this ring appears just after a stool of allergic material is passed. Dr. Doris Rapp in *Is This Your Child?* describes this sign as an indication of yeast infection in the child. Certainly, if candida (a yeast) did colonize the colon, this could bring about such a reaction, but yeast is not always cultured from these rings. Still, it is quite common for yeast and food sensitivities to go hand in hand, although the reasons for this are not entirely understood. Personally, I've been sensing that part of the phenomenon may be attributed to allergy reactions in the body to the yeast flora.

Often, diaper rash *is* candida. This yeast infection on the buttocks is often not symmetrical, may spread out from the reddest portions with red spots, and may favor the leg folds. It is a different phenomenon than the allergy ring. This kind of diaper rash could also indicate candida in the stool, and thus in the colon—a condition that may go along with food sensitivities, although yeast diaper rashes are very common in infants on antibiotics. To make matters more confusing, there is a condition of larger, symmetrical, bright red buttocks, sometimes with small sores, called "scalded buttocks," which is likely a more severe form of the allergy ring that occurs when the buttocks have been in diaper contact with allergic material for some time.

> One study found 42% of infants with gastric reflux were sensitive to cow's milk proteins.

Eczema of the diaper area will appear in irregular patches and resembles eczema rashes that appear on the face, hands, chest, and low back. This kind of "diaper rash" is likely associated with food sensitivities. A contact dermatitis rash can occur from a local skin allergy (as opposed to an internal food allergy) to detergent, softener, or other additive in the diaper itself, but would be seen only where the diaper is in direct contact with the skin. Other diaper rashes include some less common microbial infections, heat rash, and a chemical irritation rash that occurs when bacteria in the stool or on the unsterilized cloth diaper gain prolonged access to urea in the urine, causing ammonia formation and chemical burning of the skin. Diaper rashes are much more common in formula-fed babies and in babies wearing cloth diapers covered with plastic pants.

Treatment of diaper rash with steroid creams may provide temporary remission, but if the *cause* of the rash is not treated, it will only continue to return. Desitin (which has zinc and cod liver oil) or other barrier cream, and elimination of the causes of the rash, would be better choices than steroids with potentially serious side effects.

Child Avoids Certain Foods

As with other mammals, humans are born with an instinctive ability to avoid foods that have previously made them feel ill. This could be considered the first step in acquired immunity—we acquire the ability to avoid foods that will make us sick. These foods may be discerned by appearance, odor, taste, or even location. Besides simple dislike for the texture or flavor of a food, quite uncommon with dairy products, sensitivity is a common reason for a child to attempt consistently to avoid a food. Beyond the first year of life, foods may become so highly flavored and combined that it is more difficult for the subconscious brain to recognize the true culprit. This is why someone who suffered food poisoning from the potato salad at a big watermelon seed spitting contest will suddenly detest watermelon. This is also the reason why a child who usually refuses cheese or milk may quickly down a delightfully flavored chocolate shake. Of course, after one or two bad experiences with shakes, his intellect may assist his deeper instincts, and he'll avoid that food if possible. Other factors that can override this keen self-protective ability are constant encouragement or attempts to disguise foods, and outright hunger.

If a child seems to avoid dairy products, tomatoes, or some other food, it is probably best to follow his lead—especially if he suffers abdominal symptoms, stool changes, asthma, eczema, painful diaper rashes, or uncontrollable mood swings. One mother told me she had to work very hard to sneak tomatoes into her infant son's meals. Yes, they would cause him diarrhea—but she wanted him to derive the nutritional benefits and learn to enjoy a variety of ethnic dishes. The problem with this logic is that allergenic foods are tagged by the immune system to be rushed through without digestion or absorption, and any excess untagged portions can ignite a cascade of immune reactions that lead to inflamed intestinal linings, making it impossible for many other nutrients to be absorbed. Most likely there were whole pieces of undigested tomato and other foods in her son's stools. Not only will he not derive nutrition from tomatoes eaten, but he'll lose other nutrition from such a meal as well, and he may eventually learn to distrust any fancy-looking meal.

Infants who are sensitive to something in a formula—when it's their only food—may just become regularly cranky or withdrawn, slow growing, frequently waking, fussy eaters. These same infants will quickly and happily consume any solid food that is offered to them, and they will probably sleep better, given some relief from the formula.

Breastfed infants will become fussy at the breast or frequently reluctant to nurse if they are sensitive to foods in their mothers' diets. Sometimes they may learn to tell by taste or odor whether or not the current milk will be a problem for them. But when the offending food is in the milk most of the time, or when they react to multiple foods, they may just remain fussy nursers. Some of these infants become quickie-nursers who frequently need to come back for more out of hunger, and some go on nursing strikes. Unable to solve their dilemma and being frequently in discomfort, they, too, become cranky or antisocial babies most of the time.

Bedwetting and Daytime Incontinence

The inability to be in full control of one's bladder (after appropriate toilet training at an appropriate age) is known as "enuresis." Reduced bladder control is more common at night when the mind is asleep. Children who seem willing but are unable to successfully remain potty trained could have histamine-induced bladder contractions and inflammation secondary to food sensitivities.[29] Mast cells, which are initiators of most allergic responses, are most abundant in the membranes of the respiratory tract, under the skin, and in the linings of the urinary and intestinal tracts. Histamine-1 receptors, also abundant in the bladder wall, can react to immune system histamine releases just as those in the bronchii of the lungs do. Consequential inflammation and muscle contractions can cause strong urges to empty the bladder, which will cause wetting if the child cannot override them.

One analysis found that bedwetting, along with asthma and chronic illness, affected growth (*see the section on short stature, page 294*). Stunted growth was found to be even more pronounced for children suffering with bedwetting problems than for those with asthma.[30] Since no reduction in height was found in those with nonallergic chronic illnesses, allergic disease evidently plays a role in stunting growth.

Other factors often suggested as possible causes for bedwetting are hormonal imbalances, bladder immaturity, anatomical abnormalities, behavioral problems, chronic bladder infections, and dietary habits (such as drinking before bed). Bladder infections are more common in females; these infections are sometimes related to hygiene and often respond to cranberry juice. The issue of potty training is beyond the scope of this book, but I wish to caution against alarm over a child's toilet habits before kindergarten age. One would certainly want to eliminate the simpler or more likely causes of incontinence though (such as food reactions), before beginning expensive, frightening, or invasive diagnostic measures or deciding to medicate a child.

One should suspect that bedwetting is caused by allergy when other hypersensitivity symptoms are present in the child. Several studies have linked bedwetting to asthma, eczema, migraine, and hyperactivity, as well as to food intolerance. In a probe performed by Dr. Joseph Egger and his colleagues, three-fourths of children who found relief through elimination diets from migraines, hyperactivity, or both, also found relief from bedwetting problems through the diet.[31] As previously noted, a study of children diagnosed with attention-deficit hyperactivity disorder (*discussed below*) found their bedwetting to be 4.5 times that of other children.[32]

Behavior

Food intolerance reactions and other allergies or chemical sensitivities often affect the moods and behavior of children. Part of this effect is certainly a result of their discomfort, but more is learned every day about how histamine, serotonin, and prostaglandins, which are released when the body discovers allergens, act as neurotransmitters in the brain and affect mood ("shorten the fuse"). Casomorphins are endorphin-like products broken down from bovine casein (cow's milk proteins). Gliadorphins are similar products broken down from gluten (in grains). Altered absorption of these may cause behavioral symptoms as well. Scientists are only beginning to evaluate these. Generally, the reactive infant will demonstrate long or frequent inconsolable crying, a need to be bounced and walked all the time (to help override pain signals and mobilize gas bubbles), frequent waking from sleep, and general fussiness and crankiness. As the infant gets older, greater crankiness and contrariness replace much of the crying, eventually leading to tantrums. The ability to fall asleep is often poor. In younger children, fits will begin as the immune reaction begins and will rise and fall as intestinal and chemical conditions vary through a couple of days of reactivity. As reactive children get older, they may be more in control of their behavior at times, but they will also much more easily ignite into a mood they can no longer control.

The preschooler will continue with bouts of contrariness and tantrums, and may begin earning the label of "hyperactivity disorder" or "antisocial behavior." Once a child has grown too old to be diagnosed with "colic," and before he can be labeled hyperactive, there is a void where the behavior is considered normal—the "terrible twos," which in the allergic child can last from the "ones" through the "threes." Once this child enters school, the label of attention-deficit hyperactivity disorder (ADHD) is likely.

One recent investigation of 26 children diagnosed with ADHD found that 73% of these children improved on diets that eliminated common multiple allergenic foods, preservatives, and colorings.[33] The results were confirmed with double-blind, placebo-controlled challenges. An earlier but well-designed study found improvement in 82%, with full recovery in 21%, noting that concurrent symptoms such as headaches, abdominal pains, and tantrums improved as well.[34] They felt artificial colors and preservatives were big offenders although no child responded only to these. *In order to finally settle a long-time dispute between various branches of medicine and psychology, a recent analysis provided a summary of all the well-designed studies reported over a decade and concluded that diet definitely can affect the moods of children*[35] (which their mothers already knew). At about the same time, another undertaking provided evidence of electrical (EEG) alterations in beta wave brain activity in children with food-induced ADHD after they consumed response-provoking foods.[36] A study that found significant improvement in over half of hyperactive preschool boys noted the strong connection to sleep problems and also mentioned halitosis (bad breath).[37] A German investigation supports the contention that allergic children have a much higher incidence of attention-deficit disorder,[38] and a 1990 national study of 7,000 English children found a very strong association between parental reports of irritability and parental reports of food intolerance in their children.[39]

So this is it—our new and ever-growing classroom image full of "bad" behavior, "hyperactivity," antisocial behavior, ADHD...and children on drugs such as Ritalin. First came the push for detached parenting, accompanied by formula feeding, both of which we have shown to have powerful influences on children's behavior. Now, over the last 60 years, children's dairy consumption has grown from 1, then 2 glasses of milk per day, to include cheese sticks, cheese crackers, cheeseburgers, cheese and butter covered vegetables, yogurt, pudding, ice cream, cream sauces, cream cheese, sour cream dressing, buttered bread, milk at every meal, plus the added dairy ingredients in almost every prepared food on the grocery shelf.

Colic

Colic, now present in about 20% of U.S. infants, is often the first symptom in a food-sensitive child, eventually accompanied by other bowel symptoms and possibly rashes. Colic is generally defined as 3 or more hours per day of crying, for 3 or more days a week. The real distinction should be in the intensity of crying, and whether it is easy or impossible to console the child. Colicky infants often do not sleep well and will wake from sleep with screams. Studies have shown that "normal" crying in infants can be reduced by increased carrying[40] and increased attentiveness, bringing the level of crying closer to that of healthy infants in less industrialized nations. However, another study showed that increased carrying time may not reduce the crying of a baby with colic[41] (although jiggling and bouncing may help relieve some immediate pain). Herein lies the key: A so-called normal baby may cry from a lack of body contact and a need for stimulation or security, as well as from overstimulation. But there is another kind of cry, one that causes parents to instinctively feel concern. A colicky infant's cries are forceful, pleading, and inconsolable. The parents know the child is in pain and distress despite the comforting advice these parents may receive from well-meaning advisors. *Remember that today a majority of these same infants once diagnosed with colic are now diagnosed with reflux.* All of my same comments and treatment attempts apply.

Bovine protein found in milk-based formulas or in the milk of dairy-consuming mothers is by far the greatest cause of colic. Other foods can cause colic, too, but in almost all cases, the multiple food-intolerant infant will react to cow's milk among other irritating foods. Certainly, colic can be caused by other disorders as well (found in 3 to 5%), but the percentage of infants who recover through dietary measures alone is very high.

Figure 12-1 summarizes eight investigations into the effects of diet on infant colic. Of course it's difficult to find funding for such investigations and most are performed on formula-fed infants. Six of these studies involved infants with colic who were fed milk-based formula. In three studies, cow's milk proteins (CMP) were eliminated from these infants' diets by substituting soy-based formulas (which contain the strong allergens of soy and corn). The percentage of colicky infants who responded in each trial is listed in the table. In two studies, those who did not respond to soy formula were then placed on hypoallergenic formulas made from hydrolyzed milk proteins where most of the bovine proteins are broken down into nonallergenic pieces. The total number of infants who recovered or improved significantly on either soy or hypoallergenic formula is listed. Three more trials tested CMP hydrolysate alone. The weighted average of these trials demonstrates that the chief source of colic, in 67% of infants, is intolerance of cow's milk proteins (relieved by soy formula). Eliminating soy and sometimes corn as well (hydrolysate formula) suggests allergens are the source of colic in 84%.

Other investigations demonstrate that many infants who do not respond to the hydrolyzed-protein formulas, which still contain small amounts of intact proteins, will still recover on experimental highly hydrolyzed formulas, lamb-based formulas, or elemental diets (which use proteins totally broken down into amino acids). One trial found that 90% of the infants who failed to improve with hydrolysate formula recovered on elemental formula.[42] Thus, the number of cases of infant colic that can be reduced or relieved by removal of cow's milk proteins and other allergens may approach 100%. Some who initially improve with CMP hydrolysate eventually become sensitive to the small amounts of bovine protein remaining in these formulas and will do better on elemental diets.[43] There are new amino acid (elemental) formulas available on store shelves today, but corn ingredients have crept into these as well as prescription versions. I suspect this corn may be a problem in a portion of sensitive infants.

Some professionals, still eager to protect cows' reputations, insist that relief from intestinal diseases from an elemental diet does not prove there was an allergy at all; rather, this diet simply gives the intestines a rest. A rest from what? When elimination of most milk protein alone gives extremely high recovery rates, and additional elimination of other allergens provides even greater results, then clearly an elemental diet, which removes *all* traces of milk protein and other allergens, is an extension of the ability to successfully remove allergens.

A 1986 study helped to confirm the connection between bovine protein and colic from a different angle. A study performed on breastfeeding mothers and their infants demonstrated that the presence and extent of colic in infants (as well as diarrhea, vomiting, and eczema) strongly correlates to the levels of bovine protein in their mothers' milk.[44] The quantities of bovine milk proteins in these women's milk did not correlate well with their level of dairy intake, but varied from mother to mother. The amounts also did not correlate with the level of allergy in the mothers (leaving the question as to what does cause the appearance of cow's milk proteins in the mothers' milk). Cow's milk protein levels in mother's milk would certainly approach zero if dairy were eliminated from the mothers' diets.

When a breastfeeding mother eliminates dairy from her diet, her infant may still react to other foods she is eating. When mothers of breastfeeding infants who are sensitive to multiple foods take measures to find and eliminate all the offending foods, their children do just as well as those who are on elemental diets. Moreover, a breastfeeding infant's nutrition, development, and immunity will be superior. These infants will have the tools needed to recover more quickly from health challenges and keep from developing infections resultant from inflammatory reactions.

In comparison to the dietary changes above, a once common drug (Bentyl, dicyclomine) showed about 53% effectiveness in reducing symptoms in these trials. In contrast to the safety of dietary alterations, dicyclomine and similar infant colic medications occasionally lead to breathing difficulties, including cases of apnea (lack of breathing) and cyanosis (life-threatening lack of oxygen).[45] A link to cancer has also been suggested.[46] More common side effects are constipation, irregular heart rhythms, and overheating in hot

Colicky Infants Recovery[47-54]

	Sample Size	No Cow's Milk Protein (Soy)	Hydrolysate	Medication
Formula-fed Studies				
Oggero 1994	120	66%	95%	53%
Iacono 1991	70	71%		
Merritt 1990	21		71%	
Campbell 1989	19	58%	68%	
Lothe 1989	27		89%	
Weissbluth 1984	24			62%
Lothe 1982	60		71%	
Breastfed Study: Mother Had No Cow's Milk Protein				
Jakobsson 1983	66	53%		

Figure 12-1 Percentage of colicky infants who recover with elimination of cow's milk protein, hypoallergenic formula, or medication.

weather. Dental cavities may also result from these medications as salivation is decreased. Colic is no longer listed as a recommended use for this drug.

Two investigations on the relationship between colic and gas formation in the infant colon were performed by measuring the amount of hydrogen released in the breath of infants. One study found that colicky infants produce 3 times the amount of gas as those without colic.[55] Another found a two-thirds reduction in gas formation when fussy infants who had been fed milk-based formula were placed on soy formulas, resulting in a 40% reduction in their usual fussing.[56] Excess gas formation results from the increase in undigested and unabsorbed proteins and carbohydrates passed into the colon as a result of immune system tagging of antigens. The gas is created by fermentation of this material by the colon flora. Excess gas distends the bowel and causes abdominal pain.

The colons of newborns are quite leaky to large proteins compared to mature, healthy systems. This is by design to take advantage of mother's milk components. This situation allows for some of the sensitization to foods that occurs in young infants. In the food-sensitized individual, at any age, the inflammation and cellular damage that occur as a result of immune responses cause the gut to be more leaky. A Swedish pediatrician and professor and her colleagues set out to demonstrate this and its relevance to colic.[57] They used a human milk protein as a marker protein. They found this protein in colicky breastfed infants at a blood level 6 times that in the non-colicky nursers, thereby demonstrating the amount of intact protein that was able to pass through the colon wall into the blood is higher in colicky infants. This same marker protein was added to infant formulas and then found in formula-fed colicky infants at levels 12 times that of those without colic, again demonstrating the high level of leaking in colicky infant colons.

> *Ninety percent of the infants who failed to improve with hydrolysate formula recovered on elemental formula. Thus, the number of cases of infant colic that can be reduced or relieved by removal of cow's milk proteins and other allergens may approach 100%.*

Color of Stools

A newborn's stools are normally a very dark green-black. After that, soft, mustard yellow stools, possibly seedy looking, are the normal color for breastfed infants before solid foods or formula supplements are in their diet, at which point the stools gradually turn brown. Formula-fed stools are normally firm and brown. Be wary that food colorings in icings, Jell-O, candies, and other treats may persist as bright colors in the stools. Little tiny stringy or wormy looking things may be undigested banana. Red spots in the stools need to be examined to determine whether they are just pieces of tomato or spots of blood, which can be associated with food intolerance reactions. Fresh red streaks are more likely due to slight tears in the rectum walls from hard stools. Black stools may result from high iron intake. Black portions of stool may also be blood from higher up in the intestines, also a possible sign of food reaction. An infant with frequent blood in her stools with no obvious reason should be examined. Bright green color in the stools may be from bile, due to either a viral infection or foods being passed quickly through due to sensitivity reactions, or some say a foremilk/hindmilk imbalance. Pieces of food in the stools are usually a sign that the baby is not ready to digest those foods yet or that foods have washed quickly through the bowels as in diarrhea of any cause.

Constipation

There are many causes of constipation. Sometimes a child continually ignores the urge to pass stool. More and more water is then absorbed from the stool, making it harder and more uncomfortable to pass. This source of constipation may occur in an active child from the age of potty training on, but generally cannot be used as an explanation for infant constipation. Retraining of proper bowel habits can reverse this cycle. An Iowa doctor found relief in 52% of constipated infants one year after training treatment began.[58] Insufficient fluids (especially in hot weather), inactivity, and changes in diet or routine are other common causes. A formula-fed baby will generally have firmer stools than his breast-fed counterpart.

Food sensitivity should be considered when constipation is chronic, and simple measures such as increasing fluids and exercise do not work. One study found that infants were relieved from chronic constipation in 21 out of 27 cases (78%) when cow's milk protein alone was removed from their diets.[59] Laboratory testing confirmed sensitivity in most of these, and constipation returned in all of the infants when milk was returned to their diets. A larger, double-blind study by the same researchers found the same improvement in 68% of those tested.[60] One-fourth of these

> *A study performed on breastfeeding mothers and their infants demonstrated that the presence and extent of colic in infants (as well as diarrhea, vomiting, and eczema) strongly correlates to the levels of bovine protein in their mothers' milk.*

had other allergic symptoms such as rashes, runny nose, or asthma. Three-fourths of them had laboratory confirmation of bovine protein sensitivity. Other studies have found strong correlation between cow's milk and constipation as well.[61] This symptom may be more delayed and long-lasting than diarrhea and other food reactions.

Diarrhea

Diarrhea is the major manifestation of bovine protein sensitivity in infants and is a predominant symptom in children with other food intolerance. Food intolerance is the most likely cause of "nonspecific" or "noninfectious" diarrhea. However, as the inflammatory process continues, chronic inflammation or even infection sometimes sets in and many cases diagnosed as chronic infectious diarrhea, colitis, or some other pathology are the end result of food hypersensitivity reactions.

> *Diarrhea is the major manifestation of bovine protein sensitivity. Many cases diagnosed as chronic infectious diarrhea, colitis, or some other pathology are the end result of food hypersensitivity reactions.*

The following table summarizes the recovery rates reported with diets eliminating allergens and the improvement from common medication, for various diarrhea-related diagnoses. Some studies used only IgE antibody reactions when designing allergen-eliminating diets. IgE is associated mostly with immediate allergic reactions, which occur within minutes, not with delayed allergic reactions that may take hours or days to manifest. These studies found lower success rates than more inclusive studies that tested for IgG antibodies and other indicators, especially those that included food challenges. Food challenges selectively offer suspect foods one at a time to see whether symptoms are reproduced.

In one study, which revealed 87% improvement in relieving diarrhea by eliminating milk and other allergenic foods, 23% of the participants admitted they had not adhered well to the diet. This same finding had been reported in other dietary studies as well.

Recovery with Elimination Diet or Medication [62–70]

Study	Diagnosis	Sample	Nonallergenic Diet	Medication
Machida 1994	Colitis	31 infants	61%	
Jenkins 1984	Colitis	8 infants	100%	
Malchow 1990	Crohn's	40 adults	21/22 95%	80% for 6 weeks
Drisko 2006	Irritable Bowel	20 adults	100%	
Malchow 1984	Crohn's 192 adults			40% for 2 years
Meta-analysis 1994	Irritable Bowel	26 studies		27% standard drugs
Grazioli 1993	Irritable Bowel	153 infants	87%	97% cromolyn
Jones 1985	Irritable Bowel	21 adults	67%	
Xanthakos 2005	Rectal Bleeding	56 infants	64%	

Figure 12-2 Percentage recovery seen for certain diseases in various studies using either elimination dieting or medication.

The typical conclusion by researchers (well educated by the dairy industry) is that dietary management is too difficult to bother with. My conclusion is that diet is apparently the cause of the disease in genetically susceptible children. People should at least be encouraged to try eliminating suspected foods first.

In one investigation, 70 infants with food intolerance diarrhea were examined, and all had inflammation and infection of the stomach and duodenum (chronic gastroduodenitis). One-third of these suffered from destruction of the nutrient absorbing villi of the intestinal lining.[71] An immune system attack on allergenic foods will cause diarrhea and will decrease the local defenses of the mucous lining of the intestines, allowing microorganisms to adhere to the digestive tract and multiply, resulting in infectious diarrhea.[72] This damage contributes to malabsorption of nutrients, which, along with the diarrhea itself, is a very common source of failure to thrive in infants. These inflammations and infections are also responsible for several distinctive types of damage that will eventually earn diagnoses such as colitis, ulcer, or Crohn's disease, depending on the main mechanism involved.[73] The microbe that causes the destructive infection in Crohn's disease (*Mycobacterium paratuberculosis*) happens to come from cow's milk as well.[74] Another diagnosis sometimes given for chronic intestinal upset is eosinophilic gastroenteritis. Eosinophils are allergy-responding cells. When a certain amount of them are found in a tissue sample, the diagnosis is made. Again, allergen elimination is the known successful treatment though usually drugs are the only course prescribed, without great success.

The incidence of diarrhea in formula-fed infants from industrialized nations is at least double that in breastfed infants, with 5 to 7 times as many prolonged episodes in formula babies.[75-77] The immune properties of breastmilk and the more friendly flora of breastfed infants help to prevent infection of the intestinal walls.

Ear Infections

Middle ear fluid buildup (known as serous otitis, chronic otitis, or otitis media with effusion) and middle ear infections (acute otitis media) have increased greatly over the last several decades, particularly in infants,[78] just as other symptoms of allergy and food sensitivity have. Two-thirds of children in the United States experience at least 1 ear infection, and one-third experience multiple episodes.[79] The small mucous membrane lining of children's ear tubes swells up with inflammatory allergic reactions, blocking off the middle ear and allowing fluid to accumulate and eventually bacteria to multiply. The evidence is unquestionable that food allergies are the most common cause for otitis when it is persistent in children, yet this is seldom told to parents, unless by other parents who have discovered this information for themselves.

One researcher using detailed laboratory techniques found allergies present in 97% of children who had persistent serous otitis.[80] Dr. Nsouli and his colleagues used food challenge testing and found food allergy in 78% of chronic otitis children.[81] Significant long-term improvement occurred in 86% of the food-allergic children with food elimination diets. The source of this success was then confirmed when otitis returned in 94% of these children when they were challenged with foods that had been found suspect through laboratory testing and previous food challenges. Twenty-five percent of those with no dietary modification or medication improved.

Higher amounts of anti-bovine IgE and IgM antibodies have been found in children who suffer recurrent otitis than in those who do not.[82] Anti-bovine IgG antibodies have also been discovered within the fluid in otitis media cases, and it is proposed that these activate inflammatory chemical releases within the middle ear cavity.[83]

An investigation of the usefulness of "allergy shots" for recurring serous otitis media reported 65% recovery with this therapy, stating that all those who did not respond to therapy recovered on food elimination diets.[84] Another study

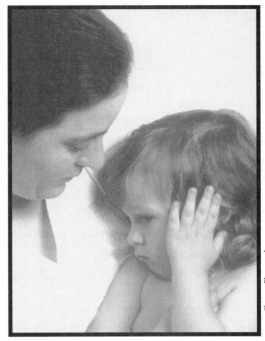

Shugrue Photography

used shots and diet, noting improvement in 80% of those found to be allergic. The adherence to diet was strongly associated with outcome.[85]

We have seen earlier that antibiotic treatments afford minimal, if any, help with ear infections. The inability of drug and surgical treatments to bring long-term recovery of otitis suggests the cause is not being addressed. In light of the positive and permanent results reported with dietary elimination, and the lack of side effects involved, it seems prudent to investigate this possibility in chronic cases of otitis media. It's difficult to find financial backers for food allergy studies, since the cure (eliminating allergenic foods) lines no pockets, while there is plenty of money to promote medications and to squash rumors about certain foods. For this reason, many a family has had to reinvent the wheel in finding the sources of their child's ear infections. Many more have had to suffer through the ongoing illnesses and the side effects of medications and chronically impaired hearing.

Epilepsy

In a study on 63 children with epilepsy, 45 of them also had migraines, hyperactivity, and abdominal symptoms. Of the 45 with these food sensitivity symptoms, 25 were cured and 11 more improved on diets that eliminated most common allergens. Other symptoms improved in most of the 45 as well. None of the 18 who had epilepsy alone improved on the diet.[86]

Eyes

Dark circles, bags, and skin folds under the eyes are visible signs of allergic children. Itchy eyes often result from allergies or sensitivities to airborne substances, although they have been reported with food sensitivities as well.

Fatigue

Studies often report links between fatigue in children (some with "chronic fatigue syndrome") and food or other allergies.[87] Studies on fatigue syndromes beyond infancy find a high correlation with other symptoms,[88] such as irritable bowel and headache, strongly associated with allergies and food intolerance in laboratory testing and double-blind challenges. One probe found irritable bowel syndrome in 63% of fatigue sufferers.[89]

Psychiatrists have taken the symptoms commonly associated with fatigue syndromes and designed psychological diagnoses to fit them. Now someone with these symptoms can easily be labeled as suffering a psychological problem. When laboratory analyses or double-blind food challenge tests are performed, the relationship between a patient's fatigue and his reported food intolerance is generally found to be a valid physical immune reaction. The younger the patient, the more likely it is that laboratory and diet testing will be performed, although many practitioners often do not have enough awareness to request the proper testing.

After performing detailed blood tests, one study found a very high correlation between allergy-related blood indicators and chronic fatigue syndrome complaints.[90] This study also found an absence of personality disorders in these subjects. It did, however, find some symptoms correlated with the psychiatric diagnoses (which, as we've said, are merely labels that were designed around typical fatigue reaction symptoms). The study concluded that the symptoms of fatigue syndrome resulted from "abnormal psychological response to the disordered expression" of allergic immune reactions, which degrades the fatigue sufferer, but I suppose it was an attempt to distinguish between allergy sufferers who complain of fatigue and those who do not. Interestingly, when fatigue (lethargy), gastrointestinal symptoms, and rashes are displayed in dogs, food sensitivity and not psychological disorder is assumed to be the cause. Elimination diet is the recommended course of care in dogs.[91,92]

Headaches

Headaches are not believed to be very common in young children, becoming more common and more severe after the age of 5 or so. Although headaches come from many different causes, the frequent relationship between headaches, especially migraine, and food or chemical sensitivities is well known and seldom disputed. A test of 88 children with migraine found recovery in 93% of them by providing nonallergenic diets.[93] Associated symptoms such as abdominal pain, behavior problems, tantrums, eczema, and asthma improved as well. A study of older children suffering from migraine found significant or complete remission from headaches in 92% of those who followed low-antigen diets designed for each patient through elimination diets with double-blind challenges, as well as laboratory studies.[94] Hazelnuts, egg, and cocoa were among the foods implicated. Migraine is usually induced by different types of foods than most of what is being described in this chapter.[95] Cow's milk is not often connected with

> Psychiatrists have taken the symptoms commonly associated with fatigue syndromes and designed psychological diagnoses to fit them. When laboratory analyses or double-blind food challenge tests are performed, the relationship between a patient's fatigue and his reported food intolerance is generally found to be a valid physical immune reaction.

migraine headaches. A well-designed investigation found the immune system chemicals histamine and certain prostaglandins to be affecting the brain in people who suffer food-related headaches.[96] MSG (which goes under dozens of names) and aspartame cause headaches in some sensitive individuals, as confirmed by double-blind studies.[97,98] These are chemically induced effects that are different from the immune reactions we have covered.

Rashes

Eczema appears as dry, scaly, usually red, and often itchy patches of skin. Curiously, this type of rash is often called "atopic dermatitis," which means "allergic skin condition," even when the probability that allergy is causing the condition is not being acknowledged. The majority of eczema cases result from delayed intestinal food reactions, so it is often difficult to make the connection. Eczema may take several days to develop after an exposure. Generally occurring on the face, especially the cheeks and around the mouth, as well as the upper chest, wrists, and hands, eczema may also occur inside the bends of the elbow and knees, and around the ankles and over the feet. Sometimes pimples concentrate around the mouth area. In others, eczema may arise over the chest and low back. Sometimes it is accompanied by cradle cap.

Two other skin conditions that commonly go along with food sensitivities are angioedema, a swelling of the blood vessels beneath the skin seen as redness and puffiness on the face and body, and hives, which are raised, red, itchy areas.[99] These conditions are loosely included when speaking about atopic dermatitis or eczema.

Eczema is commonly associated with other food sensitivity symptoms such as diarrhea or asthma. Sometimes other symptoms are not obvious, but the condition should still not be ignored. *A 1992 study of 52 children with eczema and no intestinal complaints showed that all suffered immune compromising digestive tract inflammation, even if diarrhea was absent.*[100] Intestinal biopsy studies have demonstrated that intact proteins are being absorbed across the intestinal wall in children with eczema at a rate 10 times higher than in normal children.[101] This is the leaky gut described in the case of cow's milk and other food sensitivity reactions.[102,103] Food hypersensitivity was found in 64% of children with eczema in one study that used double-blind, placebo-controlled challenges.[104] Other studies have reported higher cor-relations. Intestinal inflammation (gastroduodenitis) and damage to villi contribute to the increased occurrence of failure to thrive that is found with infants who have eczema. What does this mean? It means that lack of efforts to find and eliminate the sources of eczema (not just covering it up with steroid creams) can allow the child's health and development to be compromised.

Many food-intolerant or otherwise allergic infants may display only a few little pimples around the mouth, or no rashes at all; eczema is the most commonly found of the many food-related symptoms. Eczema is also strongly associated with asthma and allergic stuffy noses. I have described its preva-lence in food sensitivities, and thus the association with bowel symptoms. Many researchers report its occurrence in association with other symptoms, often without recognizing the probable common origin. Dr. Kathi Kemper, author of *The Holistic Pediatrician*, notes that children with eczema often suffer sleep problems, behavior problems, and "difficult temperaments" as well. She associates these behaviors with the itching skin. She has found the correlations, but she may be missing the bigger picture.

Respiratory Symptoms: Rhinitis, Chronic Cough, and Asthma

Chronic runny or stuffy nose (rhinitis), and lung symptoms, common in the better-known airborne allergies, are sometimes brought on by food sensitivity reactions. Lung symptoms include chronic coughing fits that can be either mild asthma or a pre-asthma condition. Coughing fits can also be caused by bronchitis resulting from a bronchial infection, such as may occur after a cold. There is little shortness of breath involved, but by placing your ear on the chest, a rattling can be heard during deep breathing. The food-sensitive individual with respiratory responses can be more disposed to chronic bron-chitis because excess mucus in the airways provides a good breeding ground for microorganisms. Asthma presents itself as attacks of wheezing and the inability to catch your breath. Also referred to as bronchospasm, it results from contractions in the involuntary muscle tissues of the bronchi and the smaller bronchii (branching air tubes) of the lungs. Asthma attacks occur predominantly after exercise or other stress, or during the night.

Dr. D.S. Feigin describes the changes that occur in the lungs based on the type of sensitivity reaction experienced. Immediate (type 1) reactions obstruct the airways with mucus and produce the bronchial spasms of asthma with which we are most familiar. Delayed (type 2, 3, and 4) responses, which would be food reactions, come in a few varieties, causing hemorrhage, inflammation, or enlarged lymph nodes.[105] Airborne allergens have been cited as the most common irritants in asthma, including dust mites, animal dander, molds, and pollens. After these, foods, food additives, and certain drugs are indicted. Fumes such as fresh paint, perfumes, and pesticides can significantly provoke respiratory problems, evidently more often with age or chronic exposure. Smoking and air pollution are also major contributing factors,[106] and secondhand smoke has been shown to play a major role in childhood respiratory distress.

> *Thousands of children and adults in the United States die each year of asthma even though asthma was almost never considered fatal before the 1950s.*

Hospital admissions for asthma increased nearly twentyfold from 1960 to 1995 for young children to the age of 4.[107] Thousands of children and adults in the United States die each year of asthma, even though asthma was almost never considered fatal before the 1950s. Certainly part of the problem is indoor and outdoor air pollution. While air pollution peaked in the 1960s, asthma death rates continued to grow, but cyclically, not steadily. Early introduction of formula and solids may account for much of the increase in this disease, but not the rise and falls in death rates. According to Dr. John Mansfield, author of *Asthma Epidemic*, death rates surge in accordance with increases in drug prescription rates with the advent of each new kind of asthma drug.[108] The safeties of nearly a dozen newer asthma drugs have been challenged since his 1997 book. While asthma deaths are down over the last decade, the majority of these deaths in children can be attributed to two twenty-first century drugs.[109]

Among children with food hypersensitivities and eczema, 59% also suffer respiratory reactions of some kind.[110] Children whose food allergies are persistent beyond 2 years of age have a 3.4 times higher incidence of rhinitis and a 5.5 times higher risk of becoming asthmatic than those who "grow out" of their food allergies early.[111]

While often little or no mention of allergy is made by a physician treating asthma, it has been determined that 80% of asthmatics and 90% of children with rhinitis suffer immediate type 1 allergies.[112] The remaining 20% and 10% respectively are most likely accounted for by delayed-reaction food sensitivities, with much overlap of conditions as well. The lungs are lined with a great number of H-1 histamine receptors and spasms of the little branches in the lungs (bronchioles) occur when these respond (or overre-spond) to histamine releases. Unfortunately, to date, studies of asthma-food relationships tend to focus on immediate reactions; moreover, trials do not incorporate common additional stressors. Typically, asthmatic reactions to foods require larger doses of allergen than do nasal reactions.[113] All asthma attacks are much more apt to occur with additional stressors such as exercise and emotional distress, as well as cigarette smoke and high pollen or smog counts. It is known that antihistamines, drugs that reduce histamine responses, are not always effective for asthmatics. This may be because susceptible lung tissues are being irritated by other chemicals and roaming antigen-antibody complexes created from intestinal reactions to foods. The actions of such chemicals and immune complexes are not well blocked by H-1 antihistamines alone.

An early link between asthma and food allergies is indicated by the finding that formula feeding before 3 months of age is a major risk factor for persistent asthma.[114] About half of young asthmatic children are still suffering at age 4. Most who are still asthmatic at 4 will continue to suffer into adulthood. Some children first develop asthma after the age of 4. Often, these children had earlier allergic signs, such as rashes or colic.

Reports that cow's milk is a mucus-producing food are strongly defended by some, but found not reproducible by others. Those who suffer chronic rhinitis or bronchial problems due to cow's milk sensitivity most likely account for the common reports of milk being a "mucus food."

Cow's milk sensitivity has been incriminated in some cases of pulmonary hemosiderosis—a condition where iron builds up in the lungs, causing iron deficiency anemia, poor lung performance, and eventually heart failure.[115]

Several studies report correlations between asthma and other sensitivity symptoms: One of these cites food allergy, eczema, frequent ear infections, and frequent sinus attacks.[116]

Short Stature

Several studies show that children with moderate to extensive eczema, and to a lesser extent those with asthma, grow to a shorter average height than do nonallergic children.[117] These children seem to obtain normal leg lengths, but shorter sitting statures.[118]

Children with untreated food sensitivities (those who don't successfully avoid foods to which they react) maintain high levels of inflammation and damaged villi much of the time and thus suffer from various degrees of malabsorption throughout their important growing years, and malabsorption means malnutrition. This could certainly explain the stunted growth seen in asthmatic and eczematous children. Medical studies express concern over the possibility that steroid medications used to treat asthma (inhaled) as well as eczema (applied topically) could be the cause of reduced growth, and this needs further investigation. However, the greatest reduction in expected height is seen in children with bedwetting problems, another symptom associated with food sensitivity reactions, for which corticosteroid medication is not standard treatment. Also, height reduction has been shown to occur chiefly in those asthmatic children who were considered the most allergic, as opposed to those who demonstrated little evidence of hypersensitivity reactions. The extent of stunting also correlated with the degree of allergic suffering.[119]

Dr. T. David suggests that if short stature is due to disease, and disease remits before puberty, then catch-up growth should occur. However, if the stunted growth is caused by steroid therapy, or if allergic disease lasts into adult life, catch-up growth would not be expected.[120] He suggests that the sleeplessness of atopic children could contribute to stunting as well. Theoretically, according to Dr. David's suggestions, if allergens are avoided as much as possible, and if steroid use is avoided, the child should have a good chance of obtaining near-optimal growth.

Sleeplessness

Sleeplessness, frequent waking, and difficulty falling asleep are strongly associated with food intolerance and are mentioned by many food allergy researchers in their studies of other symptoms. One small study looked specifically at sleep difficulties. To investigate the sleeplessness of 17 children whose poor sleep could not be blamed on inappropriate sleep habits, cow's milk was experimentally removed from their diets. Sleep patterns normalized in 16 of the 17, and double-blind crossover challenges confirmed these results.[121]

Tonsillitis

We have seen that food and other allergies can lead to chronically inflamed mucous membranes and mucus production. The tonsils and adenoids are little bundles of immune-reacting tissues in the back of the throat situated right in the middle of these problems. These can become chronically congested by inflammatory immune cells in response to food or other allergy, even with little noticeable sinus congestion. When this occurs, they can then harbor viruses and bacteria, becoming very enlarged, and contributing to frequent throat infections and illnesses. This chronic enlargement also often leads to snoring. The huge trend of removing the tonsils in children, which became popular just after formula and cow's milk became very popular, has since settled down. Once tonsils are removed, chronic congestion, leading to chronic illness, still occurs in the mucous membranes of the throat, nasal passages, and lungs. The procedure is often unsuccessful for reducing illness because the true source of the problem, allergy, is not being addressed.

Formula feeding before 3 months of age is a major risk factor for persistent asthma.

Others

Vomiting has not been mentioned but frequent vomiting is commonly related to diet. Weight loss and failure to thrive are frightening results of chronic intolerance and need quick attention. Furrows in the tongue, lacy tongue edges, geographic tongue (patterns of ulcers on tongue surface which incidentally are similar to damage seen in intestinal mucosa),

Conditions Responding to Elimination Diets

Symptom	Cow's Milk	Multiple Foods
ADHD		80%
Colic	67%	84%
Add Elemental Diet for Colic		98%
Constipation	71%	
Chronic otitis media		86%
Diarrheal diseases		82%
Migraines		93%
Sleeplessness	94%	

Figure 12-3 Weighted averages of cases shown to respond to eliminating cow's milk or multiple allergenic foods from the diet, taken from multiple studies, as presented in the text.

and atrophic tongue (smooth surface portions where taste buds are barely apparent) are often seen in allergic and food-intolerant children and adults.[122] Poor memory, learning disorders, autism,[123] ADHD, muscle weakness, vertigo, palpitations, blurred vision, bad breath, and red ears, cheeks, and noses have at times been implicated in allergy and food intolerance in certain children. The known allergy connections to autism are now building every day.

Several studies report a very high occurrence of allergy, and especially sensitivity to cow's milk protein, in several forms of glomerulonephritis, a degenerative disease of the kidney in children.[124,125]

Among children with cystic fibrosis (a lung disease increasingly prevalent over the last century) who also suffered diarrhea, 90% improved when allergenic foods were discovered and eliminated from their diets.[126]

Summary

Typically, food intolerance can be suspected when multiple symptoms are present, but it has also been shown that children whose parents report only eczema often also harbor irritated or damaged intestinal linings. Symptoms such as diarrhea, constipation, mood swings, and rashes are very common indicators; however, everybody responds differently, presenting a wide range of symptoms. The number of infants and children whose comfort and health could be greatly improved through dietary corrections is staggering. The previous table summarizes the percentage of patients found to recover from various problems through food elimination diets according to a review of medical literature.

Strange Genes

I present this section more for entertainment (mine) than for any kind of diagnostic value. The factors of cause and effect are unknown, although many plausible hypotheses could be made.

Many investigations over the last fifteen years have confirmed a significant prevalence of non-right-handedness (partial or dominant left-handedness) in allergic people.[127,128] At least one study ties in musical talent as well.[129] Several more studies also correlate near-sightedness, altered verbal skills, high IQ, and strong math abilities with allergics.[130–132] Other probes bring to light a high correlation between head circumference at birth and the possibility of developing allergies. Those with head circumferences of 14 inches or more (associated with higher IQ) develop allergies more than 4 times as often as those

Among children with

cystic fibrosis (a lung

disease increasingly

prevalent over the last

century) who also suffered

diarrhea, 90% improved

when allergenic foods were

discovered and eliminated

from their diets.

with head circumferences of 13 inches or less.[133,134] A 1998 report sites several chromosomes thought to be in play.[135] Type 1 immediate allergies are more common in males, while chemical sensitivities are more common in females.

If you find your child suffers from allergies, the evidence is that allergic individuals are more often intelligent (and some say limited in athletic abilities). Surely you have heard people say that a "difficult" baby's behavior could be a sign of intelligence. Fussiness, contrariness, and irritability are common symptoms of sensitivities. A restless fetus could be an early sign as well, as sensitization can begin in utero (thus, that kicker may not be the football hero).

The word for allergy, "atopy," means "strange disease."

13

Allergy Matters

THE NUMBER OF ADULTS SUFFERING FROM BOWEL SYNDROMES HAS more than tripled over the last 50 years. Autoimmune diseases and allergies have similarly increased. The percentage of children developing diabetes and hyperactivity has increased tremendously throughout the past century. What does all of this have to do with hypersensitivity reactions in babies? Are these problems connected to the decline in breastfeeding and to the new baby foods: cow's milk formulas, soy formulas, and cow's milk?

Why the Concern?

A century ago, the incidence of childhood and adult allergies was reported to be 15%. Today, more than half of all infants suffer from some kind of sensitivity reactions. Changes in our environment and parenting styles are responsible. Colic, constipation, diarrhea, vomiting, failure to thrive, diaper rashes, eczema, fussiness, chronic middle ear fluid and infections, difficulty sleeping, waking with screams during naps, chronic stuffiness, asthma, loss of appetite or refusal of the breast—all these are signs of reactions to foods in the infant. The toddler may also exhibit uncharacteristic bouts of contrary and uncontrollable behavior. The school-age child may have daytime wetting and bedwetting problems, may suffer with headaches, or may be labeled with attention-deficit hyperactivity disorder (ADHD).

Early introduction of solid foods, especially the heavy cow proteins present in infant formulas and in the breastmilk of mothers who drink cow's milk, has been one cause of the growing sensitivity rates. While the pain and suffering experienced by food-sensitive infants provide enough motivation to try to avoid the development of food sensitivities, we now also understand that when sensitivity reactions occur, the cellular damage that goes along with inflammatory responses can predispose children to developing many major diseases later in life. Additionally, in the case of intestinal reactions, malabsorption syndrome can occur, robbing a child of important immune-building, brain-building, and body-developing nutrients.

> *When sensitivity reactions occur, the cellular damage that goes along with these inflammatory responses can predispose these children to developing many major diseases later in life.*

There are long-term ramifications to allowing babies to "tough it out," as some parents are advised. Treating only symptoms without attempting to find and eliminate the causes can lead to harm—for instance, repeatedly applying steroid creams to baby rashes, or supplying sedatives and sleep aids to colicky infants can lead to unwanted side effects. Taxing the immune system with allergens early on and ignoring the reactions has led to large increases in cases of arthritis and other autoimmune diseases, irritable bowel syndrome, colitis, Crohn's disease, diverticulitis, asthma, childhood diabetes, and certain forms of cancer.

Over 14.6 million Americans suffer from asthma. Over 35 million doctor visits per year are for disorders of the digestive system. The percentage of infants suffering from these diseases has rapidly increased over the last 75 years, and adult manifestations of disease have similarly risen over the last 50 years. A large portion of our society is suffering from annoying, weakening, or crippling sensitivity-related conditions that we now have the knowledge and power to prevent, starting at infancy.

Bowel Diseases and Cancer

When food-related gastrointestinal complaints are dismissed, or more often, not even considered, children are diagnosed with colic, GERD, chronic gastroenteritis, colitis, irritable bowel syndrome, Crohn's disease, or ulcerative colitis. Research is now confirming that these diseases are most commonly entangled with chronic delayed immune reactions to foods, which lead to serious complications that could have been prevented. In the absence of acute infection, symptoms such as abdominal pains, watery stools, bloody stools, chronic diarrhea, and even constipation are signs of inflammatory reactions going on in the intestines. Most often these are caused by food sensitivities.[1,2]

Childhood sensitivity symptoms may change with age, but, untreated, these problems often present themselves throughout much of the child's life. The more troubling symptoms may abate for many years, only to return after a stressful lifestyle reduces immune function in adulthood. The infant with chronic constipation or diarrhea and rashes very often becomes the adult with chronic headaches and troubling irritable bowel syndrome. The child with bouts of altered behavior, chronic fatigue syndrome, wild tantrums, or ADHD becomes the adult suffering from depression or anxiety.

Colitis is a term often used when inflammation and damage occur in the large intestine, the colon. The diagnosis of irritable bowel syndrome is often used for inflammatory conditions of either the large or small intestine. Crohn's disease is another such condition, with a slightly different and more severe diagnostic picture. With ulcerative colitis (or irritable bowel or whatever term is used) destruction of the intestinal walls is occurring with every reaction, and long-standing symptoms (8 years or more) predispose the individual not only to debilitating malabsorption syndrome, but also to the development of intestinal cancer.[3-5]

Those suffering from gluten sensitivity (celiac disease) are found to have a mortality rate nearly double that of the general population. A large study showed that the increased deaths resulted from cancers of the digestive tract, including the throat.[6] Infection with *Helicobacter pylori*, especially common in dairy allergy, is associated with a tripled risk of stomach cancer.[7] *Even adolescents and young adults are at risk for intestinal cancer if they have suffered long-standing inflammatory intestinal conditions.* One probe found that nearly 25% of these young individuals presented precancerous cells, and 1 in the 35 studied was found to already have cancer.[8]

> *If a parent could actually see this damage, they would probably be much more concerned. Additionally, it is this regular irritation of the digestive system linings that predisposes one to cancer.*

Intestinal biopsies of food-sensitive infants have demonstrated that destructive inflammatory reactions occur deep in the mucosal linings of the intestines. Wasting of the tiny finger-like villi along the intestinal walls, important for exchange of nutrients, is seen, along with other destructive alterations.[9–11] Sometimes fissures and ulcers can be seen in the child's mouth and tongue, as can sores around the mouth. These provide a small picture of what may be going on in intestinal tissues.

Although often nothing is seen by parents using the naked eye, painful-looking destruction is occurring inside the infant who reacts to foods. If a parent could actually see this damage, they would probably be much more concerned. Additionally, it is this regular irritation of the digestive system linings that predisposes one to cancer.

More Diabetes Connections

In Chapter 11 we discussed the strong link between intolerance of cow's milk proteins and development of childhood diabetes. Other disorders that are highly associated with food intolerance are seen much more often in diabetics than in the non-allergic population. Ulcered tongue (atrophic and geographic tongue) is seen in 30% of diabetics.[12] There is a high rate of atrophic gastritis among diabetics as well, where the lining of the stomach is worn down by chronic inflammatory reactions. This condition has been shown to be strongly correlated with infection by *Helicobacter pylori* in child-hood.[13] Other researchers point out that in diabetic children, childhood *H. pylori* infection is strongly associated with the presence of cow's milk anti-bodies in their blood.[14]

What Causes Hypersensitivity Reactions?

Various sources indicate that there is a 60 to 100% chance that when both parents have some kind of allergy, their children will have allergies. If only one parent has allergies, the likelihood for the children is quoted between 30 and 50%. While there are surely other causes, many children are genetically predisposed to overreact to certain allergens. The kinds of responses and the locations that will be affected seem to be predetermined to some degree, but the food and environment they are exposed to are the determining factors for the extent of their allergic disease. Approximately 20% of children with low genetic risk develop allergies as well.[15]

Gastrointestinal infections (more common in formula-feeding) can initiate food sensitivity problems as potential allergens are allowed to leak across irritated intestinal walls. Some other causes can be early introduction of solid foods, including formula, or high exposure to chemicals, including pesticides and secondhand smoke, and to allergens such as pets, perfumes, pollen, cigarette smoke, and dust mites. Our high exposure to antibiotics and other drugs in meat and milk, and even traces in our drinking water, are thought to be another sensitizing factor. Stress can also make a child's body more reactive to allergens (and we know that babyhood and child-hood have become more stressful). This can be clearly seen in asthmatics with certain allergies or sensitivities: They often become symptomatic only with exercise or stress.

Many look to our human roots to examine how our digestive system may have been established to process a diet much different from the one we eat today. We did not start out eating processed, refined, and drug-laden foods. Just as certainly, we did not start out dependent upon the milk of

Among all the potential causes for sensitivity problems, most studies point to cow's milk as the largest offender by far.

another very different kind of animal. The huge variety in the foods and spices we eat is also very new to our genome. Even grains are relatively new in human diets, and especially as ground and refined white flours. Hunter-gatherers would most likely have had simple diets of meat, roots, and greens. Those who could not tolerate the diet of their people simply would not live to pass on their genes. Many children with multiple food sensitivities today are found to flourish on a simple meat, potato, and greens diet.

Among all the potential causes for sensitivity problems, most studies point to cow's milk as the largest offender by far.[16–22] We now know that, although it may be packed with certain nutrients, cow's milk is not meant for humans, especially for infants. We know that the intestinal irritation and bleeding commonly associated with consumption of bovine milk proteins in infants goes on to allow heavy proteins to pass through the intestinal protective barriers, causing deleterious immune reactions and the development of other food sensitivities.

Mother's milk is designed to provide immunity and other components important to baby. It has special properties that prevent its white blood cells, antibodies, hormones, and other chemicals from being broken down before they can be used by the infant. Cow's milk contains the same preventive media only in slightly different versions. Thus, the child drinking formula or milk from cows is exposed to whole bovine white blood cells, cow antibodies that cause negative reactions in the human system, cow hormones, many of which may mimic hormonal effects in human systems, antibiotics and other drugs in a highly absorbable media, and whole bacteria that exist in highly infected cows, several strains of which easily escape the short, low-temperature pasteurization process.[23] Milks are very unique foods with several unique proteins, and again, they're designed to protect and pass certain of these proteins and other components on. There is something about the very close similarity between animal milks and human milk that seems to light up our immune systems, much as we'll reject other human blood when not entirely matching our own type. Egg whites are rather the milk for baby chicks, and eggs are the second most common allergen in youngsters. Infants and young children are the most vulnerable to food reactions as their digestive and immune systems are immature.

Beta-lactoglobulin, one of the several bovine milk proteins, is much larger than the proteins found in human milk. In fact, it is probably larger than any protein found in any other foods we eat. These pose digestive problems locally in the intestine and poorly digested proteins may pass through the intestinal walls, causing sensitization in the infant's immune system to cow's milk. Now immune system cells lining the infant's intestines become armed to react to any further exposures. Even infants who are breastfed may be subjected to cow's milk proteins from dairy products in their mothers' diets. Many breastfeeding mothers are encouraged to offer supplemental formula bottles to their babies as well.

What Can We Do?

Parental actions can help reduce the development of allergies; breastfeeding and delaying solid foods are two of the most effective. Beyond this, watching for signs of allergic reactions, such as rashes and stool abnormalities, is an important step in guarding the lifelong health of your child. Prevention is the best health care for a baby and the adult he or she will become. Diminishing the amount of damage that occurs in infancy will provide a healthier and more comfortable childhood and can decrease the chance that diseases will develop in adulthood.

In many European countries, parents are advised to determine the likelihood of allergies before their child is born, based on family history. The mother can then avoid certain foods or other allergens during the second half of her pregnancy in an attempt to avoid sensitizing the baby's immune system. More apt to breastfeed, she may also automatically avoid key allergens in her diet while nursing. If unable to breastfeed, she could provide a hypoallergenic formula to her child before sensitivities are ever detected. Good statistical results in reducing childhood and adult hypersensitivities are obtained using this procedure.[24,25] Food sensitivity rates in children are going back down in some countries, including Spain.[26]

The Ignored Diagnosis

Now that you're familiar with the major symptoms of food sensitivities and the importance of recognizing them, you're probably wondering what to do if and when allergy is suspected. Because allergy is so prevalent in infants and so poorly recognized by a large portion of the medical community, I will give you a bare bones presentation of the science of these reactions, the diagnosis, and the treatment choices. If you don't need this information right now, you may wish to only glance through the next two chapters, saving them for future reference.

Some medical papers still report that only 15 to 25% of our population is suffering from allergies. These are not extensive studies, however. These numbers come from confirmed standard IgE test results on complaining patients. They do not include most of those with delayed hypersensitivity reactions, those who do not consider themselves allergic, and those who do not demonstrate blood or skin test reactions.

I cannot recount the number of times I've observed congested patients or heard them complain about sinus pain during our infamous San Diego Santa Ana days, when the pollen count soars. In response to my remarks about their allergies, the common reply is: "No, I just have 'sinus.'" What exactly is "sinus"? Unless it results from anemia or a cold, sinusitis is inflamed membranes reacting to irritants—which are allergens. Some "sinus" is even less easily sleuthed, since it results from delayed sensitivity reaction to milk or other foods.

It is important to understand that frequent abdominal pain, gas, diarrhea, constipation, or vomiting are simply not normal for a healthy infant. Vomiting includes any excessive spitting up. When these symptoms occur, less than desirable actions are occurring within the digestive system.

Before 1925, allergy was simply defined as any undesirable bodily response to something that is generally safe for most of the population. A patient would describe what symptoms he suffered, and the doctor would assist in tracing the causes.

Then IgE antibodies were discovered. These agents, found in the blood, are frequently overproduced when an allergic person is exposed to an allergen from the environment, such as pollen. Hives, difficulty breathing, itchy eyes, sneezing, and runny nose are some responses that are associated with this. Commonly associated with peanuts or sulfites, the severe allergic reaction of anaphylactic shock is generally an IgE-conducted response as well.

Once this discovery was made, the areas of the body generally associated with this type of reaction were defined. The most provable sources of this reaction were listed, and allergy was given a new, clean definition. There was certainly much excitement over this discovery, and it was thought the new definition of allergy would provide for more precise diagnoses. Unfortunately, in order for a patient's complaints or a child's colic to be diagnosed as an allergy, symptoms had to fit into the new parameters, which covered only a portion of the possible irregular reactions to food, those with obvious, immediate manifestation. To be labeled allergic, patients had to exhibit IgE antibodies in their blood (RAST test) or have swelling in reaction to scratch tests. Curiously, this new mind-set about what defined an allergy coincided with a new explosion of delayed reactions such as rashes, asthma, and intestinal symptoms in infants who were being fed progressively more of the highly promoted milk formulas.

Since this time, the diagnosis of delayed allergic reactions (most food reactions) is usually missed altogether, though some pediatricians and GI specialists are catching on. When a child's symptoms do not fit the strict (limited) definition of allergy, physicians often perform more invasive diagnostic workups, which are either inconclusive or lead to one of many vague diagnoses, such as colitis, GERD, or irritable bowel.

Most health practitioners will tell you that only the immediate, sneezy-wheezy kind of reactions (IgE antibody responses) are the result of immune system reactions. This is not true, however. Those who spend their lives researching such matters know there are many immune system responses connected to delayed reactions, including IgG, IgM, and IgA antibodies. There are other kinds of immune system responses involving histamine and other chemical releases leading to inflammation, and altered behaviors of various white blood cells. Certain T-cell behaviors and specific cytokine reactions also occur. Informed researchers use the term "allergy" for these delayed reactions as well, not just for immediate reactions, but allergists do not. Today, with the voices of hundreds of thousands of food allergy sufferers trying to be heard, some who disallow the term "allergy" are allowing the use of "sensitivity" or "intolerance" for delayed immune reactions. Here in this text, as is often done today, I use these terms interchangeably.

I just have to take you aside for a moment and tell you about my experience with a doctor whose anger was building to a face-reddening, vein-pulsating level over my attempts to explain that "these symptoms only happen when my husband has milk."

"Why does it make you so angry when I tell you this?" I asked him.

His frustrated response: "You wouldn't believe how many of my patients try to tell me that."

Well…what does that tell you???

Sometimes even double-blind studies do not confirm the patient's or parent's claims that food is causing symptoms. The reasons for this will be explained later. Around the 1940s, many adults and children whose complaints were not confirmed by IgE tests, and in whom no other diseases were found, were considered "frustrated" individuals (or babies with frustrated parents). Borrowing from the then rapidly growing field of psychology, it was often decided these complaints had psychological causes, and this mind-set persists today.

It is true that certain psychological symptoms of stress and frustration are commonly found in people with diseases that can't be diagnosed. Actually, recent studies show these symptoms are found in asthma patients, heart patients, and others with chronic illnesses. Most people dealing with a frustrating disease, especially one that is not easily diagnosed by others, suffer some level of irritability, depression, or frustration—these being the result of the disease (and others' reactions to the disease), not the cause.

The Immune Response

Airborne, food, or chemically related sensitivity reactions are essentially caused by an overreaction of the immune system (or under action of certain dampening factors). The immune system is our body's defense against invasion; it uses antibodies and certain cells and chemicals. Invasion is generally some kind of bacteria or virus, but in the case of allergy, the body treats some "non-harmful" agents as though they were invaders. In a food-sensitive individual, the body may create an inordinate amount of antibody to certain foods, pollens, or other agents (antigens) that generally do not irritate other people. These antibodies then wait in the mast cells residing in the respiratory, digestive, and urinary tissues, and deep in the skin. When antigens appear, the antibodies signal for several chemical reactions to occur. Histamine and other chemicals are released in response to this adversarial encounter, which causes inflammation, tissue damage, and other symptoms.

Histamine can cause involuntary muscles to contract, such as those in the lungs (asthma) and intestines (colic). Serotonin regulation is altered by its local release, and breakdown products of serotonin cause irritation of the local tissues. Because serotonin also acts as a neurotransmitter in the brain, the substance is probably responsible for some of the behavioral changes or mood swings seen in sensitivity reactions. While serotonin is often thought to have a calming effect, elevated levels have also been linked with anxiety and aggressive behaviors.[27,28] Serotonin is often blamed for migraine headaches as well.[29] Prostaglandins and bradykinins cause pain. Prostaglandins, as well as histamine, may also be responsible for some mood effects.

> *Standard blood or scratch tests for allergies, which only measure IgE responses, will often be negative in cases of food reactions initiated in the intestines.*

Immediate Hypersensitivity Reactions

IgE antibodies are produced in allergic responses to airborne antigens such as pollen or animal dander. They are also produced in cases of sudden food allergic reactions. The ensuing histamine releases lead to symptoms such as coughing, wheezing, hives, sneezing, and runny nose. Hence, IgE antibodies are intimately involved in standard immediate or type 1 allergic reactions. These are the reactions that can be detected with RAST IgE blood testing and scratch tests.

A very intense immediate response is anaphylactic shock. In response to a strong allergen, such as peanuts, shrimp, penicillin, insect venom, or a vaccine, the body of a highly sensitive individual can react quickly and severely. Along with sudden anxiety, anaphylactic shock involves difficulty breathing and dropping blood pressure, sometimes leading to death.

Chemical Sensitivity Reactions

Ill feelings resulting from airborne or internal exposure to various chemicals such as paint fumes, cigarette smoke, perfumes, cleaning agents, sulfites, and MSG are currently even more poorly understood than delayed food reactions. Characterized by symptoms such as fatigue, rash, stuffy nose, headache, and drowsiness, IgE responses are occasionally detected,[30] but more often not. It's difficult to tell how much these are involved in symptoms shown by infants and young children. Little research has existed on these types of reactions, although this is beginning to change. One-third of the population report suffering ill feelings in response to some kind of chemical exposure.[31] Most rats also suffer ill effects when exposed to these chemicals in the lab.[32] Common drug reactions are chemical sensitivities, too. Yet, many doctors claim chemical sensitivities are extremely rare, are "not immune reactions," and most complaints are psychological, making exceptions for sulfite reactions and recently recognized latex sensitivities.

The good news is that a whole new research branch is evolving, called developmental immunotoxicity. DIT scientists are studying the effects that our new huge spectrum of chemical exposures is having on fetal and infant development. New studies are also discovering the immune reactions that lead to the symptoms of chemical sensitivities. Among other things, basophils, a kind of white blood cell that is very few in number, are found to be mediators of chemical sensitivities.[33] Over 70,000 different man-made chemicals are being used in our environment today, a sharp contrast from only 100 years ago. Few of the 3,000 listed as high-volume usage have had even basic toxicity testing performed on them.[34] Since illness is known to occur in reaction to many types of chemical exposures, the enormous bombardment of chemicals may be causing illnesses in ways we are barely aware of.

Delayed Hypersensitivity Reactions

Delayed reactions are those that begin 45 minutes to a few days after exposure to an allergen, typically consumed foods or chemicals. Most commonly they begin between 1 to 5 hours after exposure. As it takes time for food to empty from the stomach and reach the intestines, these reactions take time to mount. Reactions such as diarrhea and painful distention take time to build to noticeable levels once reactive chemical releases begin. Intestinal transit time varies greatly depending upon diet, stress, and other factors. Hence the delay and the wide variance in the time until symptoms are noticed.

The key antibody defenses launched by the intestinal tract generally include various antibodies, IgG, IgM, and IgA, and antibody-like T cells. These agents incite local release of histamine along with serotonin and other chemicals. These cause inflammation, intestinal muscle contractions, and tissue damage. Standard blood or scratch tests for allergies, which only measure IgE responses, will often be negative in cases of delayed food reactions initiated in the intestines.[35] Fifty percent of food allergies are non-IgE mediated.[36] This is a very important point because so many parents go to allergists for answers, receive IgE blood tests or scratch tests with negative findings, and are then told there are no allergies. New IgG blood tests provide fair results, but are only

> *Amazingly, milk provides a double assault in the case of Crohn's disease, acting as an allergen to cause reduced intestinal resistance, then supplying the infecting agent.*

beginning to infiltrate the medical field, and have high rates of both false positives and false negatives. Other new tests are being developed as well and patch tests are looking good but still none come close to elimination and challenge.[37]

Following the Delayed Reaction

Although histamines are initially released in the intestines during delayed food sensitivity reactions, they often find their way into the bloodstream where they can alert histamine receptors in any organ that is genetically disposed to overreact. The bladder has many histamine receptors. Bedwetting problems (enuresis) can often be caused by swelling and contraction of the bladder lining in response to environmental or food sensitivity reactions.[38,39] Histamine receptors also reside in the walls of the uterus, and uterine contractions have been well demonstrated in response to histamine. I have not been able to find any studies investigating a relationship between allergic mothers and preterm contractions, although I personally know one very allergic mother who wishes she knew about this correlation during her months on horrible labor-inhibiting drugs.

In a sensitized system, many events occur after cow's milk proteins or other antigens enter the mouth and make their way into the small intestines. IgA antibodies tag the foods and try to rush them through the system without provoking irritation. When these tagged foods are rushed through, no digestion takes place, and a green or watery stool occurs.

Any proteins that are not vomited or rushed through will find their way into the lining of the intestines and become recognized by sensitized, waiting antibodies. As described before, inflammation occurs locally with tissue damage. As a result, the intestinal walls become more leaky and, at times, some undigested proteins of any kind can pass through the intestinal walls.[40-42] This is very common in young infants, although it occurs throughout adulthood.[43,44] Once these proteins, or possibly products of the inflammatory process, make their way into the bloodstream, more alarms go off and histamine is released throughout the system. Further and more varied delayed symptoms can now occur, including eczema, nasal stuffiness, and asthma. Histamine receptors are located nearly everywhere in the body, including the brain. Symptoms of delayed food reactions can thus manifest in the muscles, joints, nasal passages, lungs, bladder, and brain.

When antibodies attach to proteins to form immune complexes and deposit along the walls of blood vessels, arterial plaque gradually develops, and eventually, heart disease occurs. Deposits in the kidneys lead to kidney damage called "nephritis." Immune complexes can even deposit in the brain.[45] (One wonders whether this could be connected to Alzheimer's disease?)

While all this is going on in the blood, a cascade of chemical releases continues in the intestines, increasing inflammatory damage, and now causing more symptoms of diarrhea or possibly constipation, along with decreased uptake of nutrients.

Infection and Disease: Beyond the Delayed Reaction

Now that the natural protective barrier of the intestinal walls has been compromised, the immune system has been taxed, and nutrient status has diminished, the stage is set for opportunistic infection. With defenses down, bacteria or other microbes can establish themselves. Commonly, candida yeast will take hold in the lower intestinal walls. This reduces the protective barrier even more, allowing more proteins to pass through the walls, leading to more antibody reactions and chemical releases throughout the body.

Another common intestinal infection that follows the disrupted immune defenses of the intestinal wall is *Helicobacter pylori*, recently found to be present in most ulcers, and more recently suspected in some cases of SIDS. This bacterium is most likely responsible for much of the intestinal wall destruction (ulceration) in ulcerative colitis, common in infants.

Studies have found *Mycobacterium paratuberculosis* to be associated with the development of Crohn's disease.[46] This bacteria is passed to humans via cow's milk. Why doesn't everyone exposed to this bacteria develop Crohn's disease? Because for infection to take hold, the natural barrier defenses and immune defenses of the intestinal walls need to be regularly broken down by other frequent illnesses, such as hypersensitivity reactions to cow's milk. *The bacteria are not the problem; they simply take advantage of a vulnerable situation, causing further disease.* Amazingly, milk provides a double assault in the case of Crohn's disease, acting as an allergen to cause reduced intestinal resistance, then supplying the infecting agent. Genetic susceptibility is the only other necessary ingredient.

Potentiation

Potentiation, aversion, and masking are processes that occur in delayed reactions that greatly complicate the diagnosis, misleading parent and health professional alike. Alone, infrequently, and in lesser quantities, a weaker allergen may cause no detectable reaction, but there is an additive effect of multiple irritants or of multiple exposures to the same irritant. This is called "potentiation."

One exposure to an antigen in an untaxed system may result in little symptomatic effect, but can still incite antibody production. If the same agent is introduced again in a day or so, the body is now armed with higher amounts of antibodies and is ready

> As one comes down from the morphine high or suffers a serotonin low, another dose of the allergenic food can relieve the down feeling. In this way, it is thought that individuals can start to crave the very food that is causing chronic destruction inside their bodies.

to produce symptoms. Additionally, if the immune system is already in high gear from one kind of exposure or from stress, it may now react more strongly to other kinds of exposure. Since the leaking of undigested proteins through the intestinal linings may persist for several days, symptoms from one exposure can last for many days, and then a strong reaction can occur to what was previously only a mild irritant. As a result, the relationship between symptoms and foods ingested may not be at all obvious.[47]

Certainly, consuming several allergenic foods close together will create an enhanced reaction. At the same time, the presence of airborne allergies will increase food reactions. Seasonal colic is reported by some parents and could be related to the pollens of summer. Cigarette smoke, pet dander, and a high level of air pollutants can all add to the allergic response—so can stress, both mental and physical. It is well known that asthma attacks are much more common with exercise or on days of heavy smog. Many partially attribute the increasing occurrence of all kinds of sensitivities to our ever-growing environmental pollution. Diesel exhaust has been shown to be particularly offensive in promoting increased allergic reactions.[48] I've seen many food sensitivity studies where the researchers will provide a one-time food challenge of a food a child has been avoiding, see no reaction, and conclude (with this insufficient test) that the intolerance does not exist.

Aversion

Animals and humans are born equipped with an innate ability to determine when a food has caused them to feel ill, so they can learn to avoid foods that are spoiled, poisonous, or otherwise undesirable. This instinctual ability, promoted by the nervous system, allows for the survival of a species.

In a child, especially an infant, the body's natural system for learning to avoid poisonous and otherwise harmful foods is very much intact. For this reason, especially when the diet is simple, as it usually is for infants, these babies and young children will attempt to refuse a food that has previously caused an uncomfortable sensitivity reaction. These foods may be recognized by smell, taste, or sight. When a parent says, "My child won't eat much cheese or milk," there is probably a reason.

Even a breastfed baby will fuss or refuse the breast if he tastes or smells an odor that his body has associated with ill feeling. The avoidance may eventually become associated with the sight or smell of the breast itself. He may then accept breastmilk from a bottle for a while, but the refusal can return if the mother's diet does not change.

As we get older, our diets become more complicated, and we are taught to ignore our body's signals; as a result, the ability to subconsciously recognize offending foods is partially lost. Frequently, when forced to continually consume an offending food, a different phenomenon, the craving of such foods, will occur.

Masking

In one sense, the closer allergen exposures are in time, the greater the antibody and inflammatory reactions will be. With regular daily exposures, however, the body learns to defend itself to some degree against the painful response. It is thought that in this case natural morphine-like chemicals are released by the body to make the individual more comfortable.[49] This can create a pleasant, almost "high" feeling for part of a day. At least it brings a reduction in the chronic symptoms from the

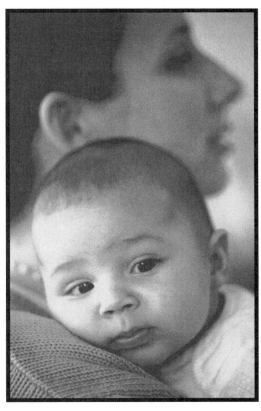

chronic exposures. This masking effect, an addiction of sorts, can hide the exposure-to-symptom relationship, making diagnosis difficult.[50] While the inflammatory destruction may be somewhat lessened, chronic damage continues, often undetected, as does immune complex deposition—leading to the insidious development of chronic diseases.

As one comes down from the morphine high or suffers a serotonin low, another dose of the allergenic food can relieve the down feeling. In this way, it is thought that individuals can start to crave the very food that is causing chronic destruction inside their bodies. Eliminating the allergenic food for a day or two now brings about withdrawal symptoms. The morphine high is lost, serotonin is low, and one can now feel the pain from the low-level reactions going on—further complicating the ability to associate consumed foods with symptoms. Simply put, consuming an offending food actually makes you feel better for a while. This masks the damaging effect of eating a food. A person feels various symptoms of illness much of the time, but the foods causing it are not easily recognized.

It once was standard advice for ulcer sufferers to drink milk regularly. Since milk is commonly a cause of ulcers, a masking effect could bring about temporary relief for many—and initially increased pain when milk was withdrawn. Since it was learned that milk consumption actually causes ulcers to be prolonged (and that men on this milk-sipping diet had high heart attack rates), this advice has been rescinded.

Protecting Baby

Allergic reactions, especially food allergies, rob baby of her greatest potential for lifelong health. Just waiting for her to "grow out" of her reactions allows ongoing damage to occur. While the number of children expressing certain kinds of food reactions drops with age, many retain their allergies. Fewer than we think "grow out" of their allergies; the way they express their discomfort merely changes with age. While they may have grown out of their colic, they have often grown into new problems such as tantrums, sleep difficulties, irritability, poor behavior, chronic diarrhea or constipation, vomiting, and so on. Eczema and other atopic rashes often give way to rhinitis and respiratory symptoms.

If no attempt is made to limit intestinal irritation, if it is indeed occurring, the child's chance of developing some form of irritable bowel syndrome or even cancer as an adult increases many times over. If immune complexes are allowed to roam through the child's body frequently, heart disease, stroke, arthritis, diabetes, or other debilitating disease may be waiting as well.

14

Discovering, Preventing, and Treating Food Allergies

"A number of differences between medicine and pure science...can result in some medical innovations being ignored or rejected without an adequate assessment. Social-organizational factors in medicine appear to favor the acceptance of theoretically glamorous, pharmaceutical, and high technology innovations over simpler and less profitable ones."
—Dr. Robert Forman, University of Toledo[1]

"A wise man ought to realize that health is his most valuable possession and learn how to treat his illnesses by his own judgment."
—Hippocrates[2]

AN ANGRY PHONE CALL FROM A PATIENT OFTEN COMES TO MIND WHEN I discuss the diagnosis of food sensitivities.

Carol brought her 8-year-old daughter into my office one day to see if I had any help for the child's daily abdominal pains. She had been to see many other doctors, and her 8-year-old was taking tranquilizers and sleep aids every day with no improvement. I took a thorough history, including the daughter's typical diet and the timing of the pains, and saw a rather strong possibility that she was sensitive to gluten. I gave materials to the mother and suggested she provide her daughter a gluten-free diet for a short trial.

Two days later came the phone call. Carol was upset and overwhelmed with the amount of work required to provide her daughter foods without wheat or any other source of gluten. She asked me where she was supposed to find the time. I empathized with the difficulty of changing her daughter's diet, but encouraged the mother to stick with the trial.

Fourteen days later she called me again to say her daughter had been following the diet and was entirely free of symptoms. In the end, the mother couldn't have been more happy than to see the end to her daughter's constant suffering.

In attempting to diagnose and treat food hypersensitivity, remember that the inconvenience is a means to an end—hopefully, a very happy, healthy end to pain or some other difficulty.

Food intolerance and other allergies are far more common in babies and children than most people think—and they are becoming more prevalent all the time. While medical acceptance of this scientific fact is slow in coming, many common difficulties with youngsters can be avoided by parents who work to prevent, diagnose, and treat hypersensitivity reactions. Moreover, the potential for adult allergies is decreased, and many diseases, including autoimmune diseases, bowel disease, and even cancer, may be thwarted by preventive measures such as avoiding foods or environmental allergens.

Not only are some of the better blood tests not available in the United States, but the ability of U.S. medical doctors to recognize food allergies is far behind that in other nations. A University of Maryland report on celiac disease occurrence in the United States and Europe demonstrates this perfectly.[3] While celiac disease remains the most accepted of any food-allergy diagnosis in the United States (though they think it's some disease entity unto itself), statistics still reveal an amazing paucity of celiac cases in the United States compared to Europe. The author of this report has performed studies, however, that suggest the actual occurrence of celiac disease in Americans and Europeans is similar—U.S. cases are simply not being diagnosed and many Americans are suffering needlessly. Let us, as parents, make a change for our new generation.

Laboratory Diagnosis

Many parents have suspected food allergies in their children and have taken a child to a pediatrician or allergist. Generally, the doctor performs the standard tests for allergy, either a RAST IgE blood test or skin scratch tests. These two tests only look for IgE-conducted, immediate hypersensitivity (type 1) reactions—those that fit under the strict definition of allergy that was created *after* these tests were developed, to fit the limits of these tests. Most of the time these IgE tests come back negative. The parents are then told they are making too much of their child's symptoms, or when digestive tract symptoms are significant, that their child needs to see a gastroenterologist. In the latter case tests involving radiation and other procedures are performed to search for underlying disease; usually to no avail. The child may end up with some vague diagnosis of "nonspecific diarrhea of infancy," colic, or colitis.

A study on how well immune reactions to foods are diagnosed in Crohn's disease sufferers illustrates the weakness of IgE testing for digestive disorders.[4] The patients were evaluated through extensive laboratory procedures and were compared to controls. All were found to have low to negative blood levels of IgE to all four major food allergens tested, while a few had elevated blood IgE levels to inhaled allergens. Scratch testing showed some positive reactions to foods. On the other hand, blood IgG levels were negative in all cases in response to inhaled allergens, but were quite elevated in response to various foods. Furthermore, a highly sensitive lymphocyte test, presently used only in research settings, was the most sensitive test for detecting an immune response to milk protein. Nearly all children and adults diagnosed with Crohn's disease remained in "remission" after allergenic foods were eliminated from their diets.

RAST IgE blood tests and skin scratch tests are valuable for diagnosing airborne allergens and immediate-reaction food allergies. These tests have very low sensitivity to the immune mechanisms in delayed-reaction food intolerance.[5] Fortunately, for healthcare practitioners aware of the need, laboratory testing is now commercially available that can help diagnose some greater portion of delayed food reactions, those mediated by IgG antibodies. An intestinal biopsy can provide good diagnostic assistance at times. Although this procedure is generally too invasive to be used in most cases, it sheds light on the number and behavior of certain white blood cells in the intestinal walls and detects any damage to intestinal villi.[6,7] Biopsy provides visual evidence of the food reactions and the destruction they cause. In addition, colonoscopy (visually looking into the colon with a scope) will reveal signs such as erythema (redness), ulceration, bleeding, and loss of vascular pattern.[8]

Biopsies frequently find an increased number of eosinophils, the allergy-related blood cells of the immune system. Thus, a diagnosis of "eosinophilic gastroenteritis" is provided. Sometimes, mast cells are more numerous, and "mastocytosis" is the diagnosis. These diagnoses are merely descriptions of the ongoing allergic processes. Common steroid treatment for these diagnoses is harmful to the body, and damage or illness will continue if irritating foods aren't avoided.

In the research laboratory, performing multiple tests for various immunological indicators provides high concordance with food challenge results. Of tests currently commercially available, even the best can only claim 75% to 85% sensitivity in detecting allergenic foods, with some false positive findings as well. One report found that only ELISA testing of IgM antibodies (not a commercially available test) is specific for diagnosing milk protein intolerance as it relates to chronic ear infections in 3-year-olds, while IgE testing was more accurate in 1-year-olds.[9] In another study, ELISA IgG testing missed diagnoses for 20% of celiac disease patients, who had proven sensitivity to gluten from grains.[10] In a large base of patients who altered their diets based almost entirely on the results of an IgG ELISA test, 67% found good improvement or recovered from symptoms.[11] Other investigations report a much higher recovery rate when actual food challenges are included in the diagnostic workup.

Using IgE tests for immediate (type 1) allergic reactions is not foolproof either: Scratch tests show only 60 to 70% sensitivity for detecting immediate reaction allergies (higher if fresh food extracts are used[12]). Some practitioners require positive test results to make their diagnosis, which makes these tests 100% reliable to them. I have shown that rhinitis and lung symptoms, usually assumed to be immediate allergic reactions, are often the result of IgG-conducted food sensitivities or other chemical sensitivity reactions. Children with these demonstrate obvious allergic symptoms, but may show up negative on all scratch and blood tests. These children are often diagnosed with nonallergic (or non-atopic) rhinitis or asthma, but further investigation through other means can discover delayed reactions and chemical sensitivities in most, which can lead to relief from symptoms with proper diet. For reasons poorly understood, even children with anaphylactic (severe respiratory) reactions to certain elements, especially to a food, can come up with negative IgE results—but the many of these will then show up positive on IgG testing.

The best way to diagnose which foods are causing symptoms is to use elimination diets. First you remove all possible allergens from the diet until the body recovers, then you offer each suspected food one at a time to see whether symptoms are reproduced.

In blood testing, just as with food challenges, it is common for an allergenic food that has not been consumed for some time to produce a negative result, because over time, especially with mild offenders, the antibodies in the body diminish. But food challenges repeated 2 or 3 days in a row will uncover these foods. To obtain the best blood test results, patients must consume most of their dietary repertoire a few times during the weeks preceding their blood tests. Many times foods will provoke immune reactivity in the laboratory, but cause no apparent reactions in the patient. This is what's called a false positive test and these are common as well. These are only some of the reasons why blood testing cannot be relied upon completely. Except in the case of a severely reacting child, any blood test results, whether positive or negative, should be followed by food challenges to make sure that foods are not needlessly eliminated, that intolerant foods are not missed, and that foods are truly the problem.

Elimination Diets

We have arrived at the heart of diagnosing food intolerance—does an ingested food provoke a symptom in the body or not? Elimination dieting with sequential challenging of different foods works because all possible allergenic substances are removed from the diet for several days *before* the body is challenged with substances one at a time, then responses are observed. In this manner, chronic reactivity and masking efforts are removed, making positive reactions clear and definite.

For diagnosing food intolerance, there are two extremes of testing. For the greatest accuracy, one consumes only a few foods that are low on the common allergen scale and that are not usual foods to their diet, until improvement is seen, then adds foods back at the rate of 1 new food every

1 to 3 days. The new food needs to be eaten at least 3 times before adding another, watching for symptoms. On the other end of the spectrum, one can simply eliminate 1 suspected food from the diet for 3 to 10 days, look for improvement, and then reintroduce the food and look for a response. More often than not, eliminating only 1 food and then challenging with it will not tell the whole story, but it is simple and may be all that is needed. The real solution may be somewhere between these two extremes.

The gold standard medical version of elimination diet testing requires a patient to swallow capsules that contain either a suspected food or a placebo, then have a professional monitor results. Because of placebo effects, many medical doctors will refuse to consider any conclusions not obtained in this fashion; however, they are also not quick to offer this testing (and some forget that standard placebos contain corn). To truly satisfy these criteria, a physician would have to be present to observe a child's responses over a 48-hour period for at least 3 separate challenges for every food of interest. Additionally, accuracy cannot be achieved unless all reactive antigens have been eliminated from the diet for some days prior to a food challenge to eliminate masking effects and reactions to foods consumed prior to the test. This kind of testing is far from practical. In research studies, food samples are provided in multiple double-blind challenges, and results are compared to one or more blood studies, and in some cases, biopsies. Some doctors claim that since proving beyond a doubt that a food causes a symptom is so difficult, the diagnosis is not worth considering. This mind-set is a product of a drug-oriented approach. Doctors have been strongly influenced by industry partners to believe there is a dangerous health risk in any diet excluding dairy, thus food elimination should not be considered. I hope you understand by now that this is far from true.

Undoubtedly, the placebo effect *is* a confounding factor. The attitude of the parent who provides the food and evaluates the symptoms is just as suspect for lack of objectivity as is the child's anticipation, but placebo effect is fairly unlikely in infants. If concerned, one caretaker can be kept in the dark about what is being tested so this individual will have more objectivity while observing symptoms. In any event, the key is that *over time, either the child's chronic symptoms will go away with food elimination, or they won't.* If the symptoms are gone, there is no other disease to be concerned with. If symptoms do not go away with cautious elimination, something else is going on.

Where to Begin

Several food allergy books recommend rotation diets for finding offending foods. Only members from a few food families are eaten at a time, eliminating other food families. Then a new set of food families is tried. While there is some treatment value to rotation dieting, this technique is weak diagnostically. A look at the lists of offending foods for many different people will actually reveal very little correlation between food families and sensitivity to the foods within these families. For instance, one may react to soy and peanuts, but thrive on peas, kidney beans, and carob, all members of the legume family. One may not tolerate strawberries or raspberries, in the rose family, but do fine with cherries, almonds, and blackberries, all in this family as well. Rotary elimination diets are designed to allow ample food selection during the testing period; however, in practice, the entire experiment could be in vain.

The level of elimination attempted depends upon how chronic and severe baby's symptoms are, as well as how motivated the parent is to relieve suffering, improve nutritional status, and prevent future disease. At the beginning of the test, the goal is to reduce all immune hyperactivity to a minimum level, so that the true effects of the food challenges can be seen. Many families and even researchers eliminate and challenge only milk. When no positive results are found, they assume allergy is not the problem. If there is one more food in the child's diet causing symptoms, it can prevent this test from revealing the milk sensitivity.

> Some doctors claim that since proving beyond a doubt that a food causes a symptom is so difficult, the diagnosis is not worth considering.

To help determine the appropriate level of an elimination diet, refer to Figure 14-1. To use this table, find the appropriate level for each symptom listed, add up the numbers from each box, and use the point ranges below to select the appropriate food elimination process.

The Formula-Fed Infant

Detecting food allergens in the bottle-fed infant may be simple, though today there are no 100% allergen-free formulas available. Amino acid formulas contain corn, and corn-free liquid hydrolyzed milk formulas contain trace milk proteins. A compounding pharmacy can create something allergen-free, but it's recently become apparent that some of the chemical processes used in creating these may cause chemical sensitivity responses. Regardless, the easiest first attempt is a switch to soy-based formula. It is best to look for a soy formula that has no corn syrup, cornstarch, or corn solids, although currently this may be impossible in the United States. Regardless, soy formula eliminates all dairy and can be tried for infants in any of the categories in Figure 14-1, with a better chance for success when the infant is in a lower score range. Try the new formula for 5 to 14 days. If desirable improvement is achieved, the soy formula can be used as the sole source of nutrition. Many infants who initially improve on soy formula eventually develop a sensitivity to the soy or corn, and a hydrolysate or elemental formula may then be needed.

If no improvement occurs with soy, try a protein hydrolysate. U.S. formulas labeled as hypoallergenic are made from cow's milk proteins that are mostly broken down (hydrolyzed by enzymes) into smaller pieces so the body will not recognize them as allergens. None of the hydrolysate formulas available presently in the United States are hydrolyzed enough to prevent eventual immune reactions in a moderate portion of sensitive infants. Hydrolyzed soy is available in some countries and has been found to be quite adequate for sensitive infants. Lamb-based formulas are also available in some other countries, as well as more completely hydrolyzed cow's milk formulas. Liquid Alimentum hydrolysate has no corn and may be the best first choice in the United States.

If adequate recovery is not seen with hydrolyzed formula, then the small remaining amounts of cow's milk protein could be the problem. The final effort is to try an amino acid formula (now commercially available) or elemental diet (such as Vivonex). A child who initially improves on standard hydrolysate may eventually react to it as well and will need to be placed on an elemental diet. Elemental formula is a complete nutrition formula with no intact proteins or complex sugars. It should be entirely hypoallergenic; that is, it should not cause allergic reactions, although I'm currently unable to find any in the United States that are free of corn syrup solids. These are very expensive and health insurance won't cover the cost, but remember, it is only a test. Try elemental formula for at least 7 days. If the child recovers from his symptoms, then his health will improve if he stays on this formula. At 5 or 6 months of age, a nutritionist can help you figure out how to replace much of the formula with more affordable solid foods and nutrient supplements. Using rice, oat, almond, or soy milks instead of formula is not sufficient as a sole source of nutrition for infants.

Sensitivity Symptoms for Determining Level of Elimination Diet

Degree of Symptoms	Skin	Colic	Stools	Sinuses	Behavior
Mild	Light, occasional rash **1**	Occasional signs of intestinal discomfort **1**	Occasional loose stools or missed days **2**	Occasional stuffiness **1**	Occasional unexplained fussiness or misbehavior **1**
Moderate	Frequent light rash, occasional allergy rings or large rashes **2**	Frequent mild or occasional great discomfort **3**	Frequent loose or missed stools, occasional diarrhea or constipation **3**	Frequent stuffiness or occasional ear fluid **2**	Frequent fussiness, or occasional episodes of great contrariness **3**
Severe	Frequent large or open sore rashes, regular allergy rings **3**	Frequent great discomfort **4**	Frequent diarrhea or constipation **4**	Regular stuffiness or ear fluid, or occasional ear infection **3**	Frequent episodes of great fussiness or contrariness **4**

Figure 14-1 Based on the score from symptoms in the chart, select the appropriate level of elimination diet.

LEVEL I (3–5 points) Try dairy elimination along with any suspected foods first.

LEVEL II (6–9 points) Try elimination of dairy, egg, wheat, corn, peanuts, fish, chicken, citrus, strawberry, and tomato, and any suspected foods first. Eliminate goat or soy also if it has been regular in diet (not counting soy oil).

LEVEL III (10+ points) Best to start with comprehensive elimination diet.

LEVEL IV (Severe illness) Begin with elemental diet for nursing mom or solid-food-consuming or formula-feeding child.

Lactose-Free Is Not the Answer

Some formulas are made without lactose to help prevent gas and diarrhea in baby. Consider, however, that mother's milk contains far more lactose than cow's milk. Although testing sometimes suggests otherwise, lactose intolerance as a primary problem in infants is incredibly rare and would show up in the first days of an infant's life. True, when infants suffer from intestinal damage due to food intolerance reactions or infectious diarrhea, they may demonstrate lactase enzyme deficiency or sugar malabsorption, but they will also be deficient in many other enzymes and will suffer malabsorption in many other ways. Removing all cow's milk products from the diet is important for treating diarrhea from any cause, but as soon as immune reactions are gone, an infant's body will straighten out the handling of lactose.

The Nursing Infant

The nursing mother of a symptomatic infant needs to follow an elimination diet herself, watching for symptoms in her child. From the following information, select what foods to eliminate and be 100% meticulous with ingredient avoidance if possible, or the entire effort might be wasted. One hundred percent elimination of all traces of corn is so difficult that it is not worth the full effort until it is positively suspected. Often within a day of elimination one will see improvement in baby. In other babies, it may take a few days and there are many reports of infants who do not respond for 10 days to 2 weeks. Watch for all the signs you have available, such as behavior, sleep patterns, spitting up, and stool changes. Vomiting should reduce quickly. Eczema is usually slow to respond. Blood in the stools may take several weeks to subside, but do not go by this symptom alone. If baby is clearly happier in other ways, there is no need to wait for bleeding to stop before beginning to add foods back.

Add food ingredients back one at a time in the beginning, remembering that prepared foods have many ingredients. Start with what you most desire rather than with what you most suspect, to give baby's system a little longer break from any offending food. Now negative responses to offending foods should occur within hours or a day, except eczema, which can take a day longer. If a baby appears to be tolerating a food after 3 introductions, you can go on to the next food. Eventually, once you get a better picture of what is going on, foods can be tried in combinations so that the diet can be increased more rapidly.

Along with cow's milk, cruciferous vegetables in mother's diet are especially known for causing colic in breastfed infants.[13] These include cabbage, cauliflower, broccoli, and turnips. Onion and garlic, from a similar vegetable family, are often added to this list. These are often referred to as gas foods and the source of discomfort may be something digestive other than the

Common Allergens in Commercial Formulas					
Company	**Brand (Type)**	**Cow's Milk Derivatives**	**Corn Derivatives**	**Soy Derivatives**	**Oils**
Ross	Similac	Nonfat Milk** Whey**			Coconut, Soy, Safflower
Ross	Alimentum (Protein Hydrolysate)	Casein-Hydrolysate*			Coconut, Soy, Safflower
Wyeth Laboratory	Babysoy (Soy Protein Milk-Free)	Beef Fat (Oleo)	Corn Syrup Solids**	Soy Protein Isolate** Lecithin* Soy Oil*	Lard (Oleo) Coconut, Soy, Safflower
Mead Johnson	Enfamil LactoFree (Lactose Free)	Milk Protein Isolate**	Corn Syrup Solids**	Soy Oil*	Coconut, Palm, Soy, Sunflower
Mead Johnson	Enfamil Nutramigen (Hypo-aller-genic)	Casein-Hydrolysate*	Corn Syrup Solids** Corn Starch**	Soy Oil*	Coconut, Palm, Soy, Sunflower
Mead Johnson	Enfamil Next Step	Nonfat Milk**	Corn Syrup Solids**	Soy Oil*	Coconut, Palm, Soy, Sunflower

Figure 14-2 *Mild Allergen **Strong Allergen

immune system process of delayed-reaction food sensitivities. Either way, if they cause symptoms, they should be discovered and eliminated. Chocolate and caffeine are also frequently implicated. Some have seen that babies can react negatively to Mom's prenatal vitamins. Iron is the suspected culprit by some and the B vitamins are suspect by others. Mom should have ample stores in her body of every needed nutrient, except for vitamin C, to make fully nutritious milk for at least a couple of weeks (and truly beyond, with the foods she's eating). After that point, if wanted, non-irritating vitamin sources will need to be explored. If doing a trial elimination of vitamin supplements, and also eliminating most fruits and vegetables, Mom needs to try to find a non-citrus source of vitamin C to take daily. Hopefully it will be without corn starch as well. There are rosehip- and acerola-derived versions available in some stores, and the pure chemically derived ascorbic acid might be the only good option found.

Elimination Diet on Solid Foods

Once a mother finds which foods she needs to avoid to maintain the health and comfort of her infant, she can generally assume that these foods should not be fed to her child when he grows into solid foods. It is also likely the child will demonstrate reactions to other foods beyond these—but often only after the third or fourth exposure. If mother and food-allergic child are happy with their nursing diet and relationship, there should be no rush to push solid foods. After a few bad experiences, the food-intolerant infant often has less interest in solid foods beyond curiosity and play. In the first year or two, other foods are only replacing the higher nutrition of mother's milk and should be considered more as entertainment.

If the nursing child has begun supplemental foods and has had no problems before the introduction of a particular supplemental formula or other food, there is little need for the mother to follow a restricted diet as well. If the nursing toddler has had long-term symptoms and is pretty attached to having solid foods, then mother and child need to follow the diet together. Still, only one food can be introduced at a time—in mother, child, or both at the same time.

When a mother suspects or discovers for sure that her child is suffering reactions to foods in mother's milk, this is by no means an indication to stop nursing. This child will almost certainly have difficulties with formulas or solid foods. The best way to ensure optimum nutrition is to preserve the benefits of mother's wonderful milk, minus the offending foods in her diet. This will also provide baby with the healthiest possible digestive tract—thereby helping to prevent further sensitization and speed any "growing out" of sensitivities. Once the offending foods are gone, mother's milk also has many qualities that will speed the child's intestinal healing and reduce risks for many potential future diseases. Since allergy is a highly genetic condition, the mother may also end up reaping improved health from this process. Some doctors push hydrolyzed formulas for babies who may be reacting to Mom's milk. I'm all for this—for Mom to consume, not baby. Mom can drink the formula, alone or along with other low-allergy foods, and convert it to a fully nutritious, hypoallergenic, healing, growth, and immune-providing diet for baby.

If swelling of the tongue or difficulty breathing has ever been seen in a child, introduction of suspicious foods, especially nuts, shellfish, and sulfites, should only be made under medical supervision. Generally, anaphylactic attacks occur rapidly after ingestion of a food; determining which food is the problem is not difficult. Elimination dieting is most often used to discover regularly eaten foods that may be causing rashes, gastrointestinal problems, behavior changes, or other delayed reactions. In this case, eliminating and challenging is no more dangerous than feeding the child his normal diet.

For milder, less problematic symptoms, where there is less allergy-related "disease" running in the family, parents may choose to begin by eliminating only dairy products. Or, if any one food is highly suspect, it makes sense to eliminate this food first. If there is a good recovery, the answer is simple. If a good response is not seen, it is best to eliminate this food along with others in a new trial. Do not be discouraged if eliminating one food provides no answers. Immediate-response food allergy to one single food is common, but those who develop delayed food reactions more often develop sensitivity to a few or several foods.

The key to successfully eliminating offending foods is learning to read labels and being very thorough. So many times I've heard people say their dairy elimination provided no relief, only to find out later they were never quite able to give up that evening bowl of ice cream. Poor restriction will most likely invalidate your entire efforts, so the decision has to be made— either you want to find answers or you don't. You will best survive diet changes by learning to be proud and optimistic about your efforts, and by being creative. The elimination measures necessary to completely avoid certain foods for testing purposes will likely be more extreme than those eventually needed to maintain a symptom-free diet. Eventually, during the treatment phase, you learn which foods can be tolerated on an occasional basis in minute quantities as an added ingredient (like wheat starch), and which ones are highly allergenic and need to be avoided at all cost.

Where Do You Find Milk Hidden in Foods?

I've had many patients spout to me that dairy could not possibly be their problem because they eat dairy products all the time. To which I usually reply, "You tell me you are sick all the time." Eliminating dairy is much more complicated than you might think, but it is very possible once you learn to read labels and prepare simple foods at home.

Cheese and yogurt must be eliminated along with all other dairy products even though these two foods are reputed to be slightly less problematic for a couple of reasons. For adolescents or adults who have decreasing lactose tolerance, much of the lactose has been consumed by the bacteria that produce the cheese or yogurt, making these more tolerable for lactase-deficient individuals. Some of the proteins are predigested as well, but likely not enough to avoid reactions by most allergic individuals.

Of course, eliminating dairy means eliminating milk, cheese, butter, cottage cheese, cream, yogurt, and ice cream, but dairy products are hidden in maybe half the packaged foods in the grocery store. Still, the grocery store or health food store is the safest source for meals for the elimination diet because the foods have ingredient labels.

The ingredients to look for on labels when eliminating dairy are milk, milk fat, milk solids, cheese, cream, butter, whey, casein, caseinate, lactose, hydrolyzed protein, and protein solids.

"Natural flavor" can be a problem because it can mean a lot of things, including hydrolyzed caseinate, which is a way to make MSG out of milk protein for flavor enhancement. Some foods that may sound very safe often are not:

- Margarine often contains whey, lactose, or casein.

- "Nondairy" on a label usually indicates that the product is lactose-free but contains the allergenic milk protein casein.

- Soy or vegetarian cheese almost always contains casein or whey. Look for vegan.

- Chicken breasts in fast-food and most other restaurants, where they are purchased already infused with several flavorings, generally include whey, caseinate, or butter. Also breading and French fries often contain whey.

- In non-fast-food restaurants, hamburgers, meats, and fish are often grilled in butter, as are hamburger buns, and butter is commonly added to the vegetables. Fish is sometimes soaked in milk overnight.

Some ingredients that sound like dairy derivatives that are not dairy are lactylate, calcium lactate, and cocoa butter.

One must read the label of any packaged food. Some form of dairy will be found in many foods:

- Most breads contain some whey. Ready-made and large restaurant chain pizza crusts usually contain cheese. Many fast-food buns are made with whey.

- Cereals, pastries, pancakes, waffles, muffins, cakes, cookies, crackers, granola bars, soups, chocolates, salad dressings, fat-free products, low-fat hot dogs, whole turkeys, and flavored chips often have dairy products in them.

When dairy products need to be avoided, remember that green vegetables and many other foods are superior sources of calcium (and other vitamins and minerals), and much less calcium is needed than the USRDA recommends when milk products and meat protein levels are not high in the diet. Remember also that *most products that claim to be nondairy are full of the bovine protein caseinate, or some other dairy component.* Health food stores provide many good dairy alternatives. Anything marked as vegan (or Kosher for Passover) should be entirely milk-free.

Wheat

Due to marketing techniques, many people believe that white flour is not wheat. But any flour that does not specifically say otherwise is wheat flour. Some food labels list "starch" or "modified food starch" as an ingredient. This is more often corn, but could be wheat. Spelt and kamut are wheat but buckwheat is not. Wheat is the main ingredient in nearly all breads, including white bread, corn bread, and rye bread, rolls, crackers, even graham crackers, cookies, even arrowroot cookies, cakes, waffles, pancakes, and most cereals. Wheat is a common thickener in ice creams, dressings, soups, and gravies, and it is the breading for foods such as fried chicken and onion rings. It also may be hidden in seemingly benign products such as French fries.

Corn

Corn ranks up there with dairy for being difficult to avoid. Corn, popcorn, corn chips, and corn bread are obvious sources. Generally when a food item lists "starch," it is cornstarch, found in many foods. Asian sauces are thickened with cornstarch. Hydrolyzed vegetable protein (another source of MSG) is often made from corn, and 99.9% of all candies, condiments, and other sweetened treats or sauces are sweetened with corn syrup or another corn derivative. Dextrose, fructose, and glucose are all safe natural fruit sugars, but when they are added ingredients in foods, they are made from corn and will certainly bother most moderately corn sensitive individuals. It may be due to remaining traces of corn proteins. Corn syrup or dextrose is added to most hot dogs and hams. Sucrose is table sugar (cane or beet sugar) and is safe for most people allergic to corn. A few are also allergic to cane, which is in the same food family as corn (the grass family), but they should tolerate beet sugar. Hypoglycemia is a different problem (of insulin regulation) and concerns all sugars.

The ingredients to look for on labels when avoiding corn are starch, cornstarch, corn syrup, dextrin, dextrose, malt, maltose, maltodextrin, maltitol, glucose, fructose, inulin syrup, invert sugar, caramel, sorbitol (also called starch hydrolysate), natural flavor, hydrolyzed vegetable protein, and cold-pressed corn oil.

Corn-derived sugars very occasionally make their way into orange juice, apple juice, honey, and maple syrup. This practice is illegal when the ingredient is not listed, but the FDA is well aware of its sporadic but continued occurrence. Companies are finding ways to make added ingredients rather "invisible" to laboratory tests. I used to avoid off-brands and trust the large brands, but I once saw problems with these and now stick to organic, without incident (so far). Corn is a prominent ingredient in many French fries, as is wheat. Someone who has extreme reactions to corn should be aware that it is found in miniscule amounts in many more, often hard to believe places (no licking postage stamps for instance). Even iodized salt contains dextrose from corn.

Other Foods Eliminated on a Level II Diet

Citrus includes orange, lemon, lime, citron, tangerine, kumquat, and grapefruit. Peanuts can be hidden in some cereals and cookies, and some restaurants cook with peanut oil. Warnings about peanut contents are fairly common on labels nowadays. Tiny amounts of peanut are generally not a problem for those with intestinal food sensitivities, but peanut allergic individuals who display breathing difficulties are at risk for anaphylactic shock from even traces of peanuts. Eggs are common baking ingredients and are listed as eggs, egg whites, or albumin. Natural strawberry flavor contains strawberry allergens, but artificial strawberry flavor is "safe."

The best way to follow a level II elimination diet is to select most foods from the "low" and "seldom" columns in Figure 14-3.

Designing the Level III Diet

A highly restricted diet can be a problem for a young child, but with sincere effort, ample nutrition can be provided, especially since most of the restrictions last for less than 2 weeks.

For the first days of the diet, select 1 or 2 meats, fruits, vegetables, and grains from the last two columns of Figure 14-3. Choose mostly foods that were seldom consumed, that are not suspect, and for infants, that were not often consumed by Mom during the second half of her pregnancy (if possible). *Lamb, brown rice, sweet potato, lettuce greens, table sugar or real maple syrup, and pear is a recommended diet and will provide more than adequate nutrition for a week or two.* With the addition of another dark fruit or vegetable, this will provide a complete diet. Use apple cider vinegar mixed with a commercial canola oil or non-virgin olive oil on lettuce. Healthier, cold-pressed oils have traces of allergens. Non-iodized salt can be used. A popularly published elimination diet includes pepper but pepper is a very common irritant. Millet is commonly suggested but millet is very close to corn. Remember, the more foods included, the greater the chance you will include a food your child is sensitized to, and the less the chance there is for diagnostic success. I generally push for only one food from each of the meat or nut, vegetable, fruit, and grain groups. If an infant has been experiencing great intestinal trauma and mother has been consuming much rice already, the child could have developed sensitivity to rice as well. I suggest then going without any grain. Amaranth or quinoa can be used. Some moms use hemp milk for a diet enhancement as it's often a new food to their diet.

You should be eliminating and challenging with spices as well, except for non-iodized salt, which is never a problem. Testing food colorings and other additives may be advisable, since the prevalence of additive intolerance is thought to be between .15 and 2%,[14,15] and is probably much higher. The most commonly implicated additives are sulfites (metabisulfite, disulfite), benzoates (in Sprite but not 7UP for example), and tartrazine (FD&C Yellow No. 5). The drug aspirin, which is salicylate, is also known to provoke reactions. These are all better known for their type 1 allergic associations, but other types of intolerance have been reported.[16] MSG sensitivity is more common, but less likely to cause several of the food sensitivity symptoms discussed. In most cases MSG causes headaches, nausea, or sudden, overwhelming fatigue. Accent is a pure source of MSG that can be used in testing if desired. Truly, MSG is a dangerous neurotoxin and should not be in the diet of an infant or child regardless of reaction.

Preventing Allergies

When allergies run in a family or have been experienced by either parent, or if irritable bowel syndrome, colitis, Crohn's, arthritis, or asthma are found in the family, many researchers suggest that attempts should be made to prevent sensitization in the infant. There is a high correlation between these familial conditions and allergies in infants, but little correlation between the specific types of reactions. A highly pollen-allergic parent may produce a bovine protein sensitive child and a parent with irritable bowel syndrome may produce a child with immediate-type peanut allergy. The intensity of the preventive measures implemented should depend on the frequency and severity of the symptoms in the family. If sensitization is prevented early on, a reduced level of allergic reaction seems to be maintained throughout the growing years.

Expecting parents can attempt to avoid sensitization in their unborn child by reducing potential allergens in the pregnant mother's environment and diet, especially during the last 3 months of pregnancy. Enough research has been performed that we can be relatively certain that elimination will help to some degree, but we still cannot predict the actual degree of protection and lifetime benefit. Maternal smoking during pregnancy certainly increases the development of asthma in the child,[17] as does secondhand smoke exposure.

Once baby is born, exclusive breastfeeding itself provides good protection against the development of allergies. When the lactating mother avoids dairy and other common allergens, this is even better. The effect of cow's milk in the mother's diet has been studied the most intensively, because bovine proteins are the biggest offenders by far. Avoiding milk during the last third of pregnancy as well as during lactation has been shown to provide a definite benefit, at least against early allergy.[18] One investigation found no long-term statistical reduction of allergies in children whose mothers avoided cow's milk and eggs during the last 12 weeks of gestation,[19] while other small studies suggest otherwise.

The artificially fed infant can be started on hydrolysate immediately, avoiding any exposure to regular milk formula, and the nursing infant who is weaned early or who starts on supplements can receive the same. Although dairy hydrolysate is often poorly tolerated by infants already sensitized to bovine proteins, either from regular milk formulas or from exposure *in utero*, infants without this exposure are less likely to develop bovine protein intolerance from the lower concentrations in hydrolysates. These measures have been shown to reduce the chances of allergic disease in at-risk children (those with allergic parents) by 50% in a 5-year follow-up study.[20] This same Canadian study revealed no long-term preventive benefit with soy formulas.

The longer you wait before exposing your child to bovine proteins and

Allergy- or Sensitivity-Provoking Foods

High	Medium	Medium	Low	Seldom
Casein/Whey	Butter	Cream	Ghee	
Cow Milk	Cheese	Goat Milk	Goat Cheese	
Egg White	Egg Yolk	Yogurt		
Shellfish	Beef	Fish	Pork	Buffalo
	Chicken		Turkey	Lamb
Brazil Nut	Cashew	Mustard	Almond	Amaranth
Sunflower	Chocolate	Pecan	Hazelnut	
	Coconut	Sesame		
	Flax	Walnut		
Corn	Buckwheat	Oat	Barley	Arrowroot
Wheat	Kamut	Rye	Quinoa	Poi
	Millet	Spelt	Rice	Tapioca
Grapefruit	Banana	Mango	Apple	Date
Lemon	Blackberry	Melon	Apricot	Lychee Fruit
Lime	Blueberry	Nectarine	Cherry	Persimmon
Orange	Fig	Peach	Cranberry	
Strawberry	Grape	Pineapple	Papaya	
Tangerine	Guava	Plum	Prune	
	Loquat	Raspberry	Raisin	
Peanut	Kidney Bean	Peas	Green Bean	
Soy	Miso	Tofu	White Bean	
Tomato	Bell Pepper	Ginger	Asparagus	Agave Nectar
	Black Pepper	Mushroom	Avocado	Baby Lettuce
	Broccoli	Onion	Beet	Iceberg Lettuce
	Cabbage	Radish	Carrot	Maple
	Celery	Squash	Cauliflower	
	Cucumber	White Potato	Leafy Greens	
	Garlic	Yam	Sweet Potato	
	Cold Pressed Oils	Virgin Olive Oil	Palm Oil	Refined Oils
	Balsamic Vinegar	Cider Vinegar	Rice Vinegar	Distilled Vinegar
	Honey	Molasses	Cane Sugar	Beet Sugar

Figure 14-3 Foods known for high, medium, or low capacity to provoke allergy or sensitivity reaction, and those seldom implicated. From multiple sources.

other likely allergens, the lower your child's chances of developing sensitivity. A Belgian investigation that evaluated hydrolysate formula against regular formula found a sixfold reduction in bovine protein sensitivity in the hydrolysate group at the age of 6 months, and just as above, a 50% advantage after 5 years, measured in terms of milk protein sensitivity.[21] Colic in infants was reduced fourfold. Researchers who previously discovered these effects suggested that no infant should ever be exposed to cow's milk proteins during their first 4 weeks of life.[22] All the evidence strongly agrees with this conclusion. In fact, the American Academy of Pediatrics released an advisory stating that milk products should not be provided during the first year of life. Milk formulas should certainly be included in this advisory since the chief motivation for this particular announcement was development of childhood diabetes. Studies report that cow's milk exposure from formula feeding during the first few months of life is the biggest risk from dairy for developing diabetes. Since formula companies provide large amounts of monetary funding to pediatric schools, associations, researchers, and practitioners, it is difficult for the AAP to promote its own recommendation to any extent.[23]

Developing food intolerances or other allergies may be unavoidable in those with stronger genetic programming, because allergic responses are highly hereditary maladies. Attempting to prevent reactions may at least reduce or delay symptoms. The big disappointment (and benefit) in preventive medicine is that you generally don't know what has been prevented in any individual case. DHA supplements and probiotic supplements for nursing mother or formula-fed baby may help reduce allergic potentials as well.

Treatment Choices

There are some old and new immune therapies that aim to reduce sensitivity reactions, and there are also medicines that may reduce or prevent symptoms, all with varying levels of success and number of drawbacks.

The best treatment today is to avoid aggravating factors and to support the immune system. Even though Drs. F. Savino and R. Oggero suggest drugs as the second treatment of choice for colic (after comforting), they go on to state that dietary modifications (their third choice) provide superior results, without the side effects of medications.[24] In many cases, long-term avoidance can reduce or erase one's sensitivity to a given allergen.[25] Studies on celiac disease (gluten intolerance) show that intestinal damage continues to occur in most who believe they have outgrown this intolerance.[26]

Clinical Treatment Methods

For nearly a century allergy shots have been given for type 1 allergies (immunotherapy). Progress has been made, but results are still only moderate, and the therapy must be received several times per month for 3 to 5 years. Benefit is mostly found for pollen, dust mite, and bee venom allergies. To date, this therapy is not recommended for food sensitivities and is not useful for food-related symptoms such as eczema. Therapy for severe anaphylactic food reactions such as peanut allergies is sometimes tried in an attempt to prevent disastrous results from accidental exposure. Doctors from the National Jewish Center for Immunology and Respiratory Medicine are having excellent results with this.[27] On the other hand, doctors at John Hopkins University found no reduction in the need for medications in an immunotherapy-treated group of allergic children with seasonal asthma.[28] Sometimes immunotherapy only makes symptoms worse, as often occurs with animal dander treatments.[29]

Provocation-neutralization is an evolving technique popular in some ear, nose, and throat and environmental medicine practices. The largest study of the provocation-neutralization method, performed by supporters of the technique following a study design approved by the American Academy of Otolaryngic Allergy, seems to be the best source for judging the technique's efficacy. This multicenter, triple-blind, placebo-controlled study reports 75% beneficial outcomes.[30] In reviewing this report, however, I find apparent weaknesses in the study design and conclusions. Still, one can see benefits in more than half the subjects. Although good benefits resulted for rhinitis, headache, and lung symptoms—symptoms that also generally respond to traditional allergen injection therapy—gastrointestinal symptoms do not appear to have improved.

Medications

Medications are commonly used to reduce symptoms of disorders such as asthma and gastrointestinal problems. The use of several medications for colic and the like has been mostly discontinued due to unacceptable levels of adverse side effects. Steroids are used for many symptoms that relate to hypersensitivity reactions—everything from eczema to bowel syndromes to asthma—offering temporary relief but also potentially serious side effects. Proton pump inhibitors (such as Prilosec and Prevacid) are now commonly prescribed for colic and other symptoms, using GERD as the diagnosis.

Avoiding milk during the last third of pregnancy as well as during lactation has been shown to provide a definite benefit, at least against early allergy.

The main concern with true, excessive reflux is that there can be severe repercussions from mucous membranes being chronically "burned" by stomach acid. Anemia can develop as well due to blood loss from bleeding tissues. The medical paradigm is that acid blocking drugs are beneficial in serious cases to prevent further consequences. The term GERD is assumed by most to represent these extreme cases that may warrant medication. Although reflux (GER) is common in infants, authoritative sources report only 1 in 300 babies as actually having the "disease," GERD. This sounds more reasonable, but the number of babies prescribed drugs for reflux is 10 to 15 times this amount. Currently, hundreds of thousands of babies and toddlers are prescribed expensive PPI drugs each year in the United States (a total of 2 million children up to the age of 16).

Some parents report gradual improvement in their infants on PPIs over time. Of course, a majority of babies naturally out-grow colic/GER symptoms during their first year whether medicated or not. Sudden withdrawal from acid blocking drugs can cause symptoms in any person as the body adjusts to regular acid reduction by creating greater amounts of acid. An increase of symptoms upon removal of the drug does not necessarily prove it was helping.

More often, parents find that PPI drugs provide little, if any, help. Multiple studies performed by these very drug manufacturers support this observation. Current studies reveal that there is great randomness to the symptoms used to diagnose GER,[31] meaning that true diagnosis is rather ambiguous. Additionally, there is little correlation found between symptoms and the gold standard esophagus examinations: endoscopy and biopsy.[32]

There is even little correlation found between these two tests. Even measuring a child's response to PPI drugs does not correlate to a diagnosis of GER; their response does not correspond to the amount of acid measured in their esophagus.[33]

It has also been shown that while the drugs reduce acid in the stomach and esophagus, they do not reduce baby's colic symptoms or other symptoms that initially led parents to seek treatment[34]—so does the acid really need reducing? GERD drugs increase pneumonia[35] and triple the risk of gastrointestinal infections,[36] while long-term safety tests are nonexistent. Other side effects of PPI drugs include headache, constipation, vomiting, stomach pain, and rashes. Absorption of nutrients is reduced, and prolonged use can lead to anemia and osteoporosis. Additionally, a systematic review of PPI studies in treatment of reflux determines that they provide no more benefit than placebos.[37] If a family finds that these help, they are the best judges, and a group called Marci Kids is exploring higher and more detailed dosing. Still, it makes sense to also try to eliminate foods that may be causing the reflux in the first place.

Epinephrine is a lifesaving emergency drug for anaphylactic reactions. Many drugs available for asthma can assist with acute reactions, but have serious side effects and (as previously discussed) are possibly responsible for the cyclical increases in asthma deaths as each new drug is introduced.

The good news is that some of the best medications for food sensitivity reactions are over-the-counter drugs with minimal side effects. While your doctor may be less aware of the drugs' food allergy values, he or she may be ready to guide you in what would be safe to try. Histamine-1 blockers (antihistamines), such as Chlortrimeton, are very valuable for allergic rhinitis and other allergic symptoms. What is not commonly known is that medications such as Zantac (ranitidine) and Tagamet (cimetadine), commonly called histamine-2 blockers, are valuable drugs for reducing the effects of food intolerance reactions,[38,39] since most histamine receptors in the intestines are histamine 2 type. These drugs, popularly known for their use with ulcers and reflux, can block H-2 receptors from responding to histamine releases related to food sensitivity and thus can reduce symptoms from food reactions—hopefully reducing damage as well. This effect often unknowingly accounts for some of the success of these drugs in ulcer and GERD treatments. H-1 blockers may be somewhat beneficial in reducing some intestinal reactions as well, and a medically supervised combination of these two drugs may work well for many. Simple anti-inflammatory medications such as ibuprofen (Advil) and aspirin may be helpful too, affecting different parts of the reaction. Unfortunately, these can also damage some already irritated stomachs and need to be used with care.

Other symptoms associated with a child's intestinal food sensitivities should respond to these drugs as well. Improvement is often seen in behavior, eczema, and other symptoms. Serotonin action is only partly blocked by H-2 blockers,[40] so all behavioral effects may not be mitigated by H-2 blockers, or by any one drug. H-2 blockers work better for symptom treatment than for prevention. By reducing stomach secretions, they reduce the ability to digest proteins. Most allergens are proteins, and less-digested proteins will only cause more reactions.

Ketotifen is a prescription drug with H-1 antihistamine activity and mast cell stabilizing action as well. Used only outside of the United States, it has been proven in many trials to be especially beneficial for treating food-sensitive patients.[41,42]

Cytoprotective drugs, prescription drugs that help to protect the intestinal mucosal lining in other ways, can be helpful for reducing food reaction symptoms and damage,[43,44] but these have more potential side effects (and should never be used during pregnancy). Pepto-Bismol is a mild and reportedly safe over-the-counter cytoprotective drug used by some.

Cromolyn sodium seems to be a valuable prescription for preventing hypersensitivity reactions in many.[45,46] Cromolyn is sometimes used in preemies experiencing various allergic reactions who cannot tolerate riskier drugs. This drug works preventively when taken one-half hour before consuming an offending food (or a mystery meal). It is not useful once a reaction is already occurring. Cromolyn works very well for some people and not for others.[47] This is a result of the wide variation of immune response mechanisms among individuals and the amount of damage already present.

In the United States, however, this drug is not classified for food hypersensitivity reactions (since we all know they don't really exist). Technically, cromolyn *is* prescribed here for the condition called "mastocytosis." This disease is described as extremely rare. It is defined as having too many mast cells and is diagnosed with biopsy. Remember, mast cells are responsible for recognizing food allergens and initiating the allergic inflammatory response. While this condition is described as severe (or needs to be severe in order to be diagnosed as mastocytosis), and it reportedly more commonly affects the skin, the symptoms of intestinal mastocytosis are indistinguishable from those of intestinal food sensitivity.

Drugs only block portions of food reactions even when they help. Drugs have potential negative side effects, and are absolutely no substitute for prudent allergen avoidance. Other, more natural treatments are shown to be more beneficial than current drugs and are without harmful side effects.

Natural Treatments

Vitamin C has been shown in several small studies to reduce histamine levels. Breastfeeding mothers can take extra vitamin C supplements, pass extra vitamin C on to baby, and reduce baby's potential to mount allergic reactions.[48]

Hundreds of thousands of babies are prescribed expensive PPI drugs each year in the United States, but they do not reduce baby's colic symptoms or other symptoms that initially led parents to seek treatment.

Antioxidants are known to reduce intestinal allergic reactions. Grapeseed extract, resveratrol, quercetin, and turmeric (curcumin) are a few powerful antioxidants. Selenium and zinc were found to be low in children with allergic colitis, probably used up by the inflammatory process.[49] Thus, supplementing these elements might be beneficial. These antioxidants and minerals can be passed to baby in higher levels through mother's milk when mother consumes higher levels.

Fatty acids are strongly associated with allergic reactions. We now know that hydrogenated vegetable oils (trans fats) increase allergic and other inflammatory reactions while omega-3 fatty acids (especially DHA and EPA) reduce them.[50–52] Some studies are beginning to discover the benefits of these specifically for delayed food intolerance reactions.[53] Trans fats should be out of the diet of breastfeeding mothers, children, and everyone really, for all kinds of health reasons. Breastfeeding mothers can take fish oil supplements (or vegan algae forms) and pass higher amounts of DHA and EPA to their nurslings, with the potential for reducing allergic/intolerance reactions.[54,55] There is a vegan version of these made from algae that might be less allergenic as well. Fat soluble antioxidants, vitamins A and E, have been shown to reduce the negative effects of "bad" fats.[56]

Probiotics are a certain step to take. *Lactobacillus rhamnosus* and *Bifidobacteria lactis* have been shown to reduce food sensitivity in children.[57] Finnish researchers have shown *Lactobacillus acidophilus* is beneficial for further reducing food allergy symptoms when used along with dietary measures, as compared with using dietary measures alone.[58] Some of these same researchers have shown that Lactobacillus may actually promote the protective IgA immune response and reduce permeability defects in the intestinal lining, reducing food sensitivity reactions.[59]

Again, breastfeeding mothers can consume probiotic supplements and pass the benefits on to baby.[60] Powdered Lactobacillus supplements (keep refrigerated before use) can be added to formula (add after warming formula). As discussed earlier, many different strains of bacteria have been shown to have beneficial effects. My recommendation is to simply find a nondairy probiotic product that contains many different strains. Yogurts seldom contain live bacteria, and dairy products should usually be avoided in treating food allergy anyway.

Aloe Vera has anti-inflammatory and healing effects in the intestine (its effect through breastmilk has not been studied)[61] and Boswellia is shown to reduce intestinal reactions and damage.[62]

Many practitioners also recommend building up the body's overall health for better immune system function by using good nutrition, regular exercise, stress reduction, and ample rest. There is certainly nothing wrong with this advice, and it will probably help. The immune system certainly functions best when nutrition, exercise, and rest are plentiful. Asthma attacks, even when surely allergy-related, are well known to increase with stress, including the stress of otherwise poor health. Cortisol (the stress hormone) release alerts the immune system, and allergic reactions can increase in response.

Many other natural modalities can also be explored such as massage, osteopathy, chiropractic, naturopathy, and acupuncture. Many of these help by reducing the body's stress level or stress reactions and improving the body's overall functioning. Good nutritional guidance can often be obtained from such practitioners as well.

Knowing and avoiding the potentially harmful effects of sensitivity

reactions on your child demonstrates the same love and devotion as nursing, close bonding, and informed healthcare decisions. What we feed our
children matters; how we parent them matters. These measures will lead
to the best health, comfort, and happiness available to a child. Parents
have the power to create and enjoy healthier, happier children with
brighter futures.

Epilogue

The New Old Way

The baby care practices that attachment parents have found to provide optimal physical and emotional health and intellectual development include the following:

- Responding to baby's cries

- Holding and carrying baby closely much of the day

- Nighttime parenting promoted by flexible sleep arrangements, especially sharing sleep with baby

- Exclusive breastfeeding on cue

- Continued breastfeeding beyond solid foods; avoiding forced premature weaning

- Speaking to and interacting with baby frequently, responding to cues

- Interpreting exploration as mind development rather than as "naughty behavior"

- Validating baby's feelings

- Enriching dialog and guidance as opposed to violent discipline or meaningless dogma

- Nonviolent toys and play

Respecting the feelings and needs of every member in the household is just as important, albeit giving baby some priority.

Notes

Chapter 2: The Attachment Advantage

1. John B. Watson, *Psychological Care of Infant and Child* (New York: W. W. Norton, 1928).
2. D.R. Pederson et al., "Maternal sensitivity and the security of infant–mother attachment: a Q-sort study," *Child Dev* (Canada) 61, no. 6 (Dec 1990): 1974–83.
3. T. Jacobsen et al., "Children's ability to delay gratification: longitudinal relations to mother–child attachment," *J Genet Psychol* 158, no. 4 (Dec 1997): 411–26.
4. M.H. van Ijzendoorn and S. van Vliet-Visser, "The relationship between quality of attachment in infancy and IQ in kindergarten," *J Genet Psychol* (Netherlands) 149, no. 1 (Mar 1988): 23–8.
5. A.G. Bus and M.H. van Ijzendoorn, "Attachment and early reading: a longitudinal study," *J Genet Psychol* (Netherlands) 149, no. 2 (Jun 1988): 199–210.
6. E.S. Harris et al., "Quality of mother–infant attachment and pediatric health care use," *Pediatrics* 84, no. 2 (Aug 1989): 248–54.
7. D.C. van den Boom, "The influence of temperament and mothering on attachment and exploration: an experimental manipulation of sensitive responsiveness among lower-class mothers with irritable infants," *Child Dev* (Netherlands) 65, no. 5 (Oct 1994): 1457–77.
8. D.C. van den Boom, "Do first-year intervention effects endure? Follow-up during toddlerhood of a sample of Dutch irritable infants," *Child Dev* (Netherlands) 66, no. 6 (Dec 1995): 1798–816.
9. G. Kochanska, "Multiple pathways to conscience for children with different temperaments: from toddlerhood to age 5," *Dev Psychol* 33, no. 2 (Mar 1997): 228–40.

10. E. B. Lehman et al., "Soft object and pacifier attachments in young children: the role of security of attachment to the mother," *J Child Psychol Psychiatry* 33, no. 7 (Oct 1992): 1205–15.

11. A.W. Wolf and B. Lozoff, "Object attachment, thumb-sucking, and the passage to sleep," *J Am Acad Child Adolesc Psychiatry* 28, no. 2 (Mar 1989): 287–92.

12. K.D. Mickelson et al., "Adult attachment in a nationally representative sample," *J Pers Soc Psychol* 73, no. 5 (Nov 1997): 1092–106.

13. E.A. Carlson, "A prospective longitudinal study of attachment disorganization/disorientation," *Child Dev* 69, no. 4 (Aug 1998): 1107–28.

14. M. Mikulincer and I. Erev, "Attachment style and the structure of romantic love," *Br J Soc Psychol* (Israel) 30, part 4 (Dec 1991): 273–91.

15. T.L. Morrison et al., "Attachment and the representation of intimate relationships in adulthood," *J Psychol* 131, no. 1 (Jan 1997): 57–71.

16. E. Moss et al., "Correlates of attachment at school age: maternal reported stress, mother–child interaction, and behavior problems," *Child Dev* 69, no. 5 (Oct 1998): 1390–405.

17. S.L. Warren et al., "Child and adolescent anxiety disorders and early attachment," *J Am Acad Child Adolesc Psychiatry* 36, no. 5 (May 1997): 637–44.

18. J.P. Allen et al., "Attachment and adolescent psychosocial functioning," *Child Dev* 69, no. 5 (Oct 1998): 1406–19.

19. K.A. Brennan and P.R. Shaver, "Attachment styles and personality disorders: their connections to each other and to parental divorce, parental death, and perceptions of parental care-giving," *J Pers* 66, no. 5 (Oct 1998): 835–78.

20. B.A. van der Kolk and R.E. Fisler, "Childhood abuse and neglect and loss of self-regulation," *Bull Menninger Clin* 58, no. 2 (Spring 1994): 145–68.

21. D.S. Rosenstein and H.A. Horowitz, "Adolescent attachment and psychopathology," *J Consult Clin Psychol* 64, no. 2 (Apr 1996): 244–53.

22. J.P. Allen et al., "Attachment theory as a framework for understanding sequelae of severe adolescent psychopathology: an 11-year follow-up study," *J Consult Clin Psychol* 64, no. 2 (Apr 1996): 254–64.

23. K.D. Mickelson et al., "Adult attachment in a nationally representative sample," *J Pers Soc Psychol* 73, no. 5 (Nov 1997): 1092–106.

24. T. Sato et al., "Dysfunctional parenting as a risk factor to lifetime depression in a sample of employed Japanese adults: evidence for the 'affectionless control' hypothesis," *Psychol Med* (Japan) 28, no. 3 (May 1998): 737–42.

25. C. Duggan et al., "Quality of parenting and vulnerability to depression: results from a family study," 28, no. 1 (Jan 1998): 185–91.

26. J.I. Escobar, "Immigration and mental health: why are immigrants better off?" *Arch Gen Psychiatry* 55, no. 9 (Sep 1998): 781–2.

27. W.A. Vega et al., "Lifetime prevalence of DSM-III-R psychiatric disorders among urban and rural Mexican Americans in California," *Arch Gen Psychiatry* 55, no. 9 (Sep 1998): 771–8.

28. National Research Council and the Institute of Medicine, "From generation to generation: The health and well-being of children in immigrant families," *National Research Council and the Institute of Medicine Report* (Washington, D.C.: National Academy Press, 1998).

29. B. Bower, "Immigrants go from health to worse," *Science News* 154, no. 12 (Sep 19, 1998): 180.

30. D.A. Cohn, "Child–mother attachment of six-year-olds and social competence at school," *Child Dev* 61, no. 1 (Feb 1990): 152–62.

31. B. Renken et al., "Early childhood antecedents of aggression and passive withdrawal in early elementary school," *J Pers* 57, no. 2 (Jun 1989): 257–81.

32. F.I. De Zulueta, "Human violence: a treatable epidemic," *Med Confl Surviv* (London) 14, no. 1 (Jan–Mar 1998): 46–55.

33. J.N. Constantino, "Early relationships and the development of aggression in children," *Harv Rev Psychiatry* 2, no. 5 (Jan–Feb 1995): 259–73.

34. J.D. Coie et al., "Predicting early adolescent disorder from childhood aggression and peer rejection," *J Consult Clin Psychol* 60, no. 5 (Oct 1992): 783–92.

35. J.A. Graber et al., "The antecedents of menarcheal age: heredity, family environment, and stressful life events," *Child Dev* 66, no. 2 (Apr 1995): 346–59.

36. M. Wierson et al., "Toward a new understanding of early menarche: the role of environmental stress in pubertal timing," *Adolescence* 28, no. 112 (Winter 1993): 913–24.

37. T.E. Moffitt et al., "Childhood experience and the onset of menarche: a test of a sociobiological model," *Child Dev* 63, no. 1 (Feb 1992): 47–58.

38. B.A. Stroll, "Western diet, early puberty, and breast cancer risk," *Breast Cancer Res Treat* (England) 49, no. 3 (Jun 1998): 187–93.

39. J.S. Suh et al., "Menstrual and reproductive factors related to the risk of breast cancer in Korea. Ovarian hormone effect on breast cancer," *J Korean Med Sci* (Korea) 11, no. 6 (Dec 1996): 501–8.

40. J. Belsky et al., "Childhood experience, interpersonal development, and reproductive strategy: an evolutionary theory of socialization," *Child Dev* 62, no. 4 (Aug 1991): 647–70.

41. Dr. Ken Magid and Carole A. McKelvey, *High Risk: Children without a Conscience* (New York: Bantam Books, 1987), 61–3.

42. Lawrence Wright, *Twins and What They Tell Us About Who We Are* (New York: John Wiley & Sons, Inc., 1997).

43. V. Jockin et al., "Personality and divorce: a genetic analysis," *J Pers Soc Psychol* 71, no. 2 (Aug 1996): 288–99.

44. Dr. Ken Magid and Carole A. McKelvey, *High Risk: Children without a Conscience* (New York: Bantam Books, 1987).

45. J.L. Phelps, J. Belsky, and K. Crnic, "Earned security, daily stress, and parenting: a comparison of five alternative models," *Dev Psychopathol* 10, no. 1 (Winter 1998): 21–38.

46. M. Main, "Introduction to the special section on attachment and psychopathology: 2. Overview of the field of attachment," *J Consult Clin Psychol* 64, no. 2 (Apr 1996): 237–43.

47. K.D. Mickelson et al., "Adult attachment in a nationally representative sample," *J Pers Soc Psychol* 73, no. 5 (Nov 1997): 1092–106.

Chapter 3: Bonding: The Inside Story

1. C.S. Carter, "Neuroendocrine perspectives on social attachment and love," *Psychoneuroendocrinology* 23, no. 8 (Nov 1998): 779–818.

2. S.S. Knox and K. Uvnas-Moberg, "Social isolation and cardiovascular disease: an atherosclerotic pathway?" *Psychoneuroendocrinology* 23, no. 8 (Nov 1998): 877–90.

3. N. Frasure-Smith et al., "Gender, depression, and one-year prognosis after myocardial infarction," *Psychosom Med* (Canada) 61, no. 1 (Jan–Feb 1999): 26-37.

4. T.R. Insel, "Oxytocin—a neuropeptide for affiliation: evidence from behavioral, receptor autoradiographic, and comparative studies," *Psychoneuroendocrinology* 17, no. 1 (1992): 3–35.

5. E. Nissen et al., "Elevation of oxytocin levels early post partum in women," *Acta Obstet Gynecol Scand* (Sweden) 74, no. 7 (Aug 1995): 530–3.

6. K.M. Kendrick et al., "Changes in the sensory processing of olfactory signals induced by birth in sheep," *Science* (England) 256, no. 5058 (May 1992): 833–6.

7. K. de Geest et al., "Plasma oxytocin in human pregnancy and parturition," *J Perinat Med* 13, no. 1 (1985): 3–13.

8. E. Nissen et al., "Different patterns of oxytocin, prolactin but not cortisol release during breastfeeding in women delivered by caesarean section or by the vaginal route," *Early Hum Dev* (Sweden) 45, nos. 1–2 (Jul 1996): 103–18.

9. E. Nissen et al., "Oxytocin, prolactin, milk production and their relationship with personality traits in women after vaginal delivery or Cesarean section," *J Psychosom Obstet Gynaecol* (Sweden) 19, no. 1 (Mar 1998): 49–58.

10. T.R. Insel and T.J. Hulihan, "A gender-specific mechanism for pair bonding: oxytocin and partner preference formation in monogamous voles," *Behav Neurosci* 109, no. 4 (Aug 1995): 782–9.

11. P. Popik and J. Vetulani, "Opposite action of oxytocin and its peptide antagonists on social memory in rats," *Neuropeptides* (Poland) 18, no. 1 (Jan 1991): 23–7.

12. D.A. Battin et al., "Effect of suckling on serum prolactin, luteinizing hormone, follicle-stimulating hormone, and estradiol during prolonged lactation," *Obstet Gynecol* 65, no. 6 (Jun 1985): 785–8.

13. K. Uvnas-Moberg et al., "Oxytocin and prolactin levels in breast-feeding women. Correlation with milk yield and duration of breast-feeding," *Acta Obstet Gynecol Scand* (Sweden) 69, no. 4 (1990): 301–6.

14. H. Varendi et al., "Attractiveness of amniotic fluid odor: evidence of prenatal olfactory learning?" *Acta Paediatr* (Estonia) 85, no. 10 (Oct 1996): 1233–7.

15. J.C. Molina and M.G. Chotro, "Association between chemosensory stimuli and cesarean delivery in rat fetuses: neonatal presentation of similar stimuli increases motor activity," *Behav Neural Biol* (Argentina) 55, no. 1 (Jan 1991): 42–60.

16. H. Varendi et al., "Soothing effect of amniotic fluid smell in newborn infants," *Early Hum Dev* (Estonia) 51, no. 1 (Apr 1998): 47–55.

17. R.H. Porter et al., "An assessment of the salient olfactory environment of formula-fed infants," *Physiol Behav* 50, no. 5 (Nov 1991): 907–11.

18. S. Takeda et al., "Concentrations and origin of oxytocin in breast milk," *Endocrinol Jpn* (Japan) 33, no. 6 (Dec 1986): 821–6.

19. A. Powell, "Children need touching and attention, Harvard researchers say," *Harvard University Gazette* (Apr 9, 1998).

20. D.J. Gubernick et al., "Oxytocin changes in males over the reproductive cycle in the monogamous, biparental California mouse, *Peromyscus californicus*," *Horm Behav* 29, no. 1 (Mar 1995): 59–73.

21. B. Schaal and L. Marlier, "Maternal and paternal perception of individual odor signatures in human amniotic fluid—potential role in early bonding?" *Biol Neonate* (France) 74, no. 4 (Oct 1998): 266–73.

22. D.M. Witt et al., "Enhanced social interactions in rats following chronic, centrally infused oxytocin," *Pharmacol Biochem Behav* 43, no. 3 (Nov 1992): 855–61.

23. Theresa L. Crenshaw, MD, *The Alchemy of Love and Lust* (New York, New York: Pocket Books, 1997), 117.

24. M. Bamshad et al., "Cohabitation alters vasopressin innervation and paternal behavior in prairie voles (*Microtus ochrogaster*)," *Physiol Behav* 56, no. 4 (Oct 1994): 751–8.

25. Z. Wang et al., "Role of septal vasopressin innervation in paternal behavior in prairie voles (*Microtus ochrogaster*)," *Proc Natl Acad Sci USA* 91, no. 1 (Jan 1994): 400–4.

26. T.R. Insel and T.J. Hulihan, "A gender-specific mechanism for pair bonding: oxytocin and partner preference formation in monogamous voles," *Behav Neurosci* 109, no. 4 (Aug 1995): 782–9.

27. Theresa L. Crenshaw, MD, *The Alchemy of Love and Lust* (New York, New York: Pocket Books, 1997), 106.

28. C.S. Carter, "Neuroendocrine perspectives on social attachment and love," *Psychoneuroendocrinology* 23, no. 8 (Nov 1998): 779–818.

29. M. Engelmann et al., "Behavioral consequences of intracerebral vasopressin and oxytocin: focus on learning and memory," *Neurosci Biobehav Rev* (Germany) 20, no. 3 (Autumn 1996): 341–58.

30. E.E. Nelson and J. Panksepp, "Brain substrates of infant–mother attachment: contributions of opioids, oxytocin, and norepinephrine," *Neurosci Biobehav Rev* 22, no. 3 (1998): 437–452.

31. R.S. Bridges, "The role of lactogenic hormones in maternal behavior in female rats," *Acta Paediatr Suppl* 397 (Jun 1994): 33–9.

32. R.E. Brown et al., "Hormonal responses of male gerbils to stimuli from their mate and pups," *Horm Behav* (Canada) 29, no. 4 (Dec 1995): 474–91.

33. A.S. Fleming et al., "Testosterone and prolactin are associated with emotional responses to infant cries in new fathers," *Horm Behav* (Canada) 42, no. 4 (Dec 2002): 399–413.

34. W.L. Castro and K.S. Matt, "The importance of social condition in the hormonal and behavioral responses to an acute social stressor in the male Siberian dwarf hamster (*Phodopus sungorus*)," *Horm Behav* 32, no. 3 (Dec 1997): 209–16.

35. R.J. Windle et al., "Endocrine and behavioral responses to noise stress: comparison of virgin and lactating female rats during non-disrupted maternal activity," *J Neuroendocrinol* 9, no. 6 (Jun 1997): 407–14.

36. T.E. Ziegler et al., "Hormonal responses to parental and nonparental conditions in male cotton-top tamarins, *Saguinus oedipus*, a New World primate," *Horm Behav* 30, no. 3 (Sep 1996): 287–97.

37. L.G. Sobrinho, "Emotional aspects of hyperprolactinemia," *Psychother Psychosom* (Portugal) 67, no. 3 (1998): 133–9.

38. B. Lozoff et al., "Serum prolactin levels and behavior in infants," *Biol Psychiatry* 37, no. 1 (Jan 1995): 4–12.

39. W.G. Roper, "The etiology of male homosexuality," *Med Hypotheses* 46, no. 2 (Feb 1996): 85–8.

40. E.M. Alder et al., "Hormones, mood and sexuality in lactating women," *Br J Psychiatry* 148 (Jan 1986): 74–9.

41. L.G. Sobrinho, "The psychogenic effects of prolactin," *Acta Endocrinol (Copenh)* (Portugal) 129, suppl. 1 (Jul 1993): 38–40.

42. E.E. Nelson and J. Panksepp, "Brain Substrates of Infant-Mother Attachment: Contributions of Opioids, Oxytocin, and Norepinephrine," *Neurosci Biobehav Rev* 22, no. 3 (May 1, 1998): 437–52.

43. E.E. Nelson and J. Panksepp, "Brain substrates of infant–mother attachment: contributions of opioids, oxytocin, and norepinephrine," *Neurosci Biobehav Rev* 22, no. 3 (1998): 437–452.

44. S.R. Robinson et al., "Experience with milk and an artificial nipple promotes conditioned opioid activity in the rat fetus," *Dev Psychobiol* 26, no. 7 (Nov 1993): 375–81.

45. E.E. Nelson and J. Panksepp, "Brain substrates of infant–mother attachment: contributions of opioids, oxytocin, and norepinephrine," *Neurosci Biobehav Rev* 22, no. 3 (1998): 441.

46. W.P. Smotherman and S.R. Robinson, "Prenatal experience with milk: fetal behavior and endogenous opioid systems," *Neurosci Biobehav Rev* 16, no. 3 (Fall 1992): 351–64.

47. L.G. Sobrinho, "The psychogenic effects of prolactin," *Acta Endocrinol (Copenh)* (Portugal) 129, suppl. 1 (Jul 1993): 38–40.

48. G.L. Kovacs et al., "Oxytocin and addiction: a review," *Psychoneuroendocrinology* (Hungary) 23, no. 8 (Nov 1998): 945–62.

49. Theresa L. Crenshaw, MD, *The Alchemy of Love and Lust* (New York, New York: Pocket Books, 1997), 134–5.

50. G.W. Kraemer et al., "A longitudinal study of the effect of different social rearing conditions on cerebrospinal fluid norepinephrine and biogenic amine metabolites in rhesus monkeys," *Neuropsychopharmacology* 2, no. 3 (Sep 1989): 175–89.

51. J. Winberg and R.H. Porter, "Olfaction and human neonatal behavior: clinical implications," *Acta Paediatr* (Sweden) 87, no. 1 (Jan 1998): 6–10.

52. K. Stern and M.K. McClintock, "Regulation of ovulation by human pheromones," *Nature* 392, no. 6672 (Mar 1998): 177–9.

53. J. Winberg and R.H. Porter, "Olfaction and human neonatal behavior: clinical implications," *Acta Paediatr* (Sweden) 87, no. 1 (Jan 1998): 6–10.

54. D. Trotier et al., "[The vomeronasal organ—a rediscovered sensory organ]," *Tidsskr Nor Laegeforen* (Norway) 116, no. 1 (Jan 1996): 47–51.

55. M.K. McClintock, "On the nature of mammalian and human pheromones," *Ann N Y Acad Sci* 855 (Nov 30, 1998): 390–2.

56. L.M. Katz et al., "Inhibition of GH in maternal separation may be mediated through altered serotonergic activity at 5-HT2A and 5-HT2C receptors," *Psychoneuroendocrinology* 21, no. 2 (Feb 1996): 219–35.

57. M.S. Oitzl et al., "Continuous blockade of brain glucocorticoid receptors facilitates spatial learning and memory in rats," *Eur J Neurosci* (Netherlands) 10, no. 12 (Dec 1998): 3759–66.

58. E.M. Albers et al., "Maternal behavior predicts infant cortisol recovery from a mild everyday stressor," *J Child Psychol Psychiatry* (The Netherlands) 49, no. 1 (Jan 2008): 97–103.

59. D.B. Bugental et al., "The hormonal costs of subtle forms of infant maltreatment," *Horm Behav* 43, no. 1 (Jan 2003): 237–44.

60. M. Schieche and G. Spangler, "Individual differences in biobehavioral organization during problem-solving in toddlers: the influence of maternal behavior, infant-mother attachment, and behavioral inhibition on the attachment-exploration balance," *Dev Psychobiol* (Germany) 46, no. 4 (May 2005): 293–306.

61. D. Liu et al., "Maternal care, hippocampal glucocorticoid receptors, and hypothalamic–pituitary–adrenal responses to stress," *Science* (Canada) 277, no. 5332 (Sep 1997): 1659–62.

62. K. Lyons-Ruth, "Attachment relationships among children with aggressive behavior problems: the role of disorganized early attachment patterns," *J Consult Clin Psychol* 64, no. 1 (Feb 1996): 64–73.

63. L. Hertsgaard et al., "Adrenocortical responses to the strange situation in infants with disorganized/disoriented attachment relationships," *Child Dev* 66, no. 4 (Aug 1995): 1100–6.

64. A.B. Fries et al., "Neuroendocrine dysregulation following early social deprivation in children," *Dev Psychobiol* 50, no. 6 (Sep 2008): 588–99.

65. M. Altemus et al., "Suppression of hypothalamic–pituitary–adrenal axis responses to stress in lactating women," *J Clin Endocrinol Metab* 80, no. 10 (Oct 1995): 2965–9.

66. K. Kendall-Tacket, "A new paradigm for depression in new mothers: the central role of inflammation and how breastfeeding and anti-inflammatory treatments protect maternal mental health," *Int Breastfeed J* 2 (Mar 30, 2007): 6.

67. M. Heinrichs et al., "Effects of suckling on hypothalamic-pituitary-adrenal axis responses to psychosocial stress in postpartum lactating women," *J Clin Endocrinol Metab* (Germany) 86, no. 10 (Oct 2001): 4798–804.

68. M.L. Laudenslager et al., "Total cortisol, free cortisol, and growth hormone associated with brief social separation experiences in young macaques," *Dev Psychobiol* 28, no. 4 (May 1995): 199–211.

69. P. Rosenfeld et al., "Maternal regulation of the adrenocortical response in preweanling rats," *Physiol Behav* 50, no. 4 (Oct 1991): 661–71.

70. H.J. van Oers et al., "Maternal deprivation effect on the infant's neural stress markers is reversed by tactile stimulation and feeding but not by suppressing corticosterone," *J Neurosci* 18, no. 23 (Dec 1, 1998): 10171–9.

71. M.A. Smith of Dupont Merck Research Labs as reported by JohnTravis of *Science News* 152 (Nov 8, 1997): 298.

72. D. Waynforth, "The influence of parent-infant cosleeping, nursing, and childcare on cortisol and SIgA immunity in a sample of British children," *Dev Psychobiol* (United Kingdom) 49, no. 6 (Sep 2007): 640–8.

73. E.R. de Kloet et al., "Brain-corticosteroid hormone dialogue: slow and persistent," *Cell Mol Neurobiol* (Netherlands) 16, no. 3 (Jun 1996): 345–56.

74. H. Anisman et al., "Do early-life events permanently alter behavioral and hormonal responses to stressors?" *Int J Dev Neurosci* 16, no. 3–4 (Jun–Jul 1998): 149–64.

75. M. Nachmias et al., "Behavioral inhibition and stress reactivity: the moderating role of attachment security," *Child Dev* 67, no. 2 (Apr 1996): 508–22.

76. M.R. Gunnar et al., "Stress reactivity and attachment security," *Dev Psychobiol* 29, no. 3 (Apr 1996): 191–204.

77. G. Spangler and K.E. Grossmann, "Biobehavioral organization in securely and insecurely attached infants," *Child Dev* 64, no. 5 (Oct 1993): 1439–50.

78. M.R. Gunnar, "Quality of care and buffering of neuroendocrine stress reactions: potential effects on the developing human brain," *Prev Med* 27, no. 2 (Mar–Apr 1998): 208–11.

79. C. Caldji et al., "Maternal care during infancy regulates the development of neural systems mediating the expression of fearfulness in the rat," *Proc Natl Acad Sci* (Canada) 95, no. 9 (Apr 1998): 5335–40.

80. M.J. Meaney et al., "Early environmental regulation of forebrain glucocorticoid receptor gene expression: implications for adrenocortical responses to stress," *Dev Neurosci* (Canada) no. 1-2 (1996): 49–72.

81. R. Rosmond and P. Bjorntorp, "The hypothalamic-pituitary-adrenal axis activity as a predictor of cardiovascular disease, type 2 diabetes and stroke," *J Intern Med* (Sweden) 247, no. 2 (Feb 2000): 188–97.

82. L.J. Luecken, "Childhood attachment and loss experiences affect adult cardiovascular and cortisol function," *Psychosom Med* 60, no. 6 (Nov–Dec 1998): 765–72.

83. D.M. Vazquez et al., "Regulation of glucocorticoid and mineralcorticoid receptor mRNAs in the hippocampus of the maternal deprived infant rat," *Brain Res* 731, no. 1–2 (Aug 1996): 79–90.

84. J. Raber, "Detrimental effects of chronic hypothalamic–pituitary–adrenal axis activation. From obesity to memory deficits," *Mol Neurobiol* 18, no. 1 (Aug 1998): 1–22.

85. H.J. Krugers et al., "Exposure to chronic psychosocial stress and corticosterone in the rat: effects on spatial discrimination learning and hippocampal protein kinase Cgamma immunoreactivity," *Hippocampus* (Netherlands) 7, no. 4 (1997): 427–36.

86. M. Carlson and F. Earls, "Psychological and neuroendocrinological sequelae of early social deprivation in institutionalized children in Romania," *Ann N Y Acad Sci* 807 (Jan 15, 1997): 419–28.

87. L.D. Dorn et al., "Biopsychological and cognitive differences in children with premature vs. on-time adrenarche," *Arch Pediatr Adolesc Med* 153, no. 2 (Feb 1999): 137–46.

88. M. Walter et al., "Cortisol response to interpersonal stress in young adults with borderline personality disorder: a pilot study," *Eur Psychiatry* (Switzerland) 23, no. 3 (Apr 2008): 201–4.

89. D. Simeon et al., "A preliminary study of cortisol and norepinephrine reactivity to psychosocial stress in borderline personality disorder with high and low dissociation," *Psychiatry Res* 149, no. 1-3 (Jan 15, 2007): 177–84.

90. J. Raber, "Detrimental effects of chronic hypothalamic–pituitary–adrenal axis activation. From obesity to memory deficits," *Mol Neurobiol* 18, no. 1 (Aug 1998): 1–22.

91. M. Deuschle et al., "Effects of major depression, aging and gender upon calculated diurnal free plasma cortisol concentrations: a reevaluation study," *Stress* (Germany) 2, no. 4 (Jan 1999): 281–87.

92. J. Jokinen and P. Nordstrom, "HPA axis hyperactivity and attempted suicide in young adult mood disorder inpatients," *J Affect Disord* (Sweden) Epub ahead of print (Dec 1, 2008).

93. C.L. Coe and C.M. Erickson, "Stress decreases lymphocyte cytolytic activity in the young monkey even after blockade of steroid and opiate hormone receptors," *Dev Psychobiol* 30, no. 1 (Jan 1997): 1–10.

94. G.R. Lubach et al., "Effects of early rearing environment on immune responses of infant rhesus monkeys," *Brain Behav Immun* 9, no. 1 (Mar 1995): 31–46.

Chapter 4: Crying and Caring

1. B.S. McEwen, "Steroid hormones and the brain: linking 'nature' and 'nurture,'" *Neurochem Res* 13, no. 7 (Jul 1998): 663–9.

2. L. Eisenberg, "The social construction of the human brain," *Am J Psychiatry* 152, no. 11 (Nov 1995): 1563–75.

3. C. Acebo and E.B. Thoman, "Role of infant crying in the early mother–infant dialogue," *Physiol Behav* 57, no. 3 (Mar 1995): 541–7.

4. G.C. Anderson, "Risk in mother–infant separation postbirth," *Image J Nurs Sch* 21, no. 4 (Winter 1989): 196–9.

5. W.H. Frey II and M. Langseth, *Crying: The Mystery of Tears* (San Francisco: Harper, 1985).

6. M.R. Gunnar, "Reactivity of the hypothalamic-pituitary-adrenocortical system to stressors in normal infants and children," *Pediatrics* 90, no. 3, pt. 2 (Sep 1992): 491–7.

7. J.E. Brazy, "Effects of crying on cerebral blood volume and cytochrome aa3," *J Pediatr* 112, no. 3 (Mar 1998): 457–61.

8. S.M. Labott et al., "The physiological and psychological effects of the expression and inhibition of emotion," *Behav Med* 16, no. 4 (Winter 1990): 182–9.

9. J.J. Gross et al., "The psychophysiology of crying," *Psychophysiology* 31, no. 5 (Sep 1994): 460–8.

10. C.C. Lambesis et al., "Effects of surrogate mothering on physiologic stabilization in transitional newborns," *Birth Defects Orig Artic Ser* 15, no. 7 (1979): 201–3.

11. P.M. Taylor et al., "Extra early physical contact and aspects of the early mother–infant relationship," *Acta Paediatr Scand Suppl* 316 (1985): 3–14.

12. R.G. Barr et al., "Crying in !Kung San infants: a test of the cultural specificity hypotheses," *Dev Med Child Neurol* (Canada) 33, no. 7 (Jul 1991): 601–10.

13. K. Lee, "The crying pattern of Korean infants and related factors," *Dev Med Child Neurol* (Korea) 36, no. 7 (Jul 1994): 601–7.

14. Sharon Heller, PhD, *The Vital Touch* (New York: Henry Holt and Co., 1997).

15. S.K. Dihigo, "New strategies for the treatment of colic: modifying the parent/infant interaction," *J Pediatr Health Care* 12, no. 5 (Sep–Oct 1998): 256–62.

16. R.G. Barr and M.F. Elias, "Nursing interval and maternal responsivity: effect on early infant crying," *Pediatrics* (Canada) 81, no. 4 (Apr 1988): 529–36.

17. E.M. Baildam et al., "Duration and pattern of crying in the first year of life," *Dev Med Child Neurol* 37, no. 4 (Apr 1995): 345–53.

18. B. Lozoff and G. Brittenham, "Infant care: cache or carry," *J Pediatr* 95, no. 3 (Sep 1979): 478–83.

19. J.R. Bemporad, "Cultural and historical aspects of eating disorders," *Theor Med* 18, no. 4 (Dec 1997): 401–20.

20. J.E. Pate et al., "Cross-cultural patterns in eating disorders: a review," *J Am Acad Child Adolesc Psychiatry* 31, no. 5 (Sep 1992): 802–9.

21. S.W. Hurt et al., "A comparison of psychopathology in eating disorder patients from France and the United States," *Int J Eat Disord* 22, no. 2 (Sep 1997): 153–8.

22. D. Neumark-Sztainer et al., "Lessons learned about adolescent nutrition from the Minnesota Adolescent Health Survey," *J Am Diet Assoc* 98, no. 12 (Dec 1998): 1449–56.

23. P.S. Zeskind and R.G. Barr, "Acoustic characteristics of naturally occurring cries of infants with "colic," *Child Dev* 68, no. 3 (Jun 1997): 394–403.

24. B.F. Fuller et al., "Acoustic analysis of cries from 'normal' and 'irritable' infants," *West J Nurs Res* 16, no. 3 (Jun 1994): 243–53.

25. V.A. Howard and F.W. Thurber, "The interpretation of infant pain: physiological and behavioral indicators used by NICU nurses," *J Pediatr Nurs* 13, no. 3 (Jun 1998): 164–74.

26. Aletha J. Solter, PhD, *Tears and Tantrums* (Goleta, California: Shining Star Press, 1998.)

27. J.J. Gross and R.W. Levenson, "Hiding feelings: the acute effects of inhibiting negative and positive emotion," *J Abnorm Psychol* 106, no. 1 (Feb 1997): 95–103.

28. Benjamin Spock, MD, and Michael B. Rothenberg, MD, *Dr. Spock's Baby and Child Care*, (New York: Pocket Books, 1998), 237, 257–8.

29. F.E. Gardner, "The quality of joint activity between mothers and their children with behaviour problems," *J Child Psychol Psychiatry* 35, no. 5 (Jul 1994): 935–48.

30. S.M. Labott et al., "The physiological and psychological effects of the expression and inhibition of emotion," *Behav Med* 16, no. 4 (Winter 1990): 182–9.

31. M.S. Zeedyk, "What's life in a baby buggy like?: The impact of buggy orientation on parent-infant interaction and infant stress," University of Dundee, School of Psychology (Nov 21, 2008).

32. J.S. Rosenblatt, "Psychobiology of maternal behavior: contribution to the clinical understanding of maternal behavior among humans," *Acta Paediatr Suppl* 397 (Jun 1994): 3–8.

33. Ashley Montagu, *Touching, The Human Significance of the Skin*, third edition (New York: Perennial Library, 1986).

34. C.M. Kuhn and S.M. Schanberg, "Responses to maternal separation: mechanisms and mediators," *Int J Dev Neurosci* 16, no. 3–4 (Jun–Jul 1998): 261–70.

35. T.M. Field et al., "Tactile/kinesthetic stimulation effects on preterm neonates," *Pediatrics* 77, no. 5 (May 1986): 654–8.

36. H. Im and E. Kim, "Effect of Yakson and Gentle Human Touch versus usual care on urine stress hormones and behaviors in preterm infants: A quasi-experimental study," *Int J Nurs Stud* 46, no. 4 (Apr 2009): 450–8.

37. D. Acolet et al., "Changes in plasma cortisol and catecholamine concentrations in response to massage in preterm infants," *Arch Dis Child* 68, no. 1 (Jan 1993): 29–31.

38. G. Ironson et al., "Massage therapy is associated with enhancement of the immune system's cytotoxic capacity," *Int J Neurosci* 84, no. 1–4 (Feb 1996): 205–17.

39. H.J. Polan and M.J. Ward, "Role of mother's touch in failure to thrive: a preliminary investigation," *J Am Acad Child Adolesc Psychiatry* 33, no. 8 (Oct 1994): 1098–105.

40. S. Lowinger et al., "Maternal social and physical contact: links to early infant attachment behaviors," *J Genet Psychol* 156, no. 4 (Dec 1995): 461–76.

41. H. Lugt-Tappeser and B. Wiese, "[Prospective study of maternal behavior in the neonatal period: a pilot study]," *Prax Kinderpsychol Kinderpsychiatr* (Germany) 43, no. 9 (Nov 1994): 322–30.

42. D. Liu et al., "Maternal care, hippocampal glucocorticoid receptors, and hypothalamic–pituitary–adrenal responses to stress," *Science* 277, no. 5332 (Sep 1997): 1659–62.

43. G.E. Carvell and D.J. Simons, "Abnormal tactile experience early in life disrupts active touch," *J Neurosci* 16, no. 8 (Apr 15, 1996): 2750–7.

44. Sharon Heller, PhD, *The Vital Touch* (New York: Henry Holt and Co., 1997), 83.

45. E. Anisfeld et al., "Does infant carrying promote attachment? An experimental study of the effects of increased physical contact on the development of attachment," *Child Dev* 61, no. 5 (Oct 1990): 1617–27.

46. U.A. Hunziker and R.G. Barr, "Increased carrying reduces infant crying: a randomized controlled trial," *Pediatrics* 77, no. 5 (May 1986): 641–8.

47. R.G. Barr et al., "Carrying as colic 'therapy': a randomized controlled trial," *Pediatrics* 87, no. 5 (May 1991): 623–30.

48. E.M. McCall et al., "Interventions to prevent hypothermia at birth in preterm and/or low birthweight infants," *Cochrane Database Syst Rev* (Ireland) 1 (Jan 23, 2008): CD004210.

49. K. Christensson, "Fathers can effectively achieve heat conservation in healthy newborn infants," *Acta Paediatr* (Sweden) 85, no. 11 (Nov 1996): 1354–60.

50. J Bauer et al., "Metabolic rate and energy balance in very low birth weight infants during kangaroo holding by their mothers and fathers," *J Pediatr* (Germany) 129 no. 4 (Oct 1996): 608–11.

51. K. Christensson et al., "Separation distress call in the human neonate in the absence of maternal body contact," *Acta Paediatr* (Sweden) 84, no 5 (May 1995): 468–73.

52. C.C. Lambesis et al., "Effects of surrogate mothering on physiologic stabilization in transitional newborns,"

Birth Defects Orig Artic Ser 15, no. 7 (1979): 201–23.

53. L. Vaivre-Douret et al., "[Kangaroo method and care]," *Arch Pediatr* (France) 3, no. 12 (Dec 1996): 1262–9.

54. R.A. Kambarami et al., "Kangaroo care versus incubator care in the management of well preterm infants—a pilot study," *Ann Trop Paediatr* 18, no. 2 (Jun 1998): 81–6.

55. S.G. Ferber and I.R. Makhoul, "The effect of skin-to-skin contact (kangaroo care) shortly after birth on the neurobehavioral responses of the term newborn: a randomized, controlled trial," *Pediatrics* (Israel) 113, no. 4 (Apr 2004): 858–65.

56. E. Mörelius et al., "Salivary cortisol and mood and pain profiles during skin-to-skin care for an unselected group of mothers and infants in neonatal intensive care," *Pediatrics* (Sweden) 116, no. 5 (Nov 2005): 1105–13.

57. P.R. Messmer et al., "Effect of kangaroo care on sleep time for neonates," *Pediatr Nurs* 23, no. 4 (Jul–Aug 1997): 408–14.

58. S.M. Ludington-Hoe et al., "Birth-related fatigue in 34–36-week preterm neonates: rapid recovery with very early kangaroo (skin-to-skin) care," *J Obstet Gynecol Neonatal Nurs* 28, no. 1 (Jan–Feb 1999): 94–103.

59. C.J. Tornhage et al., "Plasma somatostatin and cholecystokinin levels in preterm infants during kangaroo care with and without nasogastric tube-feeding," *J Pediatr Endocrinol Metab* 11, no. 5 (Sep–Oct 1998): 645–51.

60. K. Gloppestad, "Parents' skin to skin holding of small premature infants: differences between fathers and mothers," *Vard Nord Utveckl Forsk* (Norway) 16, no. 1 (Spring 1996): 22–7.

61. L. Gray et al., "Skin-to-Skin Contact is Analgesic in Healthy Newborns," *Pediatrics* 105, no. 1 (Jan 2000): e14.

62. C.C. Johnston et al., "Enhanced kangaroo mother care for heel lance in preterm neonates: a crossover trial," *J Perinatol* (Canada) 29, no. 1 (2009): 51–56.

63. R.R. Kostandy et al., "Kangaroo Care (skin contact) reduces crying response to pain in preterm neonates: pilot results," *Pain Manag Nurs* 9, no. 2 (Jun 2008): 55–65.

64. N.M. Hurst et al., "Skin-to-skin holding in the neonatal intensive care unit influences maternal milk volume," *J Perinatol* 17, no. 3 (May–Jun 1997): 213–7.

65. P. De Chateau and B. Wiberg, "Long-term effect on mother–infant behavior of extra contact during the first hour post partum. I. First observations at 36 hours," *Acta Paediatr Scand* 66, no. 2 (Mar 1977): 137–43.

66. G. Gale et al., "Skin-to-skin (kangaroo) holding of the intubated premature infant," *Neonatal Netw* 12, no. 6 (Sep 1993): 49–57.

67. A. Tan et al., "The characterization and outcome of stereotypical movements in nonautistic children," *Mov Disord* 12, no. 1 (Jan 1997): 47–52.

68. W.E. MacLean Jr. and A.A. Baumeister, "Effects of vestibular stimulation on motor development and stereotyped behavior of developmentally delayed children," *J Abnorm Child Psychol* 10, no. 2 (Jun 1982): 229–45.

69. T. Farrimond, "Sudden infant death syndrome and possible relation to vestibular function," *Percept Mot Skills* (New Zealand) 71, no. 2 (Oct 1990): 419–23.

70. J. Groswasser et al., "Reduction in obstructive breathing events during body rocking: a controlled polygraphic study in preterm and full-term infants," *Pediatrics* (Belgium) 96, no. 1 pt. 1 (Jul 1995): 64–8.

71. M.P. Sammon and R.A. Darnall, "Entrainment of respiration to rocking in premature infants: coherence analysis," *J Appl Physiol* 77, no. 3 (Sep 1994): 1548–54.

72. G. Malcuit et al., "Cardiac and behavioral responses to rocking stimulations in one- and three-month-old infants," *Percept Mot Skill* (Canada) 66, no. 1 (Feb 1988): 207–17.

73. T. Farrimond, "Sudden infant death syndrome and possible relation to vestibular function," *Percept Mot Skills* (New Zealand) 71, no. 2 (Oct 1990): 419–23.

74. D.L Clark et al., "Effects of rocking on neuromuscular development in the premature," *Biol Neonate* 56, no. 6 (1989): 306–14.

75. L. Cordero et al., "Effects of vestibular stimulation on sleep states in premature infants," *Am J Perinatol* 3, no. 4 (Oct 1986): 319–24.

76. K.E. Barnard and H.L. Bee, "The impact of temporally patterned stimulation on the development of preterm infants," *Child Dev* 54, no. 5 (Oct 1983): 1156–67.

77. A.F. Korner et al., "Effects of vestibular–proprioceptive stimulation on the neurobehavioral development of preterm infants: a pilot study," *Neuropediatrics* 14, no. 3 (Aug 1983): 170–5.

78. K.A. Waters et al., "Neuronal apoptosis in sudden infant death syndrome," *Pediatr* (Canada) 45, no. 2 (Feb 1999): 166–72.

79. J. Lehtonen et al., "The effect of nursing on the brain activity of the newborn," *J Pediatr* (Finland) 132, no. 4 (Apr 1998): 646–51.

80. R.G. Campos, "Rocking and pacifiers: two comforting interventions for heelstick pain," *Res Nurs Health* 17, no. 5 (Oct 1994): 321–31.

81. N.F. Butte et al., "Heart rates of breast-fed and formula-fed infants," *J Pediatr Gastroenterol Nutr* 13, no. 4 (Nov 1991): 391–6.

82. N.F. Butte et al., "Sleep organization and energy expenditure of breast-fed and formula-fed infants," *Pediatr Res* 32, no. 5 (Nov 1992): 514–9.

83. J.A. Bier et al., "Comparison of skin-to-skin contact with standard contact in low-birth-weight infants who are breast-fed," *Arch Pediatr Adolesc Med* 150, No. 12 (Dec 1996): 1265–9.

84. D.M. Treloar, "The effect of nonnutritive sucking on oxygenation in healthy, crying full-term infants," *Appl Nurs Res* 7, no. 2 (May 1994): 52–8.

85. G.C. McCain, "Facilitating inactive awake states in preterm infants: a study of three interventions," *Nurs Res* 41, no. 3 (May–Jun 1992): 157–60.

86. E.A. Mitchell et al., "Dummies and the sudden infant death syndrome," *Arch Dis Child* (New Zealand) 68, no. 4 (Apr 1993): 501–4.

87. M. Arnestad et al., "Is the use of dummy or carry-cot of importance for sudden infant death?" *Eur J Pediatr* 156, no. 12 (Dec 1997): 968–70.

88. Laura Flynn McCarthy, "Snooze Alarm: How to Coax a Wailing Baby into a Sound Sleep," *Parenting* May 1994, http://www.pathfinder.com/ParentTime/Growing/snooze.html.

89. B. Ogaard et al., "The effect of sucking habits, cohort, sex, intercanine arch widths, and breast or bottle feeding on posterior crossbite in Norwegian and Swedish 3-year-old children," *Am J Orthod Dentofacial Orthop* (Norway) 106, no. 2 (Aug 1994): 161–6.

90. H. Turgeon-O'Brien et al., "Nutritive and nonnutritive sucking habits: a review," *ASDC J Dent Child* 63, no. 5 (Sep–Oct 1996): 321–7.

91. P. Ollila et al., "Prolonged pacifier-sucking and use of a nursing bottle at night: possible risk factors for dental caries in children," *Acta Odontol Scand* (Finland) 56, no. 4 (Aug 1998): 233–7.

92. L. Righard and M.O. Alade, "Breastfeeding and the use of pacifiers," *Birth* (Sweden) 24, no. 2 (Jun 1997): 116–20.

93. L. Righard, "Are breastfeeding problems related to incorrect breastfeeding technique and the use of pacifiers and bottles?" *Birth* (Sweden) 25, no. 1 (Mar 1998): 40–4.

94. E. Larsson, "Orthodontic aspects on feeding of young children. 1. A comparison between Swedish and Norwegian-Sami children," *Swed Dent J* (Sweden) 22, no. 3 (1998): 117–21.

95. K. A. Freudigman and E.B. Thoman, "Infants' earliest sleep/wake organization differs as a function of delivery mode," *Dev Psychobiol* 32, no. 4 (May 1998): 293–303.

96. K.A. Waters et al., "Neuronal apoptosis in sudden infant death syndrome," *Pediatr* (Canada) 45, no. 2 (Feb 1999): 166–72.

97. R.K. Scragg et al., "Infant room-sharing and prone sleep position in sudden infant death syndrome. New Zealand Cot Death Study Group," *Lancet* (New Zealand) 347, no. 8993 (Jan 6, 1996): 7–12.

98. P. Blair et al., "Babies Sleeping with Parents: Case-Control Study of Factors Influencing the Risk of Sudden Infant Death Syndrome. CESDI SUDI Research Group," *British Medical Journal* (England) 319, no. 7223 (Dec 4, 1999): 1457-61.

99. R. Scragg et al., "Public health policy on bed sharing and smoking in the sudden infant death syndrome," *N Z Med J* (New Zealand) 108, no. 1001 (Jun 14, 1995): 218–22.

100. P. Blair et al., "Sudden Infant Death Syndrome and Sleeping Position in Pre-Term and Low Birthweight Infants: An Opportunity for Targeted Intervention," *Archives of Disease in Childhood* (England) 91, no. 2 (Feb 2006): 101–6.

101. R.E. Gilbert et al., "Bottle feeding and the sudden infant death syndrome," *BMJ* (England) 310, no. 6972 (Jan 14, 1995): 88–90.

102. H.S. Klonoff-Cohen et al., "The effect of passive smoking and tobacco exposure through breast milk on sudden infant death syndrome," *JAMA* 273, no. 10 (Mar 1995): 795–8.

103. J. Schellscheidt et al., "Epidemiological features of sudden infant death after a German intervention campaign in 1992," *Eur J Pediatr* (Germany) 156, no. 8 (Aug 1997): 655–60.

104. J.J. McKenna et al., "Bedsharing promotes breastfeeding," *Pediatrics* 100, no. 2, part 1 (Aug 1997): 214–9.

105. C. McGarvey et al., "An Eight-Year Study of Risk Factors for SIDS: Bed-Sharing vs. Non Bed-Sharing," *Archives of Disease in Childhood* (Ireland) 91, no. 4 (Apr 2006): 318–23.

106. D. Weinert et al., "The development of circadian rhythmicity in neonates," *Early Hum Dev* (Germany) 36, no. 2 (Feb 1994): 117–26.

107. P.J. Schwartz, et al., "Prolongation of the QT interval and the sudden infant death syndrome," *N Engl J Med* 338, no. 24 (June 11, 1998): 1709–14.

108. R.M. Harper et al., "Periodicity of sleep states is altered in infants at risk for the sudden infant death syndrome," *Science* 213, no. 4511 (Aug 28, 1981): 1030–2.

109. V.L. Schechtman et al., "Sleep state organization in normal infants and victims of the sudden infant death syndrome," *Pediatrics* 89, no. 5, pt. 1 (May 1992): 865–79.

110. J.B. Gould et al., "The relationship between sleep and sudden infant death," *Ann N Y Acad Sci* 533 (1988): 62–77.

111. J.J. McKenna et al., "Sleep and arousal patterns of co-sleeping human mother/infant pairs: a preliminary physiological study with implications for the study of sudden infant death syndrome (SIDS)," *Am J Phys Anthropol* 83, no. 3 (Nov 1990): 331–47.

112. S. Mosko et al., "Infant arousals during mother–infant bed sharing: implications for infant sleep and sudden infant death syndrome research," *Pediatrics* 100, no. 5 (Nov 1997): 841–9.

113. S. Mosko et al., "Maternal sleep and arousals during bedsharing with infants," *Sleep* 20, no. 2 (Feb 1997): 142–50.

114. M. Gantley et al., "Sudden infant death syndrome: links with infant care practices," *BMJ* 306, no. 6869 (Jan 1993): 16–20.

115. J. Winberg and R.H. Porter, "Olfaction and human neonatal behavior: clinical implications," *Acta Paediatr* 87, no. 1 (Jan 1998): 6–10.

116. S. Farooqi et al., "Ethnic differences in infant-rearing practices and their possible relationship to the incidence of sudden infant death syndrome (SIDS)," *Paediatr Perinat Epidemiol* (England) 7, no. 3 (Jul 1993): 245–52.

117. N. Watanabe et al., "Epidemiology of sudden infant death syndrome in Japan," *Acta Paediatr Jpn* (Japan) 36, no. 3 (Jun 1994): 329–32.

118. E.J. Adams et al., "Changes in the epidemiologic profile of sudden infant death syndrome as rates decline among California infants: 1990–1995," *Pediatrics* 102, no. 6 (Dec 1998): 1445–51.

119. B.H. Wolf and M.O. Ikeogu, *Ann Trop Paediatr* (Zimbabwe) 16, no. 2 (Jun 1996): 149–53.

120. C.L. Lee and T.L. Chung, "The trend of sudden infant death syndrome in Taiwan from 1984 to 1993," *Chung Hua Min Kui Hsiao Erh Ko I Hsueh Hui Tsa Chih* (Taiwan) 36, no. 6 (Nov–Dec 1995): 431–3.

121. J. McKenna, "International Lactation Consultants Association Conference" (lecture, Atlanta, Georgia, July 1994).

122. Nakamura et al., "Review of hazards associated with children placed in adult beds," *Arch Pediatr Adolesc Med* 153, no. 10 (Oct. 1999): 1019–23.

123. D.P. Southall et al., "Severe hypoxaemia in pertussis," *Arch Dis Child* (England) 63, no. 6 (Jun 1988): 598–605.

124. First Alert. "Facts About Fire," http://www.firstalert.com/pdfs/Facts_About_Fire.pdf 2007 (accessed April 2009).

125. Tine Thevenin, *The Family Bed* (Wayne, New Jersey: Avery, 1987), 35.

126. D. Waynforth, "The influence of parent-infant cosleeping, nursing, and childcare on cortisol and SIgA immunity in a sample of British children," *Dev Psychobiol* (United Kingdom) 49, no. 6 (Sep 2007): 640–8.

127. T. Doan et al., "Breast-feeding increases sleep duration of new parents," *J Perinat Neonatal Nurs* 21, no. 3 (Jul–Sep 2007): 200–6.

128. Tine Thevenin, *The Family Bed* (Wayne, New Jersey: Avery, 1987), 42.

129. W.P. Fifer and C.M. Moon, "The role of mother's voice in the organization of brain function in the newborn," *Acta Paediatr Suppl* 397 (Jun 1994): 86–93.

130. A.W. Wolf and B. Lozoff, "Object attachment, thumbsucking, and the passage to sleep," *J Am Acad Child Adolesc Psychiatry* 28, no. 2 (Mar 1989): 287–92.

131. V. Gedaly-Duff and J. Huff Slankard, "Sleep as an indicator for pain relief in an infant: a case study," *J Pediatr Nurs* 13, no. 1 (Feb 1998): 32–40.

132. A. Kahn et al., "Insomnia and cow's milk allergy in infants," *Pediatrics* 76, no. 6 (Dec 1985): 880–4.

133. A. Kahn et al., "Milk intolerance in children with persistent sleeplessness: a prospective double-blind crossover evaluation," *Pediatrics* (Belgium) 84, no. 4 (Oct 1989): 595–603.

Chapter 5: Brighter Babies, Not Super Babies

1. J. Lehtonen et al., "The effect of nursing on the brain activity of the newborn," *J Pediatr* (Finland) 132, no. 4 (Apr 1998): 646–51.

2. M.C. Temboury et al., "Influence of breast-feeding on the infant's intellectual development," *J Pediatr Gastroenterol Nutr* (Spain) 18, no. 1 (Jan 1994): 32–6.

3. C.D. Florey et al., "Infant feeding and mental and motor development at 18 months of age in first born singletons," *Int J Epidemiol* (England) 24, suppl. 1 (1995): S21–6.

4. D. L. Johnson et al., "Breast feeding and children's intelligence," *Psychol Rep* 79, no. 3, part 2 (Dec 1996): 1179–85.

5. A. Lucas et al., "Breast milk and subsequent intelligence quotient in children born preterm," *Lancet* 339, no. 8788 (Feb 1992): 261–4.

6. J.L. Pollock, "Long-term associations with infant feeding in a clinically advantaged population of babies," *Dev Med Child Neurol* 36, no. 5 (May 1994): 429–40.

7. C.I. Lanting et al., "Neurological differences between 9-year-old children fed breast-milk or formula-milk as babies," *Lancet* (Holland) 344, no. 8933 (Nov 1994): 1319–22.

8. L.J. Horwood and D.M. Fergusson, "Breastfeeding and later cognitive and academic outcomes," *Pediatrics* (New Zealand) 101, no. 1 (Jan 1998): E9.

9. G. Der et al., "Effect of breast feeding on intelligence in children: prospective study, sibling pairs analysis, and meta-analysis," *BMJ* (United Kingdom) 333, no. 7575 (Nov 2006): 945.

10. M.S. Kramer et al., "Breastfeeding and child cognitive development: new evidence from a large randomized trial," *Arch Gen Psyciatry* (Canada) 65, no. 5 (May 2008): 578–84.

11. C.R. Gale and C.N. Martyn, "Breastfeeding, dummy use, and adult intelligence," *Lancet* 347, no. 9008 (Apr 1996): 1072–5.

12. F.C. Barros et al., "Breastfeeding, pacifier use and infant development at 12 months of age: a birth cohort study in Brazil," *Paediatr Perinat Epidemiol* (Brazil) 11, no. 4 (Oct 1997): 441–50.

13. J. Worobey, "Feeding method and motor activity in 3-month-old human infants," *Percept Mot Skills* 86, no. 3, part 1 (Jun 1998): 883–95.

14. C.I. Lanting et al., "Breastfeeding and neurological outcome at 42 months," *Acta Paediatr* (Holland) 87, no. 12 (Dec 1998): 1224–9.

15. B. Lozoff et al., "Iron-deficiency anemia and infant development: effects of extended oral iron therapy," *J Pediatr* 129, no. 3 (Sep 1996): 382–9.

16. E. Riva et al., "Early breastfeeding is linked to higher intelligence quotient scores in dietary treated phenylketonuric children," *Acta Paediatr* (Italy) 85, no. 1 (Jan 1996): 639.

17. I.F. Wallace et al., "Interactions of African American infants and their mothers: relations with development at 1 year of age," *J Speech Lang Hear Res* 41, no. 4 (Aug 1998): 900–12.

18. D.L. Coates and M. Lewis, "Early mother-infant interaction and infant cognitive status as predictors of school performance and cognitive behavior in six-year-olds," *Child Dev* 55, no. 4 (Aug 1984): 1219–30.

19. J.R. Smith et al., "Correlates and consequences of harsh discipline for young children," *Arch Pediatr Adolesc Med* 151, no. 8 (Aug 1997): 777–86.

20. J. Raber, "Detrimental effects of chronic hypothalamic–pituitary–adrenal axis activation. From obesity to memory deficits," *Mol Neurobiol* 18, no. 1 (Aug 1998): 1–22.

21. H.J. Krugers et al., "Exposure to chronic psychosocial stress and corticosterone in the rat: effects on spatial discrimination learning and hippocampal protein kinase C gamma immunoreactivity," *Hippocampus* 7, no. 4 (1997): 427–36.

22. M. Carlson and F. Earls, "Psychological and neuroendocrinological sequelae of early social deprivation in institutionalized children in Romania," *Ann N Y Acad Sci* 807 (Jan 15, 1997): 419–28.

23. R. Feldman et al., "Comparison of Skin-to-Skin (Kangaroo) and Traditional Care: Parenting Outcomes and Preterm Infant Development," *Pediatrics* (Isreal) 110, no. 1 (July 2002): 16–26.

24. M.M. McGrath et al., "Maternal interaction patterns and preschool competence in high-risk children," *Nurs Res* 47, no. 6 (Nov–Dec 1998): 309–17.

25. B.M. Lester et al., "Developmental outcome as a function of the goodness of fit between the infant's cry characteristics and the mother's perception of her infant's cry," *Pediatrics* 95, no. 4 (Apr 1995): 516–21.

26. J. Belsky et al., "Maternal stimulation and infant exploratory competence: cross-sectional, correlational, and experimental analyses," *Child Dev* 51, no. 4 (Dec 1980): 1168–78.

27. M.W. Yogman et al., "Father involvement and cognitive/behavioral outcomes of preterm infants," *J Am Acad Child Adolesc Psychiatry* 34, no. 1 (Jan 1995): 58–66.

28. S.E. Cohen and L. Beckwith, "Preterm infant interaction with the caregiver in the first year of life and competence at age two," *Child Dev* 50, no. 3 (Sep 1979): 767–76.

29. J.D. Morrow, "The eyes have it: visual attention as an index of infant cognition," *J Pediatr Health Care* 74, no. 4 (Aug–Jul 1993): 150–5.

30. M. Zuckerman, "Attention must be paid," *U.S. News and World Report* (Aug 18 and Aug 25, 1997): 92.

31. K.E. Smith et al., "The relation of medical risk and maternal stimulation with preterm infants' development of cognitive, language and daily living skills," *J Child Psychol Psychiatry* 37, no. 7 (Oct 1996): 855–64.

32. N. Weisglas-Kuperus et al., "Effects of biological and social factors on the cognitive development of very low birth weight children," *Pediatrics* (Netherlands) 92, no. 5 (Nov 1993): 658–65.

33. L. Beckwith and A.H. Parmelee, Jr., "EEG patterns of preterm infants, home environment, and later IQ," *Child Dev* 57, no. 3 (Jun 1986): 777–89.

34. R.L. Goldenberg et al., "Pregnancy outcome and intelligence at age five years," *Am J Obstet Gynecol* 175, no. 6 (Dec 1996): 1511–5.

35. K.E. Barnard and H.L. Bee, "The impact of temporally patterned stimulation on the development of preterm infants," *Child Dev* 54, no. 5 (Oct 1983): 1156–67.

36. D.L. Clark et al., "Effects of rocking on neuromuscular development in the premature," *Biol Neonate* 56, no. 6 (1989): 306–14.

37. T. Field et al., "Massage therapy reduces anxiety and enhances EEG pattern of alertness and math computations," *Int J Neurosci* 86, nos. 3–4 (Sep 1996): 197–205.

38. H. Montgomery-Downs and E.B. Thoman, "Biological and behavioral correlates of quiet sleep respiration rates in infants," *Physiol Behav* 64, no. 5 (Jul 1998): 637–43.

39. Robert Karen, PhD, *Becoming Attached* (New York: Oxford University Press, 1998), 21–2.

40. P.A. Ferchmin et al., "Genetic learning deficiency does not hinder environment-dependent brain growth," *Physiol Behav* 24, no. 1 (Jan 1980): 45–50.

41. F. Gonzalez-Lima et al., "Metabolic activation of the brain of young rats after exposure to environmental complexity," *Dev Psychobiol* 27, no. 6 (Sep 1994): 343–51.

42. P.D. Wadhwa et al., "Prenatal psychosocial factors and the neuroendocrine axis in human pregnancy," *Psychosom Med* 58, no. 5 (Sep–Oct 1996): 432–46.
43. K. Sjostrom et al., "Maternal anxiety in late pregnancy and fetal hemodynamics," *Eur J Obstet Gynecol Reprod Biol* 74, no. 2 (Aug 1997): 149–55.
44. L.K. Takahashi et al., "Prolonged stress-induced elevation in plasma corticosterone during pregnancy in the rat: implications for prenatal stress studies," *Psychoneuroendocrinology* 23, no. 6 (Aug 1998): 571–81.
45. C. Brezinka et al., "[The fetus and noise]," *Gynakol Geburtshilfliche Rundsch* (Germany) 37, no. 3 (1997): 119–29.
46. D.S. Richards et al., "Sound levels in the human uterus," *Obstet Gynecol* 80, no. 2 (Aug 1992): 186–90.
47. C.M. Moon and W.P. Fifer, "Evidence of transnatal auditory learning," *J Perinatol* 20, no. 8, pt. 2 (Dec 2000): S37–44.
48. D.K. James et al., "Fetal learning: a prospective randomized controlled study," *Ultrasound Obstet Gynecol* (United Kingdom) 20, no. 5 (Nov 2002): 431–8.
49. D. Chelli and B. Chanoufi, "Fetal audition, Myth or reality," *J Gynecol Obstet Biol Reprod (Paris)* (Tunisia) 37, no. 6 (Oct 2008): 554–8.
50. B.S. Kisilevsky et al., "Fetal sensitivity to properties of maternal speech and language," *Infant Behav Dev* (Canada) 32, no. 1 (Jan 2009): 59–71.
51. W.H. Dietz and V.C. Strasburger, "Children, adolescents, and television," *Curr Probl Pediatr* 21, no. 1 (Jan 1991): 8–32.
52. Ulric Neisser, ed., *The Rising Curve: Long-Term Gains in IQ and Related Measures*, Apa Science Volumes, (Washington, DC: American Psychological Association, 1998): 91.
53. R.B. Tower et al., "Differential effects of television programming on preschoolers' cognition, imagination, and social play," *Am J Orthopsychiatry* 49, no. 2 (Apr 1979): 265–81.
54. Judith Van Evra, "Television and Child Development" (Canada: University of Minnesota Children Youth and Family Consortium, 1990), http:// www.cyfc.umn.edu.
55. B.S. Centerwall, "Television and violence. The scale of the problem and where to go from here," *JAMA* 267, no. 22 (Jun 1992): 3059–63.
56. R.A. Gibson et al., "Effect of dietary docosahexaenoic acid on brain composition and neural function in term infants," *Lipids* 31, suppl. (Mar 1996): S177–81.
57. R.A. Gibson and M. Makrides, "The role of long chain polyunsaturated fatty acids (LCPUFA) in neonatal nutrition," *Acta Paediatr* (Australia) 87, no. 10 (Oct 1998): 1017–22.
58. H.A. Woltil et al., "Long-chain polyunsaturated fatty acid status and early growth of low birth weight infants," *Eur J Pediatr* (Holland) 157, no. 2 (Feb 1998): 146–52.
59. C.L. Jensen et al., "Effect of dietary linoleic/alpha-linolenic acid ration on growth and visual function of term infants," *J Pediatr* 131, no. 2 (Aug 1997): 200–9.
60. J. Woods et al., "Is docosahexaenoic acid necessary in infant formula? Evaluation of high linolenate diets in the neonatal rat," *Pediatr Res* 40, no. 5 (Nov 1996): 687–94.
61. K. Wright et al., "Formula supplemented with docosahexaenoic acid (DHA) and arachidonic acid (ARA): a critical review of the research," *J Spec Pediatr Nurs* 11, no. 2 (Apr 2006): 100–113.
62. K. Simmer et al., "Longchain polyunsaturated fatty acid supplementation in infants born at term," *Cochrane Database Syst Rev* 23, no. 1 (Jan 2008): CD000376.
63. M. Fleith and M.T. Clandinin, "Dietary PUFA for preterm and term infants: review of clinical studies," *Crit Rev Food Sci Nutr* 45, no. 3 (2005): 205–29.
64. T.W. Clarkson and J.J. Strain, "Nutritional factors may modify the toxic action of methyl mercury in fish-eating populations," *The Journal of Nutrition* (Norway) 133, no. 5, suppl. 1 (2003): 1539–43S.
65. I.B. Helland et al., "Maternal supplementation with very-long-chain n-3 fatty acids during pregnancy and lactation augments children's IQ at 4 years of age," *Pediatrics* 111, no. 1 (Jan 2003): e39–44.
66. S.T. Schultz et al., "Breastfeeding, infant formula supplementation, and Autistic Disorder: the results of a parent survey," *Autism* 12, no. 3 (May 2008): 293–307.

Chapter 6: Immune Protection Matters

1. A. Palloni et al., "The effects of breast-feeding and the pace of childbearing on early childhood mortality in Mexico," *Bulletin of the Pan American Health Organization* (Mexico) 28, no.2 (Jun 1994): 93–111.
2. WHO Collaborative Study Team on the Role of Breastfeeding on the Prevention of Infant Mortality, "Effect of breastfeeding on infant and child mortality due to infectious diseases in less developed countries: a pooled analysis," *Lancet* 355, no. 9202 (Feb 2000): 451–5.
3. D.K. Guilkey and R.T. Riphahn, "The determinants of child mortality in the Philippines: estimation of a structural model," *Journal of Development Economics* (U.S. and Germany) 56, no. 2 (Aug 1998): 281–305.
4. P. Tu, "The effects of breastfeeding and birth spacing on child survival in China," *Studies in Family Planning* (China) 20, no. 6 (Nov.–Dec. 1989): 332–342.

5. A. Palloni and M. Tienda, "The effects of breastfeeding and pace of childbearing on mortality at early ages (Peru)," *Demography* (US) 23, no. 1 (Feb 1986): 31–52.

6. S.P. Srivastava et al., "Mortality patterns in breast versus artificially fed term babies in early infancy: a longitudinal study," *Indian Pediatrics* (India) 31, no. 11 (Nov 1994): 1393–6.

7. J.P. Habicht et al., "Does breastfeeding really save lives, or are apparent benefits due to biases?" *Am J Epidemiol* 123, no. 2 (Feb 1986): 279–90.

8. C.G. Victora et al., "Infant feeding and deaths due to diarrhea. A case-control study," *Am J Epidemiol* 129, no. 5 (May 1989): 1032–41.

9. A. Lucas and T.J. Cole, "Breast milk and neonatal necrotising enterocolitis," *Lancet* (England) 336, no. 8730 (Dec 1990): 1519–23.

10. M.K. Davis, "Review of the evidence for an association between infant feeding and childhood cancer," *Int J Cancer Suppl* 11 (1998): 29–33.

11. G.P. Mathur et al., "Breastfeeding and childhood cancer," *Indian Pediatr* (India) 30, no. 5 (May 1993): 651–7.

12. M. Xanthou, "Immune protection of human milk," *Biol Neonate* (Greece) 74, no. 2 (1998): 121–33.

13. A.L. Wright et al., "Increasing breastfeeding rates to reduce infant illness at the community level," *Pediatrics* 101, no. 5 (May 1998): 837–44.

14. P.W. Howie et al., "Protective effect of breast feeding against infection," *British Medical Journal* (Scotland) 300, no. 6716 (Jan 6, 1990): 11–6.15.

15. O.S. Levine et al., "Risk factors for invasive pneumococcal disease in children: a population-based case-control study in North America," *Pediatrics* 103, no. 3 (Mar 1999): E28.

16. J. Golding et al., "Gastroenteritis, diarrhoea and breast feeding," *Early Human Development* (England) 49, suppl. (Oct 29, 1997): S83–103.

17. M.D. Blaymore Bier et al., "Human milk reduced outpatient upper respiratory symptoms in premature infants during their first year of life," *Journal of Perinatology* (Providence, USA) 22, no. 5 (Jul/Aug 2002): 354–359.

18. V.R. Bachrach et al., "Breastfeeding and the risk of hospitalization for respiratory disease in infancy: a meta-analysis," *Archives of Pediatric Adolescent Medicine* (USA) 157, no. 3 (Mar 157): 237–43.

19. J. Raisler et al., "Breast-feeding and infant illness: a dose-response relationship?" *Am J Public Health* 89, no. 1 (Jan 1999): 25–30.

20. C. van den Bogaard et al., "The relationship between breast-feeding and early childhood morbidity in a general population," *Fam Med* (Holland) 23, no. 7 (Oct–Sep 1991): 510–5.

21. M.K. Davis, "Review of the evidence for an association between infant feeding and childhood cancer," *Int J Cancer Suppl* 11 (1998): 29–33.

22. S.A. Silfverdal et al., "Protective effect of breastfeeding: an ecologic study of Haemophilus influenzae meningitis and breastfeeding in a Swedish population," *Int J Epidemiol* (Sweden) 28, no. 1 (Feb 1999): 152–6.

23. A.C. Wilson et al., "Relation of infant diet to childhood health: seven year follow up of cohort of children in Dundee infant feeding study," *BMJ* (England) 316, no. 7124 (Jan 1998): 21–5.

24. L.A. Hanson, "Breastfeeding provides passive and likely long-lasting active immunity," *Ann Allergy Asthma Immunol* (Sweden) 81, no. 6 (Dec 1998): 523–33.

25. P.G. Quie, "Antimicrobial defenses in the neonate," *Semin Perinatol* 14, no. 4, suppl. 1 (Aug 1990): 2–9.

26. M. Haeney, "Infection determinants at extremes of age," *J Antimicrob Chemother* 34, suppl. A (Aug 1994): 1–9.

27. S. Agrawal et al., "Comparative study of immunoglobulin G and immunoglobulin M among neonates in caesarean section and vaginal delivery," *J Indian Med Assoc* 94, no. 2 (Feb 1996): 43–4.

28. M.F. MacDorman, "Infant and neonatal mortality for primary cesarean and vaginal births to women with 'no indicated risk,' United States, 1998–2001 birth cohorts," *Birth* 33, no. 3 (Sep 2006): 175–82.

29. M.H. Hall and S Bewley, "Maternal mortality and mode of delivery," *Lancet* 354, no. 9180 (Aug 28, 1999): 776.

30. G. Goncalves et al., "[Anti-measles IgG concentration in maternal blood: according to the mother's vaccination status]," *Acta Med Port* (Portugal) 11, no. 10 (Oct 1998): 847–53.

31. T. Hokama et al., "Isolation of respiratory bacterial pathogens from the throats of healthy infants fed by different methods," *J Trop Pediatr* (Japan) 45, no. 3 (Jun 1999): 173–6.

32. J.L. Paradise et al., "Evidence in infants with cleft palate that breast milk protects against otitis media," *Pediatrics* 94, no. 6, pt. 1 (Dec 1994): 853–60.

33. L.A. Hanson, "Breastfeeding provides passive and likely long-lasting active immunity," *Ann Allergy Asthma Immunol* 81, no. 6 (Dec 1998): 523–33.

34. L.A. Hanson et al., "The immune response of the mammary gland and its significance for the neonate," *Ann Allergy* 53, no. 6, part 2 (Dec 1984): 576–82.

35. J.A. Peterson et al., "Milk fat globule glycoproteins in human milk and in gastric aspirates of mother's milk-fed preterm infants," *Pediatr Res* 44, no. 4 (Oct 1998): 499–506.

36. D. Newburg, "Human milk glycoconjugates that inhibit pathogens," *Curr Med Chem* 6, no. 2 (Feb 1999): 117–27.

37. D.S. Newburg, "Role of human-milk lactadherin in protection against symptomatic rotavirus infection," *Lancet* 351, no. 9110 (Apr 18, 1998): 1160–4.

38. Mark Gladwin, MD, and Bill Trattler, MD, *Clinical Microbiology* (Miami, Florida: MedMaster, Inc., 1997), 56, 219.

39. B. Fornarini et al., "Human milk 90K (Mac-2 BP): possible protective effects against acute respiratory infections," *Clin Exp Immunol* 115, no. 1 (Jan 1999): 91–4.

40. J.B. German et al., "Human milk oligosaccharides: evolution, structures and bioselectivity as substrates for intestinal bacteria," *Nestlé Nutr Workshop Ser Pediatr Program* 62 (2008): 205–22.

41. D.S. Newburg, "Neonatal protection by an innate immune system of human milk consisting of oligosaccharides and glycans," *J Anim Sci* 87, no. 13 suppl. (Apr 2009): 26–34.

42. P. McVeagh and J.B. Miller, "Human milk oligosaccharides: only the breast," *J Paediatr Child Health* 33, no. 4 (Aug 1997): 281–6.

43. D.S. Newburg, "Human milk glycoconjugates that inhibit pathogens," *Curr Med Chem* 6, no. 2 (Feb 1999): 117–27.

44. J. Portelli et al., "Effect of compounds with antibacterial activities in human milk on respiratory syncytial virus and cytomegalovirus in vitro," *J Med Microbiol* 47, no. 11 (Nov 1998): 1015–8.

45. D.V. Semenov et al., "Human milk lactoferrin binds ATP and dissociates into monomers," *Biochem Mol Biol Int* 47, no. 2 (Feb 1999): 177–84.

46. S.A. Dolan, "Inhibition of enteropathogenic bacteria by human milk whey in vitro," *Pediatr Infect Dis J* 8, no.7 (Jul 1989): 430–6.

47. J. Portelli et al., "Effect of compounds with antibacterial activities in human milk on respiratory syncytial virus and cytomegalovirus in vitro," *J Med Microbiol* 47, no. 11 (Nov 1998): 1015–8.

48. M. Hamosh, "Protective function of proteins and lipids in human milk," *Biol Neonate* 74, no. 2 (1998): 163–76.

49. J. Meinzen-Derr et al., "Role of human milk in extremely low birth weight infants' risk of necrotizing enterocolitis or death," *J Perinatol* 29, no. 1 (Jan 2009): 57–62.

50. P.M. Sisk et al., "Early human milk feeding is associated with a lower risk of necrotizing enterocolitis in very low birth weight infants," *J Perinatol* 27, no. 7 (Jul 2007): 428–33.

51. D. Dia and W.A. Walker, "Role of bacterial colonization in neonatal necrotizing enterocolitis and its prevention," *Chung Hua Min Kuo Hsiao Erh Ko I Hsueh Hui Tsa Chih* (China) 39, no. 6 (Nov–Dec 1998): 357–65.

52. F.R. Moya et al., "Platelet-activating factor acetylhydrolase in term and preterm human milk: a preliminary report," *J Pediatr Gastroenterol Nutr* 19, no. 2 (Aug 1994): 236–9.

53. D. Silvestre et al., "Effect of pasteurization on the bactericidal capacity of human milk," *J Hum Lact* (Spain) 24, no. 4 (Nov 2008): 371–6.

54. D. Silvestre et al., "Bactericidal activity of human milk: stability during storage," *Br J Biomed Sci* (Spain) 63, no. 2 (2006): 59–62.

55. N. Hanna et al., "Effect of storage on breast milk antioxidant activity," *Arch Dis Child Fetal Neonatal Ed* 89, no. 6 (Nov 2004): F518–20.

56. A.S. Goldman and R.M. Goldblum, "Transfer of maternal leukocytes to the infant by human milk," *Curr Top Microbiol Immunol* 222, no. 205 (1997): 205–13.

57. R.P. Garofalo and A.S. Goldman, "Cytokines, chemokines, and colony-stimulation factors in human milk: the 1997 update," *Biol Neonate* 74, no. 2 (1998): 134–42.

58. H.F. Bu et al, "Milk fat globule-EGF factor 8/lactadherin plays a crucial role in maintenance and repair of murine intestinal epithelium," *J Clin Invest* 117, no. 12 (Dec 2007): 3673–83.

59. M. Hamosh, "Protective function of proteins and lipids in human milk," *Biol Neonate* 74, no. 2 (1998): 163–76.

60. O.H. Braun, "[The protective effect of human milk against infections and its potential causes,]" *Klin Padiatr* (Germany) 188, no. 4 (Jul 1976): 297–310.

61. J. Levy, "Immunonutrition: the pediatric experience," *Nutrition* 14, nos. 7–8 (Jul–Aug 1998): 641–7.

62. L. Thorell et al., "Nucleotides in human milk: sources and metabolism by the newborn infant," *Pediatr Res* (Sweden) 40, no. 6 (Dec 1996): 845–52.

63. G. Capano et al., "Polyamines in human and rat milk influence intestinal cell growth in vitro," *J Pediatr Gastroenterol Nutr* 27, no. 3 (Sep 1998): 281–6.

64. A.S. Goldman et al., "Anti-inflammatory systems in human milk," *Adv Exp Med Biol* 262 (1990): 69–76.

65. E.S. Buescher and I. Malinowska, "Soluble receptors and cytokine antagonists in human milk," *Pediatr Res* 40, no. 6 (Dec 1996): 839–44.

66. N. D'Ostilio et al., "90K (Mac-s BP) in human milk," *Clin Exp Immunol* 104, no. 3 (Jun 1996): 543–6.

67. L. Densmore and S.M. Pflueger, "Using Interphase Fluorescence In Situ Hybridization (I-FISH) to Detect the Transfer of Infant Cells During Breastfeeding," *J Hum Lact* 24, no. 4 (Nov 2008): 401–5.

68. R. J. Schanler, "The role of human milk fortification for premature infants," *Clin Perinatol* 25, no. 3 (Sep 1998): 645–57.

69. G. Schoch, "[Immunologic and ethologic aspects of breast feeding]," *Monatsschr Kinderheilkd* (Germany) 134, no. 6 (Jun 1986): 396–402.

70. A.S. Goldman et al., "Immunologic factors in human milk during the first year of lactation," *J Pediatr* 100, no. 4 (Apr 1982): 563–7.

71. L.A. Hanson, "Breastfeeding provides passive and likely long-lasting active immunity," *Ann Allergy Asthma Immunol* 81, no. 6 (Dec 1998): 523–33.

72. H. Hasselbalch et al., "Decreased thymus size in formula-fed infants compared with breastfed infants," *Acta Paediatr* 85, no. 9 (Sep 1996): 1029–32.

73. M. Aronson, "Involution of the thymus revisited: immunological trade-offs as an adaptation to aging," *Mech Ageing Dev* 72, no. 1 (Nov 1993): 49–55.

74. N.C. Klein and B.A. Cunha, "Treatment of fever," *Infect Dis Clin North Am* 10, no. 1 (Mar 1996): 211–6.

75. M.J. Kluger et al., "The adaptive value of fever," *Infect Dis Clin North Am* 10, no. 1 (Mar 1996): 1–20.

76. H.A. Bernheim et al., "Fever: effect of drug-induced antipyresis on survival," *Science* 193, no. 4249 (Jul 1976): 237–9.

77. M. Vestergaard et al., "Death in children with febrile seizures: a population-based cohort study," *Lancet* (Denmark) 372, no. 9637 (Aug 9, 2008): 457–63.

78. Robert S. Mendelsohn, MD, *How to Raise a Healthy Child in Spite of Your Doctor* (Ballantine Books, 1987), 83.

79. D.M. Zerr et al., "A case-control study of necrotizing fasciitis during primary varicella," *Pediatrics* 103, no. 4, part 1 (Apr 1999): 783–90.

80. TF Doran et al., Acetaminophen: more harm than good for chickenpox? *J Pediatr* 114 no. 6 (Jun 1989): 1045–8.

81. N. Nathanson at al., "The evolution of virus diseases: their emergence, epidemicity, and control," *Virus Res* 29, no. 1 (Jul 1993): 3–20.

82. D.P. Hoa et al., "Young child feeding in a rural area in the Red River delta, Vietnam," *Acta Paediatr* (Vietnam) 84, no. 9 (Sep 1995): 1045–9.

83. J. Storsaeter et al., "Mortality and morbidity from invasive bacterial infections during a clinical trial of acellular pertussis vaccines in Sweden," *Pediatr Infect Dis J* (Sweden) 7, no. 9 (Sep 1988): 637–45.

84. M.R. Griffin et al., "No increased risk for invasive bacterial infection found following diphtheria-tetanus-pertussis immunization," *Pediatrics* 89, no. 4, part 1 (Apr 1992): 640–2.

85. Centers for Disease Control and Prevention, "Strengthening Global Immunization Systems: What Is the Public Health Issue?" http://www.cdc.gov/ncird/progbriefs/downloads/global-strengthen-imz.pdf, Feb 2007 (accessed April 2009).

86. H. Yoshida et al., "Circulation of type 1 wild poliovirus in northern Vietnam during 1991–1994," *Am J Trop Med Hyg* (Japan) 55, no. 5 (Nov 1996): 531–5.

87. S. Khalfan et al., "Epidemics of aseptic meningitis due to enteroviruses following national immunization days in Baharain," *Ann Trop Paediatr* (Arabia) 18, no. 2 (Jun 1998): 101–9.

88. S. Takimoto et al., "Enterovirus 71 infection and acute neurological disease among children in Brazil (1988–1990)," *Trans R Soc Trop Med Hyg* (Brazil) 92, no. 1 (Jan–Feb 1998): 25–8.

89. T.A. Popova et al., "[The results of monitoring enterovirus circulation among the population and in the environment of Tula Province over 10 years (1985–1994)]," *Zh Mikrobiol Epidemiol Immunobiol* (Japan) 1 (Jan–Feb 1997): 35–9.

90. E. Druyts-Voets, "Epidemiological features of entero non-poliovirus isolations in Belgium 1980–94," *Epidemiol Infect* (Belgium) 119, no. 1 (Aug 1997): 71–7.

91. K. Ishii et al., "[Epidemiology of virus-related nervous infections in Japan]," *Nippon Rinsho* (Japan) 55, no. 4 (Apr 1997): 839–48.

92. B.F. Elswood and R.B. Stricker, "Polio vaccines and the origin of AIDS," *Med Hypotheses* 42, no. 6 (Jun 1994): 347–54.

93. V. Reinhardt and A. Roberts, "The African polio vaccine-acquired immune deficiency syndrome connection," *Med Hypotheses* 48, no. 5 (May 1997): 367–74.

94. R. Cutrone et al., "Some oral poliovirus vaccines were contaminated with infectious SV40 after 1961," *Cancer Res* 65, no. 22 (Nov 15, 2005): 10273–9.

95. F. Brown, "Review of accidents caused by incomplete inactivation of viruses," *Dev Biol Stand* 81, (1993): 103–107.

96. W.J. Martin, "Simian cytomegalovirus-related stealth virus isolated from the cerebrospinal fluid of a patient with bipolar psychosis and acute encephalopathy," *Pathobiology* 64, no. 2 (1996): 64–6.

97. W.J. Martin and D. Anderson, "Stealth virus epidemic in the Mohave Valley. I. Initial report of virus isolation," *Pathobiology* 65, no. 1 (1997): 51–6.

98. F. Friedrich, "Rare adverse events associated with oral poliovirus vaccine in Brazil," *Braz J Med Biol Res* (Brazil) 30, no. 6 (Jun 1997): 695–703.

99. C.P. Howson and H.V. Fineberg, "Adverse events following pertussis and rubella vaccines. Summary of a report of the Institute of Medicine," *JAMA* 267, no. 3 (Jan 1992): 392–6.

100. M.M. Braun et al., "Report of a US public health service workshop on hypotonic-hyporesponsive episode (HHE) after pertussis immunization," *Pediatrics* 102, no. 5 (Nov 1998): E52.
101. K.R. Wentz and E.K. Marcuse, "Diphtheria-tetanus-pertussis vaccine and serious neurologic illness: an updated review of the epidemiologic evidence," *Pediatrics* 87, no. 3 (Mar 1991): 287–97.
102. D.P. Southall et al., "Severe hypoxaemia in pertussis," *Arch Dis Child* 63, no. 6 (Jun 1988): 598–605.
103. C. Lindgren et al., "Sudden infant death and prevalence of whooping cough in the Swedish and Norwegian communities," *Eur J Pediatr* 156, no. 5 (May 1997): 405–9.
104. S. Schmitt-Groge et al., "Pertussis in German adults," *Clin Infect Dis* (Germany) 21, no. 4 (Oct 1995): 860–6.
105. C.M. Ausiello et al., "Cell-mediated immune response of healthy adults to Bordetella pertussis vaccine antigens," *J Infect Dis* (Italy) 178, no. 2 (Aug 1998): 466–70.
106. J. Isacson et al., "How common is whooping cough in a nonvaccinating country?" *Pediatr Infect Dis J* (Sweden) 12, no. 4 (Apr 1993): 284–8.
107. L. Gustafsson et al., "A controlled trial of a two-component acellular, a five-component acellular, and a whole-cell pertussis vaccine," *N Engl J Med* 334, no. 6 (Feb 1996): 349–55.
108. M.A. Uberall et al., "Severe adverse events in a comparative efficacy trial in Germany in infants receiving either the Lederle/Takeda acellular pertussis component DTP (DtaP) vaccine, the Lederle whole-cell component DTP (DTP) or DT vaccine. The Pertussis Vaccine Study Group," *Dev Biol Stand* 89 (1997): 83–9.
109. J.H. Menkes and M. Kinsbourne, "Workshop on neurologic complications of pertussis and pertussis vaccination," *Neuropediatrics* 21, no. 4 (Nov 1990): 171–6.
110. J.D. Cherry et al., "The effect of investigator compliance (observer bias) on calculated efficacy in a pertussis vaccine trial," *Pediatrics* 102, no. 4, part 1 (Oct 1998): 909–12.
111. L. Gustafsson et al., "A controlled trial of a two-component acellular, a five-component acellular, and a whole-cell pertussis vaccine," *N Engl J Med* 334, no. 6 (Feb 1996): 349–55.
112. L. Squeri and A. Ioli, "[A few viral infections in the recent epidemiological evolution]," *Ann Sclavo* (Italy) 19, no. 3 (May–Jun 1977): 313–46.
113. E. Kinnunen et al., "Nationwide oral poliovirus vaccination campaign and the incidence of Guillain-Barre Syndrome," *Am J Epidemiol* (Finland) 147, no. 1 (Jan 1998): 69–73.
114. T. Lasky et al., "The Guillain-Barre syndrome and the 1992–93 and 1993–94 influenza vaccines," *N Engl J Med* 339, no. 25 (Dec 1998): 1797–802.
115. F. Friedrich, "Neurologic complications associated with oral poliovirus vaccine and genomic variability of the vaccine strains after multiplication in humans," *Acta Virol* (Brazil) 42, no. 3 (Jun 1998): 187–94.
116. N.P. Thompson et al., "Is measles vaccination a risk factor for inflammatory bowel disease?" *Lancet* (England) 345, no. 8957 (Apr 1995): 1071–4.
117. T.M. Burbacher et al., "Comparison of blood and brain mercury levels in infant monkeys exposed to methylmercury or vaccines containing thimerosal," *Environ Health Perspect* 113, no. 8 (Aug 2005): 1015-21.
118. S.T. Schultz et al., "Acetaminophen (paracetamol) use, measles-mumps-rubella vaccination, and autistic disorder: the results of a parent survey," *Autism* 12, no. 3 (May 2008): 293–307.
119. M.S. Petrik et al., "Aluminum adjuvant linked to Gulf War illness induces motor neuron death in mice," *Neuromolecular Med* (Canada) 9, no. 1 (2007): 83–100.
120. J. Savory et al., "Mechanisms of aluminum-induced neurodegeneration in animals: Implications for Alzheimer's disease," *J Alzheimers Dis* 10, no. 2-3 (Nov 2006): 135–44.
121. M. Rey et al., "Impact of measles in France," *Rev Infect Dis* 5, no. 3 (May–Jun 1983): 433–8.
122. "Rotavirus vaccine for the prevention of rotavirus gastroenteritis among children," *MMWR Morb Mortal Wkly Rep* 48, (RR-2) (Mar 19, 1999): 1–20.
123. F.E. Yazbak and K. Yazbak, "Live virus vaccination near a pregnancy: flawed policies, tragic results," *Medical Hypotheses* 59, no. 3 (September 2002): 283-288.
124. "Rotavirus vaccine for the prevention of rotavirus gastroenteritis among children," *MMWR Morb Mortal Wkly Rep* 48, (RR-2) (Mar 19, 1999): 1–20.
125. "Withdrawal of rotavirus vaccine recommendation," *MMWR Morb Mortal Wkly Rep* 48, no. 43 (Nov 5, 1999): 1007.
126. M.F. Delgado et al., "Lack of antibody affinity maturation due to poor Toll-like receptor stimulation leads to enhanced respiratory syncytial virus disease," *Nat Med* (Argentina) 15, no. 1 (Jan 2009): 34–41.
127. S. Deguen et al., "Epidemiology of chicken pox in France (1991–1995)," 52, suppl. 1 (Apr 1998): 46S–49S.
128. S.S. Chaves et al., "Safety of varicella vaccine after licensure in the United States: experience from reports to the vaccine adverse event reporting system, 1995-2005," *J Infect Dis* 197, suppl. 2 (Mar 1, 2008): S170–7.
129. INFACT Canada, "Nestlé Boycott," http://www.infactcanada.ca/Nestle_Boycott.htm.
130. M.S. Patel et al., "Herpes zoster-related hospitalizations and expenditures before and after introduction of the varicella vaccine in the United States," *Infect Control Hosp Epidemiol* 29, no. 12 (Dec 2008): 1157–63.
131. S.L. Deeks et al., "Bacterial meningitis in Canada: hospitalizations (1994-2001)," *Can Commun Dis Rep* 31, no. 23 (Dec 1, 2005): 241–7.

132. J.B. McCormick, "Epidemiology of emerging/re-emerging antimicrobial-resistant bacterial pathogens," *Curr Opin Microbiol* (France) 1, no. 1 (Feb 1998): 125–9.

133. M. Inoue et al., "Why do antimicrobial agents become ineffectual?" *Yonsei Med J* 39, no. 6 (Dec 1998): 502–13.

134. Stuart B. Levy, MD, *The Antibiotic Paradox* (New York: Plenum Press, 1992).

135. N. Cimolai et al., "Invasive *Streptococcus pyogenes* infections in children," *Can J Public Health* 83, no. 3 (May–Jun 1992): 230–3.

136. R.M. Klevens et al., "Invasive methicillin-resistant Staphylococcus aureus infections in the United States," *JAMA* 298, no. 15 (Oct 17, 2007): 1763–71.

137. L.V. McFarland, "[Risk factor for antibiotic-associated diarrhea. A review of the literature]," *Ann Med Interne Paris* (France) 149, no. 5 (Sep 1998): 261–6.

138. B.A. Jobe et al., "Clostridium difficile colitis: an increasing hospital-acquired illness," *Am J Surg* 169, no. 5 (May 1995): 480–3.

139. F.L. van Buchem et al., "Primary-care-based randomised placebo-controlled trial of antibiotic treatment in acute maxillary sinusitis," *Lancet* 349, no. 9053 (Mar 8, 1997): 683–7.

140. N.T. el-Daher et al., "Immediate vs. delayed treatment of group A beta-hemolytic streptococcal pharyngitis with penicillin V," *Pediatr Infect Dis J* 10, no. 2 (Feb 1991): 126–30.

141. S.M. Schappert, "Office visits for otitis media: United States, 1975-90," *Adv Data* 214 (Sep 8, 1992): 1–19.

142. K.G. Dewey et al., "Differences in morbidity between breast-fed and formula-fed infants," *J Pediatr* 126, no. 5, part 1 (May 1995): 696–702.

143. M.L. Sassen et al., "Breast-feeding and acute otitis media," *Am J Otolaryngol* 15, no. 5 (Sep–Oct 1994): 351–7.

144. M.M. Rovers et al., "Is pacifier use a risk factor for acute otitis media? A dynamic cohort study," *Fam Pract* (The Netherlands) 25, no. 4 (Aug 2008): 233–6.

145. A. Khafif et al., "Acute mastoiditis: a 10-year review," *Am J Otolaryngol* 19, no. 3 (May–Jun 1998): 170–3.

146. P.T. Yen et al., "Brain abscess: with special reference to otolaryngologic sources of infection," *Otolaryngol Head Neck Surg* (Taiwan) 113, no. 1 (Jul 1995): 15–22.

147. Dr. Patrick Antonelli, "Doctor's Guide to Medical and Other News: Ear infection complications on the rise, researchers report," P\S\L Consulting Group Inc., Healthcare Research Partners (Sep 17, 1998): 1–3, http://www.pslgroup.com.

148. F. Tovi et al., "[Latent, non-suppurative mastoiditis. Apropos of 62 cases]," *Ann Otolaryngol Chir Cervicofac* (France) 112, no. 6 (1995): 275–8.

149. Dr. Robert Steele, "Ask the doctor—Contagiousness of sore throat and ear infection," Village Inc. (1998): 1–2, http://www.parentsplace.com.

150. S.R. Cohen and J.W. Thompson, "Otitic candidiasis in children: an evaluation of the problem and effectiveness of ketoconazole in 10 patients," *An Otol Rhinol Laryngol* 99, no. 6, part 1 (Jun 1990): 427–31.

151. R.M. Rosenfeld et al., "Clinical efficacy of antimicrobial drugs for acute otitis media: meta-analysis of 5400 children from thirty-three randomized trials," *J Pediatr* 124, no. 3 (Mar 1994): 355–67.

152. P.P. Glasziou et al., "Antibiotics for acute otitis media in children," *Cochrane Database Syst Rev* (United Kingdom) 1 (2004): CD000219.

153. R.L. Williams et al., "Use of antibiotics in preventing recurrent acute otitis media and in treating otitis media with effusion. A meta-analytic attempt to resolve the brouhaha," *JAMA* 270, no. 11 (Sep 1993): 1344–51.

154. E.I. Cantekin et al., "Antimicrobial therapy for otitis media with effusion," *JAMA* 266, no. 23 (Dec 1991): 3309–17.

155. C.T. Le et al., "Evaluation of ventilating tubes and myringotomy in the treatment of recurrent or persistent otitus media," *Pediatr Infect Dis J* 10, no. 1 (Jan 1991): 2–11.

156. F.L. van Buchem et al., "Acute otitis media: a new treatment strategy," *Br Med J (Clin Res Ed)* 290, no. 6474 (Apr 6, 1985): 1033–7.

157. WebMD Health News, "Court Rules FDA Can Regulate Supplement Marketed for Cholesterol," http://www.webmd.com/content/article/26/1728_59776.htm, July 26, 2000.

Chapter 7: Digestion Matters

1. L.T. Weaver et al., "Small intestinal length: a factor essential for gut adaptation," *Gut* 32, no. 11 (Nov 1991): 1321–3.

2. V.M. Houle et al., "Small intestinal disaccharidase activity and ileal villus height are increased in piglets consuming formula containing recombinant human insulin-like growth factor-I," *Pediatr Res* 42, no. 1 (Jul 1997): 78–86.

3. M.A. Ortega et al., "Maturation status of small intestine epithelium in rats deprived of dietary nucleotides," *Life Sci* 56, no. 19 (1995): 1623–30.

4. L. Thorell et al., "Nucleotides in human milk: sources and metabolism by the newborn infant," *Pediatr Res* (Sweden) 40, no. 6 (Dec 1996): 845–52.

5. G. Capano et al., "Polyamines in Human and Rat Milk Influence Intestinal Cell Growth In Vitro," *Gastroenterol Nutr* 27, no. 3 (Sep 1998): 281–6.

6. E.C. Dickinson et al., "Immunoglobulin A supplementation abrogates bacterial translocation and preserves the architecture of the intestinal epithelium," *Surgery* 124, no. 2 (Aug 1998): 284–90.

7. L.L. Go et al., "Quantitative and morphologic analysis of bacterial translocation in neonates," *Arch Surg* 129, no. 11 (Nov 1994): 1184–90.

8. James M. Orten and Otto W. Neuhaus, *Human Biochemistry*, ninth edition (St. Louis: The C.V. Mosby Co., 1975): 695.

9. Y. Wang et al., "The genetically programmed down-regulation of lactase in children," *Gastroenterology* (London) 114, no. 5 (June 1998): 1230–6.

10. J.J. Ellestad-Sayed and J.C. Heworth, "Disaccharide consumption and malabsorption in Canadian Indians," *Am J Clin Nutr* 30, no. 5 (May 1977): 698–703.

11. N.W. Solomons, "[Lactose and its implications in gastroenterology. Nutrition and food sciences," *Rev Invest Clin* (Guatemala) 48, suppl. (Nov 1996): 1–13.

12. E. Savilahti et al., "Congenital lactase deficiency. A clinical study on 16 patients," *Arch Dis Child* 58, no. 4 (Apr 1983): 246–52.

13. C.L. James et al., "Neonatal screening for hereditary fructose intolerance: frequency of the most common mutant aldolase B allele in the British population," *J Med Genet* 33, no. 10 (Oct 1996): 837–41.

14. P.L. Beyer et al., "Fructose intake at current levels in the United States may cause gastrointestinal distress in normal adults," *J Am Diet Assoc* 105, no. 10 (Oct 2005): 1559–66.

15. S.S. Rao et al., "Ability of the normal human small intestine to absorb fructose: evaluation by breath testing," *Clin Gastroenterol Hepatol* 5, no. 8 (Aug 2007): 959–63.

16. G. Eschenburg et al., "[Fecal sIgS and lysozyme excretion in breast feeding and formula feeding]," *Kinderarztl Prax* (Germany) 58, no. 5 (May 1990): 225–60.

17. D.G. Schmidt et al., "Raising the pH of the pepsin-catalysed hydrolysis of bovine whey proteins increases the antigenicity of the hydrolysates," *Clin Exp Allergy* (Netherlands) 25, no. 10 (Oct 1995): 1007–17

18. S.E. Balmer et al., "Diet and faecal flora in the newborn: lactoferrin," *Arch Dis Child* 64, no. 12 (Dec 1989): 1685–90.

19. G. Eschenburg et al., "[Fecal sIgS and lysozyme excretion in breast feeding and formula feeding]," *Kinderarztl Prax* (Germany) 58, no. 5 (May 1990): 225–60.

20. M. Armand et al., "Effect of human milk or formula on gastric function and fat digestion in the premature infant," *Pediatr Res* 40, no. 3 (Sep 1996): 429–37.

21. E. Freudenberg, "A lipase in the milk of the gorilla," *Experientia* 22 (1966): 317.

22. Jonathan Brostoff and Stephen J. Challacombe, eds., *Food Allergy and Intolerance*, chapter 12 by Charlotte Cunningham-Rundles (London: Baillière Tindall, 1987): 224.

23. C. Catassi et al., "Intestinal permeability changes during the first month: effect of natural versus artificial feeding," *J Pediatr Gastroenterol Nutr* 21, no. 4 (Nov 1995): 383–6.

24. La Leche League Intl., *The Womanly Art of Breastfeeding*, sixth edition (New York: pub. by Plume, a part of Penguin Putnam Inc. by arrangement with La Leche League Intl., 1997), 341–2.

25. A.G. Marsh et al., "Cortical bone density of adult lacto–ovo–vegetarian and omnivorous women," *J Am Diet Assoc* 76, no. 2 (Feb 1980): 149–51.

26. R. Itoh et al., "Dietary protein intake and urinary excretion of calcium: a cross-sectional study in a healthy Japanese population," *Am J Clin Nutr* (Tokyo) 67, no. 3 (Mar 1998): 438–44.

27. M. Hegsted and H.M. Linkswiler, "Long-term effects of level of protein intake on calcium metabolism in young adult women," *J Nutr* 111, no. 2 (Feb 1981): 244–51.

28. R. Chierici, "Supplementation of an adapted formula with bovine lactoferrin. 2. Effects on serum iron, ferritin and zinc levels," *Acta Paediatr* 81, nos. 6–7 (Jun–Jul 1992): 475–9.

29. C.P. Anyon, "Normal haemoglobin values in urban Polynesian infants: the possible deleterious influence of artificial feeding," *N Z Med J* 84, no. 578 (Dec 1976): 474–6

30. L. Dethlefsen et al., "The pervasive effects of an antibiotic on the human gut microbiota, as revealed by deep 16S rRNA sequencing," *PLoS Biol* 6, no. 11 (Nov 2008): e280.

31. M.F. Deshchekina et al., "[Study of the formation of intestinal microflora in newborn infants staying with or separated from their mothers]," *Pediatria* (Russia) 1 (1990): 13–18.

32. O.H. Braun and W.E. Heine, "[The physiologic significance of Bifidobacteria and fecal lysozyme in the breast fed infant. A contribution on the microecology of the intestine]," *Klin Padiatr* (Germany) 207, no. 1 (Jan–Feb 1995): 4–7.

33. S.S. Arnon, "Breast feeding and toxigenic intestinal infections: missing links in crib deaths?" *Rev Infect Dis* 6, suppl. 1 (Mar–Apr 1984): S193–201.

34. F. Balli et al., "[High-dose oral bacteria-therapy for chronic non-specific diarrhea of infancy]," *Pediatr Med Chir* (Italy) 14, no. 1 (Jan–Feb 1992): 13–15.

35. M.J. Hill, "Intestinal flora and endogenous vitamin synthesis," *Eur J Cancer Prev*, 6 suppl. 1 (Mar 1997): S43–5.

36. K. Fujita et al., "Vitamin K_1 and K_2 status and faecal flora in breast fed and formula fed 1-month-old infants," *Eur J Pediatr* 152, no. 10 (Oct 1993): 852–5.

37. A. Mohan et al., "The relationship between bottle usage/content, age, and number of teeth with mutans streptococci colonization in 6–24-month-old children," *Community Dent Oral Epidemiol* 26, no.1 (Feb 1998): 12–20.

38. R.O. Mattos-Graner et al., "Association between caries prevalence and clinical, microbial and dietary variables in 1.0 to .5-year-old Brazilian children," *Caries Res* (Brazil) 32, no. 5 (1998): 319–23.

39. M.C. Moreau et al., "[Effect of orally administered bovine lactoferrin and bovine IgG on the establishment of *Escherichia coli* in the digestive tract of gnotobiotic mice and human newborn infants]," *Ann Microbiol* (France) 134B, no. 3 (Nov–Dec 1983): 429–41.

40. J.M. Dolby et al., "Bacteriostasis of *Escherichia coli* by milk. II. Effect of bicarbonate and transferrin on the activity of infant feeds," *J Hyg* (London) 78 no. 2 (Apr 1977): 235–42.

41. P.T. Quinlan et al., "The relationship between stool hardness and stool composition in breast- and formula-fed infants," *J Pediatr Gastroenterol Nutr* 20, no. 1 (Jan 1995): 81–90.

42. G. Iacono et al., "Chronic constipation as a symptom of cow milk allergy," *J Pediatr* 126, no. 1 (Jan 1995): 34–9.

43. G. Iacono, "Intolerance of cow's milk and chronic constipation in children," *N Engl J Med* 339, no. 16 (Oct 15, 1998): 1100–4.

Chapter 8: In the Womb and the First Few Days

1. C.A. Sandman et al., "Maternal stress, HPA activity, and fetal/infant outcome," *Ann N Y Acad Sci* 814 (Apr 1997): 266–75.

2. M. Weinstock, "Does prenatal stress impair coping and regulation of hypothalamic–pituitary–adrenal axis?," *Neurosci Biobehav Rev* 21, no. 1 (Jan 1997): 1–10

3. S.K. Sobrian et al., "Gestational exposure to loud noise alters the development and postnatal responsiveness of humoral and cellular components of the immune system in offspring," *Environ Res* 73, nos. 1–2 (1997): 227–41.

4. F. Benini et al., "Evaluation of noise in the neonatal intensive care unit," *Am J Perinatol* 13, no. 1 (Jan 1996): 37–41.

5. P.J. Landrigan et al., "Children's health and the environment: a new agenda for prevention research," *Environ Health Perspect* 106, suppl. 3 (Jun 1998): 787–94.

6. Richard Wiles et al., "How 'bout them apples? Pesticides in children's food ten years after alar," Environmental Working Group, (Feb 1999) http://www.ewg.org.

7. T.L. Copeland et al., "Use of probabilistic methods to understand the conservatism in California's approach to assessing health risks posed by air contaminants," *Air Waste* 44, no. 12 (Dec 1994): 1399–413.

8. L.F. Paulozzi et al., "Hypospadias trends in two US surveillance systems," *Pediatrics* 100, no. 5 (Nov 1997): 831–4.

9. J.G. Koppe, "Nutrition and breast-feeding," *Eur J Obstet Gynecol Reprod Biol* (Holland) 61, no. 1 (1995): 73–8.

10. G. Ohi, "[Endocrine disrupting chemicals and carcinogenicity]," *Gan To Kagaku Ryoho* (Japan) 26, no. 3 (Feb 1999): 263–8.

11. L.E. Gray Jr. et al., "Environmental antiandrogens: low doses of the fungicide vinclozin alter sexual differentiation of the male rat," *Toxicol Ind Health* 15, nos. 1–2 (Jan–Mar 1999): 48–64.

12. I.S. Weidner et al., "Cryptorchidism and hypospadias in sons of gardeners and farmers," *Environ Health Perspect* 106, no. 12 (Dec 1998): 793–6.

13. A.M. Garcia et al., "Parental agricultural work and selected congenital malformations," *Am J Epidemiol* 149, no. 1 (Jan 1999): 64–74.

14. C. Gupta, "Reproductive malformation of the male offspring following maternal exposure to estrogenic chemicals," *Proc Soc Exp Biol Med* 224, no. 2 (Jun 2000): 61–8.

15. K.L. Howdeshell et al., "Exposure to bisphenol A advances puberty," *Nature* 401, no. 6755 (Oct 21, 1999): 763–4

16. D. Mukerjee, "Health impact of polychlorinated dibenzo-p-dioxins: a critical review," *J Air Waste Manag Assoc* 48, no. 2 (Feb 1998): 157–65.

17. S. Patandin et al., "Dietary exposure to polychlorinated biphenyls and dioxins from infancy until adulthood: A comparison between breast-feeding, toddler, and long-term exposure," *Environ Health Perspect* (Holland) 107, no. 1 (Jan 1999): 45–51.

18. S. Patandin et al., "Effects of environmental exposure to polychlorinated biphenyls and dioxins on cognitive abilities in Dutch children at 42 months of age," *J Pediatr* 134, no. 1 (Jan 1999): 33–41.

19. B.E. Richardson and D.D. Baird, "A study of milk and calcium supplement intake and subsequent preeclampsia in a cohort of pregnant women," *Am J Epidemiol* 141, no. 7 (Apr 1995): 667–73.

20. E. Oken et al., "Diet during pregnancy and risk of preeclampsia or gestational hypertension," *Ann Epidemiol* 17, no. 9 (Sep 2007): 663–8.

21. C. Qui et al., "Dietary fiber intake in early pregnancy and risk of subsequent preeclampsia," *Am J Hypertens* (Sweden) 21, no. 8 (Aug 2008): 903–9.

22. G.J. Hofmeyr et al., "Dietary calcium supplementation for prevention of pre-eclampsia and related problems: a systematic review and commentary," *BJOG* (South Africa) 114, no. 8 (Aug 2007): 933–43.

23. C.A. Aligne and J.J. Stoddard, "Tobacco and children. An economic evaluation of the medical effects of parental smoking," *Arch Pediatr Adolesc Med* 151, no. 7 (Jul 1997): 648–53.

24. Monthly Vital Statistics Report, Centers for Disease Control and Prevention 45, no. 11, suppl. (Jun 10, 1997): 2.

25. B.A. Finette et al., "Gene mutations with characteristic deletions in cord blood T lymphocytes associated with passive maternal exposure to tobacco smoke," *Nat Med* 4, no. 10 (Oct 1998): 1144–51.

26. H. Witschi et al., "The toxicology of environmental tobacco smoke," *Annu Rev Pharmacol Toxicol* 37 (1997): 29–52

27. B.T. Ji, "Paternal cigarette smoking and the risk of childhood cancer among offspring of nonsmoking mothers," *J Natl Cancer Inst* 5, no. 89 (Feb 1997): 238–44.

28. N.G. Beratis et al., "Prolactin, growth hormone and insulin-like growth factor-I in newborn children of smoking mothers," *Clin Endocrinol (Oxf)* 40, no. 2 (Feb 1994): 179–85.

29. H. Nakajima, "Response of the newborn when gently accosted by the mother immediately after birth and subsequent growth and development," *Keio J Med* (Japan) 43, no. 3 (Sep 1994): 167–70.

30. L.G. Israels et al., "The riddle of vitamin K_1 deficit in the newborn," *Semin Perinatol* 21, no. 1 (Feb 1997): 90–6.

31. P. Reverdiau-Moalic et al., "Evolution of blood coagulation activators and inhibitors in the healthy human fetus," *Blood* (France) 88, no. 3 (Aug 1996): 900–6.

32. A.H. Sutor et al., "Late form of vitamin K deficiency bleeding in Germany," *Klin Padiatr* (Germany) 207, no. 3 (May–Jun 1995): 89–97.

33. L. Parker et al., "Neonatal vitamin K administration and childhood cancer in the north of England: retrospective case-control study," *BMJ* (England) 316, no. 7126 (Jan 1998): 189–93.

34. S.J. Passmore et al., "Case-control studies of relation between childhood cancer and neonatal vitamin K administration," *BMJ* 316, no. 7126 (Jan 1998): 178–84.

35. E. Roman et al., "Vitamin K and childhood cancer: analysis of individual patient data from six case-control studies," *Br J Cancer* (United Kingdom) 86, no. 1 (Jan 2002): 63–9.

36. M. Andrew, "The relevance of developmental hemostasis to hemorrhagic disorders of newborns," *Semin Perinatol* 21, no. 1 (Feb 1997): 70–85.

37. E. Bourrat et al., "[Scleroderma-like patch on the thigh in infants after vitamin K injection at birth: six observations]," *Ann Dermatol Venereol* (France) 123, no. 10 (1996): 634–8.

38. P.M. van Hasselt et al., "Prevention of vitamin K deficiency bleeding in breastfed infants: lessons from the Dutch and Danish biliary atresia registries," *Pediatrics* (The Netherlands) 121, no. 4 (Apr 2008): e857–63.

39. T. Nishiguchi et al., "Improvement of vitamin K status of breastfeeding infants with maternal supplement of vitamin K2 (MK40)," *Semin Thromb Hemost* (Japan) 28, no. 6 (Dec 2002): 533–8.

40. S. Bolisetty, "Vitamin K in preterm breast milk with maternal supplementation," *Acta Paediatr* (Australia) 87, no. 9 (Sep 1998): 960–2.

41. K. Hogenbirk et al., "The effect of formula versus breast feeding and exogenous vitamin K1 supplementation on circulating levels of vitamin K1 and vitamin K-dependent clotting factors in newborns," *Eur J Pediatr* 152, no. 1 (Jan 1993): 72–4.

42. A. Stewart, "Etiology of childhood leukemia: a possible alternative to the Greaves hypothesis," *Leuk Res* (England) 14, nos. 11–12 (1990): 937–9.

43. D.L. Gollaher, "From ritual to science: The medical transformation of circumcision in America," *Journal of Social History* 28, no. 1 (Fall 1994): 5–36.

44. T. To et al., "Cohort study on circumcision of newborn boys and subsequent risk of urinary-tract infection," *Lancet* (Canada) 352, no. 9143 (Dec 1998): 1813–6.

45. D.M. Fergusson et al., "Neonatal circumcision and penile problems: an 8-year longitudinal study," *Pediatrics* 81, no. 4 (Apr 1988): 537–41.

46. K.A. Gracely-Kilgore, "Penile adhesion: the hidden complication of circumcision," *Nurse Pract* 9, no. 5 (May 1984): 22–4.

47. C. Tomasini et al., "Multiple pyogenic granuloma of the penis," *Sex Transm Infect* 74, no. 3 (Jun 1998): 221–2.

48. J.R. Taylor et al., "The prepuce: specialized mucosa of the penis and its loss to circumcision," *Br J Urol* 77, no. 2 (Feb 1996): 291–5.

49. W.L. Robson and A.K. Leung, "The circumcision question," *Postgrad Med* 91, no. 6 (May 1992): 237–42.

50. Y. Erk and O. Kocabalkan, "A case report of penis reconstruction for partial penis necrosis following circumcision," *Turk J Pediatr* (Turkey) 37, no. 1 (Jan–Mar 1995): 79–82.

51. J. Orozco-Sanchez and R. Neri-Vela, "[Total denudation of the penis in circumcision. Description of a plastic technique for repair of the penis]," *Bol Med Hosp Infant Mex* (Mexico) 48, no. 8 (Aug 1991): 565–9.

52. N.K. Bissada et al., "Post-circumcision carcinoma of the penis: I. Clinical aspects," *J Urol* 135, no. 2 (Feb 1986): 283–5.

53. N. Williams and L. Kapila, "Complications of circumcision," *Br J Surg* (England) 80, no. 10 (Oct 1993): 1231–6.

54. H.J. Stang and L.W. Snellman, "Circumcision practice patterns in the United States," *Pediatrics* 101, no. 6 (Jun 1998): E5.

55. Taddio et al., "Effect of neonatal circumcision on pain response during subsequent routine vaccination," *Lancet* 349, no. 9052 (Mar 1997): 599–603.

56. C. Maden et al., "History of circumcision, medical conditions, and sexual activity and risk of penile cancer," *J Natl Cancer Inst* 85, no. 1 (Jan 1993): 19–24.

57. A.G. Maiche, "Epidemiological aspects of cancer of the penis in Finland," *Eur J Cancer Prev* (Finland) 1, no. 2 (Feb 1992): 153–8.

58. F. Levi et al., "Descriptive epidemiology of vulvar and vaginal cancers in Vaud, Switzerland, 1974–1994," *Ann Oncol* 9, no. 11 (Nov 1998): 1229–32.

59. U. Kohler et al., "[Results of an individualized surgical therapy of vulvar carcinoma from 1973–1993,]" *Zentralbl Gynakol* (Germany) 119, suppl. 1 (1997): 8–16.

60. V. Mayatula and T.R. Mavundla, "A review on male circumcision procedures among South African Blacks," *Curationis* 20, no. 3 (Sep 1997): 16–20.

61. A.J. Sasco and I. Gendre, "[Current epidemiology of vulvar cancer]," *Contracept Fertil Sex* (France) 26, no. 12, (Dec 1998): 858–64.

62. R. Barrasso, "[Cancer of the uterine cervix: epidemiology and virology]," *Rev Prat* (France) 40, no. 1 (Jan 1990): 9–11.

63. S.K. Kjaer et al., "Case-control study of risk factors for cervical neoplasia in Denmark. I: Role of the "male factor" in women with one lifetime sexual partner," *Int J Cancer* 48, no. 1 (Apr 1991): 39–44.

64. E.O. Laumann et al., "Circumcision in the United States. Prevalence, prophylactic effects, and sexual practice," *JAMA* 277, no. 13 (Apr 1997): 1052–7.

65. S. Troisier, "[Sexual mutilation in women]," *Bull Acad Natl Med* (France) 179, no. 1 (Jan 1995): 135–42.

66. R. Kelly et al., "Age of male circumcision and risk of prevalent HIV infection in rural Uganda," *AIDS* 13, no. 3 (Feb 1999): 399–405.

67. J. Seed et al., "Male circumcision, sexually transmitted disease, and risk of HIV," *J Acquir Immune Defic Syndr Hum Retrovirol* 8, no. 1 (Jan 1995): 83–90.

68. E.O. Laumann et al., "Circumcision in the United States. Prevalence, prophylactic effects, and sexual practice," *JAMA* 277, no. 13 (Apr 1997): 1052–7.

69. American Academy of Pediatrics, Task Force on Circumcision, Circumcision policy statement, *Pediatrics* 103, no. 3 (Mar 1999): 686–93.

70. National Organization of Circumcision Information Resource Centers (NOCIRC), "Medical association position papers," Feb 13, 2007, http:// www.nocirc.org (accessed Apr 2009).

71. A.A. Leibowitz et al., "Determinants and policy implications of male circumcision in the United States," *Am J Public Health* 99, no. 1 (Jan 2009): 138–45.

72. R.N. Musoke et al., "Breastfeeding promotion: feeding the low birth weight infant," *Int J Gynaecol Obstet* (Kenya) 31, suppl. 1 (1990): 57–9.

73. G.P. Mathur et al., "Breastfeeding in babies delivered by cesarean section," *Indian Pediatr* 30, no. 11 (Nov 1993): 1285–90.

74. J. Meinzen-Derr et al., "Role of human milk in extremely low birth weight infants' risk of necrotizing enterocolitis or death," *J Perinatol* 29, no. 1 (Jan 2009): 57–62.

75. P.M. Sisk et al., "Early human milk feeding is associated with a lower risk of necrotizing enterocolitis in very low birth weight infants," *J Perinatol* 27, no. 7 (Jul 2007): 428–33.

76. B.R. Vohr et al., "Beneficial effects of breast milk in the neonatal intensive care unit on the developmental outcome of extremely low birth weight infants at 18 months of age," *Pediatrics* 118, no. 1 (Jul 2006): e115–23.

77. A. Ronnestad et al., "Late-onset septicemia in a Norwegian national cohort of extremely premature infants receiving very early full human milk feeding," *Pediatrics* (Norway) 115, no. 3 (Mar 2005): e269–76.

78. W. McGuire and M.Y. Anthony, "Donor human milk versus formula for preventing necrotising enterocolitis in preterm infants: systematic review," *Arch Dis Child Fetal Neonatal Ed* (Scotland) 88, no. 1 (Jan 2003): F11–4.

79. M.A. Hylander et al., "Human milk feedings and infection among very low birth weight infants," *Pediatrics* 102, no. 3 (Sep 1998): E38.

80. J. Lemus-Contreras et al., "[Morbidity reduction in preterm newborns fed with milk of their own mothers]," *Bol Med Hosp Infant Mex* (Mexico) 49, no. 10 (Oct 1992): 671–7.

81. M. Armand et al., "Effect of human milk or formula on gastric function and fat digestion in the premature infant," *Pediatr Res* 40, no. 3 (Sep 1996): 429–37.

82. R.J. Schanler et al., "Bone mineralization outcomes in human milk-fed preterm infants," *Pediatr Res* 31, no. 6 (Jun 1992): 583–6.

83. J. Ramasethu et al., "Weight gain in exclusively breastfed preterm infants," *J Trop Pediatr* (India) 39, no. 3 (Jun 1993): 152–9.

84. N.J. Bishop et al., "Early diet of preterm infants and bone mineralization at age five years," *Acta Paediatr* (England) 85, no. 2 (Feb 1996): 230–6.

85. G. Putet et al., "Nutrient balance, energy utilization, and composition of weight gain in very-low-birth-weight infants fed pooled human milk or a preterm formula," *J Pediatr* 105, no. 1 (Jul 1984): 79–85.

86. Central Intelligence Agency, The World FactBook, 2009 Estimated Country Comparisons—Infant Mortality Rate, https://www.cia.gov/library/publications/the-world-factbook/rankorder/2091rank.html.

87. M.J. Martin Puerto et al., "[Early discharge of low-birth-weight neonates. 5-year experience]," *An Esp Pediatr* (Spain) 38, no. 1 (Jan 1993): 20–4

88. L.S. Adair et al., "The duration of breast-feeding: How is it affected by biological, sociodemographic, health sector, and food industry factor?" *Demography* 30, no. 1 (Feb 1993): 63–80.

89. K. Aisaka et al., "[Effects of mother-infant interaction on maternal milk secretion and dynamics of maternal serum prolactin levels in puerperium]," *Nippon Sanka Fujinka Gakkain Zasshi* (Japan) 37, no. 5 (May 1985): 713–20.

90. V. Nedkova and S. Tanchev, "[Serum levels of prolactin, progesterone and estradiol in nursing mothers," *Akush Ginedol (Solfiia)* (Bulgaria) 34, no. 3 (1995): 22–3.

91. C.A. Boyd et al., "Donor breast milk versus infant formula for preterm infants: systematic review and meta-analysis," *Arch Dis Child Fetal Neonatal Ed* (United Kingdom) 92, no. 3 (May 2007): F169–75.

92. M.A. Quigley et al., "Formula milk versus donor breast milk for feeding preterm or low birth weight infants," *Cochrane Database Syst Rev* (United Kingdom) 17, no. 4 (Oct 2007): CD002971.

93. R.J. Schanler et al., "Randomized trial of donor human milk versus preterm formula as substitutes for mothers' own milk in the feeding of extremely premature infants," *Pediatrics* 116, no. 2 (Aug 2005): 400–6.

94. S.J. Gross, "Growth and biochemical response of preterm infants fed human milk or modified infant formula," *N Engl J Med* 308, no. 5 (Feb 3 1983): 237–41.

95. G. Boehm et al., "[Consequences of the composition of breast milk for the nutrition of underweight newborn infants. II. Lipids and lactose]," *Kinderarztl Prax* (Germany) 57, no. 9 (Sep 1989): 443–50.

96. I. Narayanan, "Human milk for low birthweight infants: immunology, nutrition and newer practical technologies," *Acta Paediatr Jpn* (Japan) 31, no. 4 (Aug 1989): 455–61.

97. K. Pridham et al., "The effects of prescribed versus ad libitum feedings and formula caloric density on premature infant dietary intake and weight gain," *Nurs Res* 48, no. 2 (Mar–Apr 1999): 86–93.

98. R.J. Schanler and S.A. Abrams, "Postnatal attainment of intrauterine macromineral accretion rates in low birth weight infants fed fortified human milk," *J Pediatr* 126, no. 3 (Mar 1995): 441–7.

99. S. Awasthi et al., "Is high protein milk beneficial for SGA-terms?" *Indian Pediatr* 26, no. 1 (Jan 1989): 45–51.

100. G. Boehm et al., "[Protein utilization by premature infants with a birth weight less than 1,500 g during nutrition with MANSAN or breast milk protein]," *Kinderarztl Prax* (German) 59, no. 1–2 (Jan–Feb 1991): 26–30.

101. E.L. Funkquist et al., "Growth and breastfeeding among low birth weight infants fed with or without protection enrichment of human milk," *Ups J Med Sci* (Sweden) 111, no. 1 (2006): 97–108.

102. R. Quan et al., "The effect of nutritional additives on anti-infective factors in human milk," *Clin Pediatr (Phila)* 33, no. 6 (Jun 1994): 325–8.

103. A. Lucas et al., "Randomized outcome trial of human milk fortification and developmental outcome in preterm infants," *Am J Clin Nutr* (England) 64, no. 2 (Aug 1996): 142–51.

104. J. Kreuder et al., "[Efficacy and side effects of differential calcium and phosphate administration in prevention of osteopenia in premature infants]," *Monatsschr Kinderheilkd* (Germany) 138, no. 11 (Nov 1990): 775–9.

105. S.J. Gross, "Bone mineralization in preterm infants fed human milk with and without mineral supplementation," *J Pediatr* 111, no. 3 (Sep 1987): 450–8.

106. E.L. Funkquist et al., "Growth and breastfeeding among low birth weight infants fed with or without protein enrichment of human milk," *Ups J Med Sci* (Sweden) 111, no. 1 (2006): 97–108.

107. C.L. Berseth et al., "Growth, efficacy, and safety of feeding an iron-fortified human milk fortifier," *Pediatrics* 114, no. 6 (Dec 2004): e699–706.

108. R.J. Schanler et al., "Feeding strategies for premature infants: beneficial outcomes of feeding fortified human milk versus preterm formula," *Pediatrics* 103, no. 6, pt. 1 (Jun 1999): 1150–7.

109. A. Lucas et al., "Randomized outcome trial of human milk fortification and developmental outcome in preterm infants," *Am J Clin Nutr* (United Kingdom) 64, no. 2 (Aug 1996): 142–51.

110. KUSCHEL 2004

111. J. Neuzil et al., "Oxidation of parenteral lipid emulsion by ambient and phototherapy lights: potential toxicity of routine parenteral feeding," *J Pediatr* 126, no. 5, part 1 (May 1995): 785–90.

112. D.A. Kelly, "Liver complications of pediatric parenteral nutrition—epidemiology," *Nutrition* 14, no. 1 (Jan 1998): 153–7.

113. R.L. Fisher, "Hepatobiliary abnormalities associated with total parenteral nutrition," *Gastroenterol Clin North Am* 18, no. 3 (Sep 1989): 645–66.

114. K.M. Gura et al., "Reversal of Parenteral Nutrition-Associated Liver Disease in Two Infants With Short Bowel Syndrome Using Parenteral Fish Oil: Implications for Future Management," *Pediatrics* 118, no. 1 (July 2006): e197-e201.

115. K. Simmer et al., "The use of breast milk in a neonatal unit and its relationship to protein and energy intake and growth," *J Paediatr Child Health* 33, no. 1 (Feb 1997): 55–60.

116. Chan GM et al., "Growth and bone mineralization in children born prematurely," *J Perinatol* 28, no. 9 (Sep 2008): 619–23.

117. F. Ovali et al., "Effects of human milk fortifier on the antimicrobial properties of human milk," *J Perinatol* (Turkey) 26, no. 12 (Dec 2006): 761–3.

118. R. Quan et al., "The effect of nutritional additives on anti-infective factors in human milk," *Clin Pediatr (Phila)* 33, no. 6 (Jun 1994): 325–8.

119. A. Lucas and T.J. Cole, "Breast milk and neonatal necrotising enterocolitis," *Lancet* (England) 336, no. 8730 (Dec 1990): 1519–23.

120. V. Araujo et al., "Impact of oxygen therapy on antioxidant status in newborns," *Biofactors* 8, nos. 1–2 (1998): 143–7.

121. L. Daniels et al., "Selenium status of preterm infants: the effect of postnatal age and method of feeding," *Acta Paediatr* 86, no. 3 (Mar 1997) 281–8.

122. G.P. Mathur et al., "Breastfeeding in babies delivered by cesarean section," *Indian Pediatr* 30, no. 11 (Nov 1993): 1285–90.

123. J. Martin-Calama et al., "The effect of feeding glucose water to breastfeeding newborns on weight, body temperature, blood glucose, and breastfeeding duration," *J Hum Lact* 13, no. 3 (Sep 1997): 209–13.

124. R. Stocker et al., "Bilirubin is an antioxidant of possible physiological importance," *Science* 235, no. 4792 (Feb 27, 1987): 1043–6.

125. E. Heyman et al., "Retinopathy of prematurity and bilirubin," *N Engl J Med* 320, no. 4: (Jan 1989): 256.

126. S. Doré and S.H. Snyder, "Neuroprotective action of bilirubin against oxidative stress in primary hippocampal cultures," *Ann N Y Acad Sci* 890 (1999): 167–72.

Chapter 9: Baby's Nutritional Beginnings

1. S.E. Nelson, "Absorption of fat and calcium by infants fed a milk-based formula containing palm olein," *J Am Coll Nutr* 17, no. 4 (Aug 1998): 327–32.

2. L.A. Baur et al., "The fatty acid composition of skeletal muscle membrane phospholipid: its relationship with the type of feeding and plasma glucose levels in young children," *Metabolism* (Australia) 47, no. 1 (Jan 1998): 106–12.

3. P.T. Quinlan et al., "The relationship between stool hardness and stool composition in breast- and formula-fed infants," *J Pediatr Gastroenterol Nutr* 20, no. 1 (Jan 1995): 81–90.

4. C.P. Anyon, "Normal haemoglobin values in urban Polynesian infants: the possible deleterious influence of artificial feeding," *NZ Med J* 84 (1976): 474–476.

5. J. Williams et al., "Iron supplemented formula milk related to reduction in psychomotor decline in infants from inner city areas: randomised study," *BMJ* 318, no. 7185 (Mar 1999): 693–7.

6. E.K. Hurtado et al., "Early childhood anemia and mild or moderate mental retardation," *Am J Clin Nutr* 69, no. 1 (Jan 1999): 115–9.

7. P. MacDougall, "Breast milk versus cow's milk," BC Ped Res, Children and Women's Health Center of British Columbia, 1997, http://www.childhosp.bc.ca.

8. J. Williams et al., "Iron supplemented formula milk related to reduction in psychomotor decline in infants from inner city areas: randomised study," *BMJ* 318, no. 7185 (Mar 1999): 693–7.

9. E.A. Mevissen-Verhage et al., "Effect of iron on serotypes and haemagglutination patterns of *Escherichia coli* in bottle-fed infants," *Eur J Clin Microbiol* 4, no. 6 (Dec 1985): 570–4.

10. B. Lönnerdal and O. Hernell, "Iron, zinc, copper and selenium status of breast-fed infants and infants fed trace element fortified milk-based infant formula," *Acta Paediatr* 83, no. 4 (Apr 1994): 367–73.

11. F. Haschke et al., "Iron nutrition and growth of breast- and formula-fed infants during the first 9 months of life," *J Pediatr Gastroenterol Nutr* (Austria) 16, no. 2 (Feb 1993): 151–6.

12. T. Walter et al., "Prevention of iron-deficiency anemia: comparison of high- and low-iron formulas in term healthy infants after six months of life," *J Pediatr* 132, no. 4 (Apr 1998): 635–40.

13. B. Lönnerdal and O. Hernell, "Iron, zinc, copper and selenium status of breast-fed infants and infants fed trace element fortified milk-based infant formula," *Acta Paediatr* 83, no. 4 (Apr 1994): 367–73.

14. M.A. Siimes et al., "Exclusive breast-feeding for 9 months: risk of iron deficiency," *J Pediatr* 104, no. 2 (Feb 1984): 196–9.

15. B. Duncan et al., "Iron and the exclusively breast-fed infant from birth to six months," *J Pediatr Gastroenterol Nutr* 4, no. 3 (Jun 1985): 421–5.

16. A. Baykan et al., "Does maternal iron supplementation during the lactation period affect iron status of exclusively breast-fed infants?" *Turk J Pediatr* (Turkey) 48, no. 4 (Oct–Dec 2006): 301–7.

17. P.D. Scariati et al., "Risk of diarrhea related to iron content of infant formula: lack of evidence to support the use of low-iron formula as a supplement for breastfed infants," *Pediatrics* 99, no. 3 (Mar 1997): E2.

18. M.A. Siimes et al., "Exclusive breast-feeding for 9 months: risk of iron deficiency," *J Pediatr* 104, no. 2 (Feb 1984): 196–9.

19. F.A. Oski and S.A. Landaw, "Inhibition of iron absorption from human milk by baby food," *Am J Dis Child* 134, no. 5 (May 1980): 459–60.

20. E.E. Ziegler et al., "Iron supplementation of breastfed infants from an early age," *Am J Clin Nutr* 89, no. 2 (Feb 2009): 525–32.

21. E.C. Monterrosa et al., "Predominant breast-feeding from birth to six months is associated with fewer gastrointestinal infections and increased risk for iron deficiency among infants," *J Nutr* (Canada) 138, no. 8 (Aug 2008): 1499–504.

22. A. Pisacane et al., "Iron status in breast-fed infants," *J Pediatr* (Italy) 127, no. 3 (Sep 1995): 429–31.

23. P. Hemalatha et al., "Zinc status of breastfed and formula-fed infants of different gestational ages," *J Trop Pediatr* 43, no. 1 (Feb 1997): 52–4.

24. R.M. Ortega et al., "[Supplementation with iron and folates during gestation: influence on the zinc status in the mother and on the zinc content in the maternal milk]," *Med Clin (Barc)* (Spain) 111, no. 8 (Sep 1998): 281–5.

25. D. Chlubek, "[Interaction of fluoride with milk constituents]," *Ann Acad Med Stetin* (Poland) 39 (1993): 23–38.

26. K.E. Heller et al., "Dental caries and dental fluorosis at varying water fluoride concentrations," *J Public Health Dent* 57, no. 3 (Summer 1997): 136–43.

27. D.J. Brothwell and H. Limeback, "Fluorosis risk in grade 2 students residing in a rural area with widely varying natural fluoride," *Community Dent Oral Epidemiol* (Canada) 27, no. 2 (Apr 1999): 130–6.

28. M. Diesendorf et al., "*Aust N Z J Public Health* (Australia) 21, no. 2 (Apr 1997): 187–90.

29. E.H. Abdennebi et al., "Human fluorosis in Morocco: analytical and clinical investigations," *Vet Hum Toxicol* (Morocco) 37, no. 5 (Oct 1995): 465–8.

30. S Dasarathy et al., "Gastroduodenal manifestations in patients with skeletal fluorosis," *J Gastroenterol* (India) 31, no. 3 (Jun 1996): 333–7.

31. P.K. DenBesten, "Biological mechanisms of dental fluorosis relevant to the use of fluoride supplements," *Community Dent Oral Epidemiol* 27, no. 1 (Feb 1999): 41–7.

32. N.J. Wang and P.J. Riordan, "Fluoride supplements and caries in a non-fluoridated child population," *Community Dent Oral Epidemiol* (Norway) 27, no. 2 (Apr 1999): 117–23.

33. A.I. Ismail and R.R. Bandekar, "Fluoride supplements and fluorosis: a meta-analysis," *Community Dent Oral Epidemiol* 27, no. 1 (Feb 1999): 48–56.

34. P.J. Riordan, "Dental fluorosis, dental caries and fluoride exposure among 7-year-olds," *Caries Res* 27, no. 1 (1993): 71–7.

35. D.J. Brothwell and H. Limeback, "Fluorosis risk in grade 2 students residing in a rural area with widely varying natural fluoride," *Community Dent Oral Epidemiol* (Canada) 27, no. 2 (Apr 1999): 130–6.

36. C.J. Spak et al., "Fluoride in human milk," *Acta Paediatr Scand* 72, no. 5 (Sep 1983): 699–701.

37. P.J. Riordan, "The place of fluoride supplements in caries prevention today," *Aust Dent J* (Australia) 41, no. 5 (Oct 1996): 335–42.

38. M.T. Pugliese et al., "Nutritional rickets in suburbia," *J Am Coll Nutr* 17, no. 6 (Dec 1998): 637–41.

39. M.J. Park, "Bone mineral content is not reduced despite low vitamin D status in breast milk-fed infants versus cow's milk based formula-fed infants," *J Pediatr* 132, no. 4 (Apr 1998): 641–5.

40. M. Cosgrove, "Perinatal and infant nutrition. Nucleotides," *Nutrition* (England) 14, no. 10 (Oct 1998): 748–51.

41. V.Y. Yu, "The role of dietary nucleotides in neonatal and infant nutrition," *Singapore Med J* (Australia) 39, no. 4 (Apr 1998): 145–50.

42. G. Sarwar et al., "Free amino acids in milks of human subjects, other primates and non-primates," *Br J Nutr* 79, no. 2 (Feb 1998): 129–31.

43. S. Desantiago et al., "[Free amino acids in plasma and milk of Mexican rural lactating women]," *Rev Invest Clin* (Mexico) 50, no. 5 (Sep–Oct 1998): 405–12.

44. Z. Kurugöl et al., "Comparison of growth, serum prealbumin, transferrin, IgG and amino acids of term infants fed breast milk or formula," *Turk J Pediatr* 39, no. 2 (Apr 1997): 195–202.

45. W.E. Heine et al., "The importance of alpha-lactalbumin in infant nutrition," *J Nutr* 121, no. 3 (Mar 1991): 277–83.

46. B. Lönnerdal, "Effects of milk and milk components on calcium, magnesium, and trace element absorption during infancy," *Physiol Rev* 77, no. 3 (Jul 1997): 643–669.

47. B. Lönnerdal et al., "Effect of reducing the phytate content and of partially hydrolyzing the protein content in soy formula on zinc and copper absorption and status in infant rhesus monkeys and rat pups," *Am J Clin Nutr* 69, no. 3 (Mar 1999): 490–6.

48. S.R. Lynch et al., "Inhibitory effect of a soybean-protein-related moiety on iron absorption in humans," *Am J Clin Nutr* 60, no. 4 (Oct 1994): 567–72.

49. B. Lönnerdal, "Nutritional aspects of soy formula," *Acta Paediatr Suppl* 402 (Sep 1994): 105–8.

50. K.D. Setchell et al., "Isoflavone content of infant formulas and the metabolic fate of these phytoestrogens in early life," *Am J Clin Nutr* 68, no. 6, suppl. (Dec 1998): 1453S–61S.

51. A.A. Franke et al., "Isoflavones in human breast milk and other biological fluids," *Am J Clin Nutr* 68, no. 6, suppl. (Dec 1998): 1466S–73S.

52. D.M. Sheehan, "Herbal medicines, phytoestrogens and toxicity: risk:benefit considerations," *Proc Soc Exp Biol Med* 217, no. 3 (Mar 1998): 379–85.

53. James M. Orten and Otto W. Neuhaus, *Human Biochemistry*, ninth edition (St. Louis: The C.V. Mosby Co., 1975): 248–9, 694–5.

54. K. Yoneyama et al., "[Change in the concentrations of nutrient components of human milk during lactation]," *Nippon Koshu Eisei Zasshi* (Japan) 42, no. 7 (Jul 1995): 472–81.

55. G.V. Coppa et al., "Changes in carbohydrate composition in human milk over 4 months of lactation," *Pediatrics* (Italy) 91, no. 3 (Mar 1993): 637–41.

56. M.V. Karra et al., "Zinc, calcium, and magnesium concentrations in milk from American and Egyptian women throughout the first 6 months of lactation," *Am J Clin Nutr* 47, no. 4 (Apr 1988): 642–8.

57. M.A. Laskey et al., "Breast-milk calcium concentrations during prolonged lactation in British and rural Gambian mothers," *Acta Paediatr Scand* (England) 79, no. 5 (May 1990): 507–12.

58. B. Fournier et al., "Variations of phylloquinone concentration in human milk at various stages of lactation and in cow's milk at various seasons," *Am J Clin Nutr* 45, no. 3 (Mar 1987): 551–8.

59. K.G. Dewey, "Growth of breast-fed and formula-fed infants from 0 to 18 months: the DARLING Study," *Pediatrics* 89, no. 6, part 1 (Jun 1992): 1035–41.

60. K.G. Dewey et al., "Breast-fed infants are leaner than formula-fed infants at 1 year of age: the DARLING Study," *Am J Clin Nutr* 57, no. 2 (Feb 1993): 140–5.

61. M. Prokopec and F. Bellisle, "Adiposity in Czech children followed from 1 month of age to adulthood: analysis of individual BMI patterns," *Ann Hum Biol* (Czech Republic) 20, no. 6 (Nov–Dec 1993): 517–25.

62. B.S. Simic, "Childhood obesity as a risk factor in adulthood and its prevention," *Prev Med* 12, no. 1 (Jan 1983): 47–51.

63. B. Lönnerdal, "Effects of milk and milk components on calcium, magnesium, and trace element absorption during infancy," *Physiol Rev* 77 (1997): 643–669.

64. D.R. Woodward et al., "Human milk fat content: within-feed variation," *Early Hum Dev* (Australia) 19, no. 1 (Apr 1989): 39–46.

65. X. Casabiell at al., "Presence of leptin in colostrum and/or breast milk from lactating mothers: a potential role in the regulation of neonatal food intake," *J Clin Endocrinol Metab* (Spain) 82, no. 12 (Dec 1997): 4270–3.

66. S.J. Fomon et al., "Infant formula with protein-energy ratio of 1.7 g/100 kcal is adequate but may not be safe," *J Pediatr Gastroenterol Nutr* 28, no. 5 (May 1999): 495–501.

67. K.G. Dewey et al., "Do exclusively breast-fed infants require extra protein?" *Pediatr Res* 39, no. 2 (Feb 1996): 303–7.

68. K.G. Dewey et al., "Breast-fed infants are leaner than formula-fed infants at 1 year of age: the DARLING Study," *Am J Clin Nutr* 57, no. 2 (Feb 1993): 140–5.

69. E.A. Simoes and S.M. Pereira, "The growth of exclusively breastfed infants," *Ann Trop Paediatr* 6, no. 1 (Mar 1986): 17–21.

70. Naomi Baumslag, MD and Dia L. Michels, *Milk, Money, and Madness: The culture and politics of breastfeeding* (Westport, Connecticut: Bergin & Garvey, 1995).

71. M.B. Belfort et al., "Infant growth and child cognition at 3 years of age," *Pediatrics* 122, no. 3 (Sep 2008): e689–95.

72. R. von Kries et al., "Breast feeding and obesity: cross sectional study," *Br Med J* 319, no. 7203 (Jul 17, 1999): 147–50.

73. K.G. Dewey et al., "Adequacy of energy intake among breast-fed infants in the DARLING study: relationships to growth velocity, morbidity, and activity levels. Davis Area Research on Lactation, Infant Nutrition and Growth," *J Pediatr* 119, no. 4 (Oct 1991): 538–47.

74. D. Skuse et al., "Postnatal growth and mental development: evidence for a "sensitive period," *J Child Psychol Psychiatry* 35, no. 3 (Mar 1994): 521–45.

75. K.C. Mehta et al., "Trial on timing of introduction to solids and food type on infant growth," *Pediatrics* 102, no. 3, part 1 (Sep 1998): 569–73.

76. H.C. Borresen, "[A questionable guideline on introduction of solid food to breast-fed infants]," *Tidsskr Nor Laegeforen* (Norway) 114, no. 26 (Oct 30, 1994): 3087–9.

77. K.B. Simondon and F. Simondon, "Age at introduction of complementary food and physical growth from 2 to 9 months in rural Senegal," *Eur J Clin Nutr* 51, no. 10 (Oct 1997): 703–7.

78. S. Cosminsky et al., "Child feeding practices in a rural area of Zimbabwe," *Soc Sci Med* 36, no. 7 (Apr 1993): 937–47.

79. S.A. Quandt, "The effect of beikost on the diet of breast-fed infants," *J Am Diet Assoc* 84, no. 1 (Jan 1984): 47–51.

80. B. Kuate Defo, "Effects of infant feeding practices and birth spacing on infant and child survival: a reassessment from retrospective and prospective data," *J Biosoc Sci* (Canada) 29, no. 3 (Jul 1997): 303–26.

81. L.L. Birch, "Development of food acceptance patterns in the first years of life," *Proc Nutr Soc* 57, no. 4 (Nov 1998): 617–24.

Chapter 10: Baby Feeding: Facts and Fallacies

1. F.A. Oski, "Infant nutrition, physical growth, breastfeeding, and general nutrition," *Curr Opin Pediatr* 5, no. 3 (Jun 1993): 385–8.

2. H.C. Borresen, "[A questionable guideline on introduction of solid food to breast-fed infants," *Tidsskr Nor Laegeforen* (Norway) 114, no. 26 (Oct 30, 1994): 3087–9.

3. D.J. Chapman and R. Perez-Escamilla, "Identification of risk factors for delayed onset of lactation," *J Am Diet Assoc* 99, no. 4 (Apr 1999): 450–4.

4. K. Nemba, "Induced lactation: a study of 37 non-puerperal mothers," *J Trop Pediatr* 40, no. 4 (Aug 1994): 240–2.

5. M.L. Macknin et al., "Infant sleep and bedtime cereal," *Am J Dis Child* 143, no. 9 (Sep 1989): 1066–8.

6. R.R. Bainbridge et al., "Effect of rice cereal feedings on bone mineralization and calcium homeostasis in cow milk formula fed infants," *J Am Coll Nutr* 15, no. 4 (Aug 1996): 383–8.

7. R.J. Shulman et al., "Impact of dietary cereal on nutrient absorption and fecal nitrogen loss in formula-fed infants," *J Pediatr* 118, no. 1 (Jan 1991): 39–43.

8. A.A. al-Dashti et al., "Breast feeding, bottle feeding and dental caries in Kuwait, a country with low-fluoride levels in the water supply," *Community Dent Health* (England) 12, no. 1 (Mar 1995): 42–7.

9. R.O. Mattos-Graner et al., "Association between caries prevalence and clinical, microbiological and dietary variables in 1.0 to 2.5-year-old Brazilian children," *Caries Res* 32, no. 5 (1998): 319–23.

10. N. Kanou et al., "[Investigation into the actual condition of outpatients. II. Correlation between the daily habits of eating and toothbrushing and the prevalence of dental caries incidence]," *Shoni Shikagaku Zasshi* (Japan) 27, no. 2 (1989): 467–74.

11. A. Mohan et al., "The relationship between bottle usage/content, age, and number of teeth with mutans streptococci colonization in 6–24-month-old children," *Comm Dent Oral Epidemiol* 26, no. 1 (Feb 1998): 12–20.

12. V. White, "Breastfeeding and the risk of early childhood caries," *Evid Based Dent* 9, no. 3 (2008): 86–8.

13. S.Z. Mohebbi et al., "Feeding habits as determinants of early childhood caries in a population where prolonged breastfeeding is the norm," *Community Dent Oral Epidemiol* 36, no. 4 (Aug 2008): 363–9.

14. L. Lopez Del Valle et al., "Early childhood caries and risk factors in rural Puerto Rican children," *ASDC J Dent Child* 65, no. 2 (Mar–Apr 1998): 132–5.

15. A.L. Hallonsten et al., "Dental caries and prolonged breast-feeding in 18-month-old Swedish children," *Int J Paediatr Dent* (Sweden) 5, no. 3 (Sep 1995): 149–55.

16. M.I. Matee et al., "*Mutans streptococci* and lactobacilli in breast-fed children with rampant caries," *Caries Res* (Tanzania) 26, no. 3 (1992): 183–7.

17. P.R. Erickson and E. Mazhari, "Investigation of the role of human breast milk in caries development," *Pediatr Dent* 21, no. 2 (Mar–Apr 1999): 86–90.

18. C. Sheikh and P.R. Erickson, "Evaluation of plaque pH changes following oral rinse with eight infant formulas," *Pediatr Dent* 18, no. 3 (May–Jun 1996): 200–4.

19. D. Birkhed et al., "pH changes in human dental plaque from lactose and milk before and after adaptation," *Caries Res* 27, no. 1 (1993): 43–50.

20. P. Ollila et al., "Prolonged pacifier-sucking and use of a nursing bottle at night: possible risk factors for dental caries in children," *Acta Odontol Scand* 56, no. 4 (Aug 1998): 233–7.

21. H.J. Kalkwarf et al., "The effect of calcium supplementation on bone density during lactation and after weaning," *N Engl J Med* 337, no. 8 (Aug 1997): 523–8.

22. K.D. Little and J.F. Clapp III, "Self-selected recreational exercise has no impact on early postpartum lactation-induced bone loss," *Med Sci Sports Exerc* 30, no. 6 (Jun 1998): 831–6.

23. M. Sowers et al., "Changes in bone density with lactation," *JAMA* 269, no. 24 (Jun 23–30, 1993): 3130–5.

24. R.G. Cumming and R.J. Klineberg, "Breastfeeding and other reproductive factors and the risk of hip fractures in elderly women," *Int J Epidemiol* (Australia) 22, no. 4 (Aug 1993): 684–91.

25. J.H. Himes et al., "Maternal supplementation and bone growth in infancy," *Paediatr Perinat Epidemiol* 4, no. 4 (Oct 1990): 436–47.

26. L.H. Amir et al., "*Candida albicans*: is it associated with nipple pain in lactating women?" *Gynecol Obstet Invest* (Australia) 41, no. 1 (1996): 30–4.

27. L. Amir, "Candida and the lactating breast: predisposing factors," *J Hum Lact* 7, no. 4 (Dec 1991): 177–81.

28. P. Thomassen et al., "Breast-feeding, pain and infection," *Gynecol Obstet Invest* 46, no. 2 (Aug 1998): 73–4.
29. S. Matsuda, "Transfer of antibiotics into maternal milk," *Biol Res Pregnancy Perinatol* 5, no. 2 (1984): 57–60.
30. K.E. Tanguay et al., "Nipple candidiasis among breastfeeding mothers. Case-control study of predisposing factors," *Can Fam Physician* (Canada) 40 (Aug 1994): 1407–13.
31. K. Katsouyanni et al., "A case-control study of lactation and cancer of the breast," *Br J Cancer* (Greece) 73, no. 6 (Mar 1996): 814–8.
32. F.D. Gilliland et al., "Reproductive risk factors for breast cancer in Hispanic and non-Hispanic white women: the New Mexico Women's Health Study," *Am J Epidemiol* 148, no. 7 (Oct 1998): 683–92.
33. L.G. Ries et al., "SEER Cancer Statistics Review, 1973–94: Tables and Graphs," National Cancer Institute, Bethesda, MD, NIH Publication No. 97-2789, (1997).
34. V. Siskind et al., "Breastfeeding, menopause, and epithelial ovarian cancer," *Epidemiology* (Australia) 8, no. 2 (Mar 1997): 188–91.
35. M. Altemus et al., "Suppression of hypothalamic–pituitary–adrenal axis responses to stress in lactating women," *J Clin Endocrinol Metab* 80, no. 10 (Oct 1995): 2954–9.
36. K. Uvnas-Moberg et al. "Oxytocin and prolactin levels in breast-feeding women. Correlation with milk yield and duration of breast-feeding," *Acta Obstet Gynecol Scand* (Sweden) 69, no. 4 (1990): 301–6.
37. M. Petersson et al., "Oxytocin causes a long-term decrease of blood pressure in female and male rats," *Physiol Behav* 60, no. 5 (Nov 1996): 1311–5.
38. Naomi Baumslag, MD, and Dia L. Michels, "*Milk, Money, and Madness, The Culture and Politics of Breastfeeding,*" (Westport, Connecticut: Bergin & Garvey, 1995).
39. A. Pallone and M. Tienda, "The effects of breastfeeding and pace of childbearing on mortality at early ages," *Demography* 23, no. 1 (Feb 1986): 31–52.
40. B. Kuate Defo, "Effects of infant feeding practices and birth spacing on infant and child survival: a reassessment from retrospective and prospective data," *J Biosoc Sci* (Canada) 29, no. 3 (Jul 1997): 303–26.
41. R.K. Valaitis and E. Shea, "An evaluation of breastfeeding promotion literature: does it really promote breast-feeding?" *Can J Public Health* (Canada) 84, no. 1 (Jan–Feb 1993): 24–7.
42. J. Wise, "Companies still breaking milk marketing code," *BMJ* 316, no. 7138 (April 11, 1998): 1115.
43. L.S. Adair et al., "The duration of breast-feeding: How is it affected by biological, sociodemographic, health sector, and food industry factors?" *Demography* 30, no. 1 (Feb 1993): 63–80.
44. Ginty, Molly M., "Feds EnticeBlack Mothers to Bottle Feed," Nov 11, 2008, http://www.womensenews.org/article.cfm/dyn/aid/3825Industry.
45. E. Romero-Gwynn, "Breast-feeding pattern among Indochinese immigrants in northern California, *Am J Dis Child* 143, no. 7 (Jul 1989): 804–8.
46. L.B. Feldman-Winter et al., "Pediatricians and the promotion and support of breastfeeding," *Arch Pediatr Adolesc Med* 162, no. 12 (Dec 2008): 1142–9.
47. G.L. Freed et al., "Pediatrician involvement in breast-feeding promotion: a national study of residents and practitioners," *Pediatrics* 96, no. 3, part 1 (Sep 1995): 490–4.
48. P.P. Meier et al., "Breastfeeding support services in the neonatal intensive-care unit," *J Obstet Gynecol Neonatal Nurs* 22, no. 4 (Jul–Aug 1993): 338–47.
49. J.M. Riordan, "The cost of not breastfeeding: a commentary," *J Hum Lact* 13, no. 2 (Jun 1997): 93–7.
50. J.D. Skinner et al., "Transitions in infant feeding during the first year of life," *J Am Coll Nutr* 16, no. 3 (Jun 1997): 209–15.
51. Central Intelligence Agency, The World FactBook, 2009 Estimated Country Comparisons—Infant Mortality Rate, https://www.cia.gov/library/publications/the-world-factbook/rankorder/2091rank.html.
52. Unicef: State of the World's Children, Under-five mortality rankings (among 194 nations), 2007, http://www.unicef.org/sowc09/docs/SOWC09-U5MR.xls.
53. A.H. Goodman et al., "The chronological distribution of enamel hypoplasias from prehistoric Dickson Mounds populations," *Am J Phys Anthropol* 65, no. 3 (Nov 1984): 259–66.
54. L.E. Wright and H.P. Schwarcz, "Stable carbon and oxygen isotopes in human tooth enamel: identifying breastfeeding and weaning in prehistory," *Am J Phys Anthropol* 106, no. 1 (May 1998): 1–18.
55. K.M. Lanphear, "Frequency and distribution of enamel hypoplasias in a historic skeletal sample," *Am J Phys Anthropol* 81, no. 1 (Jan 1990): 35–43.
56. J. Moggi-Cecchi et al., "Enamel hypoplasias in a 19th century population from northern Italy," *Anthropol Anz* 51, no. 2 (Jun 1993): 123–9.
57. J. Wallis, "A survey of reproductive parameters in the free-ranging chimpanzees of Gombe National Park," *J Reprod Fertil* 109, no. 2 (Mar 1997): 297–307.
58. L.D. Hammer et al., "Development of feeding practices during the first 5 years of life," *Arch Pediatr Adolesc Med* 153, no. 2 (Feb 1999): 189–94.

Chapter 11: The Dangers of Cow's Milk

1. E.E. Ziegler, "Adverse effects of cow's milk in infants," *Nestlé Nutr Workshop Ser Pediatr Program* 60 (2007): 185–96.

2. J.M. Norris et al., "Lack of association between early exposure to cow's milk protein and beta-cell autoimmunity. Diabetes autoimmunity study in the young," *JAMA* 276, no. 8 (Aug 1996): 609–14.

3. R.B. Elliott et al., "Type I (insulin-dependent) diabetes mellitus and cow milk: casein variant consumption," *Diabetologia* (New Zealand) 42, no. 3 (Mar 1999): 292–6.

4. S.G. Gimeno and J.M. deSouza, "IDDM and milk consumption: A case-control study in Sao Paulo, Brazil," *Diabetes Care* (Brazil) 20, no. 8 (Aug 1997): 1256–60.

5. J. Karjalainen et al., "A bovine albumin peptide as a possible trigger of insulin-dependent diabetes mellitus," *N Engl J Med* (Canada) 327, no. 5 (Jul 30, 1992): 302–7.

6. T. Saukkonen et al., "Significance of cow's milk protein antibodies as risk factor for childhood IDDM: interactions with dietary cow's milk intake and HLA-DQB1 genotype. Childhood Diabetes in Finland Study Group," *Diabetologia* (Finland) 41, no. 1 (Jan 1998): 72–8.

7. S.M. Virtanen et al., "Diet, cow's milk protein antibodies and the risk of IDDM in Finnish children. Childhood Diabetes in Finland Study Group," *Diabetologia* (Finland) 37, no. 4 (Apr 1994): 381–7.

8. P. Vähäsalo et al., "Relation between antibodies to islet cell antigens, other autoantigens, and cow's milk proteins in diabetic children and unaffected siblings as the clinical manifestation of IDDM," *Autoimmunity* (Finland) 23, no. 3 (1996): 165–74.

9. B. Rami et al., "Risk factors for type I diabetes mellitus in children in Austria," *Eur J Pediatr* (Austria) 158, no. 5 (May 1999): 362–6.

10. Y. Fukushima et al., "Consumption of cow milk and egg by lactating women and the presence of beta-lactoglobulin and ovalbumin in breast milk," *Am J Clin Nutr* (Japan) 65, no. 1 (Jan 1997): 30–5.

11. R. Sorva et al., "Beta-lactoglobulin secretion in human milk varies widely after cow's milk ingestion in mothers of infants with cow's milk allergy," *J Allergy Clin Immunol* (Finland) 93, no. 4 (Apr 1994): 787–92.

12. F. Perez Bravo et al., "Genetic predisposition and environmental factors leading to the development of insulin-dependent diabetes mellitus in Chilean children," *J Mol Med* (Chile) 74, no. 2 (Feb 1996): 105–9.

13. D.J. Pettitt et al., "Breastfeeding and incidence of non-insulin-dependent diabetes mellitus in Pima Indians," *Lancet* 350, no. 9072 (Jul 1997): 166–8.

14. K. Dahl-Jorgensen et al., "Relationship between cow's milk consumption and incidence of IDDM in childhood," *Diabetes Care* (Norway) 14, no. 11 (Nov 1991): 1081–3.

15. A.L. Drash et al., "The interface between epidemiology and molecular biology in the search for the causes of insulin-dependent diabetes mellitus," *Ann Med* 23, no. 4 (Oct 1991): 463–71.

16. A.D. Liese et al., "The burden of diabetes mellitus among US youth: prevalence estimates from the SEARCH for Diabetes in Youth Study," *Pediatrics* 118, no. 4 (Oct 2006): 1510–8.

17. K.M. Narayan et al., "Impact of recent increase in incidence on future diabetes burden: U.S., 2005-2050," *Diabetes Care* 29, no. 9 (Sep 2006): 2144–6.

18. G. Dahlquist et al., "An increased level of antibodies to beta-lactoglobulin is a risk determinant for early-onset type I (insulin-dependent) diabetes mellitus independent of islet cell antibodies and early introduction of cow's milk," *Diabetologia* (Sweden) 35, no. 10 (Oct 1992): 980–4.

19. D. Cislak et al., "[Frequency of appearance of antibodies to bovine serum albumin in children with diabetes type I]," *Pol Arch Med Wewn* (Poland) 100, no. 2 (Aug 1998): 106–10.

20. B.E. Birgisdottir et al., "Lower consumption of cow milk protein A1 beta-casein at 2 years of age, rather than consumption among 11- to 14-year-old adolescents, may explain the lower incidence of type 1 diabetes in Iceland than in Scandinavia," *Ann Nutr Metab* (Iceland) 50, no. 3 (2006): 177-83.

21. M.G. Cavallo et al., "Cell-mediated immune response to beta casein in recent-onset insulin-dependent diabetes: implications for disease pathogenesis," *Lancet* (Italy) 348, no. 9032 (Oct 1996): 926–8.

22. L. Monetini et al., "Antibodies to bovine beta-casein in diabetes and other autoimmune diseases," *Horm Metab Res* (Italy) 34, no. 8 (Aug 2002): 455-9.

23. O. Vaarala et al., "Cow milk feeding induces antibodies to insulin in children—a link between cow milk and insulin-dependent diabetes mellitus?" *Scand J Immunol* (Finland) 47, no. 2 (Feb 1998): 131–5.

24. G. Dahlquist, "The aetiology of type 1 diabetes: an epidemiological perspective," *Acta Paediatr Suppl* (Sweden) 425 (Oct 1998): 5–10.

25. G. Dahlquist, "Viruses and other perinatal exposures as initiating events for beta-cell destruction," *Ann Med* (Sweden) 29, no. 5 (Oct 1997): 413–7.

26. S.M. Virtanen et al., "Cow's milk consumption, disease-associated autoantibodies and type-1 diabetes mellitus: a follow-up study in siblings of diabetic children. Childhood Diabetes in Finland Study Group," *Diabet Med* (Finland) 15, no. 9 (Sep 1998): 730–8.

27. D. Kitts, Y. Yaun et al., "Adverse reactions to food constituents: allergy, intolerance, and autoimmunity," *Can J Physiol Pharmacol* (Canada) 75, no. 4 (April 1997): 241–54.

28. Wikinews, "Finnish parliamentary ombudsman faults infant formula study," November 2, 2006, http://en.wikinews.org/wiki/Finnish_Infant_Formula_Study_Without_Informed_Consent

29. N. Shehadeh et al., "Importance of insulin content in infant diet: suggestion for a new infant formula," *Acta Paediatr* (Israel) 90, no. 1 (Jan 2001): 93-5.

30. D. Malosse et al., "Correlation between milk and dairy product consumption and multiple sclerosis prevalence: a worldwide study," *Neuroepidemiology* (France) 11, no. 4–6 (1992): 304–12.

31. P.J. Butcher, "Milk consumption and multiple sclerosis-an etiological hypothesis," *Med Hypotheses* 19, no. 2 (Feb 1986): 169-78.

32. K. Lauer, "Diet and multiple sclerosis," (Germany) 49, no. 2, suppl. 2 (Aug 1997): S55–61.

33. S. Winer et al., "T cells of multiple sclerosis patients target a common environmental peptide that causes encephalitis in mice," *J Immunol* (Canada) 166, no. 7 (Apr 1, 2001): 4751-6.

34. B. Banwell et al., "Abnormal T-cell reactivities in childhood inflammatory demyelinating disease and type 1 diabetes," *Ann Neurol* 63, no. 1 (Jan 2008): 98–111.

35. J. Guggenmos et al., "Antibody cross-reactivity between myelin oligodendrocyte glycoprotein and the milk protein butyrophilin in multiple sclerosis," *J Immunol* (Germany) 172, no. 1 (Jan 2004): 661-8.

36. A. Stefferl et al., "Butyrophilin, a milk protein, modulates the encephalitogenic T cell response to myelin oligodendrocyte glycoprotein in experimental auto immune encephalomyelitis," *J. Immunol* (Germany) 165, no. 5 (Sep 2000): 2859–65.

37. P. Mañá et al., "Tolerance induction by molecular mimicry: prevention and suppression of experimental autoimmune encephalomyelitis with the milk protein butyrophilin," *International Immunology* 16, no. 3 (Mar 2004): 489–499.

38. A.C. Wilson et al., "Relation of infant diet to childhood health: seven-year follow-up of cohort of children in Dundee infant feeding study," *BMJ* (England) 316, no. 7124 (Jan 1998): 21–5.

39. J.S. Forsyth et al., "Long chain polyunsaturated fatty acid supplementation in infant formula and blood pressure in later childhood: follow up of a randomised controlled trial," *BMJ* (England) 326, no. 7396 (May 3, 2003): 953.

40. R.M. Bostick et al., "Relation of calcium, vitamin D, and dairy food intake to ischemic heart disease mortality among postmenopausal women," *Am J Epidemiol* 149, no. 2 (Jan 1999): 151–61.

41. R.B. Singh et al., "Association of trans fatty acids (vegetable ghee) and clarified butter (Indian ghee) intake with higher risk of coronary artery disease in rural and urban populations with low fat consumption," *Int J Cardiol* (India) 56, no. 3 (Oct 1996): 289–98.

42. L.H. Kushe et al., "Health implications of Mediterranean diets in light of contemporary knowledge. 1. Plant foods and dairy products," *Am J Clin Nutr* 61, no. 6, suppl. (Jun 1995): 1407S–15S.

43. S. Seely, "Diet and coronary arterial disease: a statistical study," *Int J Cardiol* (England) 20, no. 2 (Aug 1988): 183–92.

44. W.B. Grant, "Milk and other dietary influences on coronary heart disease," *Altern Med Rev* 3, no. 4 (Aug 1998): 281–94.

45. M. Laugesen and R. Elliot, "Ischaemic heart disease, Type 1 diabetes, and cow milk A1 beta-casein," *N Z Med J* (New Zealand) 116, no. 1168 (Jan 24, 2003): u295.

46. M. Moss and D. Freed, "The cow and the coronary: epidemiology, biochemistry and immunology," *Int J Cardiol* (United Kingdom) 87, nos. 2-3 (Feb 2003): 203-16.

47. S. Seely, "Diet and coronary disease: a survey of mortality rates and food consumption statistics of 24 countries," *Med Hypotheses* 7, no. 7 (Jul 1981): 907–18.

48. N.S. Scrimshaw and E.B. Murray, "The acceptability of milk and milk products in populations with a high prevalence of lactose intolerance," *Am J Clin Nutr* 48, no. 4, suppl. (Oct 1988): 1079–159.

49. L.D. McBean and G.D. Miller, "Allaying fears and fallacies about lactose intolerance," *J Am Diet Assoc* 98, no. 6 (Jun 1998): 671–6.

50. James M. Orten and Otto W. Neuhaus, *Human Biochemistry*, ninth edition (St. Louis: The C.V. Mosby Co., 1975): 249.

51. "Don't Drink Your Milk," *Natural Health* (July–Aug 1994), http://www.brisbaneweb.com.au/print.php?pageid=24.

52. I. Birlouez-Aragon et al., "Disturbed galactose metabolism in elderly and diabetic humans is associated with cataract formation," *J Nutr* (France) 123, no. 8 (Aug 1993): 1370–6.

53. X. Cui et al., "Chronic systemic D-galactose exposure induces memory loss, neurodegeneration, and oxidative damage in mice: protective effects of R-alpha-lipoic acid," *J Neurosci Res* (China) 84, no. 3 (Aug 15, 2006): 647–54.

54. J.F. Ferrer et al., "Milk of dairy cows frequently contains a leukemogenic virus," *Science* 213, no. 4511 (Aug 1981): 1014–6.

55. P. Kristensen et al., "Incidence and risk factors of cancer among men and women in Norwegian agriculture," *Scand J Work Environ Health* 22, no. 1 (Feb 1996): 14–26.

56. A.S. Cunningham, "Lymphomas and animal-protein consumption," *Lancet* 2, no. 7996 (Nov 27, 1976): 1184–6.

57. K.J. Donham et al., "Epidemiologic relationships of the bovine population and human leukemia in Iowa," *Am J Epidemiol* 112, no. 1 (Jul 1980): 80–92.

58. A. Tavani et al., "Diet and risk of lymphoid neoplasms and soft tissue sarcomas," *Nutr Cancer* 27, no. 3 (1997): 256–60.

59. A. Kwiatkowski, "Dietary and other environmental risk factors in acute leukaemias: a case-control study of 119 patients," *Eur J Cancer Prev* 2, no. 2 (Mar 1993): 139–46.

60. K. Klintevall et al., "Evaluation of an indirect ELISA for the detection of antibodies to bovine leukemia virus in milk and serum," *J Virol Methods* 33, no. 3 (Aug 1991): 319–33.

61. M.C. Wu et al., "Milk and fat production in dairy cattle influenced by advanced subclinical bovine leukemia virus infection," *Proc Natl Acad Sci U S A* 86, no. 3 (Feb 1989): 993–6.

62. F.L. Pollari et al., "Effects of bovine leukemia virus infection on production and reproduction in dairy cattle," *Can J Vet Res* 56, no. 4 (Oct 1992): 289–95.

63. Y. Da et al., "Milk and fat yields decline in bovine leukemia virus-infected Holstein cattle with persistent lymphocytosis," *Proc Natl Acad Sci U S A* 90, no. 14 (Jul 1993): 6538–41.

64. M.C. Alavanja et al., "Estimating the effect of dietary fat on the risk of lung cancer in nonsmoking women," *Lung Cancer* 14, suppl. 1 (Mar 1996): S63–74.

65. M.B. Veierod et al., "Dietary fat intake and risk of lung cancer: a prospective study of 51,452 Norwegian men and women," *Eur J Cancer Prev* (Norway) 6, no. 6 (Dec 1997): 540–9.

66. R. Rylander et al., "Lung cancer, smoking and diet among Swedish men," *Lung Cancer* (Sweden) 14, suppl. 1 (Mar 1996): S75–83.

67. F. Nyberg et al., "Dietary factors and risk of lung cancer in never-smokers," *Int J Cancer* (Sweden) 78, no. 4 (Nov 1998): 430–6.

68. M.B. Veierod et al., "Dietary fat intake and risk of prostate cancer: a prospective study of 25,708 Norwegian men," *Int J Cancer* (Norway) 73, no. 5 (Nov 1997): 634–8.

69. C. La Vecchia et al., "Dairy products and the risk of prostatic cancer," *Oncology* 48, no. 5 (1991): 406–10.

70. W.B. Grant, "An ecologic study of dietary links to prostate cancer," *Altern Med Rev* 4, no. 3 (Jun 1999): 162–9.

71. F.F. Angwafo, "Migration and prostate cancer: an international perspective," *J Natl Med Assoc* (Cameroon) 90, no. 11, suppl. (Nov 1998): S720–3.

72. Y. Kakehi, "[Epidemiology and clinical features of prostate cancer in Japan]," *Nippon Rinsho* (Japan) 56, no. 8 (Aug 1998): 1969–73.

73. J.O. Ogunbiyi and O.B. Shittu, "Increased incidence of prostate cancer in Nigerians," *J Natl Med Assoc* (Nigeria) 91, no. 3 (Mar 1999): 159–64.

74. A.R. Walker, "Prostate cancer—some aspects of epidemiology, risk factors, treatment and survival," *S Afr Med J* 69, no. 1 (Jan 1986): 44–7.

75. D. Ganmaa et al., "Incidence and mortality of testicular and prostatic cancers in relation to world dietary practices," *Int J Cancer* (Japan) 98, no. 2 (Mar 10, 2002): 262-7.

76. C.J. Mettlin and P.S. Piver, "A case-control study of milk-drinking and ovarian cancer risk," *Am J Epidemiol* 132, no. 5 (Nov 1990): 871–6.

77. K.M. Fairfield et al., "A prospective study of dietary lactose and ovarian cancer," *Int J Cancer* 110, no. 2 (Jun 2004): 271–7.

78. D.W. Cramer, "Lactase persistence and milk consumption as determinants of ovarian cancer risk," *Am J Epidemiol* 130, no. 5 (Nov 1989): 904–10.

79. G. Tortolero-Luna and M.F. Mitchell, "The epidemiology of ovarian cancer," *J Cell Biochem Suppl* 23 (1995): 200–7.

80. D. Ganmaa and A. Sato, "The possible role of female sex hormones in milk from pregnant cows in the development of breast, ovarian and corpus uteri cancers," *Med Hypotheses* (Japan) 65, no. 6 (2005): 1028-37.

81. D.W. Cramer et al., "Adult hypolactasia, milk consumption, and age-specific fertility," *Am J Epidemiol* 139, no. 3 (Feb 1994): 282–9.

82. I. Kato et al., "Factors related to late menopause and early menarche as risk factors for breast cancer," *Jpn J Cancer Res* (Japan) 79, no. 2 (Feb 1988): 165–72.

83. B.A. Stoll, "Western diet, early puberty, and breast cancer risk," *Breast Cancer Res Treat* 49, no. 3 (Jun 1998): 187–93.

84. L. Ibanez et al., "Hyperinsulinemia and decreased insulin-like growth factor-binding protein-1 are common features in prepubertal and pubertal girls with a history of premature pubarche," *J Clin Endocrinol Metab* (Spain) 82, no. 7 (Jul 1997): 2283–8.

85. M.E. Herman-Giddens et al., "Secondary sexual characteristics and menses in young girls seen in office practice: a study from the Pediatric Research in Office Settings network," *Pediatrics* 99, no. 4 (Apr 1997): 505–12.

86. P. Pasquet et al., "Age at menarche and urbanization in Cameroon: current status and secular trends," *Ann Hum Biol* (France) 26, no. 1 (Jan–Feb, 1999): 89–97.

87. Laura Spinney, "Genetically Manipulated Food News: Hispanic Girls Reach Puberty Later," American Association for Cancer Research, April 12, 1999, http://home.intekom.com/tm_info/rw90415.htm#01.

88. R.M. Malina et al., "Age of menarche in Oaxaca, Mexico, schoolgirls, with comparative data for other areas of Mexico," *Ann Hum Biol* (Mexico) 4, no. 6 (Nov 1977): 551–8.

89. S. Tsuzaki et al., "Lack of linkage between height and weight and age at menarche during the secular shift in growth of Japanese children," *Ann Hum Biol* 16, no. 5 (Sep–Oct 1989): 429–36.

90. K. Liestol and M. Rosenberg, "Height, weight and menarcheal age of schoolgirls in Oslo—an update," *Ann Hum Biol* (Norway) 22, no. 3 (May–Jun 1995): 199–205.

91. B.A. Stoll, "Western diet, early puberty, and breast cancer risk," *Breast Cancer Res Treat* 49, no. 3 (Jun 1998): 187–93.

92. J.S. Suh et al., "Menstrual and reproductive factors related to the risk of breast cancer in Korea. Ovarian hormone effect on breast cancer," *J Korean Med Sci* (Korea) 11, no. 6 (Dec 1996): 501–8.

93. C.C. Hsieh et al., "Age at menarche, age at menopause, height and obesity as risk factors for breast cancer: associations and interactions in an international case-control study," *Int J Cancer* 46, no. 5 (Nov 15, 1990): 796–800.

94. C.S. Berkey, "Adolescence and breast carcinoma risk," *Cancer* 85, no. 11 (Jun 1999): 2400–9.

95. B.A. Stoll, "Western nutrition and the insulin resistance syndrome: a link to breast cancer," *Eur J Clin Nutr* 53, no. 2 (Feb 1999): 83–7.

96. *MMWR Morb Mortal Wkly Rep* 43, no. 15 (Apr 22, 1994): 279–81.

97. S.P. Gaskill et al., "Breast cancer mortality and diet in the United States," *Cancer Res* 39, no. 9 (Sep 1979): 3628–37.

98. H. Ishimoto et al., "Epidemiological study on relationship between breast cancer mortality and dietary factors," *Tokushima J Exp Med* (Japan) 41, nos. 3–4 (Dec 1994): 103–14.

99. S. Mannisto et al., "Diet and the risk of breast cancer in a case-control study: does the threat of disease have an influence on recall bias? *J Clin Epidemiol* (Finland) 52, no. 5 (May 1999): 429–39.

100. J.L. Freudenheim et al., "Exposure to breastmilk in infancy and the risk of breast cancer," *Epidemiology* 5, no. 3 (May 1994): 324–31.

101. H.A. Weiss et al., "Prenatal and perinatal risk factors for breast cancer in young women," *Epidemiology* 8, no. 2 (Mar 1997): 181–7.

102. A. Mbakop et al., "[Current epidemiology of cancers in Cameroon]," *Bull Cancer* (France) 79, no. 11 (1992): 1101–4.

103. "Deaths from Breast Cancer: United States, 1991," *MMWR Morb Mortal Wkly Rep* 43, no. 15 (Apr 22, 1994): 279–81.

104. K.B. Simondon et al., "Preschool stunting, age at menarche and adolescent height: a longitudinal study in rural Senegal," *Eur J Clin Nutr* (France) 52, no. 6 (Jun 1998): 412–8.

105. F. La Rosa et al., "[Descriptive epidemiology of malignant tumors of the colon and rectum]," *Ann Ig* (Italy) 1, no. 5 (Sep–Oct 1989): 899–922.

106. Vivien Knips, "Pro-Poor Livestock Policy Initiative, Working Paper No. 30," Developing Countries and the Global Dairy Sector Part I Global Overview, December 1, 2005, http://www.fao.org/ag/againfo/programmes/en/pplpi/docarc/wp30.pdf.

107. USDA Foreign Agricultural Service, "Fluid Milk Consumption Per Capita—Selected Countries," FASonline, http://www.fas.usda.gov/dlp2/circular/1997/97-07-Dairy/milkpcap.htm.

108. D. Ganmaa and A. Sato, "The possible role of female sex hormones in milk from pregnant cows in the development of breast, ovarian and corpus uteri cancers," *Medical Hypothesis* 65, no. 6 (Aug 24, 2005): 1028–37.

109. International Agency for Research on Cancer. CANCERMondial. GLOBOCAN 2002. http://www-dep.iarc.fr/GLOBOCAN/table2.asp?cancer=132&region=99&sex=2&sort=1&submit=Execute. Nov 12, 2008.

110. D.M. Parkin et al., "Global Cancer Statistics, 2002," *CA Cancer J Clin* (France) 55, no. 2 (Mar–Apr, 2005): 74–108.

111. A. Honegger and R.E. Humbel, "Insulin-like growth factors I and II in fetal and adult bovine serum. Purification, primary structures, and immunological cross-reactivities," *J Biol Chem* 261, no. 2 (Jan 1986): 569–75.

112. T. Nickerson and H. Huynh, "Vitamin D analogue EB1089-induced prostate regression is associated with increased gene expression of insulin-like growth factor binding proteins," *J Endocrinol* 160, no. 2 (Feb 1999): 223–9.

113. E. Petridou et al., "Insulin-like growth factor-I and binding protein-3 in relation to childhood leukaemia," *Int J Cancer* (Greece) 80, no. 4 (Feb 9, 1999): 494–6.

114. J.L. Outwater et al., "Dairy products and breast cancer: the IGF-I, estrogen, and bGH hypothesis," *Med Hypotheses* 48, no. 6 (Jun 1997): 453–61.

115. K. Robbins et al., "Immunological effects of insulin-like growth factor-I—enhancement of immunoglobulin syntheses," *Clin Exp Immunol* 95, no. 2 (Feb 1994): 337–42.

116. M.D. Holmes et al., "Dietary correlates of plasma insulin-like growth factor I and insulin-like growth factor binding protein 3 concentrations," *Cancer Epidemiol Biomarkers Prev* 11, no. 9 (Sep 2002): 852-61.

117. P. Cohen et al., "Biological effects of prostate specific antigen as an insulin-like growth factor binding protein-3 protease," *J Endocrinol* 142, no. 3 (Sep 1994): 407–15.

118. D.M. Peehl et al., "The insulin-like factor system in the prostate," *World J Urol* 13, no. 5 (1995): 306–11.

119. J.C. Chen et al., "Insulin-like growth factor-binding protein enhancement of insulin-like growth factor-I (IGF-I)-mediated DNA synthesis and IGF-I binding in a human breast carcinoma cell line," *J Cell Physiol* 159, no. 1 (Jan 1994): 69–78.

120. N. Rosen et al., "Insulin-like growth factors in human breast cancer," *Breast Cancer Res Treat* 18, suppl. 1 (May 1991): S55–62.

121. A.V. Lee et al., "Enhancement of insulin-like growth factor signaling in human breast-cancer: estrogen regulation of insulin receptor substrate-1 expression in vitro and in vivo," *Mol Endocrinol* 13, no. 5 (May 1999): 787–96.

122. E.P. Beck et al., "Identification of insulin and insulin-like growth factor I (IGF I) receptors in ovarian cancer tissue," *Gynecol Oncol* (Germany) 53, no. 2 (May 1994): 196–201.

123. M. Resnicoff et al., "Insulin-like growth factor-1 and its receptor mediate the autocrine proliferation of human ovarian carcinoma cell lines," *Lab Invest* 69, no. 6 (Dec 1993): 756–60.

124. M.S. Piver, "Prophylactic oophorectomy: Reducing the U.S. death rate from epithelial ovarian cancer. A continuing debate," *Oncologist* 1, no. 5 (1996): 326–330.

125. R.P. Glick et al., "Insulin-like growth factors in central nervous system tumors," *J Neurooncol* 35, no. 3 (Dec 1997): 315–25.

126. E.E. Wheeler and D.N. Challacombe, "The trophic action of growth hormone, insulin-like growth factor-I, and insulin on human duodenal mucosa cultured in vitro," *Gut* 40, no. 1 (Jan 1997): 57–60.

127. C.C. Kappel et al., "Human osteosarcoma cell lines are dependent on insulin-like growth factor I for in vitro growth," *Cancer Res* 54, no. 10 (May 15, 1994): 2803–7.

128. S.T. Wolford and C.J. Argoudelis, "Measurement of estrogens in cow's milk, human milk, and dairy products," *J Dairy Sci* 62, no. 9 (Sep 1979): 1458–63.

129. E.P. Diamandis and H. Yu, "Nonprostatic sources of prostate-specific antigen," *Urol Clin North Am* 24, no. 2 (May 1997): 275–82.

130. S.S. Epstein, "Unlabeled milk from cows treated with biosynthetic growth hormones: a case of regulatory abdication," *Int J Health Serv* 26, no. 1 (1996): 173–85.

131. Robert Cohen, *Milk, The Deadly Poison* (Englewood Cliffs, NJ: Argus, 1998): 310.

132. Jane Akre and Steve Wilson, "News of Lawsuit Exposing Media Coverup of Suspected Danger in Milk," Target Television Enterprises, Inc., 2004, www.foxBGHsuit.com.

133. W.T. Lee et al., "Relationship between long-term calcium intake and bone mineral content of children aged from birth to 5 years," *Br J Nutr* (Hong Kong) 70, no. 1 (Jul 1993): 235–48.

134. W.T. Lee et al., "A randomized double-blind controlled calcium supplementation trial, and bone and height acquisition in children," *Br J Nutr* (Hong Kong) 74, no. 1 (Jul 1995): 125–39.

135. J.C. Cheng et al., "Determinants of axial and peripheral bone mass in Chinese adolescents," *Arch Dis Child* (Hong Kong) 78, no. 6 (Jun 1998): 524–30.

136. J.C. Cheng et al., "Axial and peripheral bone mineral acquisition: a 3-year longitudinal study in Chinese adolescents," *Eur J Pediatr* (Hong Kong) 158, no. 6 (Jun 1999): 506–12.

137. J. Cadogan et al., "Milk intake and bone mineral acquisition in adolescent girls: randomised, controlled intervention trial," *BMJ* (England) 315, no. 7118 (Nov 15, 1997): 1255–60.

138. I.D. Griffiths and R.M. Francis, "Results in two groups are not so different," *BMJ* (England) 316, no. 7146 (Jun 6, 1998): 1747–8.

139. A.J. Lanou et al., "Calcium, Dairy Products, and Bone Health in Children and Young Adults: A Reevaluation of the Evidence ," *Pediatrics* 115, no. 3 (Mar 3, 2005): 736–43.

140. T.M. Winzenberg et al., "Calcium supplementation for improving bone mineral density in children," *Cochrane Database Syst Rev* (Australia) 2 (Apr 19, 2006): CD005119.

141. N.A. Breslau et al., "Relationship of animal protein-rich diet to kidney stone formation and calcium metabolism," *J Clin Endocrinol Metab* 66, no. 1 (Jan 1988): 140–6.

142. U.S. Barzel and L.K. Massey, "Excess dietary protein can adversely affect bone," *J Nutr* 128, no. 6 (Jun 1998): 1051–3.

143. L.H. Allen et al., "Protein-induced hypercalcuria: a long term study," *Am J Clin Nutr* 32, no. 4 (Apr 1979): 741–9.

144. M.B. Zemel, "Calcium utilization: effect of varying level and source of dietary protein," *Am J Clin Nutr* 48, no. 3, suppl. (Sep 1988): 880–3.

145. D. M. Hegsted, "Calcium and Osteoporosis," *J Nutr* 116, no 11 (Nov 1986): 2316–9.

146. R. Cohen, "Who is behind the National Osteoporosis Foundation and what is their agenda?" Dairy Education Board Archives, http://www.notmilk.com, (May 23, 1999): 1–5.

147. D.M. Hegsted, "Calcium and Osteoporosis," *Adv Nutr Res* 9 (1994): 119–28.

148. B.L. Riggs et al., "Dietary calcium intake and rates of bone loss in women," *J Clin Invest* 80, no. 4 (Oct 1987): 979–82.

149. A. Tavani et al., "Calcium, dairy products, and the risk of hip fracture in women in northern Italy," *Epidemiology* (Italy) 6, no. 5 (Sep 1995): 554–7.

150. D. Feskanich et al., "Milk, dietary calcium, and bone fractures in women: a 12-year prospective study," *Am J Public Health* 87, no. 6 (Jun 1997): 992–7.

151. W. Owusu et al., "Calcium intake and the incidence of forearm and hip fractures among men," *J Nutr* 127, no. 9 (Sep 1997): 1782–7.

152. R.L. Bauer, "Ethnic differences in hip fracture: a reduced incidence in Mexican Americans," *Am J Epidemiol* 127, no. 1 (Jan 1988): 145–9.

153. B.J. Abelow et al., "Cross-cultural association between dietary animal protein and hip fracture: a hypothesis," *Calcif Tissue Int* 50, no. 1 (Jan 1992): 14–8.

154. C. Cooper et al., "Hip fractures in the elderly: a world-wide projection," *Osteoporosis Int* 2, no. 6 (Nov 1992): 285–9.

155. T. Fujita, "Osteoporosis in Japan: factors contributing to the low incidence of hip fracture," *Adv Nutr Res* (Japan) 9 (1994): 89–99.

156. W.J. MacLennan, "History of arthritis and bone rarefaction evidence from paleopathology onwards," *Scott Med J* (England) 44, no. 1 (Feb 1999): 18–20.

157. J.P. Bilezikian et al., "Optimal calcium intake" *NIH Consensus Statement* 12, no. 4 (Jun 6–8, 1994): 1–31.

158. K.K. Kim et al., "Nutritional status of Chinese-, Korean-, and Japanese-American elderly," *J Am Diet Assoc* 93, no. 12 (Dec 1993): 1416–22.

159. E.C. van Beresteijn et al., "Relationship between the calcium-to-protein ratio in milk and the urinary calcium excretion in healthy adults—a controlled crossover study," *Am J Clin Nutr* (Netherlands) 52, no. 1 (Jul 1990): 142–6.

160. A. Host, "Cow's milk protein allergy and intolerance in infancy. Some clinical, epidemiological and immunological aspects," *Pediatr Allergy Immunol* (Denmark) 5, suppl. 5 (1994): 1-36.

161. A. Paschke and M. Besler, "Stability of bovine allergens during food processing," *Ann Allergy Asthma Immunol* (Germany) 89, suppl. 6 (Dec 2002): 16-20.

162. Brix et al., "Immunostimulatory potential of beta-lactoglobulin preparations: effects caused by endotoxin contamination," *J Allergy Clin Immunol* (Denmark) 112, no. 6 (Dec 2003): 1216-22.

163. H. Almaas et al., "In vitro studies of the allergens of the digestion of caprine whey proteins by human gastric and duodenal juice and the effects on selected microorganisms," *Br J Nutr* (Norway) 96, no. 3 (Sep 2006): 562-9.

164. H.J. Brooks et al., "Potential prophylactic value of bovine colostrum in necrotizing enterocolitis in neonates: an in vitro study on bacterial attachment, antibody levels and cytokine production," *FEMS Immunol Med Microbiol* (New Zealand) 48, no. 3 (Dec 2006):347-54.

165. M.F. Rolland-Cachera et al., "Influence of macronutrients on adiposity development: a follow up study of nutrition and growth from 10 months to 8 years of age," *Int J Obes Relat Metab Disord* (France) 19, no. 8 (Aug 1995): 573–8.

166. L.H. Kushi et al., "Health implications of Mediterranean diets in light of contemporary knowledge. 1. Plant foods and dairy products," *Am J Clin Nutr* 61, suppl 6 (Jun 1995): 1407S–1415S.

167. M. Nestle, "Food lobbies, the food pyramid, and U.S. nutrition policy," *Int J Health Serv* 23, no. 3 (1993): 483–96.

168. W.C. Willett, Department of Nutrition, Harvard School of Public Health, in "Doctors, Dairy Industry Duke it Out Over Milk," *Boston Globe*, June 8, 1999.

Chapter 12: Colic to Ear Infections, Behavior to Bedwetting

1. E. Oldak, "The incidence and clinical manifestation of food allergy in unselected Polish infants: follow-up from birth to one year of age," *Rocz Akad Med Bialymst* (Poland) 42, no. 1 (1997): 196–204.

2. Heather M. Little, "Food may be causing kids' problems," *WOMANEWS*, 29 October 1995, sec. 13.

3. F. Savino and R. Oggero, "[Management of infantile colics]," *Minerva Pediatr* (Italy) 48 (July 1996): 7–8, 313–19.

4. R. Oggero et al., "Dietary modifications versus Dicyclomine hydrochloride in the treatment of severe infantile colics," *Acta Paediatr* (Italy) 83, no. 2 (Feb 1994): 222–5.

5. G. Iacono et al., "Severe infantile colic and food intolerance: a long-term prospective study," *J Pediatr Gastroenterol Nutr* 12, no. 3 (April 1991): 332–5.

6. J.P. Campbell, "[Dietary therapy of infant colic: a double-blind study]," *Cesk Pediatr* (Czechoslovakia) 48, no. 4 (April 1993): 199–202.

7. J.J. Verwimp et al., "Symptomatology and growth in infants with cow's milk protein intolerance using two different whey-protein hydrolysate based formulas in a primary health care setting," *Eur J Clin Nutr* (Netherlands) 49, suppl. 1 (Sept 1995): S39–48.

8. T.M. Nsouli et al., "Role of food allergy in serous otitis media," *Ann Allergy* 73, no. 3 (Sep 1994): 215–9.

9. A. Ojuawo et al., "Non-infective colitis in infancy: evidence in favour of minor immunodeficiency in its pathogenesis," *Arch Dis Child* (London) 76, no. 4 (April 1997): 345–8.

10. A. Armisén Pedrejon et al., "[Colitis induced by a food allergen. A report of 20 cases]," *An Esp Pediatr* (Spain) 44, no. 1 (Jan 1996): 21–4.

11. H.R. Jenkins et al., "Food Allergy: the major cause of infantile colitis," *Arch Dis Child* 59 (1984): 326–9.

12. Jonathan Brostoff and Stephen J. Challacombe, eds., *Food Allergy and Intolerance*, chapter 6 by Stephan Strobel and John G. Shields (London: Baillière Tindall, 1987), 112–5.

13. V. Alun Jones et al., "Crohn's disease: maintenance of remission by diet," *Lancet* 2 (1985): 177–80.

14. H. Malchow et al., "European cooperative Crohn's disease study: results of drug treatment," *Gastroenterol* 86 (1984): 249–66.

15. J.O. Hunter, "Nutritional factors in inflammatory bowel disease," *Eur J Gastroenterol Hepatol* 10, no. 3 (1998): 235–7.

16. P. Knoflach et al., "Serum antibodies to cow's milk proteins in ulcerative colitis and Crohn's disease," *Gastroenterology* 92, no. 2 (Feb 1987): 479–85.

17. I. Grazioli, et al., "[Food intolerance and irritable bowel syndrome of childhood: clinical efficacy of oral sodium cromoglycate and elimination diet]," *Minerva Pediatr* (Italy) 45, no. 6 (Jun 1993): 253–8.

18. J. Egger et al., "Is migraine food allergy?" *Lancet* 2 (1983): 865–9.

19. M. Boris and F.S. Mandel, "Foods and additives are common causes of the attention-deficit hyperactive disorder in children," *Ann Allergy* 72, no. 5 (May 1994): 462–8.

20. W.G. Crook et al., "Systemic manifestations due to allergy," *Pediatric* 27 (1961): 790–9.

21. T. Uhlig et al., "Topographic mapping of brain electrical activity in children with food-induced attention-deficit hyperkinetic disorder," *Eur J Pediatr* 156, no. 7 (July 1997): 557–61.

22. J. Egger et al., "Effect of diet treatment on enuresis in children with migraine or hyperkinetic behavior," *Clin Pediatr* (Philadelphia) 31, no. 5 (May 1992): 302–7.

23. W.L. Robson et al., "Enuresis in children with attention-deficit hyperactivity disorder," *South Med J* 90, no. 5 (May 1997): 503–5.

24. Jonathan Brostoff and Stephen J. Challacombe, eds., *Food Allergy and Intolerance*, chapter 11 by W. Allen Walker (London: Baillière Tindall, 1987), 219.

25. G. Iacono et al., "Persistent cow's milk protein intolerance in infants: the changing faces of the same disease," *Clin Exp Allergy* (Italy) 28, no. 7 (Jul 1998): 817–23.

26. J.L. Eseverri et al., "[Epidemiology and chronology of allergic diseases and their risk factors]," *Allergol Immunopathol* (Spain) 26, no. 3 (May–Jun 1998): 90–7.

27. Omari et al., "Effect of omeprazole on acid gastroesophageal reflux and gastric acidity in preterm infants with pathological acid reflux," *J Pediatr Gastroenterol Nutr* 44, no. 1 (Jan 2007): 41–4.

28. F. Cavataio et al., "Gastroesophageal reflux associated with cow's milk allergy in infants: which diagnostic examinations are useful?" *Am J Gastroenterol* 91, no. 6 (Jun 1996): 1215–20.

29. Jonathan Brostoff and Stephen J. Challacombe, eds., *Food Allergy and Intolerance*, chapter 18 by John W. Gerrard (London: Baillière Tindall, 1987), 349–50.

30. C. Power and O. Manor, "Asthma, enuresis, and chronic illness: long term impact on height," *Arch Dis Child* 73, no. 4 (Oct 1995): 298–304.

31. J. Egger et al., "Effect of diet treatment on enuresis in children with migraine or hyperkinetic behavior," *Clin Pediatr* 31, no. 5 (May 1992): 302–7.

32. W.L. Robson et al., "Enuresis in children with attention-deficit hyperactivity disorder," *South Med J* 90, no. 5 (May 1997): 503–5.

33. M. Boris and F.S. Mandel, "Foods and additives are common causes of the attention-deficit hyperactive disorder in children," *Ann Allergy* 722, no. 5 (May 1994): 462–8.

34. J. Egger et al., "Controlled trial of oligoantigenic treatment in the hyperkinetic syndrome," *Lancet* 1, no. 8428 (Mar 1985): 540–5.

35. J. Breakey, "The role of diet and behaviour in childhood," *J Paediatr Child Health* 33, no. 3 (Jun 1997): 190–4.

36. T. Uhlig, "Topographic mapping of brain electrical activity in children with food-induced attention-deficit hyperkinetic disorder," *Eur J Pediatr* (Australia) 156, no. 7 (Jul 1997): 557–61.

37. B.J. Kaplan et al., "Dietary replacement in preschool-aged hyperactive boys," *Pediatrics* (Canada) 83, no. 1 (Jan 1989): 7–17.

38. N. Roth et al., "Coincidence of attention-deficit disorder and atopic disorders in children: empirical findings and hypothetical background," *J Abnorm Child Psychol* (Germany) 19, no. 1 (Feb 1991): 1–13.

39. C.E. Price et al., "Associations of excessive irritability with common illnesses and food intolerance," *Paediatr Perinat Epidemiol* (London) 4, no. 2 (Apr 1990): 156–60.

40. U.A. Hunziker and R.G. Barr, "Increased carrying reduces infant crying: a randomized controlled trial," *Pediatrics* 77, no. 5 (May 1986): 641–8.

41. R. Oggero, et al., "Dietary modifications versus dicyclomine hydrochloride in the treatment of severe infantile colics," *Acta Paediatr* (Italy) 83, no. 2 (Feb 1994): 222–5.

42. G. Iacono, et al., "Severe infantile colic and food intolerance: a long-term prospective study," *J Pediatr Gastroenterol Nutr* (Italy) 12, no. 3 (Apr 1991): 332–335.

43. R.J. Merritt, et al., "Whey protein hydrolysate formula for infants with gastrointestinal intolerance to cow milk and soy protein in infant formulas," *J Pediatr Gastroenterol Nutr* 11, no. 1 (Jul 1990): 78–82.

44. J.P. Campbell, "Dietary treatment of infant colic: a double-blind study," *J R Coll Gen Pract* 39, no. 318 (Jan 1989): 11–14.

45. L. Lothe and T. Lindberg, "Cow's milk whey protein elicits symptoms of infantile colic in colicky formula-fed infants: a double-blind crossover study," *Pediatrics* (Sweden) 83, no. 2 (Feb 1989): 262–6.

46. M. Weissbluth, et al., "Treatment of infantile colic with dicyclomine hydrochloride," *J Pediatr* 104, no. 6 (Jun 1984): 951–5.

47. L. Lothe, et al., "Cow's milk formula as a cause of infantile colic: a double-blind study," *Pediatrics* (Sweden) 70, no. 1 (Jul 1982): 7–10.

48 I. Jakobsson and T. Lindberg, "Cow's milk proteins cause infantile colic in breast-fed infants: a double-blind crossover study," *Pediatrics* (Sweden) 71, no. 22 (Feb 1983): 268–71.

49. R.G. Barr et al., "Carrying as colic 'therapy': a randomized controlled trial," *Pediatrics* 87, no. 5 (May 1991): 623–30.

50. J.A. Vanderhoof et al., "Intolerance to protein hydrolysate infant formulas: an underrecognized cause of gastrointestinal symptoms in infants," *J Pediatr* 131, no. 5 (Nov 1997): 741–4.

51. D.J. Hill et al., "Challenge confirmation of late-onset reactions to extensively hydrolyzed formulas in infants with multiple food protein intolerance," *J Allergy Clin Immunol* 96, no. 3 (Sep 1995): 386–94.

52. I. Axelsson et al., "Bovine beta-lactoglobulin in the human milk. A longitudinal study during the whole lactation period," *Acta Paediatr Scand* (Sweden) 75, no. 5 (Sep 1986): 702–7.

53. R.A. Hardoin et al., "Colic medication and apparent life-threatening events," *Clin Pediatr (Phila)* 30, no. 5 (May 1991): 281–5.

54. D. Satge et al., "Antenatal therapeutic drug exposure and fetal/neonatal tumours: review of 89 cases," *Paediatr Perinat Epidemiol* (France) 12, no. 1 (Jan 1998): 84–117.

55. J.J. Miller et al., "Breath hydrogen excretion in infants with colic," *Arch Dis Child* (Australia) 64, no. 5 (May 1989): 725–9.

56. R.G. Barr et al., "Effects of formula change on intestinal hydrogen production and crying and fussing behavior," *J Dev Behav Pediatr* (Canada) 12, no. 4 (Aug 1991): 248–53.

57. L. Lothe et al., "Macromolecular absorption in infants with infantile colic," *Acta Paediatr Scand* (Sweden) 79, no. 4 (Apr 1990): 417–21.

58. V. Loening-Baucke, "Urinary incontinence and urinary tract infection and their resolution with treatment of chronic constipation of childhood," *Pediatrics* 100, no. 2, part 1 (Aug 1997): 228–32.

59. G. Iacono et al., "Chronic constipation as a symptom of cow milk allergy," *J Pediatr* 126, no. 1 (Jan 1995): 34–9.

60. G. Iacono et al., "Intolerance of cow's milk and chronic constipation in children," *N Engl J Med* 339, no. 16 (Oct 15, 1998): 1100–4.

61. H.M. Machida, et al., "Allergic colitis in infancy: clinical and pathologic aspects," *J Pediatr Gastroenterol Nutr* (Canada) 19, no. 1 (Jul 1994): 22–6.

62. H.R. Jenkins, et al., "Food allergy: the major cause of infantile colitis," *Arch Dis Child* 59, no. 4 (Apr 1984): 326–9.

63. H. Malchow, et al., "Feasibility and effectiveness of a defined-formula diet regimen in treating active Crohn's disease. European Cooperative Crohn's Disease Study III," *Scand J Gastroenterol* (Denmark) 25, no. 3 (Mar 1990): 235–44.

64. V.A. Jones, et al., "Crohn's disease: maintenance of remission by diet," *Lancet* 2, no. 8448 (Jul 1985): 177–80.

65. H. Malchow, et al., "European Cooperative Crohn's Disease Study (ECCDS): results of drug treatment," *Gastroenterology* 86, no. 2 (Feb 1984): 249–66.

66. T. Poynard, et al., "Meta-analyses of smooth muscle relaxants in the treatment of irritable bowel syndrome," *Aliment Pharmacol Ther* 8, no. 5 (Oct 1994): 499–510.

67. I. Grazioli, et al., "[Food intolerance and irritable bowel syndrome of childhood: clinical efficacy of oral sodium cromoglycate and elimination diet]," *Minerva Pediatr* (Italy) 45, no. 6 (Jun 1993): 253–8.

68. J. Drisko et al., "Treating irritable bowel syndrome with a food elimination diet followed by food challenge and probiotics," *J Am Coll Nutr* 25, no. 6 (Dec 2006): 514–22.

69. S.A. Xanthakos, "Prevalence and outcome of allergic colitis in healthy infants with rectal bleeding," *J Ped Gastro Nutr* 41, no. 1 (July 2005): 16-22.

70. J. McGrath, "Allergy to cow's milk presenting as chronic constipation," *Br Med J (Clin Res Ed)* 288, no. 6412 (Jan 21, 1984): 36.

71. N.E. Sazanova et al., "[Immunological aspects of food intolerance in children during first years of life]," *Pediatriia* (Russia) 3 (1992): 14–18.

72. U. Fagundes-Neto, "Nutritional impact and ultrastructural intestinal alterations in severe infections due to enteropathogenic *Escherichia coli* strains in infants," *J Am Coll Nutr* (Brazil) 15, no. 2 (Apr 1996): 180–5.

73. P. McClean et al., "Surface features of small-intestine mucosa in childhood diarrheal disorders," *J Pediatr Gastroenterol Nutr* (Ireland) 23, no. 5 (Dec 1996): 538–46.

74. A.M. Scanu et al., "Mycobacterium avium subspecies paratuberculosis infection in cases of irritable bowel syndrome and comparison with Crohn's disease and Johne's disease: common neural and immune pathogenicities," *J Clin Microbiol* 45, no. 12 (Dec 2007): 3883-90.

75. K.G. Dewey et al., "Differences in morbidity between breast-fed and formula-fed infants," *J Pediatr* 126, no. 5, part 1 (May 1995): 696–702.

76. Y. Lerman et al., "Epidemiology of acute diarrheal diseases in children in a high standard of living rural settlement in Israel," *Pediatr Infect Dis J* (Israel) 13, no. 2 (Feb 1994): 116–22.

77. S.C. Fuchs et al., "Case-control study of risk of dehydrating diarrhoea in infants in vulnerable period after full weaning," *BMJ* (Brazil) 313, no. 7054 (Aug 1996): 391–4.

78. B.P. Lanphear et al., "Increasing prevalence of recurrent otitis media among children in the United States," *Pediatrics* 99, no. 3 (Mar 1997): E1.

79. Kathi Kemper, MD, MPH, *The Holistic Pediatrician* (New York: HarperCollins, 1996), 180.

80. D.S. Hurst, "Association of otitis media with effusion and allergy as demonstrated by intradermal skin testing and eosinophil cationic protein levels in both middle ear effusions and mucosal biopsies," *Laryngoscope* 106, no. 9, part 1 (Sep 1996): 1128–37.

81. T.M. Nsouli et al., "Role of food allergy in serous otitis media," *Ann Allergy* 73, no. 3 (Sep 1994): 215–9.

82. U.M. Saarinen et al., "Increased IgM-type betalactoglobulin antibodies in children with recurrent otitis media," *Allergy* 38, no. 8 (Nov 1983): 571–6.

83. M. Tachibana et al., "Experimental immune complex otitis media: localization of IgG by protein A-gold technique," *Auris Nasus Larynx* 12, suppl. 1 (1985): S86–8.

84. D.S. Hurst, "Allergy management of refractory serous otitis media," *Otolaryngol Head Neck Surg* 102, no. 6 (Jun 1990): 664–9.

85. M.J. Derebery and K.I. Berliner, "Allergic eustachian tube dysfunction: diagnosis and treatment," *Am J Otol* 18, no. 2 (Mar 1997): 160–5.

86. J. Egger et al., "Oligoantigenic diet treatment of children with epilepsy and migraine," *J Pediatr* (England) 114, no. 1 (Jan 1989): 51–8.

87. K.M. Bell et al., "Risk factors associated with chronic fatigue syndrome in a cluster of pediatric cases," *Rev Infect Dis* 13, suppl. 1 (Jan–Feb 1991): S32–8.

88. D.J. Clauw, "The pathogenesis of chronic pain and fatigue syndromes, with special reference to fibromyalgia," *Med Hypotheses* 44, no. 5 (May 1995): 369–78.

89. J.E. Gomborone et al., "Prevalence of irritable bowel syndrome in chronic fatigue," *J R Coll Physicians Lond* (England) 30, no. 6 (Nov 1996): 512–3.

90. L. Borish et al., "Chronic fatigue syndrome: identification of distinct subgroups on the basis of allergy and psychologic variables," *J Allergy Clin Immunol* 102, no. 2 (Aug 1998): 222–30.

91. S. Paterson, "Food hypersensitivity in 20 dogs with skin and gastrointestinal signs," *J Small Anim Pract* 36, no. 12 (Dec 1995): 529–34.

92. B. Ballauf, "[Feed allergy in dogs and cats—not only a gastrointestinal problem]," *Tierarztl Prax* (Germany) 21, no. 1 (Feb 1993): 53–6.

93. J. Egger et al., "Is migraine food allergy? A double-blind controlled trial of oligoantigenic diet treatment," *Lancet* 2, no. 8355 (Oct 1983): 865–9.

94. G. Guariso et al., "[Migraine and food intolerance: a controlled study in pediatric patients]," *Pediatr Med Chir* (Italy) 15, no. 1 (Jan–Feb 1993): 57–61.

95. M.L. Pacor et al., "[Migraine and food]," *Recenti Prog Med* (Italy) 80, no. 2 (Feb 1989): 53–5.

96. J.A. Anderson, "Mechanisms in adverse reactions to food: The brain," *Allergy* 50, no. 20 suppl. (1995): 78–81.

97. W.H. Yang et al., "The monosodium glutamate symptom complex: assessment in a double-blind, placebo-controlled, randomized study," *J Allergy Clin Immunol* 99, no. 6, part 1 (Jun 1997): 757–62.

98. S.K. Van den Eeden et al., "Aspartame ingestion and headaches: a randomized crossover trial," *Neurology* 44, no. 10 (Oct 1994): 1787–93.

99. A. Oehling et al., "Skin manifestations and immunological parameters in childhood food allergy," *J Investig allergol clin immunol* (Spain) 7, no. 3 (May–Jun 1997): 155–9.

100. N.E. Sazanova et al., "[Immunological aspects of food intolerance in children during first years of life]," *Pediatriia* (Russia) 3 (1992): 14–8.

101. H. Majamaa and E. Isolauri, "Evaluation of the gut mucosal barrier: evidence for increased antigen transfer in children with atopic eczema," *J Allergy Clin Immunol* (Finland) 97, no. 4 (Apr 1996): 985–90.

102. C. Dupont and M. Heyman, "Food protein-induced enterocolitis syndrome: laboratory perspectives," *J Pediatr Gastroenterol Nutr* 30, suppl. (2000): S50-7.

103. R.J. Shulman et al., "Increased gastrointestinal permeability and gut inflammation in children with functional abdominal pain and irritable bowel syndrome," *J Pediatr* 153, no. 5 (Nov 2008): 646–50.

104. J.M. James et al., "Respiratory reactions provoked by double-blind food challenges in children," *Am J Respir Crit Care Med* 149, no. 1 (Jan 1994): 59–64.

105. D.S. Feigin, "Allergic diseases in the lungs," *Crit Rev Diagn Imaging*, 25, no. 2 (1986): 159–76.

106. N.S. Zhong, "New insights into risk factors of asthma," *Respirology*, (China) 1, no. 3 (Sep 1996): 159–66.

107. John Mansfield, *Asthma Epidemic* (London: HarperCollins, 1997), 1.

108. John Mansfield, *Asthma Epidemic* (London: HarperCollins, 1997), 14–27.

109. S.R. Salpeter et al., "Meta-analysis: effect of long-acting beta-agonists on severe asthma exacerbations and asthma-related deaths," *Ann Intern Med* 144, no. 12 (Jun 20, 2006): 904[en dash]12.

110. J.M. James et al., "Respiratory reactions provoked by double-blind food challenges in children," *Am J Respir Crit Care Med* 149, no. 1 (Jan 1994): 59–64.

111. M. Kulig et al., "Long-lasting sensitization to food during the first two years precedes allergic airway disease. The MAS Study Group, Germany," *Pediatr Allergy Immunol* (Germany) 9, no. 2 (May 1998): 61–7.

112. E.R. Weeke, "Epidemiology of allergic diseases in children," *Rhinol Suppl* 13 (Sep 1992): 5–12.

113. D.C. Heiner, "Respiratory diseases and food allergy," *Ann Allergy* 53, no. 6, part 2 (Dec 1984): 657–64.

114. S.M. Tariq et al., "The prevalence of and risk factors for atopy in early childhood: a whole population birth cohort study," *J Allergy Clin Immunol* 101, no. 5 (May 1998): 587–93.

115. T.F. Boat et al., "Hyperreactivity to cow milk in young children with pulmonary hemosiderosis and cor pulmonale secondary to nasopharyngeal obstruction," *J Pediatr* 87, no. 1 (Jul 1975): 23–9.

116. U. Ones et al., "Prevalence of childhood asthma in Istanbul, Turkey," *Allergy* (Turkey) 52, no. 5 (May 1997): 570–5.

117. L.D. Voss et al., "Short stature at school entry—an index of social deprivation? (The Wessex Growth Study)," *Child Care Health Dev* (England) 24, no. 2 (Mar 1998): 145–56.

118. F. Kristmundsdottir and T.J. David, "Growth impairment in children with atopic eczema," *J R Soc Med* 80, no. 1 (Jan 1987): 9–12.

119. W.F. Baum et al., "Effect of bronchial asthma on growth and physical development," *Arztl Jugendkd* 81, no. 5 (1990): 379–83.

120. T.J. David, "Short stature in children with atopic eczema," *Acta Derm Venereol Suppl (Stockh)* (England) 144 (1989): 41–4.

121. A. Kahn et al., "Milk intolerance in children with persistent sleeplessness: a prospective double-blind cross-over evaluation," *Pediatrics* 84, no. 4 (Oct 1989): 595–603.

122. J. Jarvinen et al., "Some local and systemic factors related to tongue inflammation," *Proc Finn Dent* 85, no. 3 (1989): 199–209.

123. S. Lucarelli et al., "Food allergy and infantile autism," *Panminerva Med* (Italy) 37, no. 3 (Sep 1995): 137–41.

124. G. Rostoker et al., "Mucosal immunity in primary glomerulonephritis: II. Study of the serum IgA subclass repertoire to food and airborne antigens," *Nephron* 59, no. 4 (1991): 561–6.

125. S. Jackson et al., "IgA-containing immune complexes after challenge with food antigens in patients with IgA nephropathy," *Clin Exp Immunol* 89, no. 2 (Aug 1992): 315–20.

126. S. Lucarelli et al., "Food allergy in cystic fibrosis," *Minerva Pediatr* (Italy) 46, no. 12 (Dec 1994): 543–8.

127. S. Coren, "Handedness and allergic response," *Int J Neurosci* (Canada) 76, nos. 3–4 (Jun 1994): 231–6.

128. R.E. Weinstein and D.R. Pieper, "Altered cerebral dominance in an atopic population," *Brain Behav Immun* 2, no. 3 (Sep 1988): 235–41.

129. M. Hassler and D. Gupta, "Functional brain organization, handedness, and immune vulnerability in musicians and non-musicians," *Neuropsychologia* (Germany) 31, no. 7 (Jul 1993): 655–60.

130. C.P. Benbow, "Physiological correlates of extreme intellectual precocity," *Neuropsychologia* 24, no. 5 (1986): 719–25.

131. G. Martino and E. Winner, "Talents and disorders: relationships among handedness, sex, and college major," *Brain Cogn* 29, no. 1 (Oct 1995): 66–84.

132. V. Dolezalova and D. Mottlova, "[Relation between myopia and intelligence]," *Cesk Oftalmol* (Czechoslovakia) 51, no. 4 (Sep 1995): 235–9.

133. D.M. Fergusson et al., "Perinatal factors and atopic disease in childhood," *Clin Exp Allergy* (New Zealand) 27, no. 12 (Dec 1997): 1394–401.

134. K.M. Godfrey et al., "Disproportionate fetal growth and raised IgE concentration in adult life," *Clin Exp Allergy* (England) 24, no. 7 (Jul 1994): 641–8.

135. F. Lorente et al., "[Preventive measures for allergic disease]," *Allergol Immunopathol (Madr)* (Spain) 26, no. 3 (May–Jun 1998): 101–13.

Chapter 13: Allergy Matters

1. A. Ojuawo et al., "Non-infective colitis in infancy: evidence in favour of minor immunodeficiency in its pathogenesis," *Arch Dis Child* (London) 76, no. 4 (April 1997): 345–8.

2. M. Garcia-Careaga Jr. and J.A. Kerner Jr., "Gastrointestinal manifestations of food allergies in pediatric patients," *Nutr Clin Pract* 20, no. 5 (Oct 2005): 526[en dash]35.

3. M.J. Solomon and M. Schnitzler, "Cancer and inflammatory bowel disease: bias, epidemiology, surveillance, and treatment," *World J Surg* (Australia) 22, no. 4 (April 1998): 352–8.

4. M.B. Ribeiro et al., "Colorectal adenocarcinoma in Crohn's disease," *Ann Surg* 2, no. 223 (Feb 1996): 186–93.

5. P. Karlen et al., "Increased risk of cancer in ulcerative colitis: a population-based cohort study," *Am J Gastroenterol* (Sweden) 94, no. 4 (Apr 1999): 1047–52.

6. A. Ferguson and K. Kingstone, "Coeliac disease and malignancies," *Acta Paediatr* suppl (UK) 412 (May 1996): 78–81.

7. R. Barreto-Zuniga et al., "Significance of *Helicobacter pylori* infection as a risk factor in gastric cancer: serological and histological studies," *J Gastroenterol* (Mexico) 32, no. 3 (Jun 1997): 289–94.

8. J. Markowitz et al., "Endoscopic screening for dysplasia and mucosal aneuploidy in adolescents and young adults with childhood-onset colitis," *Am J Gastroenterol* 92, no. 11 (Nov 1997): 2001–6.

9. K. Wasowska Królikowska et al., "[Morphological, microstereological, and immunohistoenzymological studies of the jejuni of infants with recurrent constructive bronchitis and chronic diarrhea due to cow's milk protein allergy]," *Pediatr Pol* (Poland) 71, no. 5 (May 1996): 397–403.

10. Jonathan Brostoff and Stephen J. Challacombe, *Food Allergy and Intolerance* (London: Baillière Tindall, 1987), 22, 112, 129, 243–5, 575.

11. Jonathan Brostoff et al., *Immunology*, fifth edition (London: Mosby, 1998), 58.

12. T. Voros-Balog et al., "[Epidemiologic survey of tongue lesions and analysis of the etiologic factors involved," *Fogorv Sz* (Hungary) 92, no. 5 (May 1999): 157–63.

13. S. Salardi et al., "*Helicobacter pylori* and type 1 diabetes mellitus in children," *J Pediatr Gastroenterol Nutr* (Italy) 28, no. 3 (Mar 1999): 307–9.

14. M Pocecco et al., "High risk of *Helicobacter pylori* infection associated with cow's milk antibodies in young diabetics," *Acta Paediatr* 86, no. 7 (Jul 1997): 700–3.

15. E. Odak, "The incidence and clinical manifestation of food allergy in unselected Polish infants: follow-up from birth to one year of age," *Rocz Akad Med Bialymst* (Poland) 42, no. 1 (1997): 196–204.

16. A. Armisén Pedrejon et al., "[Colitis induced by a food allergen. A report of 20 cases]," *An Esp Pediatr* (Spain) 44, no. 1 (Jan 1996): 21–4.

17. I. Polanco, "Current status of digestive intolerance to food protein," *J Pediatr* 121 (Nov 1992): S108–10.

18. H.R. Jenkins et al., "Food Allergy: the major cause of infantile colitis," *Arch Dis Child* 59 (1984): 326–9.

19. J.W. Gerrard, "Familial recurrent rhinorrhea and bronchitis due to cow's milk," *JAMA* 198 (1966): 605–7.

20. J. Egger et al., "Is migraine food allergy?" *Lancet* 2 (1983): 865–9.

21. A.S. Goldman et al., "Milk allergy: I. Oral challenge with milk and isolated proteins in allergic children," *Pediatrics* 32 (1963): 425–43.

22. Jonathan Brostoff and Stephen J. Challacombe, eds., *Food Allergy and Intolerance*, chapter 18 by John W. Gerrard (London: Baillière Tindall, 1987), 344–55.

23. John Hermon-Taylor et al., "Grand Round: *Mycobacterium paratuberculosis* cervical lymphadenitis, followed five years later by terminal ileitis similar to Crohn's disease," *BMJ* 316 (1998): 449–453.

24. R.K. Chandra, "Five-year follow-up of high-risk infants with family history of allergy who were exclusively breast-fed or fed partial whey hydrolysate, soy, and conventional cow's milk formulas," *J Pediatr Gastroenterol Nutr* (Canada) 24, no. 4 (April 1997): 380–8.

25. S. Halken, A. Host et al., "[Prevention of allergy in infants. A prospective study of 159 high-risk children]," *Ugeskr Laeger* (Denmark) 156, no. 3 (Jan 17 1994): 308–12.

26. I. Polanco, "Current status of digestive intolerance to food protein," *J Pediatr* 121 (Nov 1992): S108–10.

27. F.G. Graeff et al., "Dual role of 5-HT in defense and anxiety," *Neurosoc Biobehav Rev* (Brazil) 21, no. 6 (Nov 1997): 791–9.

28. J.C. Shih et al., "Role of MAO A and B in neurotransmitter metabolism and behavior," *Pol J Pharmacol* 51, no. 1 (Jan–Feb 1999): 25–9.

29. M. Nicolodi et al., "The way to serotonergic use and abuse in migraine," *Int J Clin Pharmacol* (Italy) 17, nos. 2–3 (1997): 79–84.

30. X. Baur and A. Czuppon, "Diagnostic validation of specific IgE antibody concentrations, skin prick testing, and challenge tests in chemical workers with symptoms of sensitivity to different anhydrides," *J Allergy Clin Immunol* (Germany) 96, no. 4 (Oct 1995): 489–94.

31. W.J. Meggs et al., "Prevalence and nature of allergy and chemical sensitivity in a general population," *Arch Environ Health* 51, no. 4 (Jul–Aug 1996): 275–82.

32. B.A. Sorg et al., "Proposed animal neurosensitization model for multiple chemical sensitivity in studies with formalin," *Toxicology* 111, nos. 1–3 (Jul 17, 1996): 135–45.

33. J. Elberling et al., "Increased release of histamine in patients with respiratory symptoms related to perfume," *Clin Exp Allergy* (Denmark) 37, no. 11 (Nov 2007): 1676[en dash]80.

34. L.R. Goldman, "Chemicals and children's environment: what we don't know about risks," *Environ Health Perspect* 106, suppl. 3 (Jun 1998): 875–80.

35. S.H. Sicherer, "Food protein-induced enterocolitis syndrome: clinical perspectives," *J Pediatr Gastroenterol Nutr* 30, suppl. (2000): S45[en dash]9.

36. J. Maloney and A. Nowak-Wegrzyn, "Educational clinical case series for pediatric allergy and immunology: allergic proctocolitis, food protein-induced enterocolitis syndrome and allergic eosinophilic gastroenteritis with protein-losing gastroenteropathy as manifestations of non-IgE-mediated cow's milk allergy," *Pediatr Allergy Immunol* 18, no. 4 (Jun 2007): 360[en dash]7.

37. K.M. Saarinen et al., "Diagnostic value of skin-prick and patch tests and serum eosinophil cationic protein and cow's milk-specific IgE in infants with cow's milk allergy," *Clin Exp Allergy* (Finland) 31, no. 3 (Mar 2001): 423[en dash]9.

38. Jonathan Brostoff and Stephen J. Challacombe, eds., *Food Allergy and Intolerance*, chapter 18 by John W. Gerrard (London: Baillière Tindall, 1987), 349–50.

39. J. Egger et al., "Effect of diet treatment on enuresis in children with migraine or hyperkinetic behavior," *Clin Pediatr* (Philadelphia) 31, no. 5 (May 1992): 302–7.

40. P.F. Kilshaw and H. Hester-Slade, "Passage of ingested protein into the blood during gastrointestinal hypersensitivity reactions experiments in the preruminant calf," *Clin Exp Immunol* 6 (1980): 45.

41. P.L. Lim and D. Rowley, "The effect of antibody on the intestinal absorption of macromolecules and on intestinal permeability in adult mice," *Int Arch Allergy Appl Immunol* 68 (1982): 41–6.

42. S. Husby, "Dietary antigens: uptake and humoral immunity in man," *Institute of Medical Microbiology APMIS Suppl* (Denmark) 1 (1988): 1–40.

43. Jonathan Brostoff and Stephen J. Challacombe, eds., *Food Allergy and Intolerance*, chapter 2 by C. N. Mallinson (London: Baillière Tindall, 1987), 45.

44. J.A. Lovegrove et al., "Transfer of cow's milk beta-lactoglobulin to human serum after a milk load: a pilot study," *Gut* 34, no. 2 (Feb 1993): 203–7.

45. Jonathan Brostoff et al., *Immunology*, fifth edition (London: Mosby, 1998), 336.

46. John Hermon-Taylor et al., "Grand Round: *Mycobacterium paratuberculosis* cervical lymphadenitis, followed five years later by terminal ileitis similar to Crohn's disease," *BMJ* 316 (1998): 449–53.

47. G.C.L. Du Mont et al., "Gastrointestinal permeability in food allergic eczematous children," *Clin Allergy* 14 (1984): 55–9.

48. Jonathan Brostoff et al., *Immunology*, fifth edition (London: Mosby, 1998), 315.

49. James Braly, MD, *Dr. Braly's Food Allergy and Nutrition Revolution* (New Canaan, Connecticut: Keats Publishing, Inc., 1992), 59.

50. C.S. Miller, "Chemical sensitivity: symptom, syndrome or mechanism for disease?" *Toxicology* 111, nos. 1–3 (Jul 17, 1996): 69–86.

Chapter 14: Discovering, Preventing, and Treating Food Allergies

1. R. Forman, "Medical resistance to innovation," *Med Hypotheses* 7, no. 8 (Aug 1981): 1009.

2. *Hippocrates Writings*, edited with an introduction by G.E.R. Lloyd (Harmondsworth: Penguin, 1978), 266.

3. A. Fasano, "Where have all the American celiacs gone?," *Acta Paediatr Suppl* 412 (May 1996): 20–4.

4. M. Frieri et al., "Preliminary investigation on humoral and cellular immune responses to selected food proteins in patients with Crohn's disease," *Ann Allergy* 64, no. 4 (Apr 1990): 345–51.

5. P. Juvonen et al., "Macromolecular absorption and cow's milk allergy," *Arch Dis Child* (Sweden) 66, no. 3 (Mar 1991): 300–3.

6. G.F. Hankard et al., "Increased TIA1-expressing intraepithelial lymphocytes in cow's milk protein intolerance," *J Pediatr Gastroenterol Nutr* (France) 25, no. 1 (Jul 1997): 79–83.

7. K. Wasowska Królikowska et al., "[Morphological, microstereological, and immunohistoenzymological studies of the jejuni of infants with recurrent constructive bronchitis and chronic diarrhea due to cow's milk protein allergy]," *Pediatr Pol*, (Poland) 71, no. 5 (May 1996): 397–403.

8. A. Armisén Pedrejón et al., "[Colitis induced by a food allergen. A report of 20 cases]," *An Esp Pediatr* (Spain) 44, no. 2 (Jan 1996): 21–4.

9. U.M. Saarinen et al., *Allergy* 38, no. 8 (Nov 1983): 571–6.

10. H. Scott et al., "Measurements of serum IgA and IgG activities to dietary antigens: A prospective study of the diagnostic usefulness in adult coeliac disease," *Scand J Gastroenterol* 25, no. 3 (Mar 1990): 287–92.

11. J. Graham, "Food intolerance and its impact on the nation's health. Patient survey," (York, England: York Nutritional Laboratory, 1998).

12. F. Rance et al., "Correlations between skin prick tests using commercial extracts and fresh foods, specific IgE, and food challenges," *Allergy* (France) 52, no. 10 (Oct 1997): 1031–5.

13. K.D. Lust et al., "Maternal intake of cruciferous vegetables and other foods and colic symptoms in exclusively breast-fed infants," *J Am Diet Assoc* 96, no. 1 (Jan 1996): 46–8.

14. B. Wutrich, "Adverse reactions to food additives," *Ann Allergy* 71, no. 4 (Oct 1993): 379–84.

15. G. Fuglsang et al., "Adverse reactions to food additives in children with atopic symptoms," *Allergy* 49, no. 1 (Jan 1994): 31–7.

16. E. Novembre et al., "[Unusual reactions to food additives]," *Pediatr Med Chir* (Italy) 14, no. 1 (Jan–Feb 1992): 39–42.

17. J.P. Hanrahan and M. Halonen, "Antenatal interventions in childhood asthma," *Eur Respir J Suppl* 27 (Jul 1998): 46S–51S.

18. J.A. Lovegrove et al., "Dietary factors influencing levels of food antibodies and antigens in breast milk," *Acta Paediatr* (England) 85 no. 7 (Jul 1996): 778–84.

19. K. Falth-Magnusson and N.I. Kjellman, "Allergy prevention by maternal elimination diet during late pregnancy—a 5-year follow-up of a randomized study," *J Allergy Clin Immunol* (Sweden) 89, no. 3 (Mar 1992): 709–13.

20. R.K. Chandra, "Five-year follow-up of high-risk infants with family history of allergy who were exclusively breast-fed or fed partial whey hydrolysate, soy, and conventional cow's milk formulas," *J Pediatr Gastroenterol Nutr* (Canada) 24, no. 4 (Apr 1997): 380–8.

21. Y. Vandenplas et al., "The long-term effect of a partial whey hydrolysate formula on the prophylaxis of atopic disease," *Eur J Pediatr* (Belgium) 154 no. 6 (Jun 1995): 488–94.

22. G. Stintzing and R. Zetterstrom, "Cow's milk allergy, incidence, and pathogenetic role of early exposure to cow's milk formula," *Acta Paediatr Scand* 68, no. 3 (May 1979): 383–7.

23. Naomi Baumslag, MD, MPH, and Dia L. Michels, *Milk, Money, and Madness: The Culture and Politics of Breastfeeding* (Westport, Connecticut: Bergin & Garvey, 1995), 171–2.

24. F. Savino and R. Oggero, "[Management of infantile colics]," *Minerva Pediatr* (Italy) 48, nos. 7–8 (Jul 1996): 313–9.

25. G. Patriarca et al., "Food allergy in children: results of a standardized protocol for oral desensitization," *Hepatogastroenterology* (Italy) 45, no. 19 (Jan–Feb 1998): 52–8.

26. L.J. Chartrand and E.G. Seidman, "Celiac disease is a lifelong disorder," *Clin Invest Med* 19, no. 5 (Oct 1996): 357–61.

27. J.J. Oppenheimer et al., "Treatment of peanut allergy with rush immunotherapy," *J Allergy Clin Immunol* 90, no. 2 (Aug 1992): 256–62.

28. N.F. Adkinson Jr. et al., "A controlled trial of immunotherapy for asthma in allergic children," *N Engl J Med* 336, no. 5 (Jan 30, 1997): 324–31.

29. Alan Pressman, D.C., PhD and Herbert D. Goodman, MD, PhD, *Treating Asthma, Allergies, and Food Sensitivities* (New York: Berkley Books, 1997), 29–30.

30. W.P. King et al., "Provocation-neutralization: A two-part study. Part II. Subcutaneous neutralization therapy: A multi-center study," *Otolaryngol Head Neck Surg* 99, no. 3 (Sep 1988): 272–7.

31. P. Stavroulaki, "Diagnostic and management problems of laryngopharyngeal reflux disease in children," *Int J Pediatr Otorhinolaryngol* 70, no. 4 (Apr 2006): 579-90.

32. Morgenstein, "Gastroesophageal Reflux Disease in Infants," CME material, Children's Memorial Hospital, 2008, http://www.childrensmemorial.org/cme.

33. Aanen et al., "Diagnostic value of the proton pump inhibitor test for gastro-oesophageal reflux disease in primary care," *Aliment Pharmacol Ther* 24, no. 9 (Nov 2006): 1377–84.

34. Omari et al., "Effect of omeprazole on acid gastroesophageal reflux and gastric acidity in preterm infants with pathological acid reflux," *J Pediatr Gastroenterol Nutr* 44, No. 1 (Jan 2007): 41–4.

35. Canani et al., "Therapy with gastric acidity inhibitors increases the risk of acute gastroenteritis and community-acquired pneumonia in children," *Pediatrics* 117, no. 5 (May 2006): e817–20.

36. García Rodríguez et al., "Use of acid-suppressing drugs and the risk of bacterial gastroenteritis," *Clin Gastroenterol Hepatol* 5, no. 12 (Dec 2007): 1418–23.

37. Karkos and Wilson, "Empiric treatment of laryngopharyngeal reflux with proton pump inhibitors: a systematic review," *Laryngoscope* 116, no. 1 (Jan 2006): 144–8.

38. G.W. Canonica et al., "Cytoprotective drugs: a new perspective in the treatment of adverse reactions to foods," *Ann Allergy* (Italy) 60, no. 6 (Jun 1988): 541–5.

39. M. Kaliner and R. Lemanske, "Inflammatory responses to mast cell granules," *Fed Proc* 43, no. 13 (Oct 1984): 2846–51.

40. B. Skyzydlo-Radomanska et al., "The effect of stimulation and blocking of histamine H-2 receptors on the turnover of the serotonin in different parts of the alimentary tract and the brain of the rat," *Agents Actions* 16, nos. 3–4 (Apr 1985): 183–6.

41. N. Kondo et al., "Suppression of proliferative responses of lymphocytes to food antigens by an anti-allergic drug, ketotifen fumerate, in patients with food sensitive atopic dermatitis," *Int Arch Allergy Immunol* (Japan) 103, no. 3 (1994): 234–8.

42. G. Ciprandi et al., "Ketotifen treatment of adverse reactions to foods: clinical and immunological effects," *Curr Med Res Opin* (Italy) 10, no. 5 (1986): 346–50.

43. G.W. Canonica et al., "Cytoprotective drugs: a new perspective in the treatment of adverse reactions to foods," *Ann Allergy* (Italy) 60, no. 6 (Jun 1988): 541–5.

44. G. Ciprandi et al., "Pirenzepine treatment in urticaria-angioedema syndrome caused by adverse reactions to foods," (Italy) 17, no. 4 (Jul–Aug 1989): 189–92.

45. L. Businco et al., "Evaluation of the efficacy of oral cromolyn sodium or an oligoantigenic diet in children with atopic dermatitis: a multi-center study of 1085 patients," *J Investig Allergol Clin Immunol* (Italy) 6, no. 2 (Mar–Apr 1996): 103–9.

46. A.M. Edwards, "Oral sodium cromoglycate: its use in the management of food allergy," *Clin Exp Allergy* 25, suppl. 1 (Jul 1995): 31–3.

47. R.M. Van Elburg et al., "Effect of disodiomcromoglycate on intestinal permeability changes and clinical response during cow's milk challenge," *Pediatr Allergy Immunol* (Netherlands) 4, no. 2 (May 1993): 79–85.

48. U. Hoppu et al, "Vitamin C in breast milk may reduce the risk of atopy in the infant," *Eur J Clin Nutr* (Finland) 59, no. 1 (Jan 2005): 123-8.

49. A. Ojuawo et al., "Serum zinc, selenium, and copper concentration in children with allergic colitis," *East Afr Med J* (Nigeria) 73, no. 4 (Apr 1996): 236–8.

50. A.P. Simopoulos, "Omega-3 fatty acids in inflammation and autoimmune diseases," *J Am Coll Nutr* 21, no. 6 (Dec 2002): 495–505.

51. P. Kankaanpaa et al., "Dietary fatty acids and allergy," *Ann Med* (Finland) 31, no. 4 (Aug 1999): 282–7.

52. S.N. Han et al., "Effect of hydrogenated and saturated, relative to polyunsaturated, fat on immune and inflammatory responses of adults with moderate hypercholesterolemia," *J Lipid Res* 43, no. 3 (Mar 2002): 445–52.

53. M. Korotkova et al., "Modulation of neonatal immunological tolerance to ovalbumin by maternal essential fatty acid intake," *Pediatr Allergy Immunol* (Sweden) 15, no. 2 (Apr 2004): 112–22.

54. U. Hoppu et al., "Breast milk fatty acid composition is associated with development of atopic dermatitis in the infant," *J Pediatr Gastroenterol Nutr.* (Finland) 41, no. 3 (Sep 2005): 335–8.

55. K. Duchen et al., "Human milk polyunsaturated long-chain fatty acids and secretory immunoglobulin A antibodies and early childhood allergy," *Pediatr Allergy Immunol* (Sweden) 11, no. 1 (Feb 2000): 29–39.

56. K. Yamada et al., "Effect of unsaturated fatty acids and antioxidants on immunoglobulin production by mesenteric lymph node lymphocytes of Sprague-Dawley rats," *J Biochem* (Japan) 120 no. 1 (Jul 1996): 138–44.

57. D. Sistek et al., "Is the effect of probiotics on atopic dermatitis confined to food sensitized children?" *Clin Exp Allergy* (New Zealand) 36, no. 5 (May 2006): 629–33.

58. H. Majamaa and E. Isolauri, "Probiotics: a novel approach in the management of food allergy," *J Allergy Clin Immunol* (Finland) 99, no. 2 (Feb 1997): 179–85.

59. E. Isolauri et al., "Probiotics: effects on immunity," *Am J Clin Nutr* (Finland) 73, no. 2, suppl. (Feb 2001): 444S–450S.

60. M. Gueimonde et al., "Effect of maternal consumption of lactobacillus GG on transfer and establishment of fecal bifidobacterial microbiota in neonates," *J Pediatr Gastroenterol Nutr* (Finland) 42, no. 2 (Feb 2006): 166–70.

61. L. Langmead et al., "Anti-inflammatory effects of aloe vera gel in human colorectal mucosa in vitro," *Aliment Pharmacol Ther* (England) 19, no. 5 (Mar 1, 2004): 521–7.

62. E. Ernst, "Frankincense: systematic review," *BMJ* 337 (Dec 2008): a2813.

Glossary

AAP. American Academy of Pediatrics. A large segment of pediatricians belong to this medical organization involved in policy making and continued education.

acidophilus. Short for *Lactobacillus acidophilus*, the most commonly recognized probiotic, or "friendly" bacteria that lives in the intestines. It feeds mostly off of lactose, the milk sugar, and is popular for its use in making yogurt.

acute. Recent or sudden onset of a condition worthy of attention.

ADHD. Attention deficit hyperactivity disorder. A set of behavioral symptoms, such as lack of attention and excessive activity, classified as a specific disorder. There is a wide range of extremes among children so classified, from what many might call a normal, highly active child, to one who is strongly impaired in ability to learn.

adjuvant. An agent used in drugs and vaccines to enhance the activity of other ingredients. Aluminum adjuvant is used in many vaccines to enhance the body's response to the antigen in the vaccine.

allergen. More appropriately called an antigen. An agent, such as pollen or peanuts, that stimulates an excessive sensitivity/allergy response in vulnerable individuals.

allergy. A hypersensitivity to a food, pollen, or other exposure whereby one will exhibit certain excessive symptoms not exhibited by all individuals. In the strict usage of the term, an allergy is a response by IgE antibodies in the body, resulting in symptoms such as hives or a runny nose. In a looser sense of the term, allergy can include any non-normal physical reaction, such as intestinal symptoms of diarrhea and green stools in reaction to certain foods.

anaphylactic. Anaphylactic reaction, anaphylactic shock, or anaphylaxis. A severe hypersensitivity reaction to an allergen, involving symptoms such as swelling of the tongue and lips, difficulty breathing, dropping blood pressure, and hives; typically initiated by IgE antibodies.

anemia. A deficiency in the ability of the blood to carry enough oxygen to the tissues of the body. Among other things, iron, folic acid, and vitamin B12 are required to create hemoglobin, the oxygen carrying portion of red blood cells. Insufficient iron leads to "iron deficiency anemia." Some other anemias are vitamin B12 deficiency anemia and folic acid deficiency anemia.

antibody. Part of the immune system, also known as immunoglobulin, abbreviated as Ig. Proteins found in the blood and other sites in the body identify and neutralize foreign invaders (antigens) such as bacteria or viruses. In a sensitized individual, antibodies may attack certain food proteins, pollens, or other allergens/antigens. Antibody-antigen interactions typically instigate a cascade of other immune system responses.

antigen. Any substance entering the body that elicits an immune system response. A bacterium, fungus, or virus, and sometimes certain foods or other substances, can act as antigens in an individual.

antioxidant. A substance that reduces oxidation of other substances. A certain amount of oxidation is necessary to body functioning but it can also be damaging. Popular antioxidants are vitamin C, selenium, and grapeseed extract.

ARA. Arachidonic acid. An important omega-6 fatty acid found in the diet and in breastmilk, and found to be low in standard infant formulas. The body can create this fatty acid from other dietary fats but it is thought that this ability is low in infants, so ARA is currently an additive in many formulas.

asthma. Attacks of wheezing, coughing, and shortness of breath caused by mucus accumulation and swelling of airways. Asthma attacks can be set off by all kinds of irritants such as smoke, allergens, exercise, and cold viruses.

atopic. Allergic or prone to allergies.

autism. A disorder of brain development showing symptoms of repetitive actions, poor verbal and non-verbal communication abilities, and impaired social interactions.

bilirubin. A product of the breakdown of hemoglobin from red blood cells. When excess bilirubin builds up in the body, a yellow tint to the skin and eyes occurs, known as jaundice.

bovine. Cow.

carbohydrate. Simple or complex sugar or fiber.

caries. Dental decay or cavities.

CDC. Centers for Disease Control and Prevention. Government agency intended to protect public health and safety through provision of information about the prevention of accidents and disease.

chronic. A frequently occurring, long lasting, or slowly developing condition.

cognitive. Having to do with intellectual brain activity: thinking, remembering, and reasoning.

colic. Infant colic. Excessive crying in a baby for no known medical cause. Strictly defined as crying three days a week for more than three hours a day.

colitis. Inflammation/irritation of the large intestine, which can result from infection or other disease. In infants and young children, the most common cause of colitis is sensitivity to cow's milk protein, soy, or other allergens.

cortisol. A hormone known as the "stress hormone," produced by the same organ that produces adrenaline (epinephrine), the adrenal gland. Cortisol has a daily cycle of being high in the morning and low during the night. Newborns do not yet have this cycle. Cortisol is otherwise released in response to conditions such as pain, fear, injury, and crying. Short bursts of cortisol can be helpful in reducing inflammation and pain, and in elevating mood. Chronic elevations in an infant may lead to a life-long disordered regulation of these responses.

Crohn's disease. A disease of the small or large intestine accompanied by diarrhea, weight loss, poor nutrient absorption, and sometimes rectal bleeding. The tendency toward developing Crohn's disease may be hereditary and/or may come from *Mycobacterium paratuberculosis* (MAP) bacteria infecting a chronically irritated bowel. Most Crohn's sufferers will go into remission on a diet free of dairy proteins and possibly some other dietary modifications.

cytokines. A class of a large number of various small proteins, found in the blood and other areas of the body, that help to control and perform actions of the immune system.

delayed reaction sensitivity. Delayed reaction type allergy. A term often used to describe abnormal physical reactions to certain agents, usually foods, involving intestinal symptoms, slowly developing rashes, and occasionally mood changes, as opposed to immediate type reactions of mouth swelling, restricted breathing, and hives.

dermatitis. A general term for any kind of inflammatory skin condition; a rash. Atopic dermatitis, meaning "allergic rash," is another term for eczema.

DHA. Docosahexaenoic acid. An important omega-3 fatty acid found in fish oil and in breastmilk, and found to be low in standard infant formulas. The body can create this fatty acid from other dietary fats but it is thought that this ability is low in infants and some others. Some formulas are currently adding this ingredient, but without much beneficial result being reported. DHA is especially anti-inflammatory, heart protective, and brain building.

diabetes. Diabetes mellitus. A group of disorders that lead to high blood sugar. Long-term diabetes can lead to all kinds of damage in the body including nerve pain, blindness, loss of limbs, and heart disease. Mild forms may be controlled with diet and exercise but typically diabetics are treated with the blood sugar controlling hormone insulin.

eclampsia. An acute and life-threatening complication of pregnancy that occurs in a portion of women who exhibit preeclampsia. Following high blood pressure and proteins in the urine associated with preeclampsia, eclampsia can occur in the form of a seizure or coma. Any degree of the spectrum from preeclampsia to eclampsia may be referred to as toxemia of pregnancy.

E. coli. *Escherichia coli.* A bacterium found as a predominant part of the normal flora in adults, and in children who receive any formula or solid foods. Certain strains of E. *coli*, different from those normally found in the body, cause illness with diarrhea and other symptoms.

eczema. A persistent skin rash. Some eczema is simply a condition of dry skin, but most is allergic in nature. Most infant eczema is associated with delayed-reaction sensitivity to certain foods in their diet or in the diet of their breastfeeding mother.

elimination diet. A means of determining what foods might be causing troubling symptoms in a person by means of eliminating certain foods in the diet to see whether symptoms subside. The term usually implies that one will later re-challenge suspected foods to see whether symptoms return.

endorphins. The body's own natural pain relievers, produced during strenuous exercise, excitement, play, and smiling, creating a sense of well-being.

enteritis. Inflammation/irritation of the small intestine, which can result from infection or other disease. In infants and young children, the most common cause of this finding is sensitivity to cow's milk protein, soy, or other allergens.

enteromammary pathway. Pathway through which a mother is supplied specific immune factors in her milk according to what she has been exposed to. It has been shown that certain cells (dendritic cells) carry bacterial samples directly from the intestines to the breasts, through the lymphatic system.

Certain antibody producing cells (B lymphocytes) travel through the lymph system to the breasts as well.

eosinophil. Part of the immune system. One type of white blood cell that battles infection and parasites and is also involved in creating allergic reactions and asthma attacks.

EPA. Eicosapentaenoic acid. An important omega-3 fatty acid found in fish oil and breastmilk. The body can create this fatty acid from other dietary fats but it is thought that this ability is low in infants. EPA is not currently considered important to add to infant formulas because it is not found in the brain.

eustachian tube. Mucous membrane lined tube that connects the middle ear to the throat, providing drainage for the middle ear. Infant eustachian tubes are very narrow and become easily blocked from inflammation, allowing microbes in the middle ear to reproduce in excess, creating a middle ear infection.

fatty acids. Chief components of fats, coming in many different types with different functions in the body.

ferritin. A protein in the body that binds to iron, providing iron storage in the body. While exclusively breastfed babies born full-term seldom develop iron deficiency anemia, they commonly have low iron stores, indicated by a low serum ferritin finding.

flora. The friendly bacteria that normally live in the body, throughout the digestive tract and chiefly in the intestines. *E. coli*, bifidobacteria, and lactobacillus are examples. Normal flora help break down some undigested materials, create some vitamins, help prevent the growth of harmful bacteria, and help to regulate the intestines in other ways.

fluorosis. A condition of having too much fluoride. Dental fluorosis causes spotting and decay of the teeth. In greater excess, fluorosis can cause misshapen bones and bones that appear dense on X-ray but break easily.

galactose. A simple sugar that is very rare in the human diet except from breakdown of the baby sugar lactose found in breastmilk, dairy products, and some formulas.

gastritis/gastroenteritis. Inflammation/irritation of the stomach (gastritis) or stomach and small intestine (gastroenteritis), which can result from infection or other disease. In infants and young children, the most common cause is sensitivity to cow's milk protein, soy, or other allergens.

gastroesophageal reflux. Reflux, acid reflux, heartburn, or GER. Stomach contents of food and acid going up into the throat (esophagus) and sometimes out the mouth. Often pronounced when lying down, reflux can cause burning of the throat tissues. Reflux may be exhibited in babies as spitting up, vomiting, or coughing, and sometimes fussiness or other signs of pain.

gastroesophageal reflux disease. Reflux disease or GERD. A serious condition of chronic reflux of stomach contents up into the throat and often out the mouth or nose, causing chronic damage to esophageal tissues and, in infants, great irritability, feeding difficulties, poor sleep, and sometimes weight loss.

GER. Gastroesophageal reflux.

GERD. Gastroesophageal reflux disease.

H-1 receptor. Histamine type 1 receptor. Type of receptor located on certain cells lining the respiratory system, blood vessels, and bladder, and in the skin. These receptors detect histamine when released and perform regulatory functions. When antibodies detect certain allergens in a sensitized body, abnormally large histamine releases acting on H-1 receptors lead to allergic reactions, such as restricted breathing and hives. Other less known H-1 reactions may occur as well, such as spasms of the bladder that can lead to bedwetting. Typical antihistamines such as Benadryl block H-1 type receptor actions.

H-2 receptor. Histamine type 2 receptor. Type of receptor located on certain cells lining the stomach, intestines, and lungs, and in the skin. These receptors detect histamine when released and perform regulatory functions. When antibody actions in a body sensitized to certain foods cause excess histamine releases, symptoms such as reflux, vomiting, diarrhea, and rashes can occur. Typical antacids such as Zantac block H-2 receptor actions.

H. pylori. *Helicobacter pylori.* A bacterium that colonizes the stomach or small intestine in a portion of children and adults often causing chronic inflammation, sometimes leading to painful ulcer formation.

hemoglobin. The iron-containing portion of red blood cells that carries oxygen to all parts of the body. A hemoglobin blood test will show if the blood is too low in iron, referred to as iron deficiency anemia.

HFCS. High fructose corn syrup. An artificially created sugar that is taxing to the liver and is found in many packaged foods.

Hib. *Haemophilus influenzae* type B. A bacterium that may infect the lining around the brain, causing meningitis, or may infect some other areas of the body. Before the vaccination program for Hib, it was the chief cause of meningitis. Hib vaccination has not reduced the number of meningitis cases; it has led to a shift in which bacteria cause meningitis today.

histamine. Acts as a neurotransmitter for daily regulatory functions and is released in response to injury, or invasion by a foreign microorganism. Undesirable histamine releases are induced in a sensitized system when antibodies attach to allergens, leading to inflammation, and constriction of involuntary muscles, in various areas of the body.

hydrolyzed. Chemically broken down into smaller molecules. Hydrolyzed formulas have proteins broken down into their amino acid building blocks.

hypersensitivity. Over sensitive. An allergic or allergic-type reaction.

IBD. Inflammatory bowel disease. A condition of chronic inflammation in the large or small intestine; chiefly, Crohn's disease or ulcerative colitis. Symptoms include weight loss, abdominal pain, gas, bloating, diarrhea, and rectal bleeding. IBD can often be controlled with dietary measures while stress and flora imbalance can increase episodes.

IBS. Irritable bowel syndrome. Similar symptoms to IBD but typically with little inflammation or intestinal damage, no bleeding, and may have constipation as well as diarrhea. Can often be controlled with dietary measures while stress and flora imbalance can increase episodes.

IgA. Immunoglobulin A. A class of antibodies that help protect against invading organisms in the digestive tract and other mucous membrane tissues. IgA is secreted in high quantities in breastmilk, providing immune protection against organisms invading through the nose and mouth in nursing children. Mothers will also create and provide specific IgA antibodies against organisms the child has recently been exposed to. Food allergic children are often low in IgA antibodies, thus IgA antibodies are considered to play a role in food tolerance, yet many create IgA antibodies against certain food allergens. These antibodies tag the food proteins to be rushed through the system.

IgE. Immunoglobulin E. A class of antibodies that function in protection against parasites and cause allergic reactions to various agents in allergic people. After binding to an allergen, IgE then binds to a mast cell, causing release of histamine.

IGF-1. Insulin-like growth factor 1. Hormone found in breastmilk and dairy products and released in the body in response to growth hormone. Has some insulin type action as well as regulation of growth in children, especially during puberty. Excess IGF-1 has been linked to cancer.

IgG. Immunoglobulin G. A class of antibodies involved in a later phase of immune response to invading organisms. IgG is also often involved in intestinal responses to food allergens in delayed-reaction food sensitivity responses. IgG antibodies cross mother's placenta to be stored in the infant's system, assisting the infant in protection against many organisms the mother has immunity to, for about 6 to 9 months.

IgM. Immunoglobulin M. A class of antibodies involved in early response of the immune system to invading organisms. IgM is also often involved in intestinal delayed-reaction food sensitivity responses.

inflammation. The process of immune system response to infection or other irritation. Tiny blood vessels become leaky so that white blood cells can leak out into the assaulted area to fight invading organisms and initiate other protective and healing responses. At times inflammation can become excessive and problematic. Allergic and sensitivity reactions involve unwanted and unneeded inflammatory responses that damage tissues.

intolerance. Food intolerance. Term can be used generally to include any sort of negative reactions to certain foods or chemicals in certain sensitive people. Term is also used in a stricter sense to refer to lactase enzyme deficiency (lactose intolerance), various other digestive enzyme deficiencies, or to gluten intolerance (celiac disease), a chronic inflammatory reaction to wheat and other grains. There is no physiological similarity between gluten intolerance and lactose intolerance so this stricter use of this term relates less to logic and more to food reactions that have longer been understood medically.

iron deficiency anemia. Reduced ability of the blood to carry oxygen to the tissues of the body due to inadequate iron. Iron is needed to form hemoglobin, the oxygen carrying portion of red blood cells. A blood test result of low hemoglobin indicates iron deficiency anemia.

jaundice. Yellow discoloration of the skin and eyes commonly seen in breast-fed infants in the first days and weeks after birth. The symptom of jaundice is caused by accumulation of bilirubin, a breakdown product of red blood cells. This elevated bilirubin likely provides powerful antioxidant protection to the newborn. Excessively high levels are treated with exposure of skin to blue light, to prevent possible brain damage.

kangaroo care. A method of holding an infant so that there is optimal skin-to-skin contact. The infant wears only a diaper and is held against the adult's bare chest; often between the mother's breasts to encourage thoughts of breastfeeding. The infant is covered on the outside by the adult's shirt or by a blanket.

La Leche League, International. LLLI. An international organization of mothers dedicated to providing breastfeeding information and support to pregnant and nursing mothers. LLLI typically offers local monthly informative meetings and other modes of mother-to-mother support.

lactase. The enzyme that digests lactose; the baby sugar found in the milks of nearly all mammals, and in no other foods.

lactation. The making and providing of breastmilk.

lactobacillus. A genus, or group of bacteria that make up a small but healthy portion of normal intestinal flora. Also known as probiotics, *Lactobacillus acidophilus*, *L. casei*, and *L. brevis* are example species of beneficial lactobacillus bacteria.

lactoferrin. Found in breastmilk and in mucosal secretions such as tears and saliva, a protein that provides protection from unwanted bacteria and other microbes through binding with iron and through other means. Provides highly absorbable iron to the breastfed infant, protecting the iron from being available to undesirable bacteria.

lactose. Sugar found in milk (breastmilk, cow's milk, and nearly all milks) and only in milk. Intended for babies, adults typically lose lactase enzyme activity for lactose digestion.

leaky intestines. Leaky gut. A descriptive term for increased intestinal permeability or increased tendency for whole proteins and other factors to be able to pass through the intestinal walls easily. Young infant intestines are naturally "leaky" for passing factors from mother's milk, but otherwise a leaky gut is a result of intestinal inflammatory damage.

lysozyme. Found in saliva, tears, mucus, and breastmilk, an enzyme that can break down the walls of bacteria, providing protection from infection.

mastitis. Inflammation of the breast. Infection of breast tissue occurring chiefly in breastfeeding mothers, exhibiting redness, warmth, tenderness, and hardness of the area, and often a bright red appearance of branching blood vessels. Early treatment involves heat, massage, and increased breast-feeding or pumping.

meconium. The first stool of a newborn. Thick and greenish black, meconium is made up of shed skin and hair cells and other materials the infant filters out of the amniotic fluid as he regularly drinks the fluid and urinates the liquid portion back out.

MMR. Measles, mumps, and rubella vaccine. Typically given at 12 months and 4 to 5 years.

MRSA. Methicillin-resistant *Staphylococcus aureus*. A form of staph bacteria that has developed a resistance to a large group of standard antibiotics. MRSA is an increasing source of dangerous infection, especially in hospitals.

Mycobacterium paratuberculosis. *Mycobacterium avium* subspecies *paratuberculosis* or MAP. Bacterium that causes Johne's disease in cows and is suspect of causing Crohn's disease in humans.

neurodevelopment. The development of the brain and other nerve tissues, responsible for intellectual development and motor skills.

norepinephrine. Released in the blood to act as a hormone and released in nerve endings to act as a neurotransmitter. Similar to adrenaline (epinephrine), norepinephrine is released in response to fear, pain, and stress, and stimulates a "fight or flight" response of increased attention, energy availability, and heart rate.

omega-3 fatty acid. A class of fatty acids nutritionally important for maintaining nerves and other cells of the body. The three major types are alpha-linolenic acid (ALA), eicosapentaenoic acid (EPA), and docosahexaenoic acid (DHA). DHA and EPA come from breastmilk, fish oils, certain animal organs (seldom consumed today), krill, and algae, and are more readily used by the body. The body can also make these from ALA, found in nut and seed sources, though infants and many others have poor conversion abilities.

osteoporosis. Sometimes referred to as "thinning of the bones," describes a state of weakened bones that fracture more easily. Bone density (more dense bones appearing whiter on X-rays) is one measure of a person's tendency for osteoporosis; however, it is not a complete indicator. Fluoride consumption, for example, can make the bones appear more dense but can make bones lose twisting strength, so that they break rather than bend against force. Exercise and a wide spectrum of appropriate vitamins and minerals can prevent osteoporosis.

otitis. Otitis media. An inflammation or infection of the middle ear, the ear space behind the ear drum that drains through the eustachian tube into the back of the throat.

oxytocin. Hormone released in response to close contact, especially skin-to-skin contact. Oxytocin promotes bonding and a sense of well-being. Oxytocin is high during labor, inducing contractions, and stimulates milk let-down during breastfeeding.

personality disorder. A pattern of behavior that deviates markedly from the expectations of society, and negatively affects one's life. Two examples are antisocial behavior and obsessive compulsive disorder.

pheromones. Chemicals released through the skin that cause certain inborn responses in those sensing them through their noses. While pheromonal actions are not well recognized in humans, those in pregnant women and new mothers are well exhibited and infants are especially responsive to pheromones, particularly in recognizing their mothers and in finding their mother's nipple.

phototherapy. Exposure to full spectrum light or specific light waves for therapeutic purposes. Visible blue light rays are especially helpful for promoting beneficial bilirubin breakdown in infants with excessive jaundice.

PPIs. Proton pump inhibitors. A group of drugs, such as omeprazole, Prevacid, or Prilosec, that reduce stomach acid secretion; used to treat ulcers, reflux, and other disorders.

prebiotics. Dietary or supplemental substances that act as food for beneficial probiotic bacteria in the intestines, improving their activity. Prebiotics are typically complex carbohydrates, known as soluble fiber or nondigestible fiber.

preeclampsia. See also eclampsia. A disorder that can occur during pregnancy, exhibiting high blood pressure and protein in the urine. Rapid swelling or weight gain, headaches, or blurry vision may be warning signs but often there are no outward symptoms. Preeclampsia may lead to dangerous eclampsia, but it can also be harmful or fatal itself, to either the mother, the fetus, or both.

probiotics. Microbes, chiefly bacteria, that add to the quality of one's natural intestinal flora, potentially improving the overall health of an individual. Yogurt is made with probiotic bacteria, and they occur in other fermented foods as well. Probiotic supplements are available, such as members of the lactobacillus and bifidobacterium groups.

prolactin. A hormone that plays some role in maintaining reproductive organs and also acts as a stress hormone in non-parents. In parents, prolactin encourages caregiving behaviors, and in mothers, it encourages milk production in response to suckling.

protein. An organic compound made up of amino acid pieces. Protein provides nutrition in the diet, coming from meats, nuts, beans, breastmilk, formula, and dairy products. Many active components in the body's immune system are proteins and much of the structure of the body is made up of proteins. Proteins are the usual portion of foods that incite allergic responses. Protein detected in the urine suggests improper functioning of the kidneys.

reflux. See gastroesophageal reflux.

retinopathy of prematurity. Growth of abnormal blood vessels in the eyes of a portion of premature infants. This condition may be mild and resolve completely or can be severe and cause blindness. Oxygen therapy, often used in the neonatal intensive care unit (NICU), can worsen this condition.

Reye's syndrome. A serious syndrome occasionally resulting from the use of aspirin with viral diseases such as chicken pox, usually occurring in children. Acetaminophen (Tylenol, paracetamol) and ibuprofen (Motrin) are suspect as well. Many organs of the body may be affected and permanent brain damage or death can occur.

rhinitis. Runny nose. Inflammation of the nasal passages leading to congestion or dripping nose.

rotavirus. Virus that is the leading cause of severe diarrhea in infants and young children. Transmission is fecal-to-oral (stool to mouth) and possibly respiratory. Some level of immunity can develop after a first exposure.

sensitivity. Hypersensitivity. A term sometimes used interchangeably with the terms food intolerance and allergy, especially relating to delayed reaction type allergies.

serotonin. Acts as a hormone, chiefly in the digestive tract, and as a neurotransmitter, chiefly in the brain. Certain intestinal food reactions can cause altered serotonin in the brain, leading to altered moods.

SIDS. Sudden Infant Death Syndrome. The sudden and unexplained death of an apparently healthy infant between one month and one year old. Many suffocation deaths were once lumped in with SIDS deaths, but there are increasing efforts to distinguish between suffocation deaths and unexplained, SIDS deaths.

thimerosol. A mercury compound used as an antibacterial and antifungal agent in vaccines until 2001; now mostly used in flu virus vaccines. Thimerosol is under scrutiny for links to the development of autistic regressive disorders in young children.

trans fat. Hydrogenated vegetable oil. Oil that is unnaturally altered to remain solid at room temperature. Consumption of trans fats, typically found in pre-packaged foods and many restaurants, raises bad cholesterol (LDL) and the risks of heart disease and cancer. One must read package ingredients in order to avoid these as even a label stating zero grams per serving may contain nearly one half gram.

vasopressin. Also known as antidiuretic hormone. Acts in the body to regulate water balance but also acts in the brain, chiefly in males, to encourage bonding and parenting behaviors, stimulated by nearness to the pregnant mother and the infant.

villi. Intestinal villi. Small fingerlike projections covering the walls of the small intestine to increase the surface area for the absorption of nutrients. They are relatively undeveloped in newborns, grow rapidly in response to growth factors in mother's milk, and are stunted in those fed exclusively formula from birth.

WHO. World Health Organization. Coordinated by the United Nations, a worldwide organization that acts to promote the general health of the people of the world, campaigning specifically to boost nutrition and reduce tobacco usage, and acting to monitor, prevent, and treat infectious diseases.

Resources

Bonding and Attachment

Heller, Sharon, PhD. *The Vital Touch*. New York: Henry Holt and Co., 1997. An important complement to Montagu's *Touching*, incorporating current research and addressing modern questions, with strong documentation.

Karen, Robert, PhD. *Becoming Attached*. New York: Oxford University Press, 1998. Covers the development and findings of attachment research, and the discovered ramifications.

Montagu, Ashley, PhD. *Touching*. New York: Harper & Row, 1986. A must-read about the importance of touching and bonding to healthy development.

Food Allergy

Braly, James, MD. *Hidden Food Allergies: The Essential Guide to Uncovering Hidden Food Allergies and Achieving Permanent Relief.* Laguna, CA: Basic Health Publications, 2006. An excellent resource for understanding, diagnosing, and treating food allergies and intolerances and chemical sensitivities.

Brostoff, Jonathan, MD. *Food Allergies and Food Intolerance: The Complete Guide to Their Identification and Treatment.* Rochester, VT: Healing Arts Press, 2000. Educational, enlightened, evidence-based text about food intolerances and allergies. The author's insistence that intestinal reactions to trace amounts are not possible is very inconsistent with the actual experiences of many.

Rapp, Doris J., MD. *Is This Your Child?* New York: Harper Paperbacks, 1992. Contains good explanations of hyperactivity and other food allergy symptoms and reactions in children. The diagnosis and treatment method is weak for delayed food reactions.

Milk Dangers and Politics

Baumslag, Naomi, MD. *Milk, Money, and Madness, the Culture and Politics of Breastfeeding.* Westport, CT: Bergin & Garvey, 1995. A detailed and extremely eye-opening book about the history of breastfeeding and the politics of formula promotion.

Cohen, Robert. *Milk, the Deadly Poison.* Englewood Cliffs, NJ: Argus Publishing, 1998. Touching on other concerns over milk as well, Mr. Cohen provides 300 pages of eye-opening detailed information about how money and politics supercede health concerns in federal handling of milk safety issues.

Gordon, David B., PhD. *Milk and Mortality.* Livermore, CA: Gordon Books, 1999. A well-documented, in-depth presentation of the connections between milk drinking and coronary heart disease.

Oski, Frank A., MD. *Don't Drink Your Milk!* New York: TEACH Services, 1992. First printed in 1977, Pediatrician Oski, author of renowned standard pediatric textbooks, was well ahead of his time recognizing the medical dangers of cow's milk.

Plant, Jane, PhD. *Your Life in Your Hands, Understanding, Preventing and Overcoming Breast Cancer.* 2nd edition. London: Virgin Books, 2003. Four hundred pages and hundreds of references on how dairy consumption leads to breast cancer.

Parenting and Health

Magid, Ken, PhD. *High Risk, Children without a Conscience.* New York: Bantam, 1989. About the consequences to society of children raised without good attachment. Once you read it, you will wish to prevent it.

McKenna, James, PhD. *Sleeping with Your Baby: A Parent's Guide to Cosleeping.* Washington, D.C.: Platypus Media, 2007. Maternal-infant sleep researcher presents the evidence-based biological need of humans to be near each other during sleep and teaches how to cosleep safely.

Mendelsohn, Robert S., MD. *How to Raise a Healthy Child…in Spite of Your Doctor.* New York, NY: Ballantine Books, 1987. Timeless revelations about the pediatric care industry and their motives, and how and why 95% of medical treatments offered to children can be avoided.

Nicholson, Barbara, and Lysa Parker. *Attached at the Heart: 8 Proven Parenting Principles for Raising Connected and Compassionate Children.* i.Universe.com, 2009. From the founders of Attachment Parenting International, a beautiful how-to reference guide for practicing attachment parenting, with shared personal stories.

Sears, William, MD. *The Baby Book, Everything You Need to Know about Your Baby—from Birth to Age Two.* New York: Little, Brown and Co., 2003. A complete infant care guide using attachment parenting. Dr. Sears has other valuable parenting books as well.

Small, Meredith. *Our Babies, Ourselves.* New York: Dell Publishing Co., 1999. A look at how worldwide cultures promote infant care practices that either accommodate or neglect (such as the United States) various biological needs of infants, and the apparent outcomes of these assorted practices.

Vaccination

Cave, Stephanie, MD. *What Your Doctor May Not Tell You About Children's Vaccinations.* New York: Warner Books, Inc., 2001. Valuable information to help parents make decisions about vaccines and discuss them with their doctor.

Miller, Neil Z. *Vaccine Safety Manual for Concerned Families and Health Practitioners: Guide to Immunization Risks and Protection.* Santa Fe, NM: New Atlantean Press, 2008. Extensive guide to immunizations, including detailed safety and efficacy data.

Neustaedter, Randall, OMD. *The Vaccine Guide: Risks and Benefits for Children and Adults.* Berkeley, CA: North Atlantic Books, 2002. Presents background and philosophy of vaccination and discusses vaccine effectiveness, toxicity, and adverse effects.

Magazines and Organizations

Attachment Parenting International. Parenting information and direction to local attachment parenting support groups. www.AttachmentParenting.org

Baby Reference. Regularly updated website for *The Baby Bond* with large number of informative articles on natural parenting choices, child health and nutrition, and more. www.BabyReference.com

INFACT Canada. Online newsletter and valuable links. Excellent health-oriented and political action-oriented breastfeeding information. www.INFACTCanada.ca

La Leche League International. Information and support for breastfeeding. Telephone support and local meetings. www.LaLecheLeague.org. Publishes *New Beginnings,* a magazine that contains much information and support for the breastfeeding mother.

Mothering. Magazine and website with broad spectrum of informative and personal natural parenting wisdom. www.Mothering.com

Pathways. Quarterly magazine providing thought-provoking information from the holistic health perspective. Offers parents articles and resources to make informed health care choices for their families. www.PathwaysToFamilyWellness.org

Index

H

Harris, Judith, 29
Hazardous chemicals, in foods, 162–66
Headaches, 269, 276, 289–90, 309, 334
  and food elimination diets, 269, 289–90
Heart disease, 39, 55, 60, 103, 133, 205,
  239–40, 261, 262, 312
Helicobacter pylori, 85, 113, 302, 313
Hemoglobin. *See* iron deficiency
Hepatitis B vaccination, 131
Hiatal hernia, 273
High blood pressure, 39, 41, 52, 55, 60, 62,
  69, 166, 202, 223, 239
Hippocampus, 55–56
Hippocrates, 317
Hispanics. *See* Mexico
Histamine receptors, 311, 340–41
Histamines, 276, 290, 308–9, 311, 340–41
HIV, 113, 122, 172–73
Hives, 290, 306, 309
Holland, study of pacifiers, 77
Holt, Luther Emmett, Dr., 2, 16
Homemade formula, 261
Honey, 146
Hormones, 37
  cortisol, 53–55, 62, 71, 83, 95, 116, 239,
    343
  in cow's milk, 234, 249–51
  estrogen, 40, 42, 51, 163, 165, 200–201,
    219–20, 245–46, 248, 251
  and the father, 43–47
  growth hormones, 38, 52, 71, 167,
    249–53, 261
  oxytocin, 37–45, 50, 55, 212, 222–23,
    239
  pheromones, 51–52
  prolactin, 37, 41, 47–49, 51, 71, 167,
    176, 212, 222
  and sex drive in parents, 44, 48
  testosterone, 46
  vasopressin, 45–47
Human milk. *See* breastmilk
Hyperactivity. *See* attention-deficit disorder
Hypersensitivity reactions. *See* allergies
Hyperstimulation of infants, 68
Hypospadias, 163

I

Ibuprofen, 117, 129, 341
IgE antibodies, 284, 306, 309
IgG antibodies, 115, 284, 287, 320
Immune protection, 3, 108–16, 144, 158–
  59, 174–75, 179, 231, 285

Immune response, 282, 308–9, 312, 324,
  343
Immune system, 105–39, 152, 231
  and fever, 117
  improving function, 70, 71, 109–10
  and natural remedies, 137–38, 342–43
  reaction to allergenic foods, 11, 200,
    235–36, 239, 267, 273, 274, 282, 285,
    286, 292, 303, 308–9, 312, 319, 341
  and stress, 56, 162
  and vaccination, 118
Immune system repression, 56, 62, 116, 117
Independence, 1, 4, 9, 18, 21, 22–23, 33,
  38, 61, 65, 72
Infalyte, 118, 157
Infant contact studies, 71–72
Infant death rate. *See* infant mortality; mortality rates
Infant illnesses, and formula feeding, 106–7,
  113, 134, 174–75, 179, 285
Infant mortality, 3–4, 16, 73–74, 80–87,
  106–7, 113, 175
Infections
  in premature infants, 174–75
  See also ear infections; fever; gastrointes-
    tinal infections; sinus infections
Infectious diarrhea, 107, 112, 133, 152, 191,
  216, 267, 284, 285, 326
Inflammation
  bladder, 275
  ear tubes, 286
  intestinal (*See* intestinal inflammation)
Inflammatory bowel disease. *See* colitis;
  Crohn's disease
Influenza, 108
Injections. *See* vaccines; vitamin K
Insecure attachment, 19, 21, 32, 43, 48, 53
  reattachment, 32
Insufficient milk syndrome, 3, 212–13, 223
Insulin, 236
Intellectual development, 20, 23, 92,
  95–96, 98, 233, 345
Intelligence, 23, 92–103, 175, 298
  animal studies of, 97–98
  benefits of breastfeeding, 94–95, 101
  and educational television, 100
  effect of stress hormones on, 56, 95
  effects of parental care on, 55–56, 95–96
  electronic stimulation, 99–100
  and negative qualities of the media, 100
  stimulation of, 92–93
Intestinal bleeding, 190–91, 194, 234
Intestinal cancer, 251, 302
Intestinal flora, 112, 147, 151–52, 193